From Integration
to Inclusion

From Integration to Inclusion

A History of Special Education in the 20th Century

Margret A. Winzer

Gallaudet University Press
Washington, DC

Gallaudet University Press
Washington, DC 20002
http://gupress.gallaudet.edu

Library of Congress Cataloging-in-Publication Data

Winzer, M. A. (Margret A.), 1940–
   From integration to inclusion: a history of special education in the 20th century /
     Margret A. Winzer
   Includes bibliographical references and index.
   ISBN-13: 978-56368-365-7 (casebound : alk. paper)
   ISBN-10: 1-56368-365-2 (casebound : alk. paper)
   1. Special education—United States—History—20th century. I. Title.
   LC3981.W585 2009
   371.90973'0904—dc22   2008051439

Cover photographs: Top—Used by permission of Laura J. Bottomley, Ph.D., North Carolina State University; Bottom—from *MR 67: A First Report to the President on the Nation's Progress and Remaining Great Needs in the Campaign to Combat Mental Retardation* (Washington, DC: Government Printing Office, 1967).

Contents

Introduction

This text is designed as a comprehensive history of the field that focuses chiefly on events in the 20th century. The key hallmarks of the book are its retrospective overview of the field of special education, a critical assessment of past progress and reform, and an analysis of the theoretical diversity within the discipline. The text accomplishes these elements by offering a description, analysis, and audit of the history; by highlighting the major paradigms that have both emerged from and shaped special education; by describing the reform movements that have periodically shaken the whole of education, the field of special education, or have applied to discrete groups of exceptionality; and by examining the issues and debates that have arisen within the field of special education in the twentieth century.

In another sense, the text is prospective. It anchors present experiences to the past and details the forces that have led to today's issues and controversies. There is no question that many of today's most contentious issues have plagued the field from the outset. But joined to long-standing dilemmas, many issues have acquired a new urgency in the light of current school reform movements. Critical areas include, but are not restricted to, inclusive education for students with disabilities; over- and underrepresentation in special education; techniques and methods to provide safe and caring schools; new genetic discoveries that are revamping the field of intellectual disabilities; the recent marriage of special education and the *Diagnostic and Statistical Manual of Mental Disorders* (American Psychiatric Association, 1994, 2000); the subsequent tendency to label and categorize children with overwhelming detail; the push toward high-stakes testing and accountability; and the stress on science-based methods to both inform current issues and close the gap between research and practice.

In a completely different sense, it is hoped that the text is persuasive. As a field, special education occupies contested terrain: it is both hailed and condemned. Yet, not only its defenders but also its critics often are unaware of historical developments. North American special educators seem curiously disinterested in the foundations of their field. Historical perspectives, foundational matters,

and theoretical stances are often ignored or historical knowledge is learned inci-
dentally and unintentionally (Mostert & Crockett, 1999–2000; Winzer, 2004). For
many researchers and practitioners, the immediate demands of the present tend to
occlude a broader historical and philosophical scope. They look more favorably at
proposals for practical solutions to immediate problems and prefer to devise studies and collect data on the lived worlds of schools and teachers.

Some special educators speak to a lack of history. Others rapidly dispose of their
heritage; they suggest that we "pause and reflect but not too long" (Will, 1984, p.
11). There are some who actively reject the history of the field and lean toward dis-
paraging earlier events, programs, and pioneers in favor of contemporary models.
In doing so, they chronicle the vicissitudes of special education, point to supposed
fossilized traditions, and are uncompromisingly critical of past endeavors. To others, history becomes increasingly selective, with the past made over to suit present
intentions: they pull out the odd snippet, often to justify favored policy initiatives.

Some people in the field tend to view special education as second rate and
demeaning of those it serves: they sieze the moral high ground and lash out with
indignation at what they consider to be the injustices of the past. They deride pioneer practitioners as culpable in not granting people with disabilities dignity and
equality, and they contrast the best and most effective of contemporary treatments
with the worst of the past to create a dark and distorted vision. Those holding
these perspectives not only view the past as intrinsically worse than the present
but also see the future as likely to be more positive than the present. Related to this
perspective is the contention that today's inclusive reform brings a new and more
powerful understanding that is incompatible with past practices. This argument
leads to the simple assertion that if the current movement to include students with
special needs in schools and communities embodies the best ideals of social justice, then the past, by extension, had to be unjust.

Inherent in these positions is a steadfast unwillingness to learn from the wisdom of the accumulated past, a confirmation of Blatt's observation that "in this field
we call special education, history has not served us well. We have not learned from
it" (Blatt, 1975, p. 404). Yet, no matter how persuasive the current reforms, the notion
that special education can ignore its past is unsustainable: the field cannot afford to
dismiss or denigrate the forces that have shaped contemporary understandings.

Robert Osgood (1997) wrote that the emergence of special education as a firmly
entrenched arm of public schooling has constituted a remarkable story in the history
of American education in the 20th century. Yet from whatever route it is approached,
the history of special education is not a simple tale. Nor is it merely a story of progress culminating in a better state of affairs. Rather, it is a complex thread that weaves
in and out of a much broader social and educational tapestry. To be sure, the history
is incomplete and sometimes confusing. It is also fascinating and important: how
and why special education evolved to this point not only provides special educators
with a sense of their own history but also adumbrates enduring dilemmas.

Rather than disassociate from the past, special education needs to reflect on its
history, revisit the theoretical underpinnings of the profession, and appreciate the
subtle ways in which particular contentions have been woven together to generate
arguments for a particular ideological stance. Those interested in the field need to

assume a balanced stance that considers the progress to date, the social and political context of development, and the past innovations on which today's enterprise rests. They should examine evolving practice within its social context to illustrate the general shift in attitudes couched in eras of social reform and to show that the resolutions of special education do not emerge out of social vacuum, but within a particular social space that is filled by the interplay of history, knowledge, interest, and power. The field should celebrate the varied reforms; the mosaic of concepts, approaches, and models that have developed and that inform our current work; and the contributions—both philosophical and pragmatic—of the brilliant, innovative, often controversial and erratic pioneers. Ethical philosophies and social movements are the products of the experience of members of a society living in a particular time, and the attempts of the pioneers in the field of special education to transcend these socially and culturally set limitations deserve careful and respectful study. In a more practical vein, distinguished pioneers have provided a legacy and a "heritage rich with lessons abundantly able to inform contemporary issues in special education, particularly those related to intervention" (Mostert & Crockett, 1999–2000, p. 134).

Equally compelling is the contention that engagement with some of the tensions and dilemmas that characterize the history of special education illuminates current contentions, debates, and developments. Historical inquiry elucidates strategically significant issues and, as such, forms a vital component of the struggle to understand the ideologies and practices that have developed in special education over a span of more than two centuries.

Certainly, new assumptions and understandings may work to mitigate historical traditions, and a consideration of the historical background is not a guarantee that we will not repeat our mistakes. Further, as Polloway (1984) observed, "the nature of schools, teachers, and students today would make any attempt at direct generalization . . . an extremely doubtful practice" (p. 24). Even with these limitations, lessons from the past can illuminate contemporary dilemmas, offer guidance to current issues, and illustrate enduring patterns. Alan Dyson (2001) succinctly noted that in the field of special education, there is much reinvention of the wheel, with more focus on the structure of the wheel than on the reasons why wheels go around. The wheel may be renamed, somewhat adapted, and applied to different groups or scenarios, but basically it is a reincarnation of an already invented wheel. Pursuing this theme, "much of the field's repeated wanderings and cyclical lurches could be steadied by anchoring present and future innovations in what we have already learned from our past" (Mostert & Crockett, 1999–2000, p. 137).

APPROACHING A HISTORY OF SPECIAL EDUCATION

The historical literature in the area of special education is narrow and specialized. Save perhaps for the history of deaf education, there is so little comprehensive research that historical development remains a relatively unexplored cul-de-sac within the history of education.

Many of the early studies in the field shared a tendency toward simple description: they focused on the development of a national system of special education or the contributions of great men who were celebrated for the wisdom of their vision and the changes they wrought. Much of the work included institutional developments but, in doing so, tended to portray the students who were served as appendages to the history of the settings.

Such Whig interpretations of the history of special education provide an appealing, but simplified, version of comprehensiveness and consistency. They conceptualize the historical journey of special education as an inclined plane of "onward and upward" and often busy themselves with dividing the world into the friends and enemies of progress (Mazurek, 1981). When the focus rests on the singular institution of the school, the special education pioneers, or particular categories of exceptionality, it does so at the expense of other social forces—the religious, economic, political, and demographic variables.

A field as historically complex and diverse as special education is bound to reveal controversial issues and unsolved dilemmas as well as to reflect major social issues and trends. Complex issues seldom yield to broad generalizations, and an historical tool enables us to examine theoretical stances in different ways and challenge the inadequacies of a single explanation for complex educational movements.

In this history, two foci are central. First, the historical study of disability as well as of special schooling and service provision are interfaced with reference to systems, protocols, and practices of the broader social macrosystem. Documenting how disability and schooling relate in the broad structural categories of a society is critical. Discussions must encompass the emotional and intellectual climates prevailing in different periods; the social, political, and ideological factors that influenced societal perceptions, theory, and practice; and the degree to which crucial problems such as defining exceptional conditions and separating them from one another were formulated in contexts organized along moral, theological, legislative, medical, and social dimensions.

The underlying and inherent structure adopted in this book follows this thread and makes the forces that shaped special education explicit by mapping the themes in three core areas: social and philosophical perspectives, patterns of evolution in different areas, and the specific time and space of key events. These areas allow the reader to consider the history of special education and the clients served from a number of perspectives and levels. From the first focus, social and philosophical perspectives, themes are viewed in relation to society in general—essentially joined to the structural aspects of society, institutions, and social processes that affected people with exceptionalities and the interdependence of the individual and the social world. The history also examines the philosophical underpinnings of special education—the assumptions and the concepts used in thinking about education, society, and the treatment of people who are exceptional. Another level focuses on individual disability categories as well as the policies and provisions adopted, school interventions, curricula changes, reform movements, and the disciplines that surrounded and supported special education such as psychology and social work.

The second focus rests on the notion that evolution was neither straightforward nor linear. The history of special education cannot be viewed as a historically located sequence nor as a fixed and absolute series of developmental stages; it was more a set of trends. Rather than being an event, transformation was a slow, incremental, and multifaceted process surrounded by conflicts and scattered with the disruptions, contradictions, and tensions that are natural occurrences in an evolutionary pattern.

A number of factors are paramount in the evolutionary pattern. First of all, in the two centuries of progress toward today's philosophy and practice, reform has been the zeitgeist, a dominant theme determining goals and hoped-for outcomes. Quests for reform came from within the profession just as often as from without. Ideas have their historical roots, and natural histories and the field can catalog a long series of reforms constructed in particular eras in response to political rhetoric, social perceptions, and fiscal conditions together with etiological, educational, and pedagogical considerations.

Second, the complex history and cycles of reform in special education show a field that has been characterized by fervent appeals to new philosophies and paradigm shifts and that has always been vulnerable to the caprice of changing fashions, politics, and fads. The landscape has been dotted with zealous reformers who offered innovations and remedies promoted either as being capable of solving certain problems or challenges entirely or as offering new solutions to enduring dilemmas. Often, reform ideals and decision making were based on professional consensus and the popular way; just as often, ideological principles sought to operationalize values founded on the prevailing notions of social justice, rightness, and desirability. Sometimes, reform was erected on personal opinions or impelled by an initial sense of outrage and indignation. Occasionally, the reform reasoning was rooted in prejudice, illogical assumptions, quackery, and, perhaps, downright charlatanism. Rarely did empirical evidence underlie reform; many efforts floundered because they lacked reliable data.

Many calls to reform, restructure, and reinvent centered on specific categories of exceptionality such as oral modes of communication for those who were deaf, braille for those who were blind, and individual psychotherapy for those who were labeled emotionally disturbed. Generic and encompassing changes tended to rise from social movements or general system reforms. For example, the emotional appeal of school location—the setting of schooling and whether it should be separate and specialized or mainstream and general—made school addresses central to all reform in special education, although the balance of reform efforts have always been rooted in general social perceptions and in reform within the general system.

Finally, careful examination of the evolutionary pattern shows that however fervently those involved hold beliefs about educational innovations, many of those beliefs, although worthwhile in themselves, fail to survive and tend to be temporary. Darling-Hammond (1997) observed that "Schools chew up and spit out undigested reforms on a regular basis" (p. 22); Zigler and Hall (1986) estimated that reforms in special education have a life span of about a decade. Regularities, which tend to reassert themselves again and again, quash reform agendas. Just as often, it was not that the reform efforts did not work but that they created a spiral of new problems. At the same time, resistance and oppositional cultures counter the function of particular ideologies and even the most compelling proposals.

A major assumption of this book is that any historical study must be carried out with a constant awareness that the markers for the moral correctness of a position stand in their own time and space. However, one of the major paradoxes of historical interpretation is a given: critical as it is to develop an understanding of the past in terms of the past, not the present, historical writing inevitably mirrors the concerns of the present. Indeed, it is difficult, if not impossible, to stand outside one's own conceptual givens and not to judge past events, ideas, and actors in one's own terms.

Pertinent here are the issues of terminology and labeling—long-standing, contentious, and sensitive problems in the field. However, the point at which difference becomes disability is determined by a society and is embedded in local discourses as relayed in the terms used to describe the condition. Often, the terms were originally benign, but gathered stigma as new knowledge was amassed. Even today, the complexity of the constructs means that there is often no precise or universally accepted definition of the terms. Moreover, the pastel formulations that suit contemporary political correctness cannot capture the sensibilities of the past. Throughout this book, the most generic and historically accurate terms are used.

A second assumption is that contemporary special education draws on a long and honorable pedigree. This claim is not to suggest that the field did not detour into oppressive and dreary lanes or to propose that it needs to return to traditional models of practice anchored in deficit-driven labels, specialized and segregated settings, special pedagogies, or traditional concepts. What is does suggest is that special education was created and has proceeded with the worthiest of intentions. Pioneers did not set out to stigmatize, devalue, or dehumanize people. And, although some nasty events and images cannot be erased from our professional history, special educators do not have to adopt breast-beating and mea culpas to assuage some collective guilt. That said, oppression, discrimination, and injustice rightly invoke hostility, and they deserve critical attention.

The time frame for the focus of this history is the 20th century; the location is North America—the United States and Canada—where development has been parallel and cross-fertilization paramount. An earlier volume, *The History of Special Education: From Isolation to Integration* (Winzer, 1993b) examined the genesis and development of special education and was set largely in the 18th and 19th centuries. In dealing with early developments, it highlighted institutional openings; the contributions of pioneers; the clients served; and the sociological, pedagogical, and philosophical foundations on which special education was erected. This book plays variations of the same themes but examines the huge changes and reforms (as well as the failures and disappointments) that characterize the enterprise of special education throughout the 20th century. However, although this book is a second volume, it is written to stand alone. That is, the material should be logical and reasonable even to readers not acquainted with the first text.

Chapter 1

Revisiting the 19th Century

Difference is inevitable in a community of people. Although difference is constituted in complex ways by varying cultural configurations, the existence of a scale of prestigious and shameful differences seems to be a universal feature of social life. Different societies and cultures have looked along the range of human behavior from normal to abnormal and then made a judgment as to whether a specific individual would be classed as exceptional, different, disabled, or deviant. Such marginality has always been a fluctuating concept: cultures and eras have differed significantly in the dimensions of behavior that requires major consideration. Nevertheless, difference has always been more threatening than sameness: difference challenges conformity.

Once difference, deviance, or disability is acknowledged, a series of dilemmas are immediately brought to the forefront. Chronic behavior that exceeds or violates cultural and social norms inevitably engender sanctions for the behaver, whether the penalties manifest as perceptions, attitudes, or treatment. Responses mirror the vibrant and shifting gestalt of societal dynamics and form one critical indicator of a society's progress. In terms of the history of special education, the manner in which different societies in different eras within different social, political, economic, and religious landscapes have addressed the dilemma of human differences and disabilities forms the essential core.

Disability has a history as long as humankind itself. Positive attention to disabilities, encapsulated as the field of special education, dates back to at least the middle of the 17th century when European pedants intervened with individual deaf or blind people. After that period, permanent facilities that catered to the definitive categories of deaf, blind, and intellectually disabled emerged during the middle decades of the 18th century. Institutional facilities for students with special needs expanded and thrived in 19th century Europe, Britain, and North America.

The first two chapters of this history are located in the 19th century. Although it is important to establish the 19th century context out of which special education evolved, the period was carefully scrutinized in *The History of Special Education: From Isolation to Integration* (Winzer, 1993b). It is needless to travel the same ground again. Because the purpose of the following two chapters is to supplement rather than summarize the earlier work, only the most enduring and significant themes are considered.

THE EARLY YEARS

In the long "dark ages" before the 18th century, people with disabilities met callous, cruel, or dismissive attitudes. In early societies, the complex factors that had to be understood to conceptualize disabling conditions and place them in perspective were limited or absent. Disability was not an innocuous boundary; rather, it was a liability in social and economic participation. People perceived as disabled—whatever the type or degree of disability—were lumped under the broad categorization of "idiot." The term derived from two Greek roots, which rather than denote these people as citizens, denoted them as those who did not take part in public life, who did not have a place in the *polisi*, for example, those forbidden from marriage or from taking inheritances. The denigrating term *idiot* therefore included untrained or ignorant people, private or peculiar people, as well as those disabled individuals who were generally scorned as inferior beings and deprived of rights and privileges (Barr, 1904b; Penrose, 1949/1966).

It was widely believed that most people with disabilities were quite incapable of benefiting from instruction of any kind. Because it was also widely held that disability was inflicted by God or the devil and could therefore be cured only by divine intervention, this early period is replete with innumerable stories of healing, many imbued with an aura of the miraculous. By the close of the 15th century, the uncertain recitation of miracle and legend conceded to the more or less stable compilation of authenticated records. By the end of the next century, there was a growing literature and a spawning of ideas, most particularly in the area of hearing impairment. Chiefly, however, disability was a subject of philosophical inquiry, not the object of benevolence or philanthropy. Some faint interest in the possibilities of education for people with disabilities amounted to little more than a speculative notice.

THE FRENCH INITIATIVES

The middle decades of the 18th century witnessed the pervasive influence of the European Enlightenment. The intellectual project of the Enlightenment was to build a sound body of knowledge about the world; its humanitarian philosophy and democratic thought prompted ideas about the equality of all people and the human responsibility to take care of others, particularly individuals outside the private circle of the home and the family. Reform movements sprang up, and a new wave of humanitarianism emerged as a "sustained, collective pattern of behavior in which substantial numbers of people regularly act[ed] to alleviate the suffering of strangers" (Haskell, 1985, p. 360).

The spirit of reform crystallized most potently in the philosophers of the French Enlightenment, including Rousseau, Diderot, Voltaire, and Condillac. They discarded the speculative metaphysics of the preceding century and attempted to turn humanity from its preoccupation with God to an acute social consciousness and awareness of their fellows. Their philosophy considered the improvement of the well-being of groups of individuals, varying from poor people and slaves to prisoners and the insane to people with disabilities.

As new vistas were created, Europe and Britain turned, for the first time, toward the education of people with disabilities. Although special education emerged in a number of national contexts, France is credited with the most generous vision in the treatment of exceptionality. So pervasive were the French influences that an 1881 writer was led to observe that "the great designs and inventions for the removal or palliation of physical or mental disabilities which stand as significant indices on the road of modern civilization were all of them fostered on the fertile soil of France" (Perkins Institution for the Blind, 1881, p. 60). As innovative pedagogies to assist individuals with disabilities flourished, what was to become an almost universal progression in special education emerged. People with deafness were the first to be served, followed by those who were blind. Education and training for those with intellectual disabilities generally arrived far more tardily and only after success with the adult mentally ill population (Winzer, 1998).

A simple faith in John Locke was common to the whole European Enlightenment. In France, his philosophy was enthusiastically embraced, assimilated, and naturalized to become the official epistemology of the school of philosophers (Wilson, 1972). Particularly salient to the disabled population, Locke's philosophy moved beyond the earlier nature orientation toward a nurture view of human development. Locke abandoned notions of inborn capacities and a common human nature; instead, he developed the theory of the *tabula rasa* (blank slate) and claimed that the environment supplied all knowledge through the senses.

The Abbé Charles Michel de l'Epée (1712–1789), a French priest, assimilated Enlightenment ideals of equality, melded them to new and novel concepts about language and its development, and joined these to the sensationalist philosophy of John Locke and the French philosophers to devise innovative approaches to the education of deaf people. Earlier attempts had been made to teach deaf people, but Epée's work was of a different nature from the pioneer approaches in England, Spain, the Netherlands, and Germany. Those attempts made oralism—efficiency in speech reading and the acquisition of speech—the apex of instruction. In striking contrast, Epée speculated that "it would be possible to instruct the Deaf and Dumb with written characters, always accompanied by sensible signs" (Epée, 1860, p. 26). To create a language of signs, Epée drew on the idiosyncratic signs of his own pupils plus an already existing body of gestures, signs, and finger alphabets.

Epée's doctrine promoting a silent language of the hands was revolutionary in the context of the times. In devising and instructing through a sign language, Epée made concrete the philosophical speculations of Locke, Diderot, and Rousseau, while simultaneously giving notice that sign was the sole effective medium for the intellectual development of deaf people and that speech was no longer central in their education. Many were fascinated by the novelty of the ideas. So pronounced was Epée's influence and so genuine his commitment to his deaf charges that he promoted and guided innovations for other groups with disabilities, specifically those who were blind, deaf and blind, and intellectually disabled (Winzer, 1993b).

Philosophical speculation about the problems and potentialities of blind people was not lacking: Molyneux, Berkeley, Locke, Diderot, and others explored various aspects of blindness. Following in the wake of Epée's successful mission with deaf students, Valentin Haüy opened a small school in 1784, which is recognized as the first school in the world for the blind. Haüy taught with a raised-print method. His stress, however, lay in vocational training: pupils learned weaving, basket and mat making, chair caning, and the rope trade (Guillie, 1817).

The formal study of intellectual disability has a rich and significant history. In fact, aspects of subnormality were recognized and studied with remarkable percipience by some of the great names in medicine from the period of the Renaissance onward (Mahendra, 1985). However, mental retardation and mental illness were deeply intermeshed for centuries. Although the essential nature of the distinction between *fatuus naturalis* (born fools) and those *non compos mentis* (who have lost the use of reason) dates from at least the 13th century, abstract conceptualizations and differentiations between dementia and subnormality did not evolve until the early 1800s (Lewis, 1960; Penrose, 1949/1966). This long-held conception of mental retardation as a subtype of insanity meant that medical treatment of people with mental illness preceded educational intervention with intellectually disabled children.

Asylums for the insane became common in Europe toward the end of the 18th century. Mentally ill people in Paris and its surrounds were concentrated in the institutions of Bicêtre (for males) and Salpêtrière (for females)—lunatic hospitals that were really catch basins for the hopeless and dependent. Inmates included the truly insane, mentally retarded individuals, aged derelicts, albinos, epileptics, dissenters, heretics, and others who caused disruption to the social or religious order (Doermer, 1969). Life was characterized by harsh treatment, violent remedies, whipping, and starving. Inmates were chained naked in rat-infested cubicles below ground and were fed only bread and soup (Lane & Pillard, 1978).

Medical reform was one expression of the Enlightenment quest for social reform, clearly personified in Phillippe Pinel (1745–1826), known as the first psychiatrist in France. Pinel introduced his "moral treatment," essentially humane and methodological regimes for the mentally ill that emphasized constructive activity, kindness, minimal restraint, structure, routine, and consistent treatment (Kauffman, 1976). In doing so, Pinel was instrumental in converting the institutions for the care of mentally ill and psychotic patients from prisons to hospitals.

In keeping with the reforms introduced by Pinel, the status of those who were mentally deficient was also raised. True interest in the education of people with intellectual disabilities is usually dated from 1800 when Jean Marc Gaspard Itard (1774–1838), a young physician associated with the institution for the deaf in Paris, published the preliminary results of the first recorded attempts to educate a feral child, Victor, the so-called Wild Boy of Aveyron. However, it was Itard's pupil,

Edouard Seguin, a French physician and educator, who carried on Itard's work with increasing insight and success and who broadened and legitimized the enterprise of education for the mentally retarded (see Flugel & West, 1964).

Imbued with the spirit of the Enlightenment, Seguin was convinced that education was a universal right and that society had an obligation to improve the lot of all its members. People with mental retardation were among the neediest (Crissey, 1975). For Seguin, the task of educating them was part of the wider social movement for the abolition of social classes and the establishment of a just society (MacMillan, 1960).

In 1826, a special institute for the education of mentally defective children was established in Paris; in 1828, Ferrus formed a separate section at Bicêtre for imbeciles and idiots. The up-and-coming Seguin established a small private school in 1838; in 1842, he became head of the Bicêtre school. Methodologically, Seguin refined and elaborated Itard's methods and, commented a 1945 writer, "brought to the study of the minds of imbeciles a singularly acute and original intelligence" ("Here and there . . . ," 1943, p. 213). His comprehensive approach laid the base for almost all 19th-century institutional and educational developments for children and youth with mental retardation.

The influence of the French pedagogical initiatives was pervasive. Following the French pioneers, movements to provide services for those in the categories of deaf, blind, and intellectually disabled were contemporaneous in Europe and North America. And, taking into account national idiosyncrasies, the broad outlines of intervention were similar.

The British were not tardy in developing education for people with disabilities. Nevertheless, the revolutionary winds that fanned the American battle for freedom and the French Revolution of 1789 struck fear into British hearts and created one dominant mode in British thought during that turbulent period—animosity to all things French. Indeed, the intellectual mood of France was quite different from that of England: the British social climate that promoted education of some disabled people tended to be evangelical, not philosophical. Rather than follow the rigorous intellectual approach used by the French, the British embarked on a basically utilitarian mode of special education. Nascent education was largely an extension of schemes for managing the impecunious, the dependent, orphans, and "vicious" children.

In the pedagogical realms, British reformers, while not denying the principles of assistance, largely denounced the French advances, particularly French methodologies. For example, Seigel (1969) notes that "the revolutionary and creative speculations of the French concerning the psychology of the deaf had little or no effect on the teaching of the deaf in England" (p. 96). The sign language system developed by Epée was characterized as "altogether useless" and "an absurd and inexcusable waste of time" (Seigel, 1969, p. 115).

AMERICAN EXPERIENCES

As North America welcomed the 19th century, a laissez-faire attitude toward most social problems reigned. Poverty, misfortune, unemployment, frailty, disability, and the rest were viewed as the natural concern of the family, local community, or church. Little distinction was made between those who were incapable of earning a livelihood and those who were disinclined to do so. Many people denied the notion that unemployment and poverty were the by-products of an industrializing society and nursed the illusion that work was available for all who wanted it. Those who would not work were judged just as often as the authors as the victims of their own misfortune. Giving alms was often seen as a temporary palliative, misdirected and perhaps likely to encourage the growth of a dependent or pauper class. Charity, when extended, was often more for the benefactor's soul than for the needs of the recipient.

Nevertheless, prompted by the spirit of the new nation, Enlightenment thought, and evangelical Christianity, early 19th-century Americans began to codify the previous haphazard compassion. The propriety of benevolent intervention assumed greater proportions as reformers sought to Christianize every aspect of American life. Many people adopted novel conceptions of social responsibility, and voluntary charity lost its traditional flavor. Christian paternalism spawned reform movements that catered to the physical and spiritual well-being of the floating mass of the needy—indigent and impecunious people, the old and the frail, orphans, slaves, and individuals with disabilities—and brought new theories in penal discipline and more humane treatment of those who were considered insane.

Not uncertain in their piety, social leaders held that they were authorized by God to lead the underclasses with stern but kindly authority. For example, Thomas Hopkins Gallaudet, founder of the first permanent American institution for a disabled group in North America—the Connecticut Asylum for the Education and Instruction of Deaf and Dumb Persons (later changed to the American Asylum for the Education and Instruction of Deaf and Dumb Persons in Hartford, Connecticut)—reflected perfectly the views of upper-class Protestant New England. Gallaudet saw himself, an educated steward of society, as responsible for the moral and spiritual regeneration of the disabled, entrusted to him by God for their welfare (see Valentine, 1993).

New approaches to social problems changed the traditional organizational structure of philanthropy. The benevolence of social leaders, expressed earlier as private charity, was now channeled through corporate institutions. A committee of socially responsible leaders would form, apply to the state legislature for an act of incorporation, and then proceed to organize and start the new enterprise (see Katz, 1973). The act of incorporation allowed the election of a board of officers, the appointment of trustees, some state appropriations, and the hiring and employment of teaching and other personnel. Because they were essentially private ventures, the corporate organizations depended heavily on access to the machinery of private charity for fund-raising. Literally dozens of societies for the care of orphans, the sick, the aged, and the destitute were formed and incorporated. For example, the Connecticut State government gave $5,000 to the American Asylum; a further $17,000 was raised through private donations, and Congress granted 23,000 acres, which were sold for operating funds (Lane, 1976; Weld, 1848).

Outdoor relief (some sort of financial or other support provided by the local parish or local authorities to people in need, particularly able-bodied seasonal workers) was replaced by indoor relief—institutional settings as varied as poor houses, almshouses, county homes, houses of refuge, houses of industry, orphanages, or asylums—all designed to relieve the burdens of poverty, distress, misfortune, or disability. Regardless of setting or name, forms of indoor relief tended to serve dual purposes—to protect inmates from a cruel world and to protect society from the inmates. For example, the trustees of the New York Institution for the Deaf and Dumb boasted in 1835 that the facility constituted "a little community within itself and is as much secluded from intercourse with others, as is any situation it could possibly be" (Dunscombe, 1836, p. 199). For persons with mental illness "the security of the public and the proper treatment of patients" made it "absolutely necessary that they should be confined in some convenient place, in order to prevent the commission of crimes, to which they are all more or less liable" (Beck, 1811/1834, p. 32).

INSTITUTIONALIZING STUDENTS WITH DISABILITIES

Child savers, child shapers, reformers, and philanthropists were zealous in their quest under the aegis of private charities and philanthropic organizations to save souls and protect those who were disabled. To accomplish this mission, they established a complex of institutions, chiefly founded as corporate structures. Following the progression established in France 50 years earlier, deaf people were the first to be served with the establishment by Thomas Hopkins Gallaudet and Laurent Clerc of the American Asylum in 1817. Schooling for those who were blind began under Samuel Gridley Howe in Massachusetts in 1832. Educational facilities for students with mental retardation arrived later; between 1848 and 1851, four institutions were established.

As social philosophy, special education, encapsulated by institutional training, was reformist but not radical. The founding dates of the institutions may be seen as critical indicators that pinpoint the options that were open. Reformers guided responses to differences within their existing social, educational, and economic possibilities and limitations. In doing so, they planted the seeds that sprouted as enduring patterns that accompanied special education at least until the 1960s and, indeed, almost to the present time.

The early institutions for students with disabilities, urged on the grounds of expedience, charity, and imperative duty, reflected both the values of the larger society and the efforts of the people who founded them. Inevitably, this pattern led to a persistent theme of 19th-century special education—the mixture of the protection *of* children and the protection of society *from* those with disabilities. This mix suggests that progress and social control can be interpreted as different labels for the same events or stories. On the one hand, the public could not refute the kindly and humanitarian tenets on which institutions were founded. Such settings were the seemingly logical consequence of the urge toward protecting vulnerable children from corrupt and callous societies. Moreover, the temporary marginalization and isolation of institutional settings could be viewed as a conveyor belt that, by means of instruction and industrial training, delivered students with disabilities to adult integration into the community. On the other hand, child saving was sanctioned in the interests of control. Although the language of social control tended to be less overtly florid than that of the institutional mode, the repressive aspects should not be minimized. The institutions served as much to separate disabled children and youth from a cruel world as to relieve the world of disabled people. In this way, special schooling became a convenient place for inconvenient people and thus served the interests of advantaged members of society by maintaining and rationalizing the further marginalization of those it purported to help.

Almost universally, reformers attributed expressions of immorality, discord, and disorder to the deleterious effects of life in the cities. On the one hand, the city seemed to be a closed, confining, static environment, but on the other hand, many crusaders held that "the criminal and vicious classes seek the cities and more densely populated places as bases of operations" (Ontario, Inspector of Prisons, Asylums, and Public Charities 1876, p. 92). In contrast, they advocated, the wholesome and honest atmosphere of the country and the work of farm life would develop moral and industrious habits. Given the reformers' bent, it is not surprising that institutionalization as an idealistic reform sought to concentrate people with disabilities in environments far removed from the cities, where the daily regimes were typical of rural life. For example, in Montreal the institution for deaf females was described as being "built of stone, and . . . situated in a good position, far away from the smoky atmosphere of the city" (Widd, 1868, p. 355). By 1927, one survey (Day, Fusfeld, & Pintner, 1928) showed only 8 of 29 schools for the deaf in or near a city.

Although institutionalization of people with disabilities evolved into an important basis for public policy, few children were actually in school. The institutions predated the common schools, and academic options were unavailable. Moreover, many potential pupils came from the humbler walks of life, and apart from the necessity of children's work on the farm or in the workshop or home, many parents could not defray the costs of schooling. Parental solicitude, fealty to the sacrosanct domain of the family, the ethic of private responsibility, a lingering mistrust of the institutions, the limited apparatus of state governments, and public parsimony further acted to restrict the clientele. For attendees, education was limited. The 4 to 6 years spent in the institutions was considered "as much, perhaps, as they ought to expect from the public bounty" ("American Asylum for the Deaf and Dumb," 1826, p. 631).

Nor did institutional training serve young children. When the American Asylum opened, the average age of the pupils was 22 years, a sure indication of the desire of older persons to acquire a trade. The situation was similar in schools for the blind where pupils of ages 10 or 12 years were admitted; in some cases, they were allowed to enter up to their 30th year (Best, 1934).

Two invariable tropes were used to promote special schooling. One equated being disabled and being dependent as opposed to being able bodied and productive. The other was the evangelical ideal of a spiritual redemption made concrete in the focus on the inculcation of religious values.

In the early 19th century, the clergy regarded themselves, and were regarded by the people, as men of real ability, sound knowledge, and impeccable character. As such, they were the natural guardians of education, with the schools under their particular supervision. Clergymen such as Thomas Hopkins Gallaudet approached people with disabilities by assuming a missionary stance and an attitude of benevolent paternalism. Early schoolmen decried the lack of spiritual values and moral imperatives that were generally conceded as accompanying disabling conditions. Deaf people, for example, were characterized as "long neglected heathens" (Gallaudet, 1836, p. 217), excluded from the hopes and knowledge of Christianity and dwelling in a "moral desert" (in Barnard, 1852, p. 102). From this moral platform, students with disabilities were viewed primarily as examples of the evangelical belief that all people were capable of being saved.

Religious training was made "a matter of first importance" (Stone, 1848, p. 145) to "elevate [deaf students] to the mental and moral standards of human beings" (Ontario Institution for the Education and Instruction of the Deaf and Dumb, 1895, p. 12). Schooling for blind children was celebrated as a means to "enable them to read the scriptures themselves" (Dunscombe, 1836, p. 97). The development of religious awareness and moral rectitude was an important objective in the education of those who were mentally retarded. It was noted that it was necessary "above all, to awaken the consciousness of his responsibility to God, and of his duties toward his fellow man" (Brockett, 1856, p. 601). The personnel at the schools preached a set of norms that were an essential part of middle-class morality to accompany religious strictures. Pupils were trained in values such as honesty, thrift, and toleration.

As teachers rained a torrent of moral and religious prescriptions on people with disabilities, it appears that students quickly assimilated the nuances of the moralizing climate. John Carlin, perhaps the most eminent alumnus of the American Asylum, insisted that before Gallaudet "*all* the deaf mutes of the country were *ignorant heathens*" ("Ceremonies,"1854, p. 33, original italics). Another described those who were deaf as an "excommunicated class" ("Ceremonies," 1854, p. 29).

In their paternalistic mien, teachers and benefactors were wont to refer to people with disabilities, whatever their age, as children. Such a stance of omniscient authority by schoolmen toward their dependent charges reinforced the familiar parent-child roles of authority and dependency, not unusual in antebellum America. It was a socially endorsed ideology: obedience to authority and conformity to rules were primary features of child-care dogma and institutional settings (see Bremner, 1970, 1970–1974; Rothman, 1971; Valentine, 1993).

Traditionally, abnormal individuals were seen not only as valueless but also as generally harmful to society; besides being nonproducers, they absorbed the energy and the productive power of others. Specialized training served to turn consumers into producers. Blind people, noted a 1836 commentator, "are generally paupers; they have always been so, and the place to seek the blind has always been at the way side begging for alms" (Dunscombe, 1836, p. 97). For blind children, schooling would remove from society "so many dead weights" and prevent them from becoming "taxes on the community" (Dunscombe, 1836, pp. 97–98). Education would emancipate deaf children from "the fetters . . . imposed by their deafness" (Ontario Institution for the Education and Instruction of the Deaf and Dumb, 1895, p. 12). With respect to those who were mentally retarded, "Being consumers and not producers they are a pecuniary burden to the state. Educate them and they will become producers," (Knight, 1860, cited in Trent, 1994, p. 25).

What the institutions also confronted was the need to establish an employment role for their students. It was critical that "industrious habits were formed and preliminary training secured by the operators while at school, which enabled them to succeed after leaving" (Ontario Institution for the Education and Instruction of the Deaf and Dumb, 1893, p. 17). Industrial training became the vehicle "to transform a helpless class into happy and useful citizens" (Ontario Institution for the Education and Instruction of the Deaf and Dumb, 1885, p. 15). The goals envisaged matched generally held social expectations for the lower classes: qualifying people in those groups to act as useful cogs in their own strata of society.

As students were presented with programs that were thought consonant with their intellectual ability and later social roles, literary pursuits were deemphasized. In all the institutions, 4 hours of academic work a day was generally all that was allotted to older students. "I would not prevent them from learning to read and write, or acquiring a store of intellectual knowledge," wrote Samuel Gridley Howe, director of the first school for the blind, "but it should not be allowed to impede their way in learning their trade" (cited in Dunscombe, 1836, p. 105). At Howe's school, one class of blind children from rich parents learned geography, history, English, French, and arithmetic. Those from the poorer ranks passed their time solely in learning trades, handicraft work, and music (Perkins Institution for the Blind, 1834).

With limited official funding and a reliance on charity, the institutions were impelled to become self-sufficient congregations. Students worked for their supper, and the institutions cheerfully exploited their labor. Older students were actually an economic advantage. They contributed heavily to the upkeep of their home institution through work in the garden, farm, or sewing shops; produced articles for sale; and took part in public exhibitions of their attainments designed to raise funds.

Education for Deaf Students

North American institutions, including those for deaf students, were originally modeled on earlier European enterprises, with Canadian institutions closely following the European-inspired models of the United States.[1] After 1817, the American Asylum founded by Gallaudet (1787–1851) became more or less the model, and it provides an authoritative basis for generalizations to the nation as a whole. Schools became strikingly similar in philosophy and practice: all used the manual methods of Epée, filtered through Gallaudet and taught by the deaf teacher brought from France, Laurent Clerc. Then, as Alexander Graham Bell later chidingly observed, "The teachers trained at this school naturally became the principals of other institutions established upon its model, and thus the sign-language has been diffused over the length and breadth of our land" (Bell, 1884b, p. 52).

All orders of instruction surrounded the notion that deaf people needed to be virtuous, pious, and useful. Virtue and piety arose from knowing God and the Bible. Usefulness referred not only to daily academic education but also to the industrial training for life after the school years and to student upkeep of the institutions.

A persistent theme that characterizes the education of deaf students is the manner in which their traditions related directly to the residential institutions. To quote one school superintendent from 1900, "To the deaf, their alma mater is the true home of their minds, where their intellects were first awakened, where their first mental concepts were obtained, where their understanding was born into light and freedom" (Ontario Institution for the Education and Instruction of the Deaf and Dumb, 1900, p. 9).

In many respects, institutional living would seem to be a perverse negation, a pale imitation, of proper family life. For many students with disabilities who are arbitrarily separated from home and community, this perspective is probably true. Schooling for deaf students seems to require a different lens, although it is difficult to evaluate the overall effect of life in an institutional context. School leaders were the historical actors making grand claims, not students. Scant evidence exists about students' reactions to removal from home and family, about whether they found the paternalistic benevolence characteristic of Gallaudet and his contemporaries irksome and patronizing, or whether they bemoaned their sojourn in a setting invigilated by evangelical overseers. The institutional annual reports, written for the scrutiny of legislators, trustees, benefactors, and the public, were generally celebratory. Occasionally, they mentioned the victories of students, rarely the setbacks.

However, the testimony of letters from former students that fill the pages of institutional reports suggest that many students cherished their school experience; they referred to their school days with affection and to their teachers with respect. One former student of the Ontario Institution wrote in 1897 that "we are thankful that the institution was built for the education of the deaf. I don't know what I would be if I had not been sent to school to get educated." His brother reiterated the theme. "I don't know how I should be getting along in my life," he wrote, "had I not been sent to school. Please accept my heartfelt thanks for your kindness to me at school" (Ontario Institution for the Education and Instruction of the Deaf and Dumb, 1897, p. 37).

It is plausible to suggest that students absorbed the flavor of schooling and were amenable to new attachments. Human relationships are important determinants of the nature, quality, and consequences of educational experiences. Association with other deaf people and the elusive influence of peers may have counted more in children's lives than a family and community in which communication incongruity was the norm. Alexander Graham Bell, although adamantly opposed to institutional settings, well understood. The deaf child, he wrote, "longs for the school play-ground, and the deaf companions with whom he can converse so easily. Little by little the ties of blood and relationship are weakened, and the *institution becomes his home*" (Bell, 1884b, p. 55, original italics).

In the early schools, a high percentage of the teaching staff members were deaf men: the proportion averaged 40% in the period spanning 1817 to 1896. With deaf teachers and the language of signs, specialized curricula, and isolated settings, it is hardly surprising that the institutions became organizing elements in the world of deafness. Students began to see deafness and sign language as configuring them into a category of people with different and special abilities. The first edition of the *American Annals of the Deaf and Dumb* in 1847 noted that "the deaf and dumb constitute a distinct and, in some respect, strongly marked class of human beings" (Rae, 1847, p. 4). Identity that was intimately bound to deafness came to life as the deaf community.

Evidence of deaf communities existed long before the founding of American schools for the deaf (see e.g., Mottez, 1993). Pursuing the theme then, the American institutions could be seen as becoming cradles of deaf culture; sign language, the nurse maid. The institutional stress on factory-based trades such as carpentry and shoemaking directed deaf graduates toward urban centers as they searched for remunerative employment. For deaf school leavers, particularly those drawn to the cities, the deaf community sustained a way of life by providing for its members identification with others sharing similar experiences, a social network, support in adapting to urbanization, and links to the countryside (Winzer, 1993a). Churches eventually formed the hub, involved as they were in "social, literary, and charitable work" with the deaf population.[2]

Education for Blind Students

Throughout history, two contradictory themes have defined blindness. Sighted people, tending to react to blindness on an emotional level, perceived people blind as either dependent or heroic. The dependent notion surrounded blindness with fear, myth, and superstition, all associated with darkness, despair, loneliness, and punishment. The condition was perceived as social liability, as punishment for sin, or as uselessness to self and others (Farrell, 1956; French, 1932; Ross, 1951). The opposing theme held that blind people were compensated for their lack of sight by both psychological and physical factors. Superhuman and spiritual powers, uncanny memory ability, and musicality were all traits attributed to those who were blind.

Common perceptions in the early 19th century placed blind people not only in the beggar or pauper classes but also as potential candidates for schooling. The success of the American Asylum lent a note of optimism to proposals to educate blind people in the 1830s. Thomas Hopkins Gallaudet, who resigned from the American Asylum in 1830, was invited by the new trustees of the Massachusetts Asylum for the Blind to assume the role of principal. Citing poor health, an attachment to Hartford, as well as other charitable commitments and writing, Gallaudet declined. Instead, Samuel Gridley Howe (1801–1876), a liberal Unitarian reformer whose legacy is claimed by both general and special educators, became director of what would later become the Perkins Institution in Boston. Other schools opened in New York in 1831 (slightly before Howe's school) and Pennsylvania in 1833.

Despite the assurances of promoters to the contrary, there were many debates about the feasibility of educating blind people (Best, 1934). When the New York Institution opened, for example, there were some who "laughed at the project as a wild undertaking," while "even the benevolent looked upon it as a well-meant, but utopian scheme" (New York Institution for the Blind, 1845, pp. 14, 22). Yet, Boston's school for blind children (first called the New England Asylum for the Blind, then the Perkins Institution and Massachusetts Asylum for the Blind, and finally just the Perkins Institution) was an immediate success. The trustees announced after 5 months of operation that "their most sanguine expectations of the capacity of the blind for receiving an education have been fully verified in the progress of the interesting beings under their charge" (Dunscombe, 1836, p. 95).

Howe did not lack the theology of Gallaudet. But as a medical man, he staked out different territory by adding a scientific tinge—a phrenological framework. The principles of the pseudoscience of phrenology arose from the work of Franz Joseph Gall, who began to lecture on his theories in Germany about 1800 (Temkin, 1947). Howe, a member of the group that founded the Boston Phrenological Society, cited phrenology as the source for all his educational principles (Schwartz, 1952). Within his complicated and religiously inflected pedagogy, however, phrenology was more germane to his work with those who were mentally retarded than to work with those who were blind. Founded on phrenology and evangelical Protestantism, Howe moved toward viewing morality as a central concern in mental deficiency (Gelb, 1989).

In contrast to the choices that founders made in establishing schools for those who were deaf or intellectually disabled, founders of schools for blind children did not seek rural settings. Most schools for blind children were confined to large cities, seen as the primary sources for donations and support. In some cases, the schools were located at or near the state capital, "the more thoroughly to convince the legislators of what the blind were capable of accomplishing" (Best, 1934, p. 282). Further, private schools were not attempted for blind students, although they were prominent in other categories (see Best, 1934).

Funding was a constant issue. In 1837, in a New Hampshire farmhouse, Howe met a powerful source—Laura Bridgman, then a child age 7 years, who was robbed by scarlet fever of hearing, sight, smell, and taste. Once in school, Howe sent Laura through a series of structured lessons and exercises. Under his tutelage, she became the first deaf and blind person ever to learn to communicate through language, although she did not become fully independent and remained at Perkins until her death in 1889 (see Howe & Hall, 1903; Lamson, 1878).

The public was fascinated by this tale of intellectual resurrection (Freeberg, 1994). Howe, an artful publicist, provided musical concerts and frequent public exhibitions of his pupils, especially Laura. Thousands of tourists flocked to the school for its weekly fund-raising exhibitions. European luminaries made Perkins a mandatory stop on their American tours (Freeberg, 1994).

Education for Students With Intellectual Disabilities

The reality of institutional training for students with mental retardation waited on three events. Formal schooling in Europe and North America emerged only after the recognition of (a) a distinct category of mental disability, (b) intervention with adult mentally ill people, and (c) successful intervention with those who were deaf or blind.

Determining sophisticated distinctions between mental illness and mental retardation was an effort that confounded medical men and educators. It was not until the early decades of the 19th century that mental retardation became a recognized category of disability separate from mental illness or incorrigibility. Even then, the category of mental retardation was blurred and ill defined, marked by constant flux in classifications, definitions, and terminology. (See Chapters 6 and 7).

In the European and the American contexts, intervention with adults with mental illness paved the route for work with children with mental retardation. In North America, the first half of the 19th century saw a variety of asylum experiences (see Dwyer, 1987). The first state hospital opened in Virginia in 1773; Kentucky opened a public asylum for the insane in 1824. In the next few decades, practically every state opened public facilities for the insane as "a cult of asylums swept the country" (Rothman, 1971, p. 130). By 1860, 28 of 33 states had established public insane asylums. A sole woman, Dorothea Dix, a retired school teacher, was instrumental in the establishment of 32 hospitals for the mentally ill between 1841 and 1881 (Zilboorg & Henry, 1941).

Pinel's moral treatment, interpreted by American practitioners, considered education as conducive to mental health (Bockoven, 1956). Evidence exists of young children placed in asylums and also of educational programs (e.g., Brigham, 1845, 1847). Dr. Francis T. Stribbling (1842), director of the Western Lunatic Asylum in Virginia, reported that, of 122 patients in 1841, 11 were younger than the age of 20. Dorothea Dix spoke of an asylum where she saw "a little girl, about nine or ten years of age, who suffered the fourfold calamity of being blind, deaf, dumb and insane" (Bremner, 1970, p. 777). In addition, a few students with mental retardation were accepted at the American Asylum, the New York Institution for the Deaf and Dumb, and the Perkins Institute for the Blind (Brockett, 1860; Heck, 1940; Tuke, 1968).

Agitation for an institution solely for those who were mentally retarded began in New York in 1846 but was found to be too costly for the state (Brockett, 1856). Intent crystallized in the same year in Massachusetts when Samuel Gridley Howe launched an exhaustive 2-year inquiry into the treatment of retarded people in the Commonwealth. Howe's 1848 report to the state legislature on the status of idiots in Massachusetts skillfully combined arguments of religion, humanity, duty, and economy.

Like Seguin, Howe believed that mental retardation could be largely eliminated or at least ameliorated with proper treatment. It was a moral imperative to make the attempt and a moral offence for society to allow "beings originally made in God's image [to sink] in utter brutishness" (Howe, 1848, p. 4). The legislature responded to Howe's pleas with enthusiasm and funded the Experimental School for the Teaching and Training of Idiotic Children on a trial basis. It opened in October, 1848 in a wing of the institution already founded for blind students by Howe in South Boston.

In 1851, Howe's experimental school became permanent as the Massachusetts School for Idiotic and Feeble-Minded Children. Howe retained general oversight of the institution. Similar institutions opened contemporaneously. Hervey Wilbur, a teacher at Howe's school, opened a private facility at Barre, Massachusetts, in July, 1848, with Howe's approbation. In addition, the Pennsylvania Training School for Feeble-Minded Children was founded in 1852. Around 1871, it began to be informally called the Elwyn Institution and, in 1927, officially became the Elwyn Training School. Compared with institutions for the deaf, growth in this period was relatively slow. By the mid-1860s, there were only 10 schools catering to children with intellectual disabilities.

Political pressures in France forced Edouard Seguin to emigrate in 1848. He settled first in Ohio and, later, in New York, to practice medicine. But because the teaching of children with mental retardation was modeled on European methods, often his own, he was soon invited to assist in the development of institutions, curricula, and professional organizations. For example, details of Seguin's services as advisor and organizer of class work are found in records of the Massachusetts, New York, and Pennsylvania institutions (Penrose, 1949/1966; Talbot, 1964).

Seguin's hugely influential *Idiocy and Its Treatment by the Physiological Method* (1866) explained the training school model and his psychological method. Of the major principles that underlay the training school model, the first was that the institutions should be small. Seguin recommended accommodating no more than 150 to 200 children—the number that the superintendent could know, care for medically, plan for, and thoroughly study throughout their school careers (Talbot, 1964). For example, the New York Asylum for Idiots, which formally opened in 1855 at Syracuse, provided for 150 children at the outset (Tuke, 1968). Second, the facilities were to be in rural areas that would ensure pure air, a healthy climate, and a varied terrain. Seguin proposed a colony model. Cottages would graft the branches of home and asylum to serve as a home-like reunion for children.

Seguin's specific and systemized physiological method encompassed three major components: motor and sensory physical training, intellectual training, and moral training or socialization (see Ball, 1971; Holman, 1914; Kanner, 1960; Talbot, 1964). For his children, Seguin "sought only to bring them a few steps forward" ("Here and there . . . ," 1943, p. 213). The program proceeded in small, incremental steps from basic skills to more formal education and from play activities to useful work and vocational skills (Crissey, 1975). James Kauffman (1976) observed that the teaching techniques used were modern in many respects. They were based on individual assessments; were highly structured, directive, and multisensory; emphasized training in self-help and daily living skills; made frequent use of games and songs; and were suffused with positive reinforcement.

Determining the specific clientele of these early institutions for children with intellectual disabilities that were designed as educational in nature is somewhat troubling. The early literature is unclear about just who was served. As if to confound the issue, promoters used different, often vague, terminology. Seguin, for example, used the word *idiot* to describe mental retardation both generically and as a category. To Seguin, an idiot was an individual "who knows nothing, can do nothing, and wishes nothing; and every idiot approaches more or less to this minimum of incapacity" (Brockett, 1856, p. 78).

Some statements of early programming note that the schools were intended to serve those who could profit from instruction, that is, mildly or occasionally moderately mentally retarded children and adolescents—those children who "by deficient intellect [are] rendered unable to acquire an education in the common schools" (Powell, 1882, p. 268). Howe would not accept students who showed no promise of improvement. Other commentators (e.g., Penrose, 1949/1966) observed that "most of the educational work was carried out on subjects who would now be considered to be severely subnormal and to fall into the categories of idiots and imbeciles," people "mostly ineducable [*sic*] in the ordinary scholastic sense" (p. 6). Seguin himself preferred to work with the more severely disabled students and directed attention to their needs. In a burst of florid hyperbole, Brockett (Seguin's friend and translator) wrote that under the doctor's care "the thick veil which had enshrouded the mind of the idiot was rent asunder, and these innocent but hapless creatures were rescued from the doom of a life of utter vacuity" (1856, p. 73).

It is not surprising that Seguin's work lent a note of optimism to the entire field and entranced the public with the "cult of curability," the notion that many mental defects could be ameliorated or eliminated entirely. Brockett (1856) estimated that about one-quarter of mentally retarded persons could be improved by Seguin's treatment.

SUMMARY AND THEMES

The 18th century, like most other periods in history, is difficult to characterize in a few pages, and the influence of Enlightenment thought cannot be simplistically interpreted. The spirit of reform abroad in Europe in midcentury did not mutate into complete enlightenment, rationalism, urbanity, and good sense. But throughout Europe and Britain, the second half of the 18th century witnessed the development of special education with effective procedures devised for the training and teaching of many disabled groups. France was the crucible where innovations such as the language of signs for deaf people, raised print for blind people, and the beginnings of distinctions between retardation and insanity emerged.

The ideas flourishing in France were adopted and adapted or rejected and reviled. Either way, the brave new concepts were not ignored and, ultimately, resulted in advances for people with disabilities that were founded on a growing humanistic instinct that became characteristic of the era. Educational provisions for individuals with disabling conditions emerged in a number of national contexts. In Europe and Britain, instruction was no longer confined to isolated cases or regarded merely as a subject of philosophic curiosity. Permanent facilities were established, staffed by a cadre of teachers experimenting with novel and innovative pedagogical methods.

The French advances did not go unheeded by early 19th-century American reformers. Pioneers such as Thomas Hopkins Gallaudet and Samuel Gridley Howe crossed the Atlantic to assess and study French, British, and German philosophies and pedagogies. Back on American soil, they found a common level of sympathy to improve the lives of people who were weak, dependent, or disabled.

Early special education, developed under the aegis of the clergy and philanthropy, was presented in an expanding complex of institutional settings. From the formation of the first special institution in 1817 until about 1850, the field established itself and constructed images of disablement that ensured public sympathy and funding.

Social institutions do not exist in a vacuum nor do they appear suddenly without warning. They "emerge" as Foucault (1972) said, out of a particular historical situation; as a response to a certain set of social pressures; and within a complex frame of social, economic, philosophical, and other interactions. Institutional openings coincided with a period of wide social reform and embodied the three major principles of 19th-century child rescue—protection, separation, and dependence. Development was built on the recognition of the need for organized social responsibility and intrinsically was associated with changing social, economic, political, and religious determinants of early 19th-century American society.

Powerful and influential reformers and pioneers promoted and directed special education. Edouard Seguin, for example, provided benchmarks for the nascent field: his principles, tested in France, guided institutional development. Samuel Gridley Howe's efforts were critical both in focusing attention on mental deficiency and in establishing the first educational facility. For Thomas Hopkins Gallaudet, intervention served evangelical and social purposes: his reform activities included those who were deaf, insane, slaves, and others.

As these leaders set out to ameliorate the torturing uncertainty of poverty, old age, and unemployment, it became characteristic of reformers throughout the entire century to advocate different forms of organization. Child savers and child shapers stressed specialized and separate provisions for children; all agreed that institutionalization was the most effective solution to the dilemma of difference. Separation as the dominant motif remained a fixture of special education until at least the 1960s.

Although we cannot diminish the significance of personal virtue and the noble and benevolent intentions of philanthropy, the stances of early schoolmen emphasized the inferior status of disabled people. Paternalism, kindness, and a missionary impulse held widespread appeal and brought approval and praise to the dedicated individuals employed in the task. Yet those perspectives also pointed to the lacks in judgment and ability as well as in the discharge of moral responsibilities that were seen as inherent in disability.

It is not plausible to maintain a simplistic theory of social control—or humanitarian impulse—as a way of explaining the institutional movement. Indeed, how could any field that originated from the concerns of religious individuals as well as from the active engagement of its founders with the problems of disability not struggle with the differences between advocacy and control? It must be recognized that the institutionalization of students with exceptionalities had two faces—humanitarian and controlling—that were always in tension with each other. Reformers held a variety of motives, including both a desire to control people with disabilities and a wish to improve their lives. The two strands embraced progressive ideas on the prevention of social problems and, at the same time, ultimately contributed to people with disabilities being seen as special populations.

Curriculum was designed on two prongs. Religion and moral development, founded on an ideology of rehabilitation within Christian beliefs, formed one essential tenet of instruction. Industrial training and postschool productivity similarly occupied schoolmen. The stress on industrial training reflected an acute recognition of the social realities of industrializing American society. Through practical instruction in trades and domestic skills, the institutions sought to turn disabled people into productive, law-abiding workers. At the same time, the institutions were unable to operate without pupil labor.

There were no sharp differences in the daily routines in the various institutions for those who were deaf, blind, or mentally retarded. Apart from academic training, all students were involved in industrial training and assumed responsibilities with respect to household and domestic tasks to earn their keep. Industrial training and menial occupations were directly related to their future employment and status in society: the expectations with respect to chores and duties and the future roles of people with disabilities in the work force were identical with middle-class expectations of the lower class generally.

NOTES

1. Canada carefully followed American examples in schooling. Egerton Ryerson, founder of Canada's common schools, wrote in 1868 that it was the United States "to whose example and experience we are so much indebted for the establishment and success of our Canadian School system" (Ryerson, 1848, p. 150). Then, in planning and developing institutional settings, the provinces "followed the customary practice of borrowing heavily from American experience" (Ontario, Inspector of Prisons, Asylums, and Public Charities 1878, p. 2). Later, the success of special schools and classes in the United States "had a marked effect on public opinion in Ontario" ("Auxiliary Classes," 1910, p. 10, located at the Ontario Archives, Government Document, Education Miscellaneous Box 19, No. 7) and provided one model for Canadian segregated classes. Dr. Percival, director of Protestant Education for Quebec, further noted that "The term *special class* is used in Canada as it is in the United States" (1946–47, p. 237; original italics).

2. Letter to Mrs. W. M. Voires from P. J. Whildon, May 24, 1926. Located in Rare Pamphlets, Volta Bureau, Washington, DC.

Chapter 2

Changing Directions

In the first 3 or 4 decades of the 19th century, the American population was small, rural, and relative homogeneous. Rural life bred a traditionalism that translated into the acceptance of a fairly common set of values. Occupationally, people were bound to nature's cycles. By the middle of the century, the face of America began to undergo dramatic changes. Both the society and the social institutions that emerged from this crucible were fundamentally different from the rurally based, domestically centered socioeconomic system that preceded it.

A transformed America saw new relations between man and machine and new conceptions of time and space. At the same time, North America became the refuge of Europe and the hope of depressed millions. The population of the United States increased more than 10 times between 1800 and 1860 and doubled again by 1890. Massive immigration and imported cheap labor allowed manufacturing and urbanization to take firm hold.

Mid-century changes were attended by a perceived decline in the very fabric of society. Child labor, unemployment, and the sins of intemperance, prostitution, and gambling grew into vexatious social issues. The development of industry and the separation of people from the land resulted in an army of beggars (Jennings, 1930). The desperation of some immigrants and the exigencies of frontier life saw a swelling tide of drunkards and vagrants in the towns. This tide grew in alarming proportions; one report noted that in the United States from 1850 to 1890, the population increased 170%, and the criminal class increased 445% (MacDonnell, 1897).

Growth of cities and slums was rampant. The inner cities were densely populated; industrial areas and slum districts developed alongside one another in the older areas. Housing—cramped, unsanitary, and unpleasant—could barely keep pace with the burgeoning population. By 1893, for example, 1.5 million people crowded into Manhattan's Lower East Side, the most notorious slum in New York City (Kode, 2002). Moreover, the newcomers were not people of the traditional norm. To many, they were strange people with strange customs, alien religions, strange clothes, and strange institutions.

In the guise of an expanding institutional complex, educational programs for the normative categories of disability were in place. The second half of the 19th century, however, is remarkable for the number of initiatives undertaken for the social welfare and education of many more children—typical, disadvantaged, as well as disabled. What seems to unite many of the developers of these programs and institutions was a common ideology and rhetoric concerning the dangers of pauperism, ignorance, disability, and delinquency of the children they were trying to help. As reformers formed a community of self-conscious educational innovators who devoted their energies to social change through the school system, they included special education under their reform umbrella. Institutionalization continued apace: the institutional complex expanded dramatically and embraced a greater variety of individuals.

There was little that was truly revolutionary in the additions made to special education as practiced in institutional settings in North America in the latter half of the 19th century, with the exception of the extent to which it had become built into formal systems. Growth is better viewed as evolutionary. The reason for this conceptually circumscribed growth occurred because most new initiatives were simply grafted onto an existing tree of services and programs rather than planted separately. The precedents, forms, methodologies, terminologies, classification schemes, and even attitudes and perceptions that were designed and practiced by pioneer special school organizers were renewed, reconceptualized, and provided with a new lexicon. But the essential outlines remained in place.

What was new were special classes for students with special needs that were initiated as part of the full development of the common schools. For normally developing students, the 1850s saw public schooling established as an integral component of the new mass-industrialized society. The rhetoric of the common school ideology reflected the reformist, optimistic, and ultimately political impulses that characterized much of the educational thought in the United States during the mid-19th century. Yet, almost from the outset, the founding ideology of the common school movement—all children in one classroom—quickly stumbled. When it became apparent that a common education for all students was not possible, the response was the development of special, segregated classes. Children sent into the special placements tended to show the unholy trinity of academic retardation, low intelligence, and undesirable behavior.

THE BIRTH OF THE COMMON SCHOOLS

Education has long occupied a special place in the optimistic vision of Americans. One of the proudest claims of North American society is its support of education for all citizens: in most places, residents take pride in their nation's egalitarian educational ideals. They assess the presence and contributions of schools and other educational institutions as core elements that define, sustain, and advance their communities.

The ethical imperative to provide universal education for all children is a relatively recent phenomenon. When the United States was born, very little of the new nation's energies could be spared for the education of its children. During the Colonial period (1642 to 1776), laws provided for grammar schools, which children could enter at age 7, once they could read; children attended usually for no more than 4 or 5 years. Schooling expanded slowly in the post-Revolutionary period and was conducted by family, churches, private schools, or voluntary municipal common schools. By 1789, for example, Massachusetts required all towns with 50 families to provide 6 months of education annually for all children; in 1827, the state compelled school districts to support schools (Carrier, 1986a). By the 1820s, public concern about illiteracy and the failure of families to provide reading instruction led to the beginnings of agitation for education laws (Hewes, 1989).

The push toward a tax-supported, universal public education system was a national movement that derived its authority from an assumed admission that popular education should be in the care of the states. Massachusetts in 1837 and Connecticut in 1838 were the first to establish state boards to oversee public education. Apologists for public education systems had definite, but differing, ideas about the schools' nature, function, and responsibility. Hence, any consensus about the importance of universal schooling was marred by disagreements over the form and direction. Teachers, legislators, and religious leaders went to war over matters of school structure, funding, political authority, and classroom management.

No state has been more closely identified with the common school movement than Massachusetts and no single man more than Horace Mann (1796–1859). The year 1848 can be seen as the benchmark. As secretary of the Massachusetts State Board of Education, Mann reorganized the quasi-public school system of Massachusetts to make public education, for the first time in the United States, a state vehicle supported by taxes.

Once underway, the growth of the American public school as a major social institution was quite rapid. In a few decades, the school paradigm was transformed from a relatively informal and unsystematic minor institution catering largely to the middle class to one that was open to all levels of society. By the 1880s, the change with respect to education was so sweeping that a child took as a matter of course what had not been available to the great majority of children just half a century earlier. To be sure, it was a simple educational world; although built on the notion of schooling for all children, it typically provided no more than the rudiments of language, geography, history, and arithmetic. Rote learning remained the rule. Despite the pleas of some reformers, classroom procedures were formal and intensely structured. Curriculum was inflexible, erected on the framework of sequenced textbooks for students to memorize. Johanningmeier (1989) explains how students used the *New England Primer* and Noah Webster's *Spelling Book* to learn to read. From the *Primer*, they were expected to learn piety; from the speller, patriotism.

Educators saw early adolescence, not early childhood, as the formative years. Before the common school reform, schools tended to accept very young children. In the period that matched the development of the common schools, there occurred "a veritable outpouring of opposition to premature mental exertion in the literature of domestic advice, in the reports of educational administrators, in the rhetoric of professional pedagogues, and in the pages of professional educational journals" (Finkelstein, 1985, p. 5). Schooling, considered inappropriate for young children, was directed specifically at the 6- to 12-year-old groups. This practice meant that the concept of the standard grade, first used in Massachusetts in 1847, could be fully implemented. Children of the same ages were expected to master pretty much the same curriculum content in the same time.

Not every child attended. Even in the states that passed compulsory attendance laws before 1900, enforcement tended to be scattered and sporadic, with attendance rates often distressingly low. In fact, for most of the 19th century, only the middle class throughout the nation responded to the common schools. Rural communities, rural lifestyles, and Protestant churchgoing prompted high annual enrollments (Kaestle & Vinovskis, 1980).

One problem, it seemed, was with the poor themselves, who appeared disinterested in and disinclined to force schooling on their children. A child could not attend because "it has no clothes; it is not kept clean; the mother would not take the trouble to send it, and school boards are not always sufficiently interested to provide accommodation and enforce attendance" (Kelso, 1893–94, p. 214). For many other children, the alarmingly low rates of attendance reflected deeper social values; often, school was something to be slotted in with the other needs of the family and was a relatively minor aspect of growing up.

To Horace Mann and his fellow reformers, the tax-supported common schools served as a cloak under which a great many secondary projects and ideas sought substance and advancement. Political, social, economic, and educational domains were all part of the mix.

In the broadest political sense, children had the right to an education that would make them effective citizens, and society had an obligation to provide the instruction. Training for citizenship through education was important. Schooling was viewed as an essential component of preparing young Americans for republican citizenship, but in addition, the instillation of American values provided a bulwark against the radical social, economic, and demographic changes that threatened to destabilize American society as it raced toward industrialization and urbanization. Schools paid great attention to the special characteristics of their nation and how their nation and its forms of government differed from those of other nations.

Linked to this perspective was the dominant American ideology of assimilation—diverse cultures united into a single, homogeneous society with common lifestyles, language, and cultural practices. The common schools would create a single, cohesive public out of a diverse and fragmented population. Schooling, therefore, concerned the cultivation of national identity and selfhood as much as the execution of pedagogical theory and techniques. For newcomers, the schools were the primary founts of socialization; they represented the unique means to introduce immigrant children of varied ethnic, cultural, linguistic, and religious backgrounds to the general value system and the lifestyle of the dominant culture.

Together with social mores, the learning of moral values rested on the schools' assumption of the process. Schooling was promoted as "a preventative of pauperism and vice" (Ryerson, 1848, p. 175). Holding perhaps exalted notions of teachers' cultural power and moral suasion, child savers and educators were optimistic that societal problems could be alleviated through the mechanisms of the schools.

Moreover, society now demanded workers who could contribute to the vision of an expanding America and who could tolerate the drastic changes in the work that was itself inherent in developing technology. Many began to stress the interdependence between national prosperity and the ability of society, through its schools, to train and deliver a skilled labor force. Schooling became "a benefit to the industrial pursuits of life" (Ryerson, 1848, p. 175). It would create productive citizens by instilling in children a clear sense of adult duties and proper conceptions of work, marked by self-control and induced through the systematic inculcation of acceptable habits.

THE GENESIS OF SPECIAL CLASSES

The term *common school* had a specific meaning: a school that was attended in common by all children at no cost and in which a common political and social ideology was taught (Spring, 1994). Hence, the initial vision of the common schools embraced all students, from the docile and tractable to the deviant and the intractable. But almost from the outset, the reformist and optimistic impulses that characterized the common school ideal faltered when confronted with disobedient, rambunctious, and nonconforming students. Issues of classroom behavior touched on basic notions of child normalcy (or deviance) as well as the authority of adults and of social institutions such as schools. The school system was little willing to tolerate students who violated social mores, failed to conform to the expectations of teachers, and mounted threats to the placidity of general classrooms.

Problematic students were the troublemakers, depicted in contemporary reports, as the "morally as well as intellectually weak" and the "troublesome and obnoxious" (see Osgood, 1997, pp. 386–387). The majority were male. As Baker (1949–50) later pointed out, "boys of all ages bully, fight, and act smart aleck much more frequently than girls" (p. 203). Joining the problem group were children of immigrant backgrounds who posed administrative and educational problems to the schools.

Rapidly, the troublesome matters of deviance, difference, and delinquency were addressed, not through the general classrooms' assumption of the educational process, but through the mechanisms of ungraded classes and classes for unruly students. The movement for special classes did not arrive from France. Americans directly and indirectly adopted ideas from the German *Hilfsschulen* and *Sonderklassen* (special classes). The first classes used models developed in Halle (Germany) in 1859 that were "organized solely for the feeble-minded" (Wallin, 1914, p. 386).

The initial classes served children returning from the work force, incorrigibles, truants, and low achievers (Tropea, 1987). For example, New Haven, Connecticut, opened an ungraded class for truant, dull, and insubordinate children in 1871, which became, noted the New Haven Superintendent of Schools, "an indispensable appendage to our graded school system" (in Hoffman, 1972, p. 17). The same type of class was founded in Detroit in 1883 (Tropea, 1987). In Los Angeles in 1905, a special class was organized for persistent boy truants with a curriculum related to the life interests of the pupils (Wallin, 1938–39).

In theory, ungraded classes focused on restoration and remediation; classes for unruly students served the recalcitrant, the disobedient, and the truant. However, many school systems operated only one type of special class, which was often used merely to dispose of children who did not conform to a school's behavioral standards. Similarly, the classes for unruly students or the ungraded classes were often a hodgepodge bin, disproportionately filled with immigrant children. Elizabeth Farrell (1908) described the first special class in New York City as "made up of the odds and ends of a large school. There were over-age children, so-called naughty children, and the dull and stupid children. The ages ranged from eight to sixteen years. They were the children who could not get along in school" (p. 91).

Reformers and leading educators articulated the practical, philosophical, and pedagogical bases for the establishment of special segregated classes within the public schools using arguments about class size, teacher time, and declining standards. Placing difficult students in ungraded or in classes for unruly students, for example, would allow normal students to proceed adequately so that the "unassimilable accumulation of clinks, ballast, driftwood, or derelicts" (Wallin, 1924, p. 24) would not retard the rest of the class or absorb all the energies of the teacher.

Many of the classes that were formed before 1900 faltered or failed. Those that functioned as coaching classes to give individual attention in the content of the regular curriculum and sought to raise the pupils' standards to those of regular class members failed in their efforts at remediation. Heck (1940) observed that "Public education did not take much interest in such special schools or classes until compulsory attendance laws came into being" (p. 21). Not surprisingly, classes suffered from a lack of trained teachers, materials, official commitment, and funding.

All the early special classes carried stigma. Only small numbers attended, a condition preserved by the nonenforcement of compulsory education laws, attrition, and the notion that school attendance was a privilege that could be awarded or withheld for an individual child at the discretion of school officials. Schools tended to preserve the rights of the majority over a disruptive minority and were often antagonized by, and resisted providing for, difficult children (see Kauffman, 2001).

Many of the students were early school leavers, and the public schools were quite content to see unruly pupils leave in the interests of class management and harmony. "Few of them," observed a school superintendent, "remained long enough to attract serious attention or hinder the instruction of the more tractable and capable" (in Sarason & Doris, 1979, p. 263). Such students, said another administrator in 1909, tended "to drop out, or be forced out, of school and the problem of the exceptional child disappeared with him" (in Tropea, 1987, p. 31).

It was not until 1914 that J. E. Wallace Wallin, a leading spokesman for special education, suggested that these settings be called *special classes*. The generic phrase became widely accepted, although Wallin himself preferred more specificity in description. He called for the terms *orthogenic* or *orthophrenic* to prefix classes for "imbeciles, morons, borderline and seriously backward cases"—those children who were clearly disabled, at least 2 or 3 years overage for their grade levels, and needed both different content and differential methods (Wallin, 1914, p. 386). Wallin wanted to retain ungraded classes for students who were pedagogically backward, with the goal of remediation and restoration. He further suggested elementary industrial classes for young adolescents who were appreciably backward or who were overage and who showed themselves to be industrially inclined (Wallin, 1914).

Before Wallin and the widespread adoption of the phrase *special classes*, a hodgepodge of titles and designations matched the varied organizational and physical settings of the classes. In Europe, the prevailing tendency was to organize small, separate schools. Germany, for example, established special schools instead of classes. The English preferred *special school centers*—two or three rooms in small buildings located in a corner of the school yard and separated from the regular building by a high fence (Wallin, 1914). In the United States and Canada, the trend was toward separate classes within regular buildings, although they were often referred to as day schools. For example, by 1914, Dayton, District of Columbia, St. Louis, and Salt Lake City maintained what were described as day schools, although Wallin (1914) observed that "the schools are probably not all housed in separate buildings" (p. 391).

Two main players championed the rights of children with disabilities to attend neighborhood schools—Alexander Graham Bell and Samuel Gridley Howe. Both were unwilling to restrict educational opportunities to the institutional model.

Howe has already been introduced as a fierce evangelical reformer who established the first residential schools for those who were blind and mentally retarded. During the founding years, Howe contended that the intellects of blind children "cannot be developed by the common mode of education and it is to supply peculiar processes of instruction that our Institution is established" (Perkins Institution for the Blind, 1837, p. 5). As they were wont to do, Howe's leanings soon changed and he began to dispute the concept of "Public Charitable Institutions." In 1857, he observed that they, "like all prisons and penal establishments, are evils; and are maintained only to avoid greater ones" (cited in Kirk & Lord, 1974, p. 5). The congregating together of individuals with disabilities resulted in "stamping deeper certain original peculiarities which the teacher would fain efface" (Howe, 1871, p. 14).

Again and again, Howe argued that a common education was the birthright of every child and that the state had the moral obligation to provide an equal education to all, regardless of disability. Public-supported education was not, in his view, an act of charity. Rather, the republican ideal of a common school held an implied promise that an effective education would be offered to all. Institutionalization may have served a need for those with mental retardation, but Howe insisted that "blind children can attend common schools advantageously, and be instructed in classes with common children" (Howe, 1874, p. 119).

Bell arrived in Boston in 1871, ostensibly to teach and promote his father's method of Visible Speech at the Boston Day School for Deaf Mutes. From this toehold, his activities expanded to include his invention of the telephone in 1877, his scientific experiments, his genealogical studies, and his excursions into the fields of Social Darwinism and eugenics.[1]

The Boston school, the first day school within the system of public education, actually predated the ungraded classes and classes for unruly students (as well as Bell's 1871 arrival in Boston). It was established in 1869 on Newbury Street in Boston by Reverend Dexter King, with Sarah Fuller as the founding principal. In May 1877, the name was changed from the Boston Day School for Deaf Mutes to the Horace Mann School for the Deaf (see Numbers, 1974).

An immediate purpose of Fuller's school was to provide a more economical and convenient education for Boston's deaf children. Another purpose nestled within the curriculum and pedagogy that was used—the oral or articulation method in which all instruction depended on speech and speechreading. Sign language was not taught. The fingerspelling alphabet was used, but only temporarily with younger children. This approach meant that in administration and pedagogy—indeed, in almost all aspects—the Horace Mann School was conspicuously out of step with the traditional institutional settings for deaf children.

In one sense, Fuller's school epitomized the transplantation of special education knowledge and practice from isolated institutions to the public schools (Osgood, 1999). In another, it was an expression of the changing views of deaf people, their educability, and their role in society. It advanced the notion that hearing impaired students were not deviant or dependent but, rather, worthy of an education identical to that provided hearing children. In practical terms, Fuller's school provided a model for future day classes. Fuller promoted oralism through demonstrating the authenticity of her modes of instruction. Exhibitions of pupils were used "to excite an interest in the public mind," with the "prospect of hearing deaf-mutes talk," and simultaneously to raise subscriptions for other ventures (de Land, 1908, p. 35).

What was most critical for the future course of the education of deaf children was the manner in which the advent of the school and the advent of the oral methodology altered the distinctive characteristics of the construction of deafness. Simply put, to manual educators (manualists), deafness was a human difference best accommodated through a unique language of signs; those of the oral persuasion (oralists) saw deafness as a disability to be overcome.

When Alexander Graham Bell arrived in Boston in response to an invitation to instruct at the Boston Day School, he came well acquainted not only with the mechanics of sound, deafness, deaf education, and sign language but also with persuasive arguments in favor of oral methodologies. Like Howe, Bell did not attempt to disguise his basic antipathy toward all forms of institutionalization for children. He consistently attacked the private and relatively isolated institutional world that celebrated sign language and led inevitably to the deaf community and marriages among deaf people. "Deaf children," said Bell in 1884, "are gathered into institutions and schools that have been established for their benefit away from the general observation of the public, and even in adult life they hold themselves aloof from hearing people" (Bell, 1884b, p. 34). Bell suggested that "the instruction of deaf children should go hand in hand with the education of those who can hear and speak in the public schools" rather than be conducted in separate institutions

(Ontario Institution for the Education and Instruction of the Deaf and Dumb, 1884, p. 10). In his view, the ideal day school arrangement would be for deaf children to have separate classrooms in a public school building, mingling with hearing children outside of classes.

As a propagandist for the day school cause, Bell was tireless. He advanced the ideas most directly and conspicuously as a lobbyist for state support—so much so that one critic was led to sneer that Bell's appeal was so strong that any interest group "who will get Dr. Bell to come out and appear before the legislature . . . , is going to have a day-school law, and it is going to be drawn just according to Dr. Bell's dictates" (Wilkinson, 1905, p. 82).

When Bell marshaled cogent arguments in favor of his ideology, he took care to put day schools forward as complementing residential schools, not supplanting them. Day schools were the "most economical kind of school" (Bell & Gillett, 1884, p. 3), they improved attendance for the almost half of American deaf children who were not attending school, and they served the many pupils in schools for the deaf who were actually hard of hearing. Day schools would compel students to live and interact in the hearing world, would raise their incentive to use speech, widen their range of personal contacts, and lessen the likelihood that they would eventually intermarry and thereby perpetuate hereditary deafness (see Bell, 1884a).

The notion of day schools held wide appeal for parents and a growing band of oral educators of the deaf. Not surprisingly, teachers in institutions with manual pedagogies resisted: they held that only residential schools could comprehensively address all the needs of deaf students and characterized day schools as "cruel" and "barren of good results" (Wing, 1886, p. 22). One manual educator argued that the chances of success "are far less favorable than in boarding schools" ("Mr. Stainer's . . . ," 1884, p. 252). Another contended that "disappointment and failure have uniformly followed the attempted extension and adaptation of the common school system to the needs of deaf children" (Ontario Institution for the Education and Instruction of the Deaf and Dumb, 1885, p. 15).

Day schools for deaf children faced the same challenges as did the other special classes in the common schools—lack of funding, little official commitment, and untrained teachers. By 1900, only Michigan and Wisconsin had established laws permitting the establishment of day classes for deaf children. Wisconsin created the largest system, which Bell proclaimed to be "the most important movement of the century for the benefit of the deaf" (cited in Bruce, 1973, p. 395). By 1900, Wisconsin had 15 day schools for the deaf; by 1910, there were 20 day schools (Bush, 1942).

For blind students, approximately 10 day schools in the urban areas were established throughout the country by the opening of the 20th century. Harry Best (1934) noted that these schools were "more on the order of the regular common schools, and more distinctly an integral part of the state's educational economy" (p. 293). Again, not all traditional educators were convinced. For example, Wilkinson, then superintendent of the California School for the Deaf and Blind, protested in 1872 at a meeting of instructors of the blind against a resolution that recommended that schools for the blind "should be conducted as nearly as possible according to the manner and methods of seeing schools" (Lowenfeld, 1956, p. 53).

CHANGING ROLES OF INSTITUTIONS, CHANGING CONSTRUCTIONS OF DISABILITY

Institutional settings designed for students with exceptionalities expanded exponentially throughout the 19th century. By 1868 Pennsylvania, for example, had what were described as five insane hospitals, a feebleminded children's institution, an institution for deaf mutes, one for the blind, two reformatories, and one home for friendless children (Pennsylvania Institution for Feeble-Minded, 1868).

In 1852, there were 14 schools for the deaf in North America; 17 by 1855. By 1900, the *Association Review* could report the existence of 59 residential institutions and 55 day schools (Wing, 1902). Schools for blind children similarly expanded: by 1875, there were 30 institutions for the blind in the United States, serving a total of 3,000 pupils, and three in Canada, serving a total of 150 pupils (Halifax Institution for the Blind, 1875). Catering to individuals with mental retardation was slow until the 1880s; from then on, there was unprecedented expansion. By 1888, 14 states had institutions that admitted mentally defective children (Davies, 1959) and it was estimated that there were 4,000 residents within state and private institutions for those who were mentally retarded (Rosen, Clark, & Kivitz, 1976).

Some of the schools for students with disabilities were housed in grand Gothic buildings; others were poor stepsisters. Many early schools for blind children, for example, were modest and unpretentious. They started in a single rented room, in a church, or in the home of a teacher (Best, 1934).

Finances, funding, state appropriations, and donations were matters of grave concern to administrators. Equally compelling were the designations and titles of the segregated settings. In the opening half of the 19th century, schooling for children and youth with special needs was a charitable enterprise—worthy, but unimportant to the national interest. As components of the complex of charitable institutions, the schools were most often administered by state boards of charity in the United States and by departments of prisons, asylums, and public charities in Canada. By the middle of the century, education, which had so far been an issue for religious interests or local communities, moved to become a state responsibility; most American states assumed some responsibility for the education and training of their disabled populations. The transfer of power from the religiously evangelistic, voluntary trustees, and staff members to the bureaucratic social welfare structures and professional urban schoolmen altered the orientation of special education. The new breed introduced an ethic of disinterested public service and sought to uplift the quality of education by standardizing and systemizing.

The official rationales for the existence of institutions went through periodic changes. For students who were deaf or blind, the final 3 decades of the century witnessed mounting agitation among school administrators as they advocated for free and compulsory education under local school board jurisdiction. Charity connotations slowly dissipated; the settings transmuted into schools, albeit separate and special, but with educational goals.

The idea of a purely educational journey became increasingly manifest. Educators argued that individuals with disabilities were neither dependent nor delinquent but worthy of the same educational rights as other children. Discounting the myth of intellectual inferiority for deaf students and blind students, they asserted that their schools trained pupils in scholastic and industrial pursuits and were by no means charitable institutions or asylums but should function as a part of the total educational complex. Many institutions began to condemn the term *asylum*, finding it "altogether out of place when applied to establishments designed solely for educational purposes" (Gallaudet, 1888, p. 3). Schools for the blind dropped the word *asylum* in 1877. In a number of cases, educators asked for and received legal action to have the official names of schools changed so as to eliminate objectionable terms. As an example, in 1896, the Supreme Court of New York ruled that institutions for the deaf and the blind were chiefly educational in their purpose and were not properly classified as charitable institutions (Delehanty, 1896).

Once schools parted company with charitable connotations, positive changes ensued. The principal of the Virginia School for the Deaf wrote that after the "elevation of our school to its rightful position" they did "not have to send out agents to solicit patronage." Pupils, no longer looked on as dependents, could "appreciate the dignity of their position, and the possibilities before them, and slumbering ambition has been aroused" ("Not an asylum . . . ," 1902, pp. 11–12).

Reconstructing Deafness

The second half of the 19th century saw that designs for the education of students who were deaf ventured from the comfortable institutional world into a veritable pedagogical battleground. An array of events were key to the transformation of deaf education and the reconstruction of the concept of deafness.

Higher Education

Little did more to positively alter the social status of deaf people than the creation of an institute of higher learning with academic degrees attached. The Columbia Institution for the Deaf was incorporated by Congress in an act approved on February 16, 1857, under the name of the Columbia Institution for the Instruction of the Deaf and Dumb and Blind. The National Deaf Mute College became the highest department of the Columbia Institution. The College, under the care of the federal government and with Edward Miner Gallaudet at the helm, was given the right to confer degrees in 1864 in an act of Congress approved by the ex officio patron, President Lincoln (Lesperance, 1872). In honor of Thomas Hopkins, the name was changed to Gallaudet College in 1894; on October 24, 1986, it became Gallaudet University.

The Oral-Manual Controversy

In the early residential schools, "the noble language of signs" (C. P. Turner, 1848, p. 78) imported from France was the language of instruction and interaction. The stress on manual modes matched perfectly the evangelical romantic reform movements that stressed regeneration and salvation. Educators, concerned primarily with moral transactions held to "the self-evident axiom that *where there is no language there is no religion*" (McGann, 1863, p. 3, original italics). They never doubted their capacity to achieve the religious and secular redemption of deaf students. Sign language was the primary effective means for the cultivation of morality and knowledge of the Creator, ideal to bring deaf persons to the sacred text of the Bible.

Sign language as the general mode of communication was so widely accepted by schoolmen, students, and the public in this period that it acquired the cohesive force of a cultural compulsion. Inevitably, deaf people began to perceive themselves as a "distinct class" (Smith, 1876, p. 140). In after-school life, they established social networks and a vibrant deaf community.

Beginning in the 1850s, major challenges to universal instruction in, and use of, sign language mounted. The questions and arguments surrounding oralism and manualism were not novel; rather, this controversy is perhaps the longest-running debate in education, dating back to the 16th century. It was in mid-18th-century Europe that the blurred outline of the debate was brought sharply into focus. Epée's silent or manual method, which stressed the supremacy of sign language and manual alphabets, was challenged by an oral mode. The German oral methodology eschewed manual forms entirely, adopting as the central tenet the superiority of speech and speechreading, supplemented with writing.

The first oral salvo in North America sounded after Horace Mann and Samuel Gridley Howe toured European schools for the deaf in 1844. Their visits led them to conclude that the oral modes embraced in northern Europe were superior to other methodologies. Mann and Howe thereafter diligently stirred up educational and public opposition to the manual methods, speaking consistently in support of the superior advantages gained from oralism.

In truth, however, pedagogy was only partly the precursor of powerful change. Although the assaults on manualism emerged from distinctly different ideological perspectives, reform was most often dressed in a social garb. When wealthy parents examined the programs in institutional settings, they found them undesirable in virtually every respect. These parents could not tolerate a sign language that restricted social intercourse; they wished their children to acquire the social graces and the language competencies that would allow them access to polite society. Oralism, they thought, would provide deaf children with respectability manifested in social mobility, refined manners, good taste, respectable religion, proper speech, and literacy.

Confronted with oral ideals, the traditional manual educators were vehement in defending their system. They resented any criticisms, seeing them as a personal attack on their own competence, and were little interested in venturing into novel areas or surrendering their autonomy. Into the early 1860s, the manual views survived relatively unscathed. For example, when parents of deaf children in Massachusetts approached the legislature for the incorporation of the Clarke Institution, a residential private oral school, the petitioners were opposed by teachers from the American Asylum. As one parent reported, "they believed an articulating school would retard the education of the deaf, as it was impracticable to teach the deaf by articulation . . . and the new method was stigmatized as one of the visionary theories of Dr. Howe" (Hubbard, cited in Bell, 1884b, p. 65).

It took three attempts before the oral faction prevailed. In 1864, Harriet Rogers opened a small private oral school in Chelmsford, Massachusetts, the Clarke Institution for Deaf Children. The break with the traditional institutional training was as sharp and resounding as that of the later Horace Mann day school. Although a residential setting, the Clarke School was placed directly under the state's board of education. Whereas the manual institutions generally set admittance eligibility at the age of 10 or older, Clarke took younger children between the ages of 5 and 10 years. The period of instruction at Clarke was lengthened to 10 years and the mode was a purely oral methodology (Clarke Institution for Deaf Children, 1868). Clarke and other early oral schools exercised remarkable control over the selection of their clients by careful admission procedures. The student bodies were select, not heterogeneous. Pupils typically came from the middle and upper classes. Indigent children went to public institutions where they were instructed through sign language.

The Clarke Institution was well publicized and heavily endowed by wealthy and prominent men; it was also closely watched by critics, friendly and unfriendly. The idea that deaf people could be taught to speak, could be "demutized," was one that caught the fancy of the public (Mitchell, 1971). Together with Sarah Fuller's day school, the Clarke Institution became a convincing argument in favor of oralism. Further credence was added by the Europeans who heavily favored oral modes and legitimized oralism within the professional domain at world congresses in 1878, 1880, and 1900. For example, the resolutions declared at the Second International Congress for the Amelioration of the Condition of Deaf Mutes held in Milan in 1880 witnessed an uncompromising avowal of the oral methods.

On the American landscape, expansion of oral methods coincided with Bell's arrival and tenure in Boston. This observation is not to contend that Alexander Graham Bell was solely instrumental in bringing change. Yet there is little question that he was the most robust factor and provided oralism an eminently respectable public champion. "His magnetic personality, and the prestige of his name as inventor of the telephone," noted his friend John Wright, "gave him great influence and made him the most powerful single force that made the cause of oralism successful ("Tributes to Alexander Graham Bell at the Horace Mann School for the Deaf," 1923, p. 49).

Bell's claim to know and to do what was best for deaf people was based on a number of assumptions. First, he held that professionals possessed the objective knowledge that was needed to solve human problems. Second, he articulated the image of the scientist as a neutral, dispassionate observer. Finally, as a trained elocutionist and sometime teacher of the deaf, he assumed the right to speak to linguistics, language policies, and the needs of deaf children.

Bell's excursions into the world of Social Darwinism, genealogical studies, and eugenics are reserved for Chapter 3. Here, the discussion centers on his policies of language and oralism. Although each of Bell's claims is examined individually, it is important to remember that they were woven together to create a complex scientific and pedagogical web.

The Language Question

Virtually all the major philosophers since Plato and Aristotle have considered the problem of the origin and role of human language. During the European Enlightenment of the 18th century, a rigorous analysis of the structures and functions of language formed an important thread because the origin of speech and language was seen as the key to the history of thought (Knowlson, 1965). One set of Enlightenment arguments concerned whether or not gesture preceded speech as the natural antecedent or whether they were completely unrelated in development (Knowlson, 1965; Rudowski, 1974). It was generally held that gestural language was the original endowment of humans, more sublime than speech, and closer to creation (see Knowlson, 1965).

Later, Thomas Hopkins Gallaudet and the pioneer teachers of the deaf embraced evangelicism rather than philosophy. They saw the possession of an immortal soul as the sole defining characteristic of humans. Sign language was cherished as an effective medium to know God and His works.

The dissemination of ideas from Charles Darwin's 1859 publication of *On the Origin of the Species* caused ever-widening ripples that affected many fields— psychology, education, and philology (the study of language). Post-Darwinists lacked the theology of Gallaudet and dismissed the Enlightenment philosophers. With evolution as the dominant way of understanding the past, they assumed an entirely different meaning about the relationships between speech and sign.

Speech supplanted sign in the evolutionary competition to become the distinctly human endowment. Once this view took hold, sign language was denigrated as a kind of primitive prosthesis, lower in evolution than speech and more brutish (Baynton, 1991, 1993). References to the gesture signs of savages and deaf people became commonplace in both popular and scholarly publications. It was openly suggested that any "culture dependent upon [sign] must be proportionately inferior" (Baynton, 1997, p. 141).

People who used sign were like apes or savages and less evolved than white-skinned Americans (Baynton, 1993). Deaf people, it was said, when left to themselves "would rise no higher than orang-utangs" (Jenkins, 1890, p. 85).

Oral teachers proclaimed the salutary effects of speech and derided the brutishness of sign. One teacher admonished the pupils that "if you make signs, you behave like monkeys; do you want to be monkeys?" (Fay, 1883, p. 238).

Adding a subtle tinge were mid-19th-century ideas of language and acculturation, as interpreted by the common schools. Although the United States did not (and does not) have an official language policy but an informal national standard, American English, the schools made Anglo conformity the guiding principle. English was the sole legitimate medium for learning and instruction. Noah Webster, for example, maintained that "Provincial accents" were "the seeds of political discord" and therefore all Americans should use and pronounce the language in the same way (Webster, 1839, pp. 19–20).

A dominant thread of Bell's convictions about language was not concerned with deaf people at all but revolved around issues of immigration, race, ethnicity, assimilation, and citizenship. He adopted American notions of linguistic legitimacy, joined them to opposition to institutionalization and sign language, and couched the whole in tones of Social Darwinism and eugenics that were pointed at class, ethnicity, and culture. Although a recent arrival to American soil himself, Bell was zealous about a common American culture and consistently paraded his concern for protecting republican ideals and maintaining the Anglo dominance. "Our population is recruited from all the countries of the world," he said, "and from this source another danger threatens the Republic" (Bell, 1884b, p. 9). The threats were threefold—sources of immigration, the American birthrate, and the acculturation of immigrants.

Bell did not manifest the hatred, scorn, and oppression of hard core assimilators. Still, though not obsessed with race and ethnicity, he assumed that ethnic groups differed in temperament and intelligence. In addition, America not only was in danger of being swamped by undesirable immigrants but also had to contend with home-grown deviants. These social misfits bred larger families than did the middle class, which showed a declining birthrate. The avoidance of race suicide became a patriotic anthem. Articles in the popular media wanted to know "Is the race going downhill?" (Balch, 1926). Bell (1920) was prompted to ask, "Is race suicide possible?" and "How to improve the race?".

To Bell, citizenship was a relatively uncomplicated matter. For those who aspired to describe themselves as American, he viewed language as synonymous with acculturation. He feared the fragmentation of society into groups defined by language and therefore deemed it "important for the preservation of our national existence" that Americans should "speak one tongue" (Bell, 1920, p. 340).

Bell's views were enticingly patriotic. And it was only a wee step from non-English-speaking immigrants as poor citizenship material to sign users as subtly sinister and subversive, prone to un-American and unpatriotic instincts. Supporters of oral methods denounced "the foreign language of signs," which was limited in scope, flexibility, and expression, and "immeasurably inferior to English" (Baynton, 1997, p. 141). The language of signs was not only inferior but also sharply separated the deaf population from the wider hearing world because it lacked a common mode of communication and similar ways of expressing thought. Testifying before a Royal Commission on the Deaf in London in 1888, Bell noted that "a person who has been taught by a special language comes to look upon himself as belonging to a different race, of which he is proud. He comes to look upon himself as different from other people and glories in the fact" (Bell, 1888, p. 64).

Sign language represented the antithesis of American citizenship. Only one route led to righting the problem. Oral modes were key to bringing deaf people into the national fold and simultaneously removing the deaf minority's linguistic and cultural challenge. The extent of knowledge of English was "the main determining cause of the congregation or separation of the deaf in adult life" (Bell, 1884b, p. 75); hence, more English would operate on deaf people "to effect their absorption into society at large and to weaken the bonds that tend to bring them together" (p. 58).

Arguing for the sole use of speech and speechreading, Bell dissected arguments that were propping up the manual system. For example, he dispensed with the conclusion of Epée and Thomas Hopkins Gallaudet that "the natural language of the deaf and dumb is the language of signs" (Epée, 1860, p. 127; Gallaudet, 1847) and denied "the proposition that the sign-language is the only language that is natural to congenitally deaf children" (Bell, 1884b, p. 48). No, said Bell, "all deaf-mutes could acquire an intelligible articulation" ("Discussion at Chicago . . . ," 1884, p. 317).

Oralism as a Profession

In the final 3 decades of the 19th century, Edward Miner Gallaudet and Alexander Graham Bell became the champions for the manual and oral stances, respectively. By 1870, educators of the deaf had similarly developed "diversified and conflicting interests" and had divided into opposing camps of manualists and oralists. Instead of devoting their time to "scientific and pedagogic discussions," they directed their energies toward "political, factional, personal and sectional differences" (Goldstein, 1919, p. 339).

The debate raged almost unchecked for a couple of decades, its flames fanned by various forms of elitism, paternalism, and parochialism. While oral advocates waxed effusive about the advantages of their system, manual advocates mustered a phalanx of counterarguments. The flavor of the dissention is evident through the carps and criticisms that flooded the contemporary literature. The oral faction, contemptuous of the restrictive social intercourse and intellectual development allowed by sign language, looked on manualists as both an embarrassment and an anachronism. They directed "a continued avalanche of sneers and jeers at the so-called old-fogeyism of the manual methods" (Wright, 1915, p. 219). From their corner, the manualists disparaged the new reform group. They contended that "the logic of facts was entirely against the system of articulation" (Hubbard, 1876, p. 179). For example, they "were disposed to look upon Miss Rogers' attempt to teach congenitally deaf children to speak and read lips as an absurdity, perhaps not surprising in a woman, but certainly unworthy of serious consideration" (Moore, 1934, p. 193).

Edward Miner Gallaudet sensed the oral tide early. In 1868, he proposed a method of conciliation that coupled the politics of institutional settings with the demands of educational progress. Schools would adopt a Combined Method in which students received basic instruction in sign language but selected children who showed aptitude were provided with additional articulation training. The method was readily accepted, seen as "capable of affording the greatest good to the greatest number" (Ontario Institution for the Education of the Deaf and Dumb, 1891, p. 21).

The trajectory of thought of those of the oral persuasion went only one way, however. Oralism was promoted to the exclusion of a language of signs and the manual alphabet abandoned as "a hindrance to speech and speech-reading" (Stewart, 1892, p. 151). Bell characterized the Combined Method as the "sign method" because of its distinctive features and often remarked that it was only a cover for sign language (Bruce, 1973). Others saw the Combined Method as providing the necessary political loophole for the reappointment of sign (deaf) teachers (Goldstein, 1919, p. 141).

The manualists fought and argued from the stances of contemporary teachers, deaf teachers, and most deaf adults and cited the fairness of the Combined Method. No matter. The practical and theoretical dimensions of oralism grew increasingly popular and the manualists could not stem the rising tide. As the principal of the Pennsylvania Institution observed in 1892, "The oral instruction of the deaf, whether wisely or unwisely, is unquestionably commanding increased public attention and public sympathy" (Crouter, 1892, p. 200).

The promises of oralism—speech and speechreading for every deaf child— were enticing. The philosophy snowballed and was adopted by parents, educators, and other stakeholders. By 1897, articulation teachers became the majority among all instructors of deaf students, including superintendents and principals (American Association to Promote the Teaching of Speech to the Deaf, 1899). The percentage of students who were taught speech rose from 27% to 65% from 1884 to 1900; those taught by oral methods alone from 20% to 40% ("Statistics . . . ," 1900). By 1905, 96% of all American schools for the deaf were designated as oral schools (Crouter, 1907). In 1922, the year of Bell's death, 80% of all deaf pupils were taught by oral methods.

A brief case study of the Pennsylvania Institution for the Deaf and Dumb sums up with sufficient precision the state of affairs at the end of the 19th century. In 1881 there was a separate oral department under Emma Garret with 10% of pupils taught orally. By 1893, the percentage of orally taught pupils had risen to 50%, and in that year, legislation was passed that required that all pupils should be placed under oral instruction and maintained under oral instruction until it was shown that they could not be so taught. By 1905, 96% of deaf children in Pennsylvania were under oral instruction (Crouter, 1907).

Institutions for the Blind

Developments in the education of students who were blind tended to be more quiescent and stable than those in the other categories of students. The issue of communication modes that permeated and divided educators of the deaf was matched, though with somewhat less intensity and antagonism, by the so-called Battle of the Types.

In the founding schools for the blind, instruction focused on oral teaching, communication, and religious instruction. Pupils were exposed to reading by raised letters, to writing by special methods, and to arithmetic by the help of tangible figures or types (Perkins Institution for the Blind, 1858). Various raised types such as Moon Type, Roman, and New York Point were found in reading materials.

Louis Braille's alphabetic code as a system to assist blind people with reading and writing differed quite dramatically from the traditional raised print. Rather than print traditional letters made tactile by some means, Braille used a six-dot system designed to be read by the fingers. Braille was published in France in 1834; his music notations in 1839. The braille system for reading and writing was officially adopted at the Paris School for the Blind in 1854. Dr. Simon Pollak, one of the founders of the Missouri School for the Blind, brought braille from Europe and, from the 1850s on, Americans experimented with changing to braille.

The transition to braille was neither tranquil nor universally accepted, however. In fact, by 1890, teachers of the blind in Europe and the United States were hopelessly divided over reading methods (Perkins Institution for the Blind, 1895). Some teachers did not want to abandon the traditional systems. Others, aware of parallel issues connected with deaf education, feared the creation of a blind community. "The use of braille," they argued, "would disassociate the blind from the seeing altogether" (Perkins Institution for the Blind, 1895, p. 84).

Braille eventually prevailed. The Perkins Institution adopted the braille code in 1879, and by 1892, most schools for blind students in North America opted for the braille dot system as fundamentally the most effective tool not only for writing but also for reading. By 1917, a newly modified braille code was accepted as the American standard for the printed word, and it was decided that all literature would be transposed in that medium (Koestler, 1976).

Redefining Mental Retardation

To those who worked in the field of mental deficiency, the second half of the 19th century brought vast changes. The key constructs of mental disability were altered and expanded. The powerful reconstruction then spilled over to create subtle but dramatic shifts in the institutions, their administration and leadership, the clientele, training and pedagogy, and the growing variety of professionals circling the enterprise.

Change was most rapid and encompassing after 1880. However, the outlines were clearly delineated 2 decades earlier and can be traced directly to Darwin's 1859 publication of *On the Origin of the Species*. As discussed earlier, Darwin's speculations and conclusions changed humans' conceptions of their relationship with God and nature, which in turn created new views of mental retardation and a growing encompassing concept of degeneracy.

The middle of the century saw the appearance of a growing emphasis on exactness and definiteness in the use of terminology in all branches of science, but especially in medicine. The demand for greater particularity and accuracy ultimately translated into more cogent definitions of exceptionalities and the quest for labels that has characterized special education. Within the discrete category of mental retardation, new terminology emerged that predicted a very strict pattern of descent formulated around an ability-disability binary.

Until the 1850s, mental retardation was viewed as a somewhat monolithic condition with only crude classifications. The generic *idiot* lumped all possible people within the category together. Idiot shed its generalized roots during the 1850s when Americans adopted the concept and definition of feeblemindedness, originated by the Royal College of Physicians in London (The New Jersey Training

School, 1893). The term *feebleminded* was seen as a less harsh expression than *idiot* and appeared to satisfactorily cover the entire range of retardation. The term also came to denote the highest grade and largest class of mental retardation. Feebleminded people were "those who were defective as to judgment and in whom the defect was of similar origin to, though not as intense as, that of imbecile or idiot" (Spitzka, 1887, p. 275).

Imbecile, reserved for the next category of feeblemindedness, derived from the Latin, *bacillus*, needing a stick, and implied weakness or wanting strength of mind (Barr, 1904a). Imbecility included mildly, and some moderately, retarded persons. Imbeciles were capable of simple accomplishments but were sometimes described as "human animals" (The New Jersey Training School, 1893), unable to exercise reasoning power beyond the extent to which a child was able.

Idiot, the bottom grade of the retardation hierarchy, described those who were viewed as devoid of understanding from birth, incapable of holding communication, and therefore alone and set apart (Barr, 1904a). Some spoke of idiots as "the lowest type of humanity" (Pennsylvania Institution for the Feeble-Minded, 1868, p. 6). To Howe (1848), these "idiots of the lowest class" were "mere organisms, masses of flesh and none in human shape" (p. 7). Edward Spitzka (1887) pointed to the likelihood of multiple disabilities in idiots.

Greater specificity in terminology was boosted by changes in classification. A number of workers observed "that the appearance of idiots strikingly suggests a reversion to or imitation of certain ethnic types" (Spitzka, 1887, p. 278). John Langton Down (1826–1896), medical superintendent of the Asylum for Idiots at Earlswood, England, from 1858 to 1868, pursued this thread as he attempted to make distinctions between pathological entities of mental defect. Although Down's ethnological classification included a number of so-called throwbacks, it was the comprehensive description of the "Mongoloid" child that endured in the field, a condition later known as Down's syndrome and, today, known as Down syndrome.

Moral Imbecility

In the late-19th century, American morality was absolutist. It was assumed that adults elected a life of crime or did nothing to halt their slide once on a downward path. Criminals were born to be criminals; willpower was important only to the extent that it was acknowledged that children did not inherit willpower, rather, the capacity for judgment and for the development of willpower (Goddard, 1976).

The 19th-century use of the word *moral* was broad. At times, *moral* was used to refer to all the nonphysical aspects of human life. At other times, it referred more specifically to the emotions and was also used in the modern sense of ethical (Gelb, 1989). Early psychologists spoke of the moral treatment used with persons who were mentally ill that essentially consisted of all nonmedical techniques and specifically the therapeutic efforts that affected the patient's psychology (Carlson & Dain, 1960).

During the 1850s, the term *moral insanity* emerged in England (Walton, 1979). The construct supported the notion of diseased morality and was applied to people whose bad conduct was a lifelong enterprise. Those deemed morally insane were described as "subjects, whose reasoning powers are fair, whose memory is excellent, who are perhaps accomplished in the arts, but in whom the moral sense is either deficient or entirely absent" (Spitzka, 1887, p. 281). Once use of the term crossed the Atlantic, a loosely connected constellation of ideas about degeneracy came together, and the notion of moral insanity transmuted to moral imbecility. Isaac Kerlin, Superintendent of the Elwyn Institution for the Feeble Minded, crystallized the concept when he aired the term in the 1880s.

Although the construct of moral imbecility represented a constellation of science, pseudoscience, religion, and morality, it owed much to Franz Gall's phrenology. The essence of Gall's phrenology was the belief that the brain consisted of 37 separate faculties that were specialized for various functions. Faculties could be identified by tissue prominence, and the type and density of prominence (bumps) narrated the character, personality, and even intelligence of the subject. A person with a well-developed frontal lobe, for example, might have a natural aptitude for language but not for music, a peculiarity that would be reflected by a prominence in the area of the language organ and a deficiency in the area of the tune organ (Passinen, 1974). Faculties were not, however, immutably fixed: they could be strengthened by exercise or, conversely, weakened by disuse of improper or unnatural use (Schwartz, 1952).

Moral imbecility rested on the belief that reason and morality were separate mental faculties, with the moral faculty being the most recent development in the course of human evolution. It was also generally held that people with disabilities were evolutionary defectives, somehow arrested in a lower stage of evolutionary development. In such cases of hereditary regression to a lower form, it was to be expected that the highest faculty—morality—would drop out (Gelb, 1989). Moral imbeciles, it was said, suffered an irreparable defect of the moral faculties comparable with the intellectual damage suffered by the truly mentally retarded.

The moral imbecile was viewed as bad and "practically incurable," a growing danger to the American way of life.

Institutional Structures

Americans unearthed two salient features about mental retardation in the 1860s. First of all, the old, easy optimism—the belief that many defectives could be cured given time and patience—vanished. Exposing the myth of the "cult of curability" led to public disenchantment and professional disappointment with methodologies that had been boldly touted as the means to ameliorate or even eradicate mental retardation. Optimism, pragmatism, and inventiveness disappeared among those working in this field, and in their place grew a profound pessimism. At the same time, America discovered degeneracy. Socially constructed categories that included behavioral and social indices forged a link between personality and mental disorders.

New vistas opened for the understanding of dependency, delinquency, crime, and many forms of deviant behavior; in addition, the poor, prostitutes, criminals, the insane, and the mentally deficient were all seen to be cut from the same cloth (Cohen, 1983). With these factors in the foreground, changes in institutional organization and the clientele served were inevitable. Institutions slipped into revised roles—from the role of training of children who would return to family and community to the role of preventing mental retardation in subsequent generations through the segregation of adults.

By the 1870s, states were scrambling to build custodial facilities, and the number of institutions grew. By 1876, 34 states had institutions for people considered to be retarded, accommodating approximately 25,000 inmates (Thurston, 1876; U.S. Department of Labor, 1915). In the same year, there were more than 3,000 inmates in the New York and Pennsylvania institutions together. The Massachusetts Institution at Waverly and the associated Templeton Farm Colony served 1,500 inmates by 1913.

For the future course of special education, one of the most important institutions to develop was the New Jersey Training School for Feeble-Minded Boys and Girls at Vineland, founded by S. Ohn Garrison (1853–1900) in 1888. The Vineland school took as its motto, "Happiness first, all else follows." The school, intended for White children only, opened with a kindergarten and industrial department (see Vernon, 1942). From Vineland grew the State Home for Feeble Minded Women and the State Village for Epileptics. Similarly, the work lent impetus to developments in Colorado, Oregon, and California (The New Jersey Training School, 1908).

Literature from the late-19th century suggests that epilepsy was deeply misunderstood. As a disease, epilepsy was considered to be "hereditary in a high degree" ("Report of the New Jersey Commission . . . ," 1896, p. 32). Moreover, it was said that "probably more than two-fifths of all epileptics are, during a part of the time, insane." Even after a seizure, "slight stimulation could be sufficient to excite an insane 'furor,' which may be followed by the commission of homicide or some other crime" ("Report of the New Jersey Commission . . . ," 1896, p. 33). The severity of the condition meant that "the general hospitals refused them; that they could not keep their places with employers in the outside world because of their fits; that for the same reason they could not go to school or church; that they were burdensome at home" (Peterson, 1896, p. 43).

Because people with epilepsy "had to be disposed of in some way" (Peterson, 1896, p. 43), admission to insane hospitals or almshouses was common. However, with the expansion of the institutions for the mentally retarded in the 1880s, many were institutionalized, often in the custodial departments with idiots and the juvenile insane (The New Jersey Training School, 1893). By the 1890s, states were forming hospitals and homes specifically for people with epilepsy (The New Jersey Training School, 1896). By 1895, for example, there were state institutions for epileptics in Ohio and New York State. Epileptic patients were culled from almshouses and county jails. Those taken from almshouses and asylums were state patients; private patients were received at prices regulated by the boards of managers (The New Jersey Training School, 1896).

In parallel with the admission of people with epilepsy into the institutions, the demographics of the general clientele altered dramatically. Between 1850 and 1860, the mean age of admission for mentally retarded students was 10.8 years; by 1910, it has risen to 15.8 years (Tyor, 1977). At the same time, there was a surge toward accepting those who were less educable and required more custodial care. Parental pressure and legislative coercion forced the institutions to accept such cases, and states delegated to judges a power of commitment that opened an avenue of access previously closed, particularly for those who lived in almshouses (see Tyor, 1977). Extra concern surrounded feebleminded women who were subject to sexual abuse and who were frequently seen as responsible for enticing immoral behavior (Tyor, 1977). States modified their admission and discharge laws to place a greater emphasis on admitting women at an earlier age and retaining adult women in institutions longer than men.

Most inmates were now bound for life. Once committed to an institution, discharge was problematic. Some inmates were allowed to return to conscientious parents. Other parents were reluctant for their return; they would pauperize a family. Many had no families to which to return. For some, a return home meant a return to the almshouse. Not a few of the males took matters into their own hands and ran away. In cases where institutional staff members disputed a discharge, cases were brought before the courts for settlement (see Fernald, 1919).

With changes in size, clientele, and the duration of confinement, it soon became apparent to most service providers that the original intent of the schools could not be sustained. As the correction of mental retardation began to take a second seat to the prevention of the condition and the control of those seen to be afflicted, the educational emphasis waned. In fact, the educational programs altered to the extent that the trustees of the Massachusetts Institution charged in 1885 that "the character of our institution is rapidly changing from that of a school to that of an asylum" (Massachusetts Institution for the Idiotic and Feeble-Minded, 1885, p. 23).

Walter Fernald, principal of the institution now located at Waverly, explained in 1893 that "the essentially educational character of the earlier institutions has been maintained, but the relations of the different parts of instruction are now better understood. The strictly school exercises, in the early days the most prominent feature, still perform their necessary and proper functions, but now in harmony with and preliminary to the more practical objects of the institution" (Fernald, 1893, p. 46). In summarizing activities to be used in training "the lowest grade of defectives," Fernald (1893) noted the value of rhythmic training, games, and outings, but observed that training in polishing, scouring, sweeping, and dusting held more promise than a standard kindergarten program for this group.

Administrators were compelled to find ways to maximize the efficiency of the institutions, so economic concerns were placed on a level with individual improvements. The policy that emerged encouraged institutional self-sufficiency through the use of inmate labor. Essentially, the "practical objects" referred to by Fernald mutated into upkeep of the institutions. Rural institutions soon evolved into farm colonies consisting of a custodial department, a training school, an industrial department, and a farm. Inmates worked the heavy machinery in the laundry, print shop, or boiler room and tended the animals and farm. Females performed domestic chores as well as did the sewing, mending, and hand laundry. They also provided custodial care for low-functioning inmates (Trent, 1994). Some people worked in the community and returned to the institution after working hours.

As the institutions began to productively use the inmate's labor, the practical training and vocationally oriented programs that were originally designed to be the corridor from the institution to the community became a dead end; maintenance of the institution itself became the pressing need. Simultaneously, institutional upkeep undermined the functionality of the inmates; the nature of social relations between staff members and their charges as well as the strict regulation of daily activities meant that the clients learned to function only within institutional structures (Lasch, 1973). Alexander Johnson, for many years an institutional superintendent, noted that "the proportion of the feebleminded who are fit to go out from our schools at twenty-one to take a common man's or common woman's place in the great world, with all that it implies, is so small that it may be safely disregarded in adopting policy" (Johnson, 1900, p. 93).

SUMMARY AND THEMES

The common schools developed with the implicit mandate of providing to an increasingly complex school-age population the skills needed for contributing to an expanding, rapidly changing society. The schools not only assumed the burden of socializing and disciplining working-class children but also served as culture bearers, helping to assimilate the streams of immigrants entering the United States. Other roles for organized education included spiritual salvation, political goals, moral uplift, social stability, mental discipline, vocational efficiency, and school reform.

Diversity among students and an ever-growing concern for bureaucratic efficiency began to severely test the principles and practices of common school ideology almost from the outset. Educators hoped to remain aloof from disruptive, cantankerous, and troublesome children. They opted for mechanisms different and apart from the common classroom; in the 1870s, school jurisdictions in the United States opened classes specifically for truant, disobedient, and insubordinate children.

Within the ungraded classes and classes for unruly students, programs were designed to accomplish two primary goals. First was the identification of students whose presence in any way significantly inhibited efficient instruction and administration. Second was a two-pronged goal to isolate students seen as malevolent, if not dangerous, and simultaneously to remove trouble, disruption, and general chaos from general education classrooms. For almost all of its history, this essential dichotomy between the best interests of the school and the best interests of special learners would plague special education.

Of all the tedious debates in education, it is doubtful that any have generated more heat and shed less light than the so-called oral-manual controversy in deaf education. Ostensibly, the debate was a search for the answer to a difficult question What is the most appropriate mode of communication for deaf people? In fact, the tensions in deaf education, though expressed in terms of communication mode, were rooted in the ineradicable antagonisms between two different philosophies and their class bases. Pedagogical issues were pertinent to wider social issues that were reflected in differing viewpoints of oralists and manualists concerning the role of deaf people in society. These new language ideologies were not an isolated phenomenon unconnected to larger developments in North American culture. Rather, they reflected various social changes, the influence of new theories of heredity and evolution, and a focus on a culturally narrow society in which spoken English was paramount. In the education of deaf students, they signaled the movement from moral transactions to pedagogical considerations as the governing motif of schooling.

No one was as ready to take up the oral cause as Alexander Graham Bell. At its roots, Bell's ideology about the education of students who were deaf was deceptively simple. He saw deafness as a fundamental flaw that hindered interaction in the sole acceptable medium—hearing society. Sign language and institutionalization massaged the flaw. Fitness for citizenship was equated with linguistic normalcy and corresponded to the educational system's goal to formally assimilate pupils through the rapid acquisition of English, which was key in their minds to creating quick Americans. Bell assumed that all deaf children could attain normalcy (a state in which one has ready access to the hearing world and full rights of citizenship) only though oral methods. Abolishing sign language would emancipate deaf people and dissolve the bonds that held deaf communities together. Oralists would not contemplate any halfway measures such as the Combined Method proposed by Gallaudet. In direct philosophical contrast, those of the manualist ideology held that deafness was a human difference and, as such, deserved its own unique language. The animosity was reflected in the many confrontations between manual and oral advocates who spent much of the time refuting and castigating each other.

When mental deficiency emerged as a public issue for Americans in the 1840s, it did so in the context of concerns about morality. By the 1850s, the narrowing bounds of conduct acceptable to society wrought a moral revolution that conditioned attitudes toward a construct of moral insanity, later moral imbecility.

From the 1870s on, new constructs of mental retardation changed the service clientele from the individual to the society. The revised purpose of the institutions was to protect the public by circumscribing the growth of a potentially dangerous class of people. The populations of institutionalized people with mental retardation increased, and the characteristics and ages of the clients changed. The admission of pupils who could be successfully discharged after completing a course of study was supplemented with custodial clients. Most were seen as incurable and totally unteachable, and their eventual release was doubtful.

As a result, with the exits blocked for many, the institutions bulged. They generally assumed a more custodial character, and daily routines became more regimented. Education—expensive in terms of personnel and unspectacular in terms of results—consequently suffered most. A stress on work-related training superseded any literary curriculum. There was a move to finance institutions through client labor. Institutions hoped to become self-sufficient, with their own power, plants, gardens, and farms.

NOTE

1. When he was age 70, he wrote that "recognition of my work and interest in the education of the deaf has always been more pleasing to me then even recognition of my work with the telephone" (cited in Bruce, 1973, p. 379). Bell opened a private school in Boston in 1872 and in 1873 obtained an appointment at Boston University as professor of Vocal Physiology and Elocution. From then until his death in 1922, Bell served as the recognized leader of those who opposed the use of sign language in teaching. After inventing the telephone, Bell wrote to his mother, "Now we shall have money enough to teach speech to little deaf children" (Wooden, 1934–35b, p. 16). After the phone's successful launch in 1877, Bell donated half a million dollars, about half the fortune of the telephone, to shape deaf education in his own image (Bruce, 1973). In 1890, Bell endowed the American Association to Promote the Teaching of Speech to the Deaf with $25,000, later increased to $250,000 (Yale, 1931), and an annual donation of $1,500 (Ontario, Department of Education, 1907). In 1906, Bell donated another $75,000 to the Association to establish a normal school at the Clarke School in memory of his father (Ontario, Department of Education, 1907). In 1887, he opened the Volta Bureau "for the increase and diffusion of knowledge relating to the deaf" (de Land, 1923, p. 98). He promoted his ideas about deafness and his varied scientific experiments through ownership, or interest in, various journals, specifically *Science*, the *Association Review* (later the *Volta Review*), the *National Geographic*, and the magazine of the American Breeder's Association (later the *Journal of Heredity*).

Chapter 3

The Politics of Biology

Social and political problems beset North America as it entered the 20th century. These seemingly unresolvable and mounting issues were not novel. Although faith in the progress of America produced a conservative, well-satisfied nation in the late-19th century, it was clear that progress brought a particular set of problems.

As the movement toward urbanization and industrialization accelerated, demographic, political, and social realities shifted. For example, town dwellers formed 28.6% of the population in the United States in 1880; by 1920, they formed 51.4%. The U.S. Census of 1910 found that 84.7% of Irish people lived in towns; only 15.8% in the country (Carr-Saunders, 1926).

The United States transited from the small-town values that had previously organized social life to the establishment of a more centralized, impersonal, and bureaucratic social system that could serve an increasingly industrialized and corporate economy (Wiebe, 1966). The rurally based, largely self-sufficient family unit seen at the beginning of the 19th century was supplanted by a reorganized model of the family, with revised roles for family members. New models served to adapt to an increasingly interdependent society that was based on an economy and social order formed around wages and sales rather than one formed around relative autonomy and self-sufficiency. Work now meant new modes of production, new roles for workers, new types of labor, and the imposition of new time keeping and schedules.

By 1900, the United States was an urbanized, industrialized, heterogeneous society of racially, religiously, politically, linguistically, and ethnically mixed peoples. But the fallout of the emerging capitalist technological expansion included a realm of social ills. The decay engendered by urbanization, industrialization, and immigration was seen in heightened rates of vagabondage, labor unrest, rising divorce rates, suicides, and crime. Statistical scrutiny of the 1870, 1880, and 1890 censuses of the United States showed increases in deviant behavior and growing numbers of those considered to be defective, dependent, and delinquent. The 1880 census showed the rate of "feeble mindedness" as 153.3 per 100,000 compared with 63.6 per 100,000 for the 1870 census. The 1890 census figures, almost identical to those of 1880, confirmed that the numbers of feebleminded people in society was dangerously high (Gorwitz, 1974).

Blame for the perceived decline of society and the social problems in the United States (and Canada) was readily and easily assigned. First, the lax and unrestricted immigration policies that characterized the 19th century evolved into a national concern. By 1900, there was a growing sentiment among the American people that the influx of immigrants threatened the stability of the nation's institutions and the purity of its racial foundations. Immigrants were a "complication of the social evil" (Social Survey Commission of Toronto, 1915, p. 40); moreover, data from the U.S. Immigration Commission were taken as evidence that some foreign groups showed little capacity to adjust to American life (U.S. Immigration Commission, 1911). Joined to problems with immigration was the entire spectrum of degeneracy—that huge underclass that included virtually all groups with presumed moral, mental, and physical deficiencies. Feeblemindedness was posited as the root cause of most of the stresses and strains on American society. Individuals who, because of their innate mental deficiencies were unable to cope with the complexities of modern life, threatened the future of the nation (Goddard, 1916a, 1916b).

With the movement from a 19th-century system of beliefs rooted in Protestant ideologies to a more modern culture embedded in secular ideologies, many influential Americans acclaimed science as the new gospel. Of course, North America was a long way from secular in those decades: religion remained important to most people and could be a political minefield. Still, devotion to science and the expert grew. Medicine emerged as a dominant profession. At the same time, the fledgling field of psychology sought political legitimacy and public acceptance by claiming to have scientific ways of understanding social problems. With tests of mental ability as a bastion, psychology became a biased advisor with an overarching motive. Moral and social judgments, whether good or bad, right or wrong, were overwhelmed by a morass of half-formed ideas from the emerging discipline of psychology.

By the time of World War I, Americans were informed as never before about the threats posed to national survival arising from two chief sources—immigration and degeneracy. Over and over, the public was warned of the problems raised by feebleminded individuals in society. They not only would become criminals, prostitutes, and paupers but also would pass on their defective traits to future generations. A complex nexus between immigration, feeblemindedness, intelligence testing, and eugenics emerged. As Black (2003) observed, "Crime analysis moved race and ethnic hatred into the realm of heredity" (p. 23). Researchers, writers, and the popular media elevated the threat of those who were feebleminded to the status of a national concern and increased national misgivings with respect to the tide of immigrants then flooding into America.

The advent of World War I changed forever the face of Europe and the balance of power. The war and its aftermath recast American society, moving it into a new phase of organized social responsibilities and an accompanying sophistication in political, economic, and social matters. Turmoil followed the war. War industries laid off millions of workers, and returning soldiers sought work. Labor strikes paralyzed the nation in 1919. A record number of single-parent families generated increased dependency.

The 1920s, however, introduced a glittering new reality across North America. Industry expanded and led to a period of soaring production, concentration of capital, and the need for a more organized and skilled labor force. The central meaning of progress was revised, closely tied to the secular scientific vision that played an even greater role in postwar America. With science as their lens, many Americans reconnoitered a wide field of operation with vigilance and energy and declared that something had to be done about degeneracy and feeblemindedness. To alleviate the double threat of immigration and degeneracy, they embarked on a mission for race betterment—a quest to improve the human race. As these Americans advocated a philosophy of progress based on the application of science to society, various subcultures within a mainstream of human betterment emerged, some more fervent and extreme than others. Whatever their ilk, all were concerned with the sting of heredity.

The mainstay of the crusade for a pure America was the IQ test that introduced scientific methods into a field where previously only subjective judgment had been possible. Advocates of a better America used the measures to scour the highways and the byways for those who would not, or could not, contribute to their vision of the nation.

Social movements were one layer of the complexity of changing society. The connection between the development of social movements and special education are subtle. The ensemble of political, economic, and social movements influenced the schools, special classes, the students sorted and assigned to segregated placements, as well as the curriculum presented and the teachers who taught it. Disabilities were deconstructed and then reconstructed in light of new medical and psychological findings, public and professional sentiment, and variables inherent in school systems.

Not every social movement vying for hegemony in this period can be addressed. This chapter is designed to provide an overview of the major social movements that emerged and that affected the education and treatment of people with disabilities. Targeted areas are eugenics and its offshoots as well as the mental testing movement. Both profoundly influenced educational and social provisions for special populations, especially people who were deaf and those who were mentally retarded.

IMPROVING THE RACE

By the opening of the 20th century, the term *race* and notions about race were well established and casually used by social commentators of every stripe. Speaking to race was not an embarrassment, and the use of ethnic, nativist, or racist labels occasioned little public comment.

Although the term was readily bandied about, the precise meaning of *race* was not always clear. Despite the lack of clarity about the construct and meaning, some commonly held assumptions stood out. First, few North Americans doubted that the races were unequal, and most believed that that each race had its own forms of social and cultural behavior. Second, not many Americans could have escaped the mantra that the race was threatened by degeneration. Moreover, most assumed that the race could and should be improved. Finally, the public held the belief that scientific knowledge was a means to improve existing conditions. Improvement was not a facile task. As Alexander Graham Bell observed in 1908, "The problem of improving a race of human beings is a most perplexing one to handle" (Bell, 1908a, p. 123). Solutions required a combination of the insights of business, science, and Christianity (McLaren, 1990).

Professionals, academics, and the public embraced varied, but not necessarily matching, guides to defensive action. Two main thrusts were prominent. On the one side, many people held an inherent belief in the legislation of morality and social improvement. On the other, most believed that the struggle for survival could be aided by advances in medicine and psychology. These scientific advances included certificates of physical fitness, systematic mating, restrictive marriage laws, compulsory birth control, and forced segregation during the child-bearing years. Some advocated pacifism on the theory that war selects the strongest to be killed while the weak stay home to renew the population (see e.g., Jordan, 1915).

Eugenics, together with its intellectual arm, Social Darwinism, emerged as the most popular and pervasive of the human betterment movements. From the 1880s to the 1930s, eugenicists claimed the political, medical, and social terrain. The eugenics preoccupation colored the discussion of a vast variety of topics ranging from public health, child welfare, prison reform, human hygiene, sex education, birth control, clinical psychology, school psychology, and women's suffrage to intelligence testing, special education, social welfare, and immigration.

Social Darwinism

Charles Darwin's disturbing and controversial publication, *On the Origin of the Species* in 1859 coincided with geological and archeological discoveries. The book, in itself a revolutionary event, did more than just advance the study of biology. Rather, it was intensely significant in many respects beyond the immediate issue. Considered as either a cause or the consequence of other intellectual developments, it acted as the focal point for the spread of the materialist mode of thought (MacMillan, 1960) and spawned or revitalized a variety of trends and movements. For example, the neo-Malthusian, feminist, and socialist movements all responded in their particular ways to Darwin's shift in vision of humanity's development and future. Neo-Malthusians held that the only way in which the masses could improve their conditions was by limiting their numbers. Women's work and their place in the social hierarchy together with issues surrounding birth control engaged feminists. Socialists called for a redistribution of resources.

Popular and widely used phrases and metaphors sprang from Darwin's work or were attributed to it. For example, Darwin's meticulous empirical account precisely outlined the minute operations of natural change. Yet, as Darwin (1859,

1874) wrote about a natural world distinct from humans and espoused natural selection as the survival process, he was reticent on the matter of human evolution. The powerful complementary new phrase "survival of the fittest" was coined in the 1860s by the agnostic English philosopher, Herbert Spencer (1820–1903), who was far more widely read by the public than Darwin. Spencer subsumed the particular workings of natural and sexual selection under the larger story of the march toward natural and human perfection. In his *Social Statics* (1865), Spencer asserted that man and society followed the laws of cold science, not the will of a caring God. For Spencer, competition was key in an age of greater specialization, differentiation, and interdependence.

Similarly, the phrase "nature versus nurture" did not belong to Darwin but to his younger half cousin, Francis Galton (1822–1911), who was significantly influenced by Spencer's work. Although Galton's wording was Victorian, the question of the chief influences on human development had occupied philosophers for centuries. Aristotle promoted nature; Plato leaned more toward the nurture point of view. In the span of centuries between Classical Greece and the 18th century, the nativistic concept with its reliance on innate and hereditary characteristics formed the major philosophical premise. Then, prodded by John Locke, George Berkeley, and the philosophers of the French Enlightenment, the nurture view resurfaced. In the mid-19th century, Darwin and evolution unsettled the accepted explanations for the origin and development of humans and sent the pendulum swinging back to nature.

It was during the 1860s that notions of social planning, philosophy, and biology began to merge. Thinkers distilled the ideas of Thomas Malthus, Herbert Spencer, and Darwin into the new area of Social Darwinism, a name not validated by Darwin himself. Firmly in the nature camp, this new breed of Social Darwinists sought to view human society through Darwin's vision of the animal world (Rogers, 1972). They held that social relations could be explained by evolutionary theory and that the successes of the establishment and the failures of the misfits were readily explained through a theory of inherited intellectual potential.

Social Darwinism turned biology into destiny and made evolutionary analogies, explanations, and ways of thinking dominant. Previously, the concept of being "created equal" had implications not only for government but also for all the social institutions, including church, family, charity, and welfare. Now, the inspiring democratic conceptions of human equality were discarded; the new science left no ground for the denial of human inequality. It was held that "on every hand, innate tendencies and early environmental influences definitely condition our choices and determine the measure of our success" (Yerkes, 1917, p. 252). The distinguished father was likely to have a distinguished son; the child of the poorer classes had very little chance of becoming distinguished.

It would be unwise to argue that from the birth of the movement in the 1860s until the beginning of World War II, Social Darwinists enjoyed the unanimous confidence and approval of the public and their colleagues. They did not. Yet, although the orientation was not universally shared, for decades it was dominant among the American intelligentsia and main culture bearers.

William Graham Sumner, professor of social science at Yale University, for example, became a major spokesman for Social Darwinist thought in the United States. Sumner synthesized Darwinian theory with traditional Protestant values to argue that not only social but also biological inequality were part of an inevitable law of nature. Without inequities, Sumner insisted, society could not operate and evolve, and the law of survival would not have meaning. To Sumner and a growing band of Social Darwinists, the principles of social evolution negated the traditional American values of equality and natural rights. It was innate biological differences that made some people rich and powerful. Simultaneously, the poor and infirm were simply those members of the species who lost out in the evolutionary race owing to their innate disabilities (see Blanton, 1976).

For Alexander Graham Bell, deafness was the fundamental springboard for his theories and activities. But even as Bell was only a subplot in a much larger drama, he was a respectable and influential opinion maker and shaper and a potent influence on the entire field of special education. Early in the 1870s, Bell embraced Social Darwinism. In fact, Baynton (1993) describes him as an extreme Darwinist; Black (2003) as an "ardent eugenicist" (p. 44); Fairchild (1922) as "in the rank of the earliest explorers in the field of eugenics" (p. 198). Echoing Sumner, Bell (1908a) contended that "superior individuals on the whole have a larger proportion of superior offspring than the average of the race" (p. 122). Further, "if three or four generations of ancestors were all individually superior a thoroughbred would be produced" (p. 123).

A notion of the greater public good both drove and justified Social Darwinism. Promoters held that to attempt a program of public aid for the poor, the deviant, and the intellectually disabled was ridiculous and grossly unscientific. The environment served as "merely a means of giving good heredity a chance for expression" wrote the editor of the *Journal of Heredity* in 1916 (Shull, 1916, p. 228). Therefore, he argued, "If the good heredity is not there, it is hardly worth while to improve the environment; certainly it is a waste of time if it is done with the idea of thereby improving a stream of bad heredity in it" (p. 228). Herbert Spencer's theory of social selection precluded state aid for the poor. "The whole effort of nature," Spencer explained, is "to get rid of such, to clear the world of them and make room for the better" (Spencer, 1865, p. 414).

Social reform could not repair the defects of heredity. Human society, like nature, had to be harsh to its weaklings or it would foster within itself cankerous and destructive social ills. Joining Spencer, American Social Darwinists renounced environmental improvements as well as philanthropy, sanitation, medicine, and even education for easing the struggle in existence as giving undue advantage to those characterized as the "cacogenic" stocks. Far more logical and sensible, according to Social Darwinist thought, was an emphasis on eugenics, with a side-step into scientific racism.

Eugenics

The eugenics movement was born on converging currents of elitism, racism, Social Darwinism, social reform, and genetics. Its roots can be traced to Francis Galton's 1865 publication in *MacMillans Magazine* and more specifically to his 1869 work, *Hereditary Genius*. In the first systematic attempt to apply statistical concepts to biological development, Galton took as his subjects eminent British men who lived between 1768 and 1868. Included in his sample were statesmen, soldiers, scientists, writers, poets, artists, and ministers. Galton's interpretation of the data showed that about half of the great men of England had distinguished close relatives. Citing one concrete case, Galton found that the son of a distinguished judge had about one chance in four of becoming himself distinguished. On the other hand, the son of a man picked at random from the population had about one chance in 4,000 of becoming distinguished. From there, it was an easy step to conclude that success in life was pretty much a family affair and that genius was largely a hereditary factor.

A man of outstanding ability and wide interests, Galton was to have a far-reaching influence on science, education, and popular thinking. His work underlay the rapidly developing fields of psychology, sociology, and statistics. He created the field of eugenics, and quite direct links can be discerned in his influence on the education of gifted students.[1]

The philosophical, nonexperimental tradition of the first half of the 19th century had altered rapidly, and Galton rode the tide of the sudden emergence of experimental biology and psychology. He echoed the dominant mid-century medical leanings toward autopsy findings, collected data, and possible cause-and-effect relationships. Francis Galton was fascinated by the world of statistics: his work reflected his faith in the explanatory powers of statistical analysis. Galton's dictum, "Whenever you can, count," led him to count phenomena, things, traits, and all manner of occurrences (McLaren, 1990; Pearson, 1914). Galton was the first to assert that intelligence was a scientifically meaningful concept (McLaren, 1990). He developed methods for measuring abilities and for statistically analyzing the data collected.

Although Galton applied his counting to finding correlations, his greatest quest was prediction. In 1869, he suggested distributing intelligence, like other human characteristics, on a linear metrical scale ranging from idiocy to genius. He then proposed that all human characteristics could be analyzed by procedures comparing collected data from large groups of people. He lumped together various types of individual differences, including intelligence, character, physical prowess, and temperaments. He then attempted to show that people's natural abilities derived from inheritance in much the same way as did features such as height and eye color.

In 1883, Galton joined the Greek words for *well* and *born* to create a new word, *eugenics* (Black, 2003). Galton himself described eugenics as "the science which deals with all influences that improve the inborn qualities of a race; also with those that develop them to the utmost advantage" (Galton, 1904). Later, he defined the major goals of eugenics: "to check the birth-rate of the Unfit," and to further "the productivity of the Fit" (Galton, 1908; original spelling).

Galton's philosophy was exported throughout the world. Although eugenic thought originated in England, eugenic action began in North America. Throughout, British eugenicists, adhering to the positive Galtonian policies, shielded themselves from negative, coercive eugenics and quickly sought to separate themselves from the sham science that they saw taking root in America. The British, it was said, were more reticent about absolute principles, more forgiving of human differences (Carr-Saunders, 1926). But "Galtonian eugenics," observed Black (2003), "was reborn, recast and redirected in the United States as a purely and uniquely American quest" (p. 31). And, though in England eugenics was a biology of class, in America, it transmuted to a biology of racial, ethnic, and disabled groups. Science and prejudice walked hand in hand.

Until the opening decades of the 20th century, however, eugenics lacked details. The movement needed two advances to propel it to a sort of national crusade—specifics on the mechanisms of heredity and a scientific tool with which to sort people. These advances arrived in the guise of the rediscovery of Mendel's work and the creation of measures to assess mental ability, respectively.

Genealogical Studies

In the pre-Mendel days, heredity was explained by analyses that were said to trace the influence of innate characteristics. Cohorts of paupers, criminals, misfits, and disabled people were cataloged and tracked in attempts to assess the influence of heredity on successive generations of large families of defective stock.

Alexander Graham Bell was early shaped by the new scientific metaphors. As he joined the eugenics parade, Bell borrowed scientific theory from his animal breeding experiments. "The breeder of animals," he contended, "is fitted to guide public opinions on questions related to human heredity" (Bell, 1914, p. 2). To Bell, procreation was a social, not an individual issue, and he supported intrusive public policies. Because "human beings are undoubtedly capable of modification by selection" (Bell, 1914, p. 2), he held that people could be scientifically shaped and controlled to fulfill the nation's destiny.

Beginning in 1830, the federal government of the United States conducted censuses of the deaf. In the late 1870s, Bell was drawn into investigations of the prevalence and causes of deafness and blindness when he accepted a commission from the Massachusetts State Board of Health. He based his research on the belief that "if we could obtain a detailed account of the families of the ancestors of a large number of unrelated deaf-mute families, we might hope to throw light upon the origin of deafness by a comparison of the genealogies; whatever abnormal peculiarities the genealogies might present in common would probably have something to do with the production of deafness" (cited in de Land, 1925, p. 141).

As an underlining to his genealogies, Bell first revisited other studies on hereditary deafness (e.g., Gillett, 1890; W. W. Turner, 1848). Then, using the records of Canadian and American schools for the deaf, the ancestral records of certain families in which an inherited tendency to impairment of hearing was particularly noticeable, and census reports, Bell created his own genealogical charts. The results concerning the essential factors involved in the production of family deafness confirmed Bell's suspicions: the country was faced with the formation of a deaf variety of the human race.

To validate his conclusions, Bell sought assurances from leading academics and scientists. For example, Alpheus Hyatt, a professor at Harvard University and a member of the National Academy of Sciences, wrote that "if such marriages should continue through several generations I should regard it as almost certain that a deaf-mute race would be produced" (Bell, 1888, p. 91). Simon Newcomb, a member of the National Academy of Sciences, agreed that "the continual intermarriage of deaf-mutes through successive generations would ultimately result in the gradual formation of a deaf-mute variety," although he added the caveat that "this tendency would be very slow" (Bell, 1888, p. 98). Edward D. Cope, editor of the *American Naturalist*, wrote to Bell, saying that "according to my views of evolution it is quite possible for a deaf or deaf-mute variety of man to arise and be perpetuated" (Bell, 1888, p. 89).

Bell's reputation lent the appearance of scientific exactitude to the family studies, and his work foreshadowed future genealogies. But authoritative and persuasive as they may have been, Bell's assumptions had a narrow focus trained only on the deaf population. To the layperson, deafness did not engender the same fear as mental retardation. It was the feebleminded population that formed a much larger, more serious, and more threatening problem. Although inimical to the deaf community, Bell's discourses were drowned out on the larger stage. The spotlight focused instead on the genealogy prepared by Richard L. Dugdale (1877), an executive of the New York Prison Association.

When inspecting prisons for New York State, Dugdale discovered in a jail in rural Ulster County six relatives all being held at the same time. Dugdale was driven to document the lineages of no fewer than 42 families heavily composed of criminals, vagrants, and paupers. He collectively dubbed them the Jukes, and described the work as a study on heredity, pauperism, disease, and crime. Dugdale's story began with five mentally retarded sisters, one of whom was said to be known as "Margaret, the mother of criminals." Their descendents at the time the study was made numbered 540 people. These, together with 169 people connected with them by marriage or irregular union, made the basis of the study. Among the Jukes were 128 prostitutes, 142 habitual paupers on outdoor relief, 64 workhouse inmates, and 76 habitual criminals (Jones, 1960). The hovels, which these people created for themselves, were seen as signifying degeneracy. Dugdale (1910) described "their hovels" and "rude shelters" with "all ages, sexes, relations and strangers 'bunking' indiscriminately" (p. 13). The Jukes cost the community more than a million dollars in public expenses apart from the price of crime and pauperism. (A later study of the Jukes was undertaken in 1915 by Arthur H. Estabrook of the Eugenics Record Office in America, who concluded that over half the offspring either were mentally defective or had anti-social traits [Estabrook, 1915; Jones, 1960].)

Dugdale was cautious, blaming poor environment and calling for social reform. But an avid public focused instead on the crime, immorality, insanity, and waywardness. Environmental aspects were ignored. The work was hailed as proof of the existence of hereditary defect showing that the effect of a morbid inheritance was almost inevitably social deterioration.

Psychology

The way that human beings think and process knowledge has been of perennial interest to philosophers and educators, dating back to at least the time of ancient Greece. As a modern discipline, separate but arising from philosophy, psychology emerged during the French Enlightenment. By the opening decades of the 19th century, the essential outlines of the fields of psychiatry and psychology were drawn. Still, by 1900, psychology remained a fledgling discipline, although one determined to conquer the complexities of the human mind through the astute application of experimental science.

Right from the outset, psychology embarked on its long and controversial history of involvement in efforts to measure and explain human variations, to validate or dispute moral principles, and to account for human behavior within a scientific framework. Pioneers directed their energies to determining the answer to the nature-nurture conundrum and to devising and using tools that would scientifically measure a person's IQ, predict that person's social role, and ultimately decide that person's value to society. Although the primary interest of early scientific psychology was discovering the laws of the human mind that were common to all people (Hilgard, 1987), what was abnormal (the obvious referent for normal) reaped a harvest of attention, especially for those deemed to be feebleminded.

American psychology's conception that childhood constituted a discrete stage of development arose from G. Stanley Hall (1844–1924), an early prominent architect of the developing field of child study, first at Johns Hopkins and then at Clarke University. Hall was one of the strongest proponents of the applicability of evolutionary theory to the study of development and it is hardly surprising that his students adopted similar stances. At Clarke University, Henry Goddard (1866–1957) undertook psychological studies and experiments with psychomotor tests; he earned his PhD under Hall in 1899. Lewis Terman (1877–1956), who was to become America's most influential psychologist, investigated the measurement of intelligence and the phenomenon of individual differences. His 1905 doctoral dissertation at Clarke was titled "Genius and Stupidity: A Study of Some of the Intellectual Processes of Seven 'Bright' and Seven 'Stupid' Boys" (Terman, 1906/1975).

The Testing Movement

Historical accounts of standardized testing typically begin with Wilhelm Wundt's experimental psychology at the University of Liepzig, Germany, in 1875. Wundt (1832–1920) formulated generalized descriptions of human behavior, although he did not devise a true mental test. His legacy to measurement and assessment were the standardized conditions and procedures that he used in his experimental studies of measurement (Goodenough, 1949; Linden & Linden, 1968; Young, 1923).

Mental testing in North America arose from the work of James McKeen Cattell (1869–1944) at Columbia University, a student of both Wilhelm Wundt and Francis Galton. Cattell coined the term *mental test* in 1890, the year that he published his seminal work, *Mental Tests and Measurements*. Cattell successfully promoted the idea of mental testing as a desirable pursuit for scientific psychology but left the productive implementation of the idea for later generations. His call was taken up by his students who included Edward Lee Thorndike, E. L. Strong, and R. S. Woodworth, all of whom had a marked influence on mental testing (Luftig, 1989).

To find the first commercially viable and widely accepted test of intelligence, we must look to France in 1905. Observations in schools had indicated that a percentage of students in the beginners' classes were unable to progress in the normal way and became progressively more retarded in achievement as they passed from grade to grade. In February 1904, the Commission for the Study of the Retarded, a division of a society composed of educators, psychologists, pediatricians, and others interested in child development, proposed a three-part plan. They would use a test, begin special classes in schools, and establish a demonstration special education class.

The problem was passed to Alfred Binet (1857–1911) a member of the society renowned for his work in experimental psychology, experimental pedagogy, and the measurement of individual differences. Binet and his young assistant, Theopile Simon (1873–1961), completed the test phase in 1905.

Like Galton, Binet subscribed to the belief that the basic concept for individual differences focused on deviations from the population average. He also thought that mental tests should yield information about not only quantitative mental differences but also those that are qualitative; should be related to scholastic success; should aid teachers in the allocation of pupils to their correct grades or classes in the schools; and, rather than provide an absolute measure of ability, should rate individuals with respect to one another (Binet, 1898; Penrose, 1949/1966; Young, 1923).

Binet and Simon devised 30 subtests, sequenced in order of increasing difficulty, that required children to carry out simple verbal commands, coordinate actions, recognize and use common objects, and complete sentences (Luftig, 1989). Binet and Simon quickly recognized the weaknesses of the 1905 scale, produced as it was under time restraints. When they undertook a revision in 1908, items were added or eliminated and grouped according to age, the concept of mental age was introduced, and the scale was made more statistically representative (Binet & Simon, 1908).

Scoring of their tool, the Measuring Scale of Intelligence, was done simply by counting the number of items passed correctly, which provided a mental age. Binet and Simon did not use the term *intelligence quotient*; it was first coined in 1911 by William Stern (1871–1938), a German psychologist interested in the characteristics of prominent men (Stern, 1914). The intelligence quotient was defined as the measured mental age expressed as a percentage of the chronological age at the time of testing (Penrose, 1949/1966). Later, Lewis Terman changed the formula to MA/CA × 100.

Binet was not obsessed with the constancy of IQ. Nor did he insist that heredity was the determining factor in intelligence. Once his scale crossed to North America, however, the early adapters and adoptors used intelligence tests in ways not envisioned by Binet and Simon. Americans shifted the testing emphasis from the needs of the individual to the needs of society and transformed it into a pseudo-scientific movement that had at its core social control and a movement to cleanse society of its deviants and defectives.

The Vineland Revisions

In September of 1906, Henry Goddard was appointed as director of the Research Department at the New Jersey Institution for Feeble Minded Boys and Girls at Vineland.[2] His mandate was to find the causes of mental retardation and eradicate the condition. Neither contemporary medical or psychological knowledge was sufficient to fulfill either expectation. Goddard, however, probably did more than any other individual in the first 2 decades of the 20th century to alert the public to the dangers posed by immigration and degeneracy. In doing so, he emerged as one of the most powerful players in the fields of mental deficiency, eugenics, and testing.

Goddard hurried to France to learn about the new tests and introduced the Binet test to North America in 1908. In 1910, he adapted Simon and Binet's 1908 revision; it was translated by Elizabeth Kite, his assistant and field worker. In 1911, Goddard standardized the Binet test on 2,000 school-aged children in the Vineland public schools. He discovered that at least 2% in the sample were mentally retarded, unable to achieve in traditional classrooms (Goddard, 1910, 1911; Huey, 1910).

Before the Vineland revision of the Binet scale, the practice of intelligence testing was negligible. After the appearance of the Vineland publication, intelligence testing in the United States spread like wildfire. The Goddard revision became one of the most commonly used versions of the scale (Sattler, 1982). Within a few years, 30,000 copies of the Vineland Binet manuals had been distributed.

Fabrications of Degeneracy

Despite a plethora of constructs and folk taxonomies derived from the connotative baggage accumulated from the 1850s on, no one at the opening of the 20th century was quite sure about mental retardation. The term *feebleminded* was never adequately defined; its meaning varied from place to place, situation to situation. Explanations were laced with contradictions, and the various terms were fuzzy enough in their contours to be used interchangeably. Nevertheless, the tendency was to believe that whatever received a name must be an entity or being, having an independent existence of its own. Although problems abounded in classifying what they actually meant, the words *feeblemindedness* and *degeneracy* joined the common discourse.

Using the results of his Binet testing as a base, Henry Goddard devised a new tripartite system of classification for mental deficiency. In organizing the system, he adopted the genre used previously by Samuel Gridley Howe and by Alfred Binet, both of whom classified mentally retarded people into three groups demarcated by mental age (see Chapter 7). Goddard's entire group remained labeled as the feebleminded or the mentally deficient. They were then divided into three classes—morons, imbeciles, and idiots. For the sake of classification, the three classes were divided into the three grades of high, middle, and low (Mundie,

1919). The new scheme was adopted by the American Association for the Study of Feeble-Mindedness in 1914.

Goddard's classification of idiots and imbeciles added to the framework of his forebears; however, his creation of the *moron* in 1910 to designate the mildest degree of feeblemindedness moved in a new direction. Moron was drawn from the Greek *moros* meaning stupid or foolish. It referred to older youth and adults who tested between the age of 8 and 12 years on the Binet intelligence scale. On the deviancy spectrum, morons were both the highest type and "the largest numerical proportion of the feebleminded" (Hincks, 1918, p. 58). They were also the most difficult to handle and the most difficult to identify. The moron, it was said, "often passes muster as being of normal mentality when interviewed by an untrained examiner" (Hincks, 1918, p. 58).

Goddard's creation of the moron appropriated Isaac Kerlin's notion of moral imbecility but with a different starting point. To Kerlin, degeneracy could exist without any accompanying feeblemindedness, although he increasingly viewed crime as a group phenomenon, an inherited family trait. For Goddard, inherited feeblemindedness was the raw material from which social ills were made. Moreover, Goddard could validate his population with psychometric sources. Under Goddard, morality and intelligence were intimately united through the Binet tests.

In concert with moral imbecility, the classification of moron was vague and nebulous. As Doll (1941b) pointed out, "the term [moron] immediately appealed to both public and professional imagination and soon led to numerous differences of meaning" (p. 206). A plethora of alternate labels were used—unfit, degenerate, feebleminded, and cacogenic.

Under Kerlin, moral imbecility was applied broadly to those whose behavior was judged socially deviant, in both the presence and in the absence of other signs of mental or physical disability (Gelb, 1987). Goddard was convinced of a causal relationship between social vice and mental retardation (Trent, 1994). The category of moron served to biologize a whole range of social problems and confirmed a giant underclass; it became the bridge to span feeblemindedness and degeneracy.

It was the morons' purported contribution to crime rates that particularly disturbed observers. As a group, morons possessed such "weak will-power and deficient judgment" that they were "prone to become vagrants, drunkards, and thieves" (Fernald, 1903, p. 34) and were seen to be "mainly responsible among mental defectives for anti-social activity" (Hincks, 1918, p. 58). Specifically, "among delinquents, paupers, and those socially incompetent in other ways, the corresponding frequency [of morons] was alleged to be 50 per cent" (Penrose, 1949/1966, p. 13). Goddard (1914b) estimated that 25% to 50% of prisoners were mentally defective and incapable of managing their affairs with ordinary prudence. At least 50% of prostitutes were feebleminded, as were 50% of the inmates of almshouses (The Training School, 1914).

Although morons and moral imbeciles had many parallel traits, Goddard was skeptical about the idea of moral imbecility and questioned Kerlin's faith in the coherence of a category that tried to distinguish between the moral and the intellectual based solely on observation and intuition. Undoubtedly, part of

Goddard's disdain of Kerlin's concept arose from Goddard's own training as an experimental psychologist and his bent toward empirical methodologies. That training had broader implications because Goddard's psychological background distinguished him from the group of physicians who had traditionally led the field of mental deficiency.

In the latter third of the 19th century, medicine transited from a subordinate position to the dominant profession. The reliance and respect for science as well as innovations such as X-rays and anesthesia handed great power to the medical profession. Doctors and the medical sciences became the authorities in mental retardation, and medical men cornered the market on institutional management. As an example, Walter Fernald, who assumed the superintendency of the Waverly Institution in Massachusetts, came to Waverley after 5 years as assistant superintendent of a Wisconsin mental hospital.

Medical authority did not go unchecked. By 1910, the new profession of psychology was vying for influence. Psychologists were etching out an increasing sphere of influence in the field of mental retardation, largely founded on the new schemes of IQ measurement that lent the legitimacy and prestige that a designation of science offered and consequently provided a dramatic boost to the field.

In their attempts to mount pedigrees of unworthy families, various organizations such as the Eugenics Records Office at the Cold Spring Harbor Laboratory sent field workers threading throughout the country, unearthing family histories and scrutinizing family records. Goddard, participating in this effort, found a representative family on site at the Vineland institution when he discovered a girl named Deborah Kallikak. Goddard quickly discerned Deborah as worthy of an entire book to herself, ultimately making her "The World's Best Known moron" (Reeves, 1938, p. 199, original punctuation).

As his scientific metaphors, Goddard adopted the tradition of the Jukes. He claimed that his work was a report of a "natural experiment" in which he proved conclusively the heritability of feeblemindedness (Elks, 2005). Goddard traced the ancestry and social degeneracy back five generations before Deborah Kallikak in his first major work, published in 1912. Elizabeth Kite, Goddard's assistant, assembled the family tree of the Kallikaks.[3]

The story told of Martin Kallikak, a Revolutionary War soldier, and his two lines of descendents. From a liaison with "a nameless feeble-minded woman" (Goddard, 1912, p. 36) Kallikak had an illegitimate son, sometimes called Old Horror. This son had, in four generations, 480 descendents, of whom 143 were feebleminded, 36 were illegitimate, 24 were alcoholics, and 33 were sexually immoral. However, the 496 descendents of his union with a Quaker wife included a series of highly respected professional people. All except three were normal, and many reached high office in the state. The three failures were merely charted as being "somewhat degenerate" (Jones, 1960).

The Kallikak family book, replete with photographs, became a classic.[4] It was received with acclaim and reissued through 12 printings, one as late as 1939 (Zenderland, 2004). Hailed as "epic-making" at the time (Rogers, 1912, p. 84), Goddard's book became "the best known and most widely quoted of all the studies of defective stock" (Davies, 1930, p. 63). The Kallikak tale also triggered a wave of eugenic alarm. Goddard's data and his campaign to warn the public of the threat of the feebleminded spread panic throughout North American society. Professionals and politicians began to agree that the only way to save the world from hereditary defects was to isolate all defectives, prevent them from procreating, and remove them at birth to segregated settings.

EARMARKING THE INFERIOR

Before the advent of the IQ tests, the classification of morons, the rising tide of degeneracy, eugenics, and all the rest were simply stories to be taken on faith without proof. Lacking a number, race betterment and its far-ranging possibilities were destined to be confined to discussions within intellectual and medical circles. Testing became the requisite harbinger of grand social reconstruction: it recast eugenics as a quasi-legitimate doctrine. The creation and use of tests meant that, for the first time, the nebulous phenomenon of intelligence could be measured. Society was now armed with a technological innovation that provided numerical values attached to feeblemindedness. Everyone could be counted and classified, and there was scientific ground for making socially relevant decisions.

Of course, not every American in every nook and cranny and in every ghetto and red light district could be assessed. Rather, the predictive powers of the tests were used to socially indict many problematic groups. Researchers used the data to seed a national focus on degeneracy as well as racial and ethnic differences: they produced sweeping claims about feeblemindedness and its threat to social stability and progress. In Ontario, for example, Hincks (1918) claimed that "because of lack of provision for mental abnormals in farm colonies, buildings were burned, stores burglarized, venereal disease spread, and citizens murdered in the city of Toronto" (p. 57).

Most people accepted the thesis that the balance lay in heredity, that feeblemindedness was a simple Mendelian recessive. The so-called dangerous classes had received their qualities and tendencies from a "vicious ancestry" and were powerless to resist (Cobb, 1911, p. 254). Behaviors, mannerisms, and personal traits were lumped under genetic influence with coined terms to describe deviations. Charles Davenport, who came to dominate American breeding programs, contributed the major cluster. Those afflicted with shiftlessness, for example, were worthless and unattached in life; those with nomadism were similarly worthless and potentially dangerous (see Davenport, 1915a, 1915b).

Scientific Racism

Race and ethnicity have long formed a cogent factor in American history, life, and culture. Immigration has always been a complex, emotionally charged concept around which insistence on and resistance to racial differences have ebbed and flowed. For the American public in the opening decades of the 20th century, debates about immigration and racial differences combined unsolved issues in science with contentious disputes in politics.

The notion that hierarchal designations could be attached to humans and that differences in skin color, physiognomy, and geography were associated with scientifically measurable differences in character, aptitude, and temperament can be traced back to the late-18th century (see Smedley, 1998). Belmessous (2005) explained that "the scientific disciplines emerging from the Enlightenment searched for an explanation for differences between human societies that lay in nature rather than culture" (p. 326).

When adopted by early 20th century North Americans, this scientific approach to the idea of race took on a life of its own. Race signified a new ideology about human differences: racist structures and convictions were widespread and doctrinaire forms of racism emerged. Of central concern in the discovery of race was the identification of physical and mental differences between humans of different groups (Belmessous, 2005). As Haller (1971) pointed out, "the subject of race inferiority was beyond critical reach in the late 19th century" (p. 132). Race and ethnicity were assumed to mean something negative and divisive and were clearly associated with crime, alcoholism, and illiteracy.

Between the time of the first settlement at Jamestown in 1607 and 1920, more than 30 million European immigrants came to North America. Waves of immigration to the United States and Canada saw a preponderance of Irish in the late 1700s to the 1850s. In the mid-19th century, common antagonisms were largely directed toward these Irish Catholic immigrants. For example, Catherine Beecher railed against the "thousands of degraded foreigners and their ignorant families," who were "pouring into the nation at every avenue" (1835, p. 16). Brockett, Edouard Seguin's most favorable commentator, charged that "every arrival from Europe brings hither a host of the lower classes of European society, often ignorant, degraded, and vicious. These, if suffered to congregate in our large cities, taint the whole community, as with a moral pestilence" (1856, p. 86).

Eighteen million people immigrated to the United States between 1890 and 1920. Between 1896 and 1914, 3 million went to Canada (McLaren, 1990). A remarkable change took place in the character of immigration. The deeply maligned Irish were still arriving, but were joined by droves of southern and eastern Europeans. As one critic noted, "Southern Europe had been tapped and the stream came with a rush" (Woodsworth, 1921, p. 163). By 1910, immigrants from southern and eastern Europe made up 77%; the rest were from the traditional places such as the British Isles (Phelps, 1924). Italians began arriving in huge numbers in the 1890s. From 1890 until the start of World War I, about one quarter of immigrants to the United States were Italian. More than 4 million Italians arrived between 1890 and 1921, with 2 million arriving in the single decade between 1910 and 1920 (Winzer & Mazurek, 1998).

When Americans looked at the newcomers and then checked the map, they apprehended geography as destiny and developed the pleasing notion that the northern climate and virtue went hand in hand. A widely held perception was that the desirable immigrants were Anglo-Saxon, easily assimilated, and unmarked by the sharp physical and cultural differences of the southern and eastern newcomers. The most cherished northerners were the Dutch, the Germans, and the Swedes, all favorably captioned as vigorous and healthy—quite the opposite of their southern neighbors. It was argued that "these southern and eastern Europeans are of a very different type from the northern Europeans who preceded them" (Cubberly, 1909, pp. 15–16). Writers scorned the "two brothers from sunny Italy, lazy, degenerate, dissolute and mentally deficient" (in McLaren, 1990, p. 95). And the newcomers were not only "illiterate, docile lacking in self-reliance and initiative" but also ceded little allegiance to the "Anglo-Teutonic" ideals of law, order, and government (Cubberly, 1909, pp. 15–16).

This perspective was more than overweening cultural confidence and ethnocentric dislike. Changes in the ethnicity of immigrants stirred the embers of long-standing prejudices: they caused fear and resentment among many citizens and conveyed the notion of differences that could not be transcended. It was then an easy step for the established population to see immigrants as the source of many social problems.

In theory, incoming individuals were checked for disabilities. Doctors at Ellis Island were examining 20,000 newcomers a week by 1913, although Henry Goddard and others speculated that many feebleminded persons were passing through. To present suggestions for a more thorough culling of potential immigrants, Goddard and his associates visited Ellis Island's massive intake centers in the fall of 1912 and selected immigrants they suspected of being feebleminded (Goddard, 1913b). On a return to the intake sheds in 1913, Goddard used interpreters to administer the Binet test and some performance scales to selected immigrants, all of them steerage passengers. Goddard's staff initially selected just 20 Italians and 19 Russians, all of whom "appeared to be feeble minded" (Goddard, 1917). Ultimately 148 adult Jews, Hungarians, Italians, and Russians were chosen for examination.

When Goddard published his findings in 1917, he announced that 83% of Jews, 80% of Hungarians, 79% of Italians, and 87% of Russians were feebleminded (Goddard, 1917), scoring below the age of 12 on the Binet scale. A new scale, consisting of questions passed by 75% of the original group, was devised but still 40% of the immigrants failed (see Knox, 1914). Goddard insisted that his results applied only to immigrants traveling steerage and not to those in first or second class (Goddard, 1917).

Test results showing that two out of every five immigrants tested at Ellis Island were feebleminded proved to be devastating assessments of the intelligence of newcomers. They served to reinforce notions of the inferiority of southern and eastern Europeans and Jews and offered Americans little confidence in the abilities of the newcomers. These immigrants not only would take away jobs but also would infect the purity of the race and would fail to rapidly Americanize and contribute to the nation (e.g., Fairchild, 1917, 1924a, 1924b; Garis, 1927; Gulik, 1916; Knox, 1914; Ward, 1910).

Terman Revisions

Psychologists were unwilling to leave the IQ playing field to Goddard alone. Measures far more sophisticated than the Vineland revision rapidly appeared. Lewis Terman began to work on the Binet scale in Los Angeles and continued the project when he moved to Stanford University in 1910, supported by the Carnegie Foundation and the Commonwealth Fund (Karier, 1972). With his coworker, H. G. Childs, Terman published the Terman and Childs Revision of the Binet-Simon Scale in 1912 (Terman & Childs, 1912). In the next 4 years, the revision was further modified, extended, and standardized and, finally in 1916, published as the Stanford Revision and Extension of the Binet-Simon Intelligence Scale (Sattler, 1974). Terman expanded the number of tests given at each age and standardized it on what he believed to be a typical American sample.

So popular and influential was Terman's 1916 revision of the Binet test that it became the bible of mental testing and produced a number of results. On a practical level, Terman linked Stanford's name with the Binet test to provide the most widely known English title for the test. The Stanford-Binet also provided a model for future IQ tests and later measures of achievement. Critically, when Terman published his *The Measurement of Intelligence* in 1916, he gave full expression to the concept of IQ originated by Stern, cited the test as an exact measurement of an individual's mental inventory, made IQ synonymous with intelligence, and stressed that intelligence was a unidimensional trait determined almost entirely by genetic endowment.

Army Tests

During the Boer War, the British found that vast numbers of potential recruits were either physically or mentally unfit to serve their country overseas (McLaren, 1990). The United States took careful note of this finding when World War I brought universal military conscription. Washington struggled to classify more than 3 million drafted and enlisted men. Government testing of some sort was thought necessary "in order to weed out the inefficients and to be sure that there were none to clog the great war machine or to endanger the lives of others by their weakness" (The Training School, 1918, p. 19).

Harvard psychologist, Robert Yerkes, then president of the American Psychological Association, offered the association's services to the United States Army as America prepared to enter the war in 1917. Under a seven-man group selected by the chairman of the Eugenics Section of the American Breeders Association's Committee on the Inheritance of Mental Traits, the Army tests were written at the Vineland institution in 6 weeks from May to July 1917. Along with Yerkes were Henry Goddard, Lewis Terman, Edward Lee Thorndike, and behavioral psychologist John Watson.

The group created the Alpha test for English-speaking literates, which was based largely on a group IQ test developed by Arthur Otis (Chapman, 1981). The Beta test for nonliterates was a pictorial instrument for those who could not read or speak English. Terman's Stanford-Binet test was administered to those who did not score appreciably on either the Alpha or the Beta test.

In less than 2 years, the United States administered the Alpha and Beta tests to 1,726,966 draftees, using enlisted men for administration (see Haney, 1981; "The psychological examination . . . ," 1917). The United States discovered that "they had 700,000 men of draft age who could neither read nor write a military order and that in their whole population there were 5,500,000 over 10 years of age who could neither read nor write in any language" (Dobson, 1919, p. 136). When broken down, results showed 4% to 5% of men in the very superior range. Eight percent to 10% were superior; 15% to 18% high average; and 25% low. About 42% of the draftees were tested as very inferior with an estimated mental age of 10 or 11 years. Put another way, on the standards that had been followed, 47% of the White recruits and 98% of the colored recruits were mentally deficient (Wallin, 1927). Further analysis of the data along racial lines showed that eastern and southern Europeans scored only slightly higher than African Americans. In fact, overall, the United States Army found six feebleminded men per thousand ("Two out of . . . ;" 1917; Yerkes, 1921). With so many morons showing up, it was not possible to reject them all. The draft act brought into the army 35,000 illiterates and as many more who were almost illiterate (Dobson, 1919).

After the Army's Alpha findings were broadcast in late 1918 and in 1919, controversies raged around moot questions (see e.g., Wallin, 1927, 1949). An immediate result was the direction of public attention to the large percentage of men who, because of physical disability, mental retardation, illiteracy, or psychiatric disorders, were rejected as unfit to assume the major responsibility of citizenship. Long term, the data derived from the army testing were for many years the chief resource for studies of occupational, ethnic, racial, and geographic differences in ability in the United States (Tuddenham, 1962).[5]

The Alpha and Beta tests were not mental age scales of the Binet school; nevertheless, the data were compared with the Binet tests with devastating results. According to the data used, more than 40% of the inductees had mental ages of 12 years or under, which slotted them into the moron category created by Goddard. With the term *moron* bandied about, Goddard then fudged and claimed that moron was applicable only to those who were obviously feebleminded—that is, incapable of managing their affairs with prudence and of competing in the struggle for existence—and not to others with a tested mental age of 12 or under (Goddard, 1928). He contended that "the term *moron* is improperly used when it is applied to any person who is not feebleminded, no matter what his mentality" (Goddard, 1921, p. 49; original italics).

Nevertheless, a large section of the public believed the data and felt that America was sinking into a morass of illiteracy, crime, and feeblemindedness. Further, the tests confirmed the inferiority of non-Whites and newcomers. As one Dr. Arthur Sweeney noted, "The army tests revealed the intellectual endowments of men. . . . The Slavic and Latin countries showed a marked contrast in intelligence with the western and northern European group" (cited in Kamin, 1974, p. 23).

Post-Mendel Eugenics

The experiments on hybridization that had been conducted by Gregor Mendel, an obscure Czech monk, revealed the way in which characteristics were passed from generation to generation. Mendel's pea plant experiments were first published in 1866. When the work was rediscovered in 1900, it stimulated the fast-growing science of genetics and added the second necessary prong to the eugenics agenda.

Mendel's laws called forth the simple but elusive biological truth about hereditary transmission and provided new and alarming evidence about the transmission of hereditary traits. With Mendelian theory in hand, early 20th-century scientists and eugenicists had a rationale for attributing biological and behavioral deviations to heredity. They applied Mendel's law to the human race and claimed that it held good not only for physical characteristics but also for mental ability. Just as two black-haired parents could expect to produce black-haired children, so too could parents of outstanding ability expect to produce intelligent children. Ability of a particular kind could be transmitted: musicians sired musicians and statesmen begat statesmen. But the converse was also true. The children of criminals had criminal tendencies; the children of the feebleminded would almost certainly be defective.

Far more vocal than the laboratory-bound geneticists were the disciples of eugenics. Some claimed to be both elaborating the science of genetics and developing their own scientific branch; others held more moral convictions. Whatever the bent, the ideas were shouted from the pulpit; pounded on the schoolmaster's desk; presented by prominent citizens, psychologists, esteemed professors, and elite universities; and aired in publications such as the *Saturday Evening Post* and the *Atlantic Monthly*.[6]

Francis Galton said that "eugenics ought to be a religion" (cited in Bruce, 1936, p. 97). Following this theme, other advocates such as C. W. Saleeby (1911), a leading English popularizer of the eugenics doctrine, spoke to "the divine cause of race culture" (p. 24); he cited eugenics as a national creed or even religious faith. Many churchmen identified with groups organized to achieve the goal of racial purity. Numerous religious spokesmen within the "Protestant, Catholic, and Jewish mainstream" joined other reform-minded intellectuals and political leaders. They wrote books and articles espousing eugenics and lent their support to programs to regulate human production (Rosen, 2004, p. 4).

Eugenicists who wore the mask of respectable science attested that "there is a special field of data which can be made the subject of accurate observation and measurement in a detached frame of mind" (Carr-Saunders, 1926, p. 18). The scientific veneer was polished by representatives from those in the senior echelons of psychology, authorities on measurement, and professionals from the elite medical schools. Eminent scholars enunciated the doctrine, joined by numerous respected research bodies. Eugenics was advanced by academics such as biologist David Starr Jordan, president of Stanford University. Lewis Terman promoted the idea of the influence of heredity over environment as the major determinant of mental ability and crusaded for the eugenics initiatives as the solution to crime, poverty,

prostitution, and feeblemindedness. Canada's most eloquent defender of social-
ism, Tommy Douglas, wrote his master's thesis, "The Problems of the Subnormal
Family," on this issue (McLaren, 1990).

Race betterment was taught in colleges and universities, including elite institutions such as Harvard, Princeton, and Northwestern (Black, 2003). By 1914,
some 44 major institutions offered eugenics instruction; in a decade, the numbers
swelled to hundreds, reaching some 20,000 students annually (Black, 2003). By
1928, racial hygiene was taught in 376 American colleges and universities (Proctor,
1988). High schools adopted eugenically oriented textbooks that emphasized the
clear distinctions between superior and inferior families (Black, 2003).

Social and political leaders supplied influence and funds. Large corporate
structures, themselves a 20th-century phenomenon, moved to finance and support eugenics. For example, on January 19, 1904, the Carnegie Foundation formally inaugurated the Station for Experimental Evolution at Cold Spring Harbor,
Long Island, which became the headquarters of the eugenics movement under
its director, Harry H. Laughlin. In October 1910, the Eugenics Record Office,
a separate and larger facility, also opened at Cold Spring Harbor, directed by
Harvard-educated zoologist Charles Davenport who assumed the pivotal role
of eugenic crusader in chief. Michael Wehmeyer (2003) characterized Davenport
as "the man most closely aligned with the rise of the eugenics movement in
America and with the promulgation of negative eugenics worldwide" (p. 59). A
matching institution, the Genealogical Record Office, founded and directed by
Alexander Graham Bell in Washington, DC, devoted itself to the collection of
data with respect to longevity (Poponoe, 1915). Paul Bowman Poponoe became
the head of California's Human Betterment Foundation, which was established
solely to promote the use of eugenic sterilization for purposes of race and human
betterment (Wehmeyer, 2003).[7]

One group of prominent spokesmen came from the Eugenics Section of the
American Breeders Association, an organization of like-minded human betterment apostles, created in 1903 by the Association of Agricultural Colleges and
Experimental Stations. The mandate of the American Breeders Association related
"to human improvement by a better selection of marriage mates and the control
of the reproduction of the defective classes" ("Eugenics Section: Its Organization,"
1910, p. 235). Over time, officers included Charles Davenport, David Starr Jordan,
and Alexander Graham Bell. The sub-committee on feeble mindedness was originally chaired by Dr. A. Rogers, superintendent of the Minnesota School for the
Feeble Minded and Colony for Epileptics, with Henry Goddard serving as secretary (Davenport, 1910, p. 126).

A descriptive lexicon emerged; the quasi-scientific legitimacy of the terms
reinforced their usage. Eugenics was described as "the study of those agencies
under social control which may improve or impair the inborn qualities of future
generations of man either physically or mentally" ("*A Eugenics Catechism*," 1927,
p. 2). Constructive (positive) eugenics sought to heighten the birth rate for those
families viewed as superior. Negative eugenics was "concerned with the restrictive
reproduction of those with socially inferior hereditary endowment" (Landman,

1932, p. 4). Applied eugenics "treats of the agencies affecting the differential fecundity of the race. It deals with a conscious effort for improving the human race by such methods as the control of immigration, birth control and restrictive marriage legislation" (Landman, 1932, p. 4).

Except for the most outright eugenicists, most were too sophisticated to simply dismiss the need for environmental improvements. At the opposite end of the spectrum from the eugenicists were those of the euthenics school, who stressed environmental considerations above heredity.

Supporters of eugenics often linked the movement to improvements in public health. And, with public health in the forefront, it is not surprising that many of the most strenuous supporters and vocal defenders of eugenics arose from the medical profession. In this sense, medicine became an agent of social control as it began to present eugenics as a legitimate medical concept.

The deep empathy between medicine, eugenics, and public health in turn led to a relatively smooth linkage between medicine, institutional management, feeblemindedness, and special education. At a 1914 conference, Charles Davenport confided to the delegates that "the superintendents of state institutions were very desirous of assistance" (Davenport, 1914, p. 452). Many of the institutional medical administrators left cogent records of their ideological stances, commonly a position that regarded feebleminded people as a disease entity that threatened the welfare of an otherwise healthy society. One of the most outspoken was Martin W. Barr, director of the Pennsylvania Training School for the Feeble Minded. Confronted with a growing population of feebleminded students, Barr (1899) wrote, "We have reached that point when we must conquer it, lest it should conquer us" (p. 747).

THE DARK QUEST FOR PERFECTION

Eugenicists preached that "in mental degeneracy is to be found the poison that corrupts the well-springs of life" (Mitchell, 1919, p. 4). After their damnation of the degenerate, the eugenics gospel chorused tidings about its potential to cleanse America.

Who to eliminate was readily decided. In 1911, Harry Laughlin and members of the American Breeders Association Committee on Eugenics met to debate the problems of "cutting off the supply of defectives" (in Black, 2003, p. 57). The 10 social groups identified as socially unfit and targeted for special restraints, direction, care, and eventual elimination were the feebleminded, the pauper class, the inebriate class of alcoholics, criminals of all descriptions, epileptics, the insane, the constitutionally weak class, those predisposed to specific diseases, the deformed, and those with defective sense organs ("The Socially Inadequate," 1922).

It must not be assumed that eugenics enjoyed universality. The practical political and economic concerns of the nation such as expansion, manufacturing, railways, labor, and so on, ran counter to the ideological preoccupations of ardent eugenicists. Eugenics was a movement of the nation's elite, not the grass roots, which led Black (2003) to characterize it as "a pernicious white-gloved war" (p. xv).

Eugenicists could contend that social ineptitude and its carriers were to be stamped out through education, legislation, segregation, and sterilization and could attempt to justify intervention in defense of race and nation. Yet active hostility and disdain by many community members had to be counted. Their charges countered that the eugenics movement not only needed scientific validation and standards to exactly identify who was unfit but also required public approbation of the desire to eliminate traits of defect.

Few would not have heard politicians or medical people at one time or another expound the virtues of eugenics. The public, terrified at the prospect of the unfit multiplying thoughtlessly and suspicious of a democracy that allowed morons to vote, gravitated toward uncomplicated interpretations of human differences. Medical paradigms absolved society of complicity in the problems. McLaren (1990) observes that for the middle class, "it was a comforting notion to think that poverty and criminality were best attributed to individual weakness rather than to the structural flaws of the economy" (p. 37).

Public and political mood swayed in tune with changing conditions in the country. Gradually, the social climate grew receptive to the excesses and vulgarity of the claims and a culture of consent was created. Allegiance to and compassionate care for the dependent classes was diverted into a movement for social and biological cleansing and concerns for improving the material welfare of the genetically more competent classes.

Marriage Laws

The eugenics credo preached that decisions on breeding could no longer be left to individual whim or chance; rather, the production of children should be calculated, managed, and sharpened. Echoing A. G. Bell, advocates contended "that just as cattle breeders can fix a type, or dog fanciers evolve a Boston bull or an Airedale terrier, so can mankind breed sound or bad strains, mental degenerates or healthy honest citizens" (Mitchell, 1919, p. 4).

Worries about race suicide were bandied about. Writing in *the Journal of Exceptional Children*, Higbee (1935–36) wrote that "The differential birth rate among superior and inferior strains is probably the most alarming single danger which threatens modern civilization" (p. 12). On one side of the equation was the flagging fertility of Americans; on the other, the alarmingly high rate of fertility among immigrants and the degenerate classes. The feebleminded were seen as a rapidly increasing subgroup, with a birth rate much higher that of the rest of the population. California's Human Betterment Foundation carped in 1937 that "births among families living on public charity have increased as much as thirty per cent to fifty per cent in recent years. Self-supporting families, on the other hand, have cut down the number of their children beyond the replacement level" (p. 19).

Artificially boosting or halting unions would contribute to progress and efficiency. Marriage laws designed to stop the procreation of defectives were promoted by moderates who hoped to recast eugenics as a doctrine governing race betterment through marriages. Bell wrote that "the interests of the race demand that the best should marry and have large families, and that any restrictions upon reproduction should apply to the worst rather than the best" (1908b, p. 339). Legislation and persuasion would address the problems of differential fertility, the former for deviant groups, the latter for the middle class.

One of the first salvos on marriage laws came from Bell whose studies led him to conclude that deafness had to be constrained and controlled. Bell (1884c) in his *Memoir Upon the Formation of a Deaf Variety of the Human Race,* showed that under the conditions then existing there was "a tendency to the formation of a deaf variety of the human race in America" (p. 45) and offered suggestions to aid in counteracting the possibility. Contained within the covers of *Memoir* were speculations about restricting the marriages of congenitally deaf people and further legislation to forbid the marriages of individuals from families in which there was more than one deaf individual (Bell, 1884c, p. 45). In 1884, a bill, the first of a number on the subject, was presented to the Congress of the United States, asking that body to pass a law restricting the marriages of deaf individuals (Mitchell, 1971). The bill proceeded without Bell's knowledge, and he was later forced to sidestep and backtrack and support education rather than legislation.[8]

In the early 20th century, the pages of eugenics journals were filled with articles on hereditary blindness. Black (2003) writes that "leaders of the ophthalmology profession conducted a long and chilling campaign to round up and coercively sterilize every relative of every American with a vision problem" (p. xv). In 1921, legislation was drafted in New York to prevent the marriages of the blind, but it did not succeed.

Arguments concerning those who were deaf or blind never provided the same weight as did the fear of neglecting the mentally subnormal. For these people, marriage prohibition laws proliferated throughout the country. Marriage laws were within the purview of state legislatures, and much variation was apparent. States made marriage illegal in instances of insanity, feeblemindedness, epilepsy, alcoholism, and criminality (Carr-Saunders, 1926).

Immigration Restrictions

Many people viewed the lax immigration laws as an enduring source of debasement of American stock. It followed that restriction of immigration was a necessary condition to foster the moral, mental, economic, political, and racial health of the United States and Canada. After World War I, a contemporary writer observed that the movement to restrict immigration "was in part a response to the extraordinary conditions which prevailed in Europe and the virtual certainty of an unprecedented flood of immigrants if the door was left as wide open as the existing door required" (Fairchild, 1924b, p. 657). A highly selective immigration policy was widely advocated by eugenics proponents (Kevles, 1985). In June 1920, Harry Laughlin was appointed Expert Eugenics Agent of the U.S. Congress House Committee on Immigration and Naturalization. He testified at great length on three different occasions about the scientific basis and implications of immigration restrictions.

Goddard's testing at Ellis Island and the army data lent fuel to an already burn-ing question. The tests scientifically demonstrated the superiority of specific groups and upheld the popular bias about unassimable and inferior European stocks. The testimony of professional restrictionists repeatedly invoked the army data. In his *A Study of American Intelligence*, Princeton psychologist, Carl C. Brigham (1923) dem-onstrated the reliability of the army tests and then represented the results according to nationality. With respect to intelligence, he showed that the people with the low-est intelligence were (in descending order) born in Greece, Italy, Russia, and Poland. Madison Grant, a fanatic on race hatred, singled out the Irish and insisted that they "were of no social importance" (Grant, 1921/1936, p. 86).

As concepts of race informed the views of policymakers, they concluded that the population of the United States was on a mental decline and that there was no need to add more of the inferior races to already problematic stock. The former laissez faire state of affairs in connection with immigration was replaced by sets of regulations restricting immigration intake. In 1921, the objectified results of racist thought saw Congress pass, and Warren G. Harding sign, a bill (the Emergency Quota Act) limiting immigration to 3% of the foreign born of each nationality in the United States according to the census of 1910 (Garis, 1927, p. 143). Later, the National Origins Act, passed in 1924 and 1929, restricted the number of immigrants to 150,000 annually and set up quotas that favored people from northern and west-ern Europe. Until the 1960s, about 70% of those allowed to enter the United States were from Britain, Ireland, Scandinavia, or Germany (see Chapter 9).

Segregation

Those who were judged as feebleminded were seen as parasitic and preda-tory, often a menace and a danger to the community. The census of 1890 showed 95,571 idiotic and feebleminded people in the United States of whom 6% were in institutions (Fernald, 1893). By 1923, it was estimated that 500,000 to 1 million feebleminded people needed institutional care, although only 43,349 were actu-ally accommodated in state institutions (*A Eugenics Catechism*, 1927, p. 6). By 1939, psychologists presented the same rates: 1 million feebleminded people needed special care and supervision (Human Betterment Foundation, 1937). Among the population of 8 million in Canada, there lived an estimated 40,000 mental defec-tives ("The neglected . . .", 1919).

Something had to be done about the misfits caught in their wretched cycle of immorality, promiscuity, and improvidence. To many, segregation was the most appealing solution. Isaac Kerlin insisted on the "absolute necessity of life-long guardianship" and did so "in the name of science, of sociology, as a matter of politi-cal economy, of the protection of homes, and all that man holds dear" (Barr, 1913, p. 68). Ever moderate in his views, E. R. Johnstone, superintendent of the Vineland institution, wrote in 1914 that segregation "will appeal to the great public," because "it shocks no one's ideas of propriety, humanity and Christianity" (p. 65).

Sterilization

The more ardent of the eugenicists' clan prescribed sterilization as the way to solve the vast array of problems, remove almost every social ill, and ensure the continued progress of society. In 1908, Helen MacMurchy optimistically asserted that 80% of feeblemindedness could be eliminated within a generation by segregation; however, the ultimate weapon in the battle was sterilization (McLaren, 1990).

Although the ultimate goal was the elimination of degeneracy, diverse arguments underlaid sterilization. When, for example, Martin Barr of the Pennsylvania Training School for the Feeble-Minded pushed for sterilization of mental defectives and other degenerates, he framed it as an issue in public health. "We guard against all epidemics, are quick to quarantine small-pox, and we exclude the Chinese," said Barr, "but we take no steps to eliminate this evil from the body social" (Barr, 1902, p. 163). If vaccinations and quarantines were enforced to control disease, why not sterilization? Others presented themselves as deeply moved by the plight of the mentally deficient. Sterilization was a humane procedure: proposals were made "in the spirit of understanding and sympathy for the limitations of the defective members of our community" from whom "it would be unjust and antisocial to withhold the privilege of sterilization" (Hutton, 1936, p. 11).

Then there were the crushing financial burdens of institutionalization. In his 1912 annual report, E. R. Johnstone observed that "in theory the feeble minded should be sent at once to the State's institution. In practice this cannot be done. No State in the Union is providing for more than one-tenth of her feeble-minded and epileptics. The cost of housing all of them, feeding them, treating and training them would swamp the State treasury" (The Training School, 1912, p. 22).

In many states, the sterilization of people considered to be degenerate in some way commenced well before it was legal. The first sterilization operations used for eugenic purposes were done by Dr. Harry Sharp in 1899 at the Indiana State Reformatory at Jeffersonville. Sharp, without legal sanction, began to operate on men who had been legally committed to the institution in that year (Poponoe, 1934). By 1907, when Indiana passed a law that specifically sanctioned sterilization, Sharp had performed the procedure on 465 males (Gosney & Poponoe, 1929; Radford & Park, 1995).

Bills in favor of sterilization were introduced in Michigan in 1897 and in Pennsylvania in 1905 (Poponoe, 1934). In 1907, the Indiana legislature passed a state sterilization law that provided for the "prevention of the procreation of 'confirmed criminals, idiots, imbeciles, and rapists'" (Landman, 1932, p. 55). California's statute, first introduced in 1909, went into effect in August 1913, providing for the "sterilization of the insane and feeble-minded inmates of state hospitals and of convicts and idiots in state institutions" (Landman, 1932, p. 58). Complementary laws appeared in Alabama, 1919; Arizona, 1929; California, 1909; Connecticut, 1909; Delaware, 1923; Idaho, 1925; Iowa, 1911; Kansas, 1913; Maine, 1925; Michigan, 1913; Minnesota, 1925; Mississippi, 1928; Montana, 1923; Nebraska, 1915; New Hampshire, 1917; North Carolina, 1919; North Dakota, 1913; Oklahoma,

1931; Oregon, 1917; South Dakota, 1917; Utah, 1927; Vermont, 1931; Virginia, 1924; Washington, 1909; West Virginia, 1929; and Wisconsin, 1913 (Poponoe, 1934).

Despite active propaganda in the years around World War I, the sterilization laws were more theoretical than practical in application and consequence. Although a number of state courts went part way, the patchwork of largely inert state sterilization laws waited on further validation.

A variety of factors contributed to the hesitation. First was the contention that sterilization was an unwarranted interference with personal liberty. Then, although it was agreed that heredity played a controlling part in the blight of those who were feebleminded, scientists were not fully agreed on the law of heredity and the eugenicists could not agree on how far the law should interfere with natural selection (Landman, 1932). In addition, slight worries emerged about the safety of the operations. Sterilization of the male by means of vasectomy, a very minor operation, consisted of cutting and tying back the ducts through which the sperm flowed. Sterilization of the female by means of salpingectomy was perfected in about 1910 in Germany (Radford & Park, 1995). The procedure, which involved tying and cutting the fallopian tubes, was "a major operation requiring hospitalization for about two weeks" (Hutton, 1936, p. 10).

The states' hesitations continued until the Supreme Court of Michigan declared unmistakably on the question of the constitutionality of a law permitting the sterilization of mental defectives in 1925 with *Smith v Wayne Probate Judge* (Higbee, 1935–36). However, the landmark decision in the quest for the compulsory medical sterilization "of the mentally disordered" in the United States arrived with the decision in the case of *Buck v Bell*, decided in 1927.

After World War I, classifying promiscuous women as morons was commonplace. Once classified, Robert Yerkes explained, they were viewed as "intellectual inferiors," the "simple-minded members of the community" who were "relatively incapable of contributing to social progress" and were therefore "unfit for parenthood" (Yerkes, 1917, p. 293).

Virginia had a well-established policy of sweeping its social outcasts into homes for the feebleminded and epileptic (Black, 2003). In June 1924, Virginia adopted a sterilization measure founded on Harry Laughlin's model sterilization law, and a test case ensued. On September 20 of that year, Dr. A. S. Priddy, superintendent of the State Colony for Epileptics and Feeble-Minded, filed a petition with his board of directors in accordance with the law for the sterilization of one Carrie Buck, an inmate of the colony. While the litigation was in progress Priddy died and his successor, Dr. James H. Bell, was substituted in the case in which Carrie Buck's appointed guardian appealed the sterilization decision.

Carrie Buck was then age 18 years. To some of the good folks of Virginia, she was merely White trash from the back streets of Charlottesville. Yet, her cacogenicity was not convincingly established. She was a seemingly bright girl, a good student, and a hard worker: she had attained the sixth grade in school and was employed as a domestic from the time she was age 12 years. Her commitment to the state colony as a feebleminded individual was based on a tested mental age of 9 years and a reputation for incorrigibility. In 1923, 17-year-old Carrie was also found to be pregnant from, she said, a rape.

Carrie's mother, Emma, also a resident of the state institution, was then age 52 years with a mental age of 7 years, 11 months, and a long history of immorality and prostitution. She had three children, all of doubtful parentage. Emma Buck was declared feebleminded in 1920 and consigned for the rest of her life to Ward 5 in the State Colony. Vivian, Carrie Buck's illegitimate child, was deemed defective when she was only a few months old.

Buck v Bell was decided on May 2, 1927, by Justice Oliver Wendell Holmes of the U.S. Supreme Court. Holmes was age 86 at the time. The result was "very clear cut and decisive" (Higbee, 1935–36, p. 12). Holmes's opinion, astoundingly brief and platitudinous, saw the U.S. Supreme Court sanctify eugenics and its tactics. To Holmes, three generations of imbeciles were enough. He said in effect "that if society had the right to call on its best blood for sacrifice in time of danger, it surely had the right to insist that those who were feebleminded should forego the privilege of propagating their kind" (Higbee, 1935–36, p. 12). Carrie Buck was sterilized on October 19, 1927.

Buck v Bell was the most important case in the history of eugenic sterilization (Landman, 1932). Before 1927, eugenics had lacked an effective reinforcement mechanism. When the Supreme Court upheld the constitutionality of a properly safeguarded sterilization law as a social measure, it made the state the principal serious actor in sterilization and thereby legitimized a state's right to sterilize the unfit. Other courts upheld the principles of the decision by declaring that those statutes that approximated the Virginia statutes were constitutional.

Eugenics scripts became standardized elements legitimized by professional and political approbation. The movement for human sterilization became a panacea for the elimination of socially undesirable people (Landman, 1932). Statutes now provided that the superintendents of the state institutions for incompetents could advise vasectomy or salpingectomy in the best interests of the patient and society.

By 1934, 150 million people worldwide lived under laws providing for eugenic sterilization in selected cases (Poponoe, 1934). Thirty U.S. states had enabling legislation on the books from 1907 to 1958; two Canadian provinces, British Columbia and Alberta, had laws in effect from 1928 to 1973. More specifically, by 1921, 15 states had laws on sterilization; 2,233 people had been sterilized by January 1921 (Carr-Saunders, 1926). By the mid-1930s in the United States, more than 20,000 people with mental retardation and epilepsy had been sterilized (Hume, 1996). By the end of 1940, 35,878 men and women had been sterilized or castrated, almost 30,000 of them after the *Buck v Bell* decision (Black, 2003). California was America's most energetic state in terms of enabling eugenics. By January 1, 1928, California had sterilized 5,820 people with intellectual disabilities. By January 1, 1938, California had performed 12,180 involuntary sterilizations. It was followed by Virginia (2,916), Kansas (1,915), Michigan (1,815), Minnesota (1,459), and Oregon (1,218) (Wehmeyer, 2003).

RETHINKING EUGENICS

Even during the period when sterilization was at its height, undercurrents were sapping away the influence of the eugenics movement. Early on, it was easy to discern a different focus between British and American writers. Then, as psychology and psychiatry professionalized in the late 1920s, they tended to turn away from the cruder eugenicists. The 1920s also saw a radical decoupling of eugenics and genetics. Some geneticists began to renounce eugenics on the basis of racism; they refuted conventional notions that race played a part in IQ. Other scientists contended that science and propaganda had become inextricably confused. During this time, the German cellular biologist, August Wisemann, announced that "germ plasm," readily identified with a powerful microscope, was the true vehicle of heredity. Geneticists who increasingly understood the complexities of heredity in terms of genes, chromosomes, and mutations derided the idea of a single gene representing and developing into a single characteristic. They turned decisively away from the simplistic policies of the overzealous and overardent eugenicists.

Public and professional optimism about eugenics as the mechanism to rescue the nation from feeblemindedness either faded or was renounced. Alexander Graham Bell, for example, became a director of the Eugenics Record Office in 1912, the same year in which he was president of the International Eugenics Congress. But Bell appeared to grow increasingly uncomfortable with the constant focus on inferior traits. Although the American Breeders Association had promoted the sterilization of 100,000 deaf people in the United States (Poponoe, 1928), Bell did not support the measures. By 1916, he was queasy about Davenport's quest for sterilization and distanced himself from the ardent eugenics movement. He wrote to Davenport in 1916: "I will no longer be associated with yourself and the other directors" (cited in Black, 2003, p. 105). Bell proposed that the emphasis be changed to studying desirable characteristics and reiterated the stance that only education should be used to restrict marriages. Publicly, Goddard abandoned eugenics. Although for many years the emphasis on heredity was the chief motif of Terman's thought, he too grew less sure of hereditary notions as he grew older (Hilgard, 1987).

Many, however, still championed the pretensions of the eugenicists and maintained their support for sterilization despite attacks by eminent authorities and the hostile reviews of the practice published by a committee of the American Neurological Association in 1937 (McLaren, 1990). Germany's eugenic sterilization law came into effect on January 1, 1934,[9] and encompassed the largest number of people ever included under the scope of such legislation (Poponoe, 1934). The Nazis shifted the focus from sterilization to euthanasia. Once that shift aired, North Americans rushed to condemn their barbarous practices, and there was a general discrediting of eugenics by its association with the Nazi policies.

Summary and Themes

Darwin's evolution hypothesis was developed to account for the variation through time and habitat of plant and animal populations. Once aired, however, the effect of evolutionary theory was to turn the attention of scholars back to the nature end of the controversy and to focus attention on the functional significance of different constellations of characteristics, including behavior, as both the products and determinants of a species' evolution.

When the theory of evolution by natural selection was integrated with Mendelian genetics, many interpreted the ideas of Darwinism and the natural selection of man to mean that procreation was a social, not an individual, issue. Moreover, individuals could be scientifically shaped and controlled to fulfill the nation's destiny. Social Darwinists and eugenicists saw every aspect of a person's life, from socioeconomic status to health and educational achievement, as immutably determined by the genes they received from their parents at the moment of conception. Scientists increasingly disputed the contention that ignorance and poverty were fundamental and important causes of many of society's problems; a good environment was seen as merely a means of giving expression to good heredity, and it was deemed useless to improve environmental conditions for individuals lacking good heredity.

The coming of the 20th century spawned a new breed of moral entrepreneurs who promoted theories of race betterment. Implicit in the search for race betterment was the vision of the perfectability of humans. Tactics included segregation, sterilization, and prohibitions against marriage for those in certain groups.

Together with Mendelian genetics, eugenics was the terminus of manifold routes paved by IQ tests. The advent of tests of mental ability bolstered the claims and credibility of race-betterment movements. In the hands of eugenicists, the standardized tests became social artificers as much as scientific instruments. Tests identified those who were feebleminded for purposes of exclusion and population control and popularized the notion of racial differences in intelligence.

Conscription subjected almost the entire male population of the United States to complete physical, psychological, and psychiatric examinations. More than 1,700,000 men were given the Army Alpha and Beta tests. The results painted a bleak picture of the mental health of the United States. At the same time, accelerating immigration changed the composition of North America. The eugenicists, preoccupied with degeneracy at home, were equally appalled at the specter of being swamped by inferior immigrants.

Eugenics made the best of both fears—fear of immigrants and fear of the feebleminded. The results of tests of immigrants and those of the army tests were used to lobby for immigration restrictions. At the same time, civilized society, threatened by genetically defective strains, became hostile and repressive. The attitude was brutal; from hereditary taint, no reprieve was available. With increasing evidence that feebleminded people were in large part criminally inclined, potential perverts, and in any case dysgenic and socially dangerous, the only way to preserve the American way of life was to restrict them to segregated facilities. Given the implausibility and the staggering costs of institutionalization, many developed an enthusiasm for sterilization. People were selected because of their ancestry, national origin, race, or disability. In 1927, the problem of sterilization came before the federal Supreme Court for adjudication. Eventually, 29 states sanctioned sterilization.

During the 1920s, challenges to biological models of intelligence and behavior rapidly emerged. Many claimed that behavior could not be explained by immutable laws of biology. Eugenics as both creed and pseudoscience was eventually swamped by respectable genetics and the horrors of Nazi Germany.

NOTES

1. Francis Galton, an independently wealthy gentleman scholar, began his studies at London's King College Medical school but did not finish. Instead, he studied mathematics at Trinity College, Cambridge, and quickly immersed himself in the developing field of statistics (Galton, 1908). Galton found the law of regression, which expressed the relationship between the abilities of parents and offspring in what he called the regression or correlational coefficient. His colleague, Karl Pearson (1857–1936) carried on the work with considerable ingenuity. Galton also advanced the science of meteorology and drew up the world's first weather map; in addition, he began the forensic science of fingerprinting. When Galton moved into the study of psychology, he redefined the field from one of a normative science to one of a functional science of behavior. Galton was the first to use correlation to represent the degree of agreement between pairs of measurements of the same individual (Hilgard, 1987). He undertook some of the earliest studies of twins. He also worked on creating tests of mental ability. In 1883, Galton established what amounted to an intelligence test center in London. His Anthrometric Laboratory at the international Health Exhibition charged applicants three pence each to be evaluated (Black, 2003; Hothersall, 1984). Galton (1887) made estimates of the memory span of retarded children at North London School and at the Earlswood Asylum. Although he never produced a satisfactory measure of intelligence, Jones (1960) credits early developments in mental ability testing by J. McKeen Cattell in the United States and Alfred Binet in France to the early work of Galton.

2. Records of the New Jersey Training School for Feeble-Minded Boys and Girls at Vineland trace the origins of Goddard's laboratory to the formation of the Feeble Minded Club in March, 1902, which mandated itself to discuss the problems of mental retardation. E. R. Johnstone, director of the training school, was committed to the idea that public institutions should be considered human laboratories where problems of human growth and development could be studied under controlled conditions. In his annual report of 1906 (The New Jersey Training School, 1906), Johnstone translated the notion into policy when he recommended the establishment of a scientific laboratory. This laboratory made the Vineland institution the preeminent research site, which was funded by Philadelphia soup magnate, Samuel Fels.

3. Kite herself wrote a genealogical study of the Pineys in 1913.

4. Goddard's book contained 14 photographs, six of Deborah and eight showing her family and their present and ancestral homes (Elks, 2005). All the photographs had been retouched. Whether the alterations served to create a stronger impression of feeblemindedness or simply to enhance their reproduction remains controversial (see Fancher, 1987; Gould, 1981).

5. The U.S. army never acted on the findings of the original army tests. Despite the fact that approximately 4 million men were tested for military assignments in World War II (Tuddenham, 1962), the military testing in the second war did not receive nearly as much attention in the popular literature as had the earlier testing (Haney, 1981). Nevertheless, the high percentage of rejections because of "physical defect and mental conditions—including neuropsychiatric conditions, emotional instability, personality deviations, mental disease, and feeble mindedness" caused grave concern (Bowman, 1944, p. 33). In World War II, the army decided to accept 10% of the illiterate group through the induction stations each day.

6. The quantity of literature on eugenics is voluminous. Representative of the early work are Davenport (1915 a, 1915b), East (1923, 1924), Grant (1921/1936), Landman (1932), and Pitkin (1928).

7. Paul Bowman Poponoe was at the forefront of the eugenics movement and, as secretary of the Human Betterment Foundation, became a force in sterilization. He was educated at Stanford (although not a Stanford graduate) as a pupil of David Starr Jordan. In 1926, he became secretary of the Human Betterment Foundation, which published numerous tracts and tests promoting eugenics. He was appointed editor of the *Journal of Heredity* in which he cited in full the German sterilization law (1934, pp. 257–259).

8. Fred de Land, a major apologist for Bell, explains the events this way. Bell's *Memoir* was presented to the National Academy of Sciences in 1883 and later published by order of Congress. A representative of the Associated Press saw the volume lying on the desks of the members of Congress. As he glanced through, he saw that one portion referred to compulsory marriage laws. The reporter's conclusions that the *Memoir* advocated the adoption of laws to prevent deaf people from marrying appeared in most of the newspapers throughout the country. As Bell told it, the newspapers were at fault, not the proposals within the *Memoir*. He said lightly that "there is no man in America, I think, who has been more interviewed by newspaper reporters than I have" (Bell, 1891, p. 13).

9. Proctor (1988) makes the compelling point that a common theme of the German eugenicists both before and after the Nazi accession to power was that Germany had to catch up to the United States in its eugenic legislation. A number of prominent American eugenics books were translated into German, and the 1933 law was modeled on American laws. In turn, some American eugenicists, such as Poponoe, were impressed with the German measures.

Chapter 4

The Development of Special Classes

Throughout the 19th century, institutions formed the chief setting for the training and instruction of students who were deaf, blind, or mentally retarded. Although the clergy was conspicuous in the early genesis and development of these institutions, by mid-century, the institutions had clearly withdrawn from their historic Protestant alliance. As the 19th drew to a close, a complex of institutions was in place under the leadership of professional schoolmen and, to a growing extent, the auspices of the state.

Institutionalization was both metaphor and place, manifested in the changing constructions of various disabilities and the altered roles of the residential settings. Social Darwinism, scientific racism, and the eugenics movement, linked as they were to notions of heredity, innate human differences, nationality, race, and criminality, interacted with medical paradigms to create new sets of principles and practices. Altered constructs and the peculiarities of the pathological approach engendered profound changes in special education, particularly for those who were deaf and those who were mentally retarded. Segregation was the motif for all groups, but the course of institutional processes and structures differed dramatically after about 1880. Deafness and blindness became largely educational considerations. For those deemed to be mentally retarded—a group seen as a menace to the present society and as a threat to future generations—the educational emphasis dissipated and was almost lost within institutional milieus.

Horace Mann's vision for the common schools embraced all students. Yet almost from the outset, the system was under stress as the expectations of the common schools proved less reliable than the rhetoric surrounding them. Perversely, some children persistently refused to come to school or, when they did arrive, refused to learn in the same way, on the same schedule, and to the same depth as did other students.

The notion of shared belief as manifested in the common schools faltered in the face of the schools' unwillingness to recognize difference and opposition. Disorders, deviance, and disabilities became boundary conditions that the public schools were remarkably reluctant to confront. Unable to maintain growing numbers of unruly, disabled, low-functioning, and immigrant children, the system embarked on a sustained effort to address the obstacles that diversity created for the organizational and pedagogical structures of the schools. Seeking to maintain order, discipline, efficiency, and high standards, school districts created the community equivalents of institutions—special segregated classes.

As the 20th century opened for business, students with special needs were served in two main settings—the vital and still expanding complex of institutions and a small cadre of segregated classes or day schools. The classes established from the 1860s on were not strikingly successful. As the public schools became increasingly more structurally complex, there arose greater demands for efficiency in all branches, and diversity became more obvious and problematic. By 1910, the noncategorical ungraded classes and classes for unruly students, both of which had arrived largely unheralded in the latter half of the 19th century sprang to life in urban school systems across North America. By 1920, the public schools' responses to student heterogeneity became more organized and definite, and the institutional complex was replaced as the most viable option. At this date, two thirds of the large cities had special classes (Abraham, 1976) although "special education was very much in the experimental stage in 1922" (Warner, 1942, p. 247).

Early 20th-century education for special students was influenced by factors internal to the educational system. Of all the variables that underlay the massive expansion of special segregated classes, two stand front and center—compulsory education laws that propelled a growing and diverse population of children into the schools and the ongoing immigration that provided the expanding and diverse population of school-age children.

Immigration was dominant as a major factor supplementing compulsory education. The presence of so many immigrant children catalyzed the development of compulsory education in the United States and directly influenced the establishment of special education (Hoffman, 1975). Together with compulsory education laws, the pressures on children to attend school, and on families to send them, gained impetus from other legislation in the area of child welfare and protection, from new labor codes, and from the emergence of the nemesis of all recalcitrant students—the attendance or truant officer (see Tyack & Berkowitz, 1977).

The development of a theory of measurement and the widespread use of IQ tests was compelling. Testing advocates, delighted with what they saw as the usefulness of the Army tests, rapidly moved onto the domestic front and were met with a ready welcome. Group and individual scales for rating mental abilities appeared quickly in the schools. Members of the new breed of psychologists built their occupational identities around the process of evaluating children and then assigning them to special programs and classes.

Yet the most potent forces for change were rooted in factors outside the boundaries of the system. Despite the critical nature of compulsory education laws, the mounting population of immigrant children in the schools, and the pervasiveness of IQ testing, the growth of special segregated classes was the outcome of a host of social, economic, medical, and educational movements rather than the offspring of a single trend. The combination of new medical and scientific knowledge, the influence of new theories of heredity and evolution, increasing social fears, and a climate of interventionist social reform provided the historical context within which steadily increasing numbers of children were being identified as recipients for special education (see Osgood, 2000).

The essential nature of special education—what it did and who it served— remained relatively stable, as shown by the definitions presented over time in Table 4.1. However, with the burgeoning of segregated classes, special education evolved into an area characterized by a bewildering, complex, and complicated structure of disabilities, classes, and settings.

Mid-19th-century Americans developed an appetite to create mental categories based on various attributes that included gender, intelligence, degeneracy, and reading prowess. Special educators adopted a similar stance; from the 1850s on, they embarked on a quest for labels and categorization that served to maintain the purity of each special population by focusing on discrepant attributes—the unique and elusive characteristics that distinguished one defined area from other groups of exceptionality. As the labeling industry grew apace, classification and categorization became controversial and confusing. Even with the acute recognition that labels have their own markers in time and space, this chapter neverthess uses the encompassing "exceptional" (which includes all types and degrees of disability as well as those considered to be gifted) for continuty and clarity. Similarly, no other area has generated greater problems with terminiology than that of intellectual disabilities. This chapter uses the generic clinical term *mentally retarded* for clarity and precision. From this starting point, they organized special education into narrowly framed categories that applied to students, teachers, programs, and governance.

Diverse classifications of students emerged, each requiring attention. Along with the traditional groups of deaf, blind, and mentally retarded children, schools discovered children with a range of physical, emotional, and health difficulties. New categories included hard of hearing, speech impaired, emotionally disturbed, gifted, and dyslexic. Soon there were special classes under a variety of generic titles such as auxiliary class, opportunity class, open air class, and welfare class (see Chapter 7). More specific designations included sight-saving classes, lipreading classes, orthopedic classes, vocational and advancement classes, remedial reading programs, speech correction classes, and home instruction. In addition, steamer classes developed to serve immigrant children who could not speak English.

Almost always, events in the United States and Canada mirrored each other. In the case of special classes, however, those in the United States essentially grew from the need to serve unruly and truant students within the common school structures. Canada, certainly not unaffected by difficult children, nevertheless followed a different route. The first special day classes were established in 1906 in Montreal for children with physical problems—those who were described as crippled, sickly, or malnourished.

As special classes expanded, special educators no longer found themselves alone in considering the problems of exceptional children. Institutions, experts, and associations devoted exclusively to the study and treatment of disability emerged. Psychologists, medical personnel, nurses, speech therapists, social workers, and

Table 4–1

Definitions of Special Education

Definition	Source
Special education is a recognized instrumentality to equalize educational opportunity among children of differing physical and mental capacities.	Turner (1944, p. 216)
The purpose of special education programs is to serve all children who have serious probems of physical, intellectual, or emotional adjustment.	Martens (1946a, p. 226)
Special education assumes responsibility for those who have failed to adjust in the regular set-up.	Robb (1946, p. 239)
Special education is "that part of the school program designed for children who are unable to obtain an effective education without specialized help, not ordinarily considered essential in the general educational program.	Poole (1955–56, p. 20)
Special education exists to modulate or otherwise augment the regular education program to increase the likelihood that all children will be provided equitable social assistance in becoming self-sustaining adults.	Paul and Warnock (1980, p. 3)
Special education refers to "specially designed instruction . . . to meet the unique needs of a child with a disability."	U.S. Department of Education (1999, pp. 124–125)
Special education is an integrated system of academic and social supports designed, implemented, and monitored to ensure that students with disabilities are appropriately educated.	DiPaola, Tschannen-Moran, and Walther-Thomas (2004, p. 1)
Special education describes an extremely complex social and conceptual system designed to assist all children to reach their full potential.	Winzer (2007b)

other allied disciplines soon circled the educational core and encased exceptional children in a cocoon of professional help.

The realities of the first decades of the 20th century and those of the 1930s and 1940s were very different. In the first 2 decades of the new century, considerable public interest arose from new findings in psychology and child study as well as new directions in medicine and public health. At the same time, much alarm was caused by a host of intermeshed social factors that included mounting problems of family instability and juvenile delinquency, the shroud of degeneracy seen as sapping the energies of the nation, and the accompanying threat of the feebleminded. During the 1920s, a huge expansion of special education occurred, followed throughout the 1930s by an evaporation of the optimism that had previously surrounded special classes. Factors included the financial burdens of the Great Depression and, later, the fiscal focus of World War II. Within school systems, there was mounting dissatisfaction with inadequately planned classes that were staffed by untrained or poorly trained teachers; the complete segregation of children; the watered down curriculum; and the misinterpretation of the philosophy and practices of Progressive Education, which was essentially a child-centered curriculum and methodology that differed quite dramatically from traditional didactic approaches. School district involvement decreased dramatically, and complaints from professionals and parents mounted.

World War II brought a spirit of criticism of the old pre-war days, combined with a sense of progress and reform, both during the war and in the peace to follow. Postwar demographic shifts and swelling school enrollments refueled challenges to the organization of schools and to the practice of special education. By the late 1940s, the tendency was to reexamine and reevaluate earlier approaches, concepts, and practices. The 1950s saw the emergence of calls for better planning and teaching in the special education programs of the nation together with the entrance of the federal government into the provision of services for students with exceptionalities.

This chapter traces the development of the special segregated class paradigm in the opening half of the 20th century and examines the factors that underlay its rapid expansion. The body of material is organized in chronological order that demonstrates the changing face of special education and the humanizing attitude toward people with exceptionalities as the century progressed. Chapter 5 continues the story of special classes with an examination of reforms and developments in the 1960s and 1970s. Chapters 6 and 7 are devoted to considering the students designated as recipients of special services.

COMPULSORY EDUCATION

A key criterion for the success of schooling is the percentage of school-aged children enrolled in classes. Clearly, if schools are to work, everyone has to attend. School enrollment indicates the recognition by the parents or guardians that schooling is socially, economically, and intellectually advantageous. In addition, rates of attendance indicate with what assiduity parents pursued schooling.

The period from 1870 on established the public school as an integral part of the new, mass-industrialized society. Enrollments in the public schools expanded hugely. Between 1890 and 1915, public day school enrollment increased by 55% from 12.7 million to 19.7 million. Average daily attendance went up by 84%; the average length of the school year went from 134.7 days to 159.4 days, an increase of 18%, while the average number of days attended went from 86.3 to 121.2, a 40% increase (Chapman, 1979).

Secondary attendance slowly grew. By 1870, there were only about 80,000 students in all of the secondary schools in the United States, a figure that included only 2% of all 17 year olds. By 1900, American secondary education underwent a drastic reorganization, moving from the predominantly classical, elitist, semi-private academy to the mass public high schools. More than 8% of eligible students attended high schools, although the great majority still came from the upper and middle classes (Boyer, 1983; Gulek, 1988). By 1910, numbers of those in secondary schools had risen to 1 million students, of whom 15% were 17 year olds.

Many of the early state constitutions spoke freely and somewhat loosely about guaranteeing free public education to all children (Melcher, 1976). Massachusetts passed the first compulsory education law in 1852. By the turn of the century, nearly all the states had laws on their books that delineated public responsibility for the education of their children. Mississippi was the last in 1918.

Lawrence Cremin (1961) commented that "compulsory school attendance marked a new era in the history of American education" (p. 127). Nevertheless, the rectification of school practice with legislative mandates occurred slowly. The early laws were essentially symbolic statements that all children should be in school and that all parents should send them. It was not until the 1880s that the legislation began to be seriously enforced. By about 1910, expectations shifted. Children not in school were seen as threatening to the social order; simultaneously, the benefits of schooling were too great for children to miss. Social pressures promoted a growing awareness that school should be the social norm for all children, and reformers created elaborate legislative policies and organizational machinery to enforce compulsory attendance.

The new laws dramatically affected special education provisions and populations. With compulsory attendance, schools could no longer ignore part of the clientele; once the state ensured the right to compel attendance, then the state also had the responsibility to provide an education congruent with students' needs. As an example, labor legislation meant that schools could no longer abrogate their responsibilities by sending recalcitrant and unruly older students into the work force. The passage of child labor laws meant that under-age children had to possess work permits. Between 1900 and 1930, child labor decreased dramatically, and the balance of time that children spent in work and school shifted.

Once special classes began to emerge, enabling state-level legislation sustained growth. In 1900, only two states (Michigan and Wisconsin) had enacted laws allowing for the establishment of day classes for deaf children. Schooling for children who were deaf or blind was made compulsory in Indiana, North Carolina, North Dakota, Ohio, Utah, and Washington by 1909 (Pybas, 1909). In 1911, Massachusetts passed a law making education for mentally retarded children mandatory; in the same year, New Jersey passed the first compulsory special class laws for children who were deaf, who were blind, and who were retarded (New Jersey Commissioner, 1965). Other states followed suit. New York (1917) and Massachusetts (1920) passed legislation making it mandatory for local school boards of education to determine the number of children with special needs in their districts and to provide special classes where 10 or more mentally retarded children were found.

In 1919, Iowa passed a law for statewide care of handicapped children. Minnesota (1915), Illinois (1917), Wyoming (1919), Missouri (1919), Connecticut (1921), Washington (1921), and Oregon (1923) enacted permissive legislation, which allowed local jurisdictions to advance special education as much—or as little—as they pleased. Wisconsin (1921), Louisiana (1921), and Ohio (1921) introduced state aid. Maryland, whose compulsory education act of 1902 excluded handicapped children, passed legislation in 1914 that called for special classes at each county's discretion and, in 1930, that provided state aid. Many state departments of education formed bureaus of special education. These bureaus were soon staffed by specialists who dealt with the entire range of exceptional children.

Even with a hodgepodge of state laws, compulsory attendance did not draw in all children. Most states' early requirements were lax, with exemptions for poor families, families involved in agriculture, and families with sick or disabled children (Trent, 1994). In many jurisdictions, a disability was looked on as a type of illness and deemed sufficient cause for nonenrollment in school. As late as 1930, nine states did not have compulsory education laws for students who were blind (Koestler, 1976). Even into the 1950s, school boards were resistant to organizing programs for moderately mentally retarded pupils. Similarly, it was not until the late 1950s that the emotionally disturbed child became an item of educational interest.

Children with severe disabilities were not served. The schools made it clear that they did not want untrainables, and the institutions were reluctant to accept clients who were drains on staff time and energies and who could not contribute to the maintenance of the institutions. School boards routinely excluded large numbers of children from educational programs because of the nature or severity of their handicaps by developing strategies such as postponement, suspension, and outright denial as well as by crafting compulsory attendance laws, which in many states held that, for large numbers of handicapped children, school attendance was "inadvisable" (Weintraub & Abelson, 1975).

Apart from children who were simply excluded and left at home, another group of children were placed in alternate settings, including homes for dependent children, county poor farms, and almshouses, which continued to be used extensively. There were also children who, despite the laws and ubiquitous truant officers, simply would not go to school.

Most educators viewed schooling as the primary mechanism for social control and the obstruction of deviant behavior. However, it goes without saying that schooling was not a popular pursuit for many potentially delinquent and confirmed delinquent children and youth. The high numbers of truant students who thumbed their noses at the compulsory mandates posed a grave problem for educators and related agencies. J. E. W. Wallin was particularly unsympathetic to young truants. He complained that "society has been burdened for generations with a staggering *excess baggage* of unambitious, inefficient social nonconformists who are satisfied to live on the dole." Of itself, said Wallin, truancy is "often is a portent of eventual vagrancy, or at least of complaisant idling" (Wallin, 1938–39, p. 2, original italics).

To ensure that all eligible children attended some form of schooling, a body of professionals who were gradually added to the staffs of schools and the courts enforced the compulsory education laws. An interwoven bureaucracy of court officers, social workers, public health nurses, psychologists, attendance officers, and others circled the actual educational core (see Chapter 6).

Compulsory education laws greatly enhanced access for many youngsters. Yet, they led simultaneously to less access in a number of ways. First, there was the ongoing differentiation of children, teachers, and classes. As these distinctions occurred, the social space between regular and special education widened into a chasm. The expansion of the number and type of classes confirmed for general educators the parameters of acceptable achievement and behavior in their own classrooms. Teachers involved in special education were isolated both pedagogically and physically. On the one side, they developed mind-sets different from those of regular teachers (see Chapter 8). On the other, classes were located in obscure places in schools—in basements, down dark hallways, in former closets, or in the back of the school building. Children were often totally segregated; although in the same building, they entered and left school at different times and were kept apart at recess (Coveney, 1942).

IMMIGRANT CHILDREN IN THE SCHOOLS

Throughout the 19th century and well into the first decades of the 20th, immigration into the cities transformed a chiefly Anglo-Saxon population to one that reflected the widespread migration to the United States of people from all over the world. The first sizeable wave occurred between 1849 and 1860 and consisted primarily of people from Ireland. Between 1846 and 1855 alone, 2,300,000 immigrants from Great Britain and Ireland immigrated to America (Coleman, 1973). A second great wave began around 1880 and included immigrants from Europe, especially the southern and eastern regions. By 1900, Italians had replaced the Irish as the largest ethnic group in many northeastern states (Dworkin, 1976; Kamin, 1974).

World War I abruptly ended both the massive flow of immigrants and the protests their arrival engendered. But until the start of the war, when immigration was restricted, the public schools encountered waves of immigrant children. By 1900, approximately half of the American population was foreign born or were the children of foreign-born parents. In 1909, when the United States Immigration Commission conducted a massive study, 57.8% of children in the public schools of the 37 largest American cities were of foreign-born parentage (Cremin, 1961). Between 1900 and the beginning of World War I in 1914, New York schools experienced a 60% jump in enrollment. A single classroom with one teacher often held 60 and occasionally up to 150 children (Martz, 1993). In New York City, 71.5% of the school population was immigrant; in Chicago, 67.3%; and in Boston, 63.5% (Hoffman, 1975).

The massive immigration instigated two responses with completely incompatible endings within the same society—essentially, assimilation or segregation. Assimilation served to Americanize the hordes of foreigners: from about 1919 on, assimilation and Americanization became popular crusades that gained momentum in concert with the xenophobic and political reactions of the postwar period. Segregation, as detailed in Chapter 3, ensured that those in control in America would remain White, Anglo-Saxon, and Protestant.

Many seemed oblivious to, or at least willing to overlook, the obvious contradictions that existed between the views of immigration. The contrary currents melded in the schools. Dedicated as they were to the ideals of Americanization and patriotism, school systems searched for means to accommodate students who came from backgrounds holding very different cultural and social mores. Segregation was key. Often, a newly arrived child was assigned to a steamer class; just as often, a child was sent to backward classes "not because the backward class is the right place for him but rather because it furnishes an easy means of disposing of a pupil who, through no fault of his own, is an unsatisfactory member of a regular class" (cited in Hoffman, 1975, p. 419).

THE FIELD OF PSYCHOLOGY

The first decades of the 20th century saw the new field of psychology increasingly asserting authority and credibility. It became the primary discipline informing special education practice, although its effect extended far beyond a concern for individual achievement. Pioneer psychologists developed mental tests that quickly emerged as a fixture in social science. The tests also spawned or accelerated a set of trends and movements. On the one side, IQ measures brought the scientific investigation of individual variation, the concept of mental age, individual psychological diagnoses, and large-scale assessment. On the other, reformers operating under the banner of interlocking movements such as Social Darwinism and eugenics sought a crafted world order. For their mission, IQ tests were the critical criterion. Psychology also created the new child study movement that, in turn, led to a developing concern over child care and formal advances in early childhood education for both typical and disabled young children.

Child Study Movement

European educational theorists such as Pestalozzi and his student Froebel highlighted the importance of children's interactions with their environment through direct experiences rather than through abstractions. Another European theorist, Johann Herbart, in 1901 introduced the concept of developmental stages. Turn-of-the-century Americans, fascinated with all forms of natural science study and increasingly interested in the early development of infants and young children, readily adopted the ideas. The fledgling disciplines of psychology and sociology melded the American ideas about general human development with European notions about child development.

G. Stanley Hall's genetic psychology (which meant *human development* at the time) deserves its place as the first developmental psychology in America (Grinder, 1967). Hall established the study of child development as a legitimate field and influenced writers and educational reformers who began to conceptualize young children as learners and to promote their instruction in special environments.

Many of Hall's students, including Henry Goddard and Lewis Terman, achieved a prominence of their own. Most germane to the discrete field of child development were the psychological studies of human infants, which became popular as the universities began to open nurseries and child study laboratories. When the Clinic of Child Development opened at Yale University in 1911, Hall's student, Arnold Gesell (1880–1961), a physician and psychologist, became the director. Gesell pioneered longitudinal research methods in the study of the physical and motor development of children; he made elegant and painstaking catalogs of the acquisition of motor skills in infants and set a standard for the scientific study of human development that lasted 50 years.

Mental Ability Testing

The use of IQ tests was crucial to the advance of special education. "The widespread employment of these tests," noted Wallin (1914), "has indubitably done more than anything else to promote the organization of special classes and the introduction of differentiated courses of instruction in the public schools" (p. 46).

The very early instruments had failed to make much impression and were even viewed negatively (Freeman, 1926). Educators at the opening of the century saw little value in mental tests in the schools (Linden & Linden, 1968; Young, 1923). And, as Lawrence Cremin (1964) suggested, the feverish activity in educational testing in the early years of the century would undoubtedly have remained very much a professional phenomenon had it not been for the intervention of World War I and the testing that the military conducted, specifically the Army tests.

This single undertaking of these military tests dramatically enhanced the status of the profession of psychology. Moreover, the practical success of group psychological examining in the Army coupled with the demobilization of trained examiners made testing widespread after World War I. The years after the war saw the development and implementation of group intelligence tests. For example, a committee of psychologists previously concerned with the development of the Army tests formulated the National Intelligence Test for use in the public schools (Chapman, 1981). In less than a year, more than 575,000 copies were sold. In 1923, Lewis Terman published the Terman Group Test of Mental Ability for Grades 7 to 12, which sold more than half a million copies (Chapman, 1981). By 1926, there were more than 30 group tests on the market, designed for use in the schools (Freeman, 1926).

Individual tools developed apace. In 1921, Terman began his study of gifted children for which he designed the Stanford Achievement Test battery. In 1936, Terman and Catherine Cox issued an Attitude-Interest Analysis Test designed to measure masculinity and femininity; in 1937, Terman issued a new revision of the Stanford-Binet.

As a branch of psychology, educational psychology emerged about 1910. The term *school psychologist* first appeared in print in 1923 (Hutt, 1923). School psychology grew from the need to examine children for placement in special classes and for the diagnosis of learning, behavioral, and emotional difficulties. When Wallin surveyed 108 schools, for example, 81% of the respondents said that they provided some kind of psychological test or examination before assignments were made to special classes for the mentally handicapped (Wallin, 1958).

School districts began to constructively use the skills of the new discipline of psychology. In 1915, the Connecticut Board of Education was the first to appoint a psychologist to help plan education for backward and defective children. New

York City employed psychological examiners from the early 1900s (Fagan, 1985). By the 1920s, large urban school districts were developing extensive testing programs. They hired psychologists and other experts to teach new methods and techniques and to use standard IQ tests (see Raftery, 1988).

Before such tests were available, judgments of mental development were based on personal interpretations and indices such as head measurements, vital capacity, ability to discriminate differences, and academic failure, to say nothing of the interviewer's personal bias and "sixth sense." Once the possibility of measuring an individual's ability by a short and simple test was aired, the idea captured the imagination of professionals and the general public. The practical value of the Binet type of scale was immediately obvious to American educators. Many welcomed testing programs because they were scientific; teachers were enthralled with the new tools that would allow them to compare the mental and physical attributes of students and to understand the thinking of disabled children. Through the assiduous use of "modern psychometric tests," educators could be confident that the intelligence of a child could be "accurately measured and a very close estimate made as to what his mental development will be when he reaches adult life" (Fernald, 1924, p. 966).

In 1905, Binet and Simon created a single scale in which samples of different aspects of mental ability could be combined to provide a rough but serviceable means of appraising general intelligence. Binet's early assessment efforts were driven by a benevolent charge from the French Minister of Public Instruction to develop measures for identifying young children in need of educational assistance (Binet & Simon, 1916). In North America, however, testing became a primary component in sorting and tracking students, in assigning them to special classes, and in planning curricula. "Without scientific diagnosis and classification of these (feeble-minded, physically defective, backward, truants, incorrigibles) children," said Terman in 1916, "the educational work of the special class must blunder along in the dark" (p. 5). The tests were seen as able to identify 10% to 15% of the children needing special help—"those intellectually superior or supernormal; intellectually inferior or subnormal; intellectually dependent; and affectively or instinctively defective" (Yerkes, 1917, p. 252).

Lewis Terman, instrumental as both as test constructor and test promoter, coined the slogan, "a mental test for every child" (Chapman, 1981). He argued that all levels of intelligence could be measured and advanced the notion of the widespread use of testing to route students into appropriate educational experiences. In Los Angeles, for example, psychologists administered Binet tests, examined health and school records, and took statements from teachers and principals as part of their effort to place pupils in more clearly defined categories (Hines, 1922).

Public Health

The early 20th century brought a growing emphasis on public health and hygiene. One of the most pressing problems was the high mortality and morbidity rates of children, which were a consequence of inadequate nutrition, poor living conditions, diseases, and epidemics. Mortality was estimated at 10% for newborns (Shapiro, Schlesinger, & Nesbit, 1968). By 1914, infants in the United States were dying of gastrointestinal disorders, respiratory problems, and infant cholera (Wallin, 1914). Medical and public health advances stressed decreasing infant mortality, lowering maternal mortality, and increasing child well-being. Physical health, nutrition, and the problems of malnourishment assumed greater importance. Professionals, parents, and the public became more alert to the educational implications of physical handicaps; academic and popular writings on the effects of sight, hearing, and mental defects on learning began to motivate enquiry about and observation of many pupils for possible physical and intellectual disabilities.

School medical inspections began in Europe in the mid-19th century and spread to Britain and America in the 1890s. American reformers (who often spoke disparagingly of parental child-rearing and hygiene practices) sponsored medical inspections of schools. The great physical toll of World War I and the outbreak of the postwar influenza epidemic further sensitized school and other government officials to the importance of children's physical well-being and to a need for medical testing.

Edouard Seguin had suggested careful physical and mental scrutiny of each child. Later, Henry Goddard's first reports from the Psychological Research Laboratory at Vineland told how he "tested and measured our children at least once, many of them twice, and a few a third time" (New Jersey Training School for Feeble Minded Boys and Girls at Vineland, 1906, p. 37), examining height and weight as well as results of a stimulating diet. Following this lead, other speakers suggested that the schools "should make physical, medical and psychological examinations of the children by groups of ten to fifty" to discover "physical and mental peculiarities" as well as "defects or degrees of development which are actual or possible handicaps in school or vocational work" (Yerkes, 1917, p. 257).

By the 1920s, public health officials such as public health nurses began to move into the schools, and they identified masses of children as undernourished, turbercular, or with minor physical disorders. Medical inspection looked for emotional and mental defects as well as evidence of contagious diseases that included ringworm, impetigo, scarlet fever, diphtheria, measles, and so on (Kode, 2002).

PROMOTING SPECIAL CLASSES

Arguments for special education rest on particular ways of thinking and understanding. When special classes truly emerged in the first decades of the 20th century, the alleged purposes were highly variable: there was little consensus among the organizers and most had modest immediate goals. The various methods and agendas were not founded on one coherent theory but on a family of loosely woven ideas. In truth, most classes were not the result of any theory but had simply evolved along lines similar to a class in New York City, which "grew out of conditions in a neighborhood which furnished many and serious problems in truancy and discipline" (Farrell, cited in Sarason & Doris, 1979, p. 290).

Only two common threads can be readily discerned in the arguments for the formation of special classes in the opening decades of the 20th century. The first echoed those for the earlier ungraded classes and classes for unruly children that removed rambunctious and unruly pupils. The second responded to calls for the reduction of retardation as well as other learning and behavioral problems that were plaguing the schools. Reformers and educators may have celebrated the philosophical ideals of equal access and universal education but, pragmatically, the numbers of students who functioned below the norm magnified the pressures created by already overcrowded schools and large class sizes. The cost of laggards within the schools in terms of finances, teacher time, and classroom disruption was a constant irritant to administrators seeking order, efficiency, and economy. Stemming these costs became an important political and economic issue.

Leonard Ayres, the former superintendent of the Puerto Rican schools and a statistician and economist with the Sage Foundation, foregrounded the problems when he published *Laggards in Our Schools* in 1909, one of the earliest volumes in special education. Ayres found more boys than girls with mental retardation. The lowest percentage was among Germans; the highest, Italians. Ayres also provided an account of the discrepancy between instruction in the public schools and the poor achievement of many pupils. He reported that 33.7% of all elementary school children demonstrated an age-to-grade retardation. Older children who were retained to repeat school years thus created a phenomenal financial burden to the schools. Ayres later suggested that such children needed "a different kind of teaching and a different sort of treatment from the other children" (Ayres, 1915, p. 40). Toronto's director of auxiliary classes, Helen MacMurchy, matched the influence of Ayres's work in expanding Canadian special education through her annual reports on feeblemindedness and her 1920 popular account *The Almosts: A Study of the Feeble-Minded*.

As Ayres provided the underlying administrative rationale, Chicago provided the model. In 1899, the Educational Commission of the City of Chicago was authorized by the mayor and city council to conduct an in-depth survey of the faltering Chicago school system. The report, which provided a model for many urban school systems in the United States, urged the establishment of ungraded classes and parental (industrial) schools for children who could not be accommodated within general classrooms (Hoffman, 1975).

One of the most influential spokesmen for special education in the opening half of the 20th century was J. E. W. Wallin, a former student of G. Stanley Hall's at Clarke University, who had held posts as director of the psychoeducational clinic in the St. Louis public schools and as director of the Division of Special Education and Mental Hygiene in the Delaware State Department of Public Instruction. To Wallin, segregated classes contributed to harmonious schools. School officials complained that students with disabilities in general classrooms often exerted "an injurious influence upon the normal children" because of "their indolence, eccentricities, abnormalities, and not infrequent vicious, depraved, or immoral practices" (Wallin, 1914, p. 390). Teachers faced the unpromising task of attempting to follow a course adapted to the main group of average students while providing adequately for the below-average students who required extra help. Segregated classrooms effectively removed what Wallin (1914) called the "flotsam and the jetsam," the "hold backs and the drags" (p. 390). Thus removed from the mainstream, problem children could not disrupt classrooms or contaminate the learning of others.

In Toronto, Helen MacMurchy (1919) echoed Wallin in arguing that "the rights of the majority and the normal child must not be interfered with." Putting it simply, she said, "Nature has put the defective child in a class by himself and we should follow her example" (p. 280). An American teacher echoed the sentiment: "The misfits should be collected and put by themselves. Extremes should never be put together" ("The Training and Certification of Teachers," 1929, p. 298).

The theme of menace from those deemed to be mentally retarded and the need for custodial response was frequently repeated in discussions throughout the decade of 1910. During this period of public alarm, many opposed the placement of children with disabilities, particularly mental disabilities, in the public schools. However, special schools, it was argued, simply increased the evil they were established to cure. Moreover, educating people with mental retardation would make them more marriageable and more likely to be parents, a dire outcome because such people were viewed as "eugenically unfit for parenthood and incapable of sharing in social progress" (Yerkes, 1917, p. 293). Ultimately, it was considered far better to pursue social salvation through institutional segregation. The atypical "weaklings" required special care. Advocates suggested that "in an institution, well-managed and well-supported, these children will be much happier and progress somewhat, while running no risks, and doing no damage to anyone else" ("Defective children . . . ," 1915, p. 4).

Thus, the main function of special classes was to serve as a conveyor of exceptional children to the institutions. Ada Fitts, director of special education in Boston, explained that the "ideal condition" was "for many of the mentally defective to go from school directly to the institution, and thus safeguard the public from inefficiency, unemployment, pauperism, vagrancy, degeneracy, and all the other social consequences of feeble-mindedness" (Fitts, 1916, p. 3). Within the public schools, educators could "ensure diagnosis and treatment at an early age" and use the classes as "clearing houses for personnel segregation before adult life is reached" (Fernald, 1912, p. 9).

Because human development and competence was seen as not malleable but predetermined and inevitable—the result of a biological master plan—education for exceptional children could, at best, only ameliorate or contain the unfortunate conditions that frustrated development. Still, effective interventions had to operate selectively, based on distinctions between the dangerous and the less dangerous as well as juxtaposed to the economic price for society. Certainly, degenerates were costly. They spread disease, clogged up the school system, promoted crime and prostitution, burdened hospitals, overwhelmed charitable institutions, and raised the taxes paid by the respectable. Yet, the ultimate solutions of institutionalization and sterilization were simply unfeasible in financial and human terms. Therefore, noted Walter Fernald in 1919, "It is most important that the limited facilities for segregation be used for the many who can be protected in no other way" (1919,

p. 7). With economy to the forefront, it was hoped that the maintenance of feeble-minded children and youth in schools would at least stem some incipient truancy and delinquency.

The period from 1910 to 1930 saw a huge spurt in the enrollments in and types of special classes. By 1911, more than 100 large city school systems had established special schools and special classes for children who were exceptional, and a number of states began to subsidize special programs by paying the excess costs of maintaining special classes. By 1913, 108 cities had special classes and special schools (Trent, 1994). By 1927, 218 American cities had special or ungraded classes for about 52,000 children labeled "mental handicapped" (Osgood, 1997). Boston's services in this area grew from nine special classes in 1912 to 132 by 1930 (Boston Council of Social Agencies, 1930). In Toronto, one class in 1908 expanded to 240 by 1930 (Ontario Department of Education, 1930).

The city of Los Angeles illustrates the trend. Special schooling began in 1898 for deaf children, followed by classes for problem boys in 1905 and aid for hospitalized children in the same year. "Opportunity A" rooms were established in 1915 for students 2 years ahead of their chronological age. In 1917, blind pupils, academically maladjusted children, and those who were mentally retarded began to receive help. In 1920, classes were formed for those described as crippled. Speech correction classes began in 1921; in 1925, classes were formed for those with partial sight, hard of hearing children, tubercular youth, problem girls, and backward high school pupils (Sutherland, 1938). Similar rapid expansion was seen in other major urban areas. For example, by 1935, Chicago provided special classes and special schools such as those for unadjusted boys, physically handicapped children, and those who were crippled, deaf, blind, anemic, mentally retarded, and others (Stullken, 1935–36).

FALL FROM CERTAINTY: THE 1920S

The 1920s saw a growing reliance on research findings to settle issues relating to intelligence. Psychologists began to assess the nature-nurture conundrum and examine the importance of both heredity and environment in the biological makeup of a total human being. The eugenics preoccupation was gradually displaced by attempts to clarify the basic concepts, methods, and presuppositions of intelligence and heredity.

As methods for studying and understanding human behavior became more sophisticated and reliable, it grew clear that chromosomes, evolutionary adaptation, mental retardation, and the like could not be brought into existence simply by the intellectual activity of the people who posited them. The realization grew that both heredity and environment shaped behavior. A single, monolithic conception of mental retardation was wrong; rather, a complex map of biological, social, and psychological factors combined at every juncture in the etiology of intellectual disability. At the same time, studies attempted to highlight the social influences and genetic factors involved in giftedness (e.g., Cattell, 1915).

Accumulating clinical experience together with new research findings led psychologists and educators to reassess the propensity to order human variations as fixed, inherited traits on a gradual descending scale. From psychology came the argument that "heredity makes mental achievement possible; it does not ensure it" (Carr-Saunders, 1926, p. 116). Medicine showed that feeblemindedness was not carried on a single recessive gene, but was a condition that arose from a variety of complex causes. Alfred Strauss, for example, discarded the notion that mental retardation was a homogeneous entity simply characterized by slowness of development resulting from inherited factors (Gardiner, 1958). Other researchers took a sober look at the correlates of poverty and suggested that poor nutrition, inadequate health care, prematurity, multiple sensory and neurological defects (even though minor), and an impoverished environment were at least as deleterious as genetic factors (Crissey, 1975).

Further examinations of environmental effects used deprivational studies.[1] Skeels and Dye (1939) conducted one of the earliest studies using experimental and quasi-experimental group designs. Skeels followed a sample of children diagnosed as mentally retarded, and 21 years later, he found normalcy the rule rather than the exception. Although replete with methodological caveats, these and other deprivational studies emphasized environmental correlates. They disputed the assumed cognitive rigidity seen in persons with mental retardation by providing evidence that IQ was not fixed, that children could move from retardation to normalcy—or from normalcy to retardation.

Major developments in other areas of psychology similarly placed the weight of theoretical opinions on the side of growth and development variables rather than genetic factors. J. B. Watson held that observable behaviors should form the sole subject matter of psychology and that the goal of psychology was to control and predict behavior through the manipulation of environmental stimuli. Watson argued that conditioning and learning, not heredity, accounted for human achievement. Sigmund Freud's psychoanalytic theory placed principal emphasis on early social learning, especially within the family, as the source of most differences in personality.

Notions about adaptive behavior grew clearer. Tredgold (1908) attempted a more refined definition of mental retardation using social competence rather than only organic pathology as a primary diagnostic criteria. Potter (1922) indicated that the importance of intelligence had to be placed in perspective and that "human efficiency depends upon the adjustment to three groups of factors, namely, in their order of importance, instincts, emotions, and intelligence" (p. 22). As a construct, adaptive behavior was crystallized by Edgar A. Doll who defined social competence developmentally, progressing from dependent behavior to independent behavior to responsibility for the welfare of others to the dependency of senescence. Doll's Vineland Scale of Adaptive Behavior was first published as a series of behavioral items in April 1935 (Bradway, 1937).[2]

No psychological construct has engendered more controversy, however, than that of intelligence. No expression of intelligence has been more misused than the intelligence test. No single group was more open to the full range of indignities that stemmed from mismeasurement than those labeled as mentally retarded.

Although IQ testing came under attack almost as soon as it was introduced in the early years of the 20th century, it was during the 1920s that psychologists began to grapple with the oppositions and contradictions of IQ. Dissident groups of psychologists and commentators emerged who posed vexatious questions about IQ as the sovereign criterion in development, about the infallibility of the test results, and about the specious statistics and worrisome conclusions. For example, newspaper man Walter Lippmann, a formidable liberal thinker, embarked on an extended public debate with Lewis Terman. In six articles in the *New Republic*, Lippmann damned the army tests and castigated Terman. He summed it up when he declared that the IQ tests were "a new chance for quackery in a field where quacks breed like rabbits" (in Black, 2003, p. 84).

Researchers who reexamined the army data were led to castigate not only the technical inadequacy of the measures but also the interpretation of the results that subverted the design of the tests. The army tests, for example, had not been designed to provide mental ages, but these were the data presented to an unknowing public. Other researchers stressed the hereditary emphasis of the IQ measures in general, a criticism largely directed toward Lewis Terman (Hilgard, 1987). Still others, less concerned with ideology, held simply that the tests were untrustworthy evaluators of intelligence.

Right from the start, some researchers and workers involved in psychological measurement stressed that the tests were delicate instruments; that testers required specialized training and skills; and that assistance to individual children, rather than tracking and segregation, were the goals. Standardization and usage were constant irritants that prompted calls for structured professional guidelines, uniform standards, and judicious use (Wallin, 1911, 1914). As early as 1901, the Committee on Psychological Research of the American Association for the Study of the Feeble-Minded provided a format for an appropriate psychological examination that included mental, physical, and emotional measurements (Committee on Psychological Research, 1901). In 1906, the American Psychological Association appointed a committee to standardize tests of motor and sensory skills (Freeman, 1926). With the introduction of the Stanford-Binet test in 1916, a clinical criterion was adopted for assigning children to classes for the retarded, and the IQ score became part of the legal basis for the assignment in many states.

Early promotions of the Goddard and Terman revisions of the Binet scale held that educational usage could become universal; the step-by-step administrative and scoring instructions made possible the use of the test by any school teacher who could afford to buy the book. It therefore became popular to castigate the testers rather than the tests. Edgar Doll, who was at the Vineland institution from 1925 to 1949, carped about "inexpert Binet users." Psychologist J. E. W. Wallin, one of the most vocal and persistent of the early critics, wrote that "between 1910 and 1915 I witnessed psychological examinations and demonstration psychological clinics by persons who were not even graduates of two-year normal schools. At one demonstration I counted 17 errors in the administration of the Binet by one tester. It gave me something of a shock to hear such examiners referred to as 'our psychologists'" (Wallin, 1927).

In the face of public assaults, test constructors and test promoters could no longer defend their positions. Lewis Terman, who had advocated a unidimensional conception of intelligence, now warned that "we must guard against defining intelligence solely in terms of ability to pass the tests of a given intelligence scale" (Terman, 1921, p. 131). Carl Brigham, who had used the tests to lobby for immigration restrictions, recanted on IQ tests in 1929.[3] Robert Yerkes questioned the infallibility of IQ measures, the use of the tests, and the interpretation of the results (see Black, 2003).

Henry Goddard's tenure at the Psychological Research Laboratory at Vineland from 1906 until 1918 (when he left to become director of the Ohio Bureau of Juvenile Research) was marked by a series of historically important events, particularly in reference to his creation of the concept of the moron and to his deep involvement in mental ability testing and interpretation. The results of Goddard's family pedigree studies were regarded as a major scientific breakthrough and "found their way into scholarly journals and scientific texts, legislative debates and court cases, political speeches and popular magazines" (Zenderland, 2004, p. 165). But Goddard's findings were both too good and too bad to be true. After 1917, the Kallikak data collection and findings were seriously questioned.

The belief in an absolute and dogmatic view of mental ability was clearly reflected by Goddard in 1914 when he stated optimistically that the Binet scale was "wonderfully accurate even down to a variation of only one or two points" (Goddard, 1914, p. 86). He defended Binet's plan as perfect and asserted that it could be used by anyone (Goddard, 1913a, 1913b, 1913c). Most of the examiners of the time followed Goddard explicitly on the question of the adequacy of the Binet scale for the diagnosis of mental deficiency, on the accuracy of the scale, and on the correctness of his system of classification (see Wallin, 1958). J. E. W. Wallin wrote in 1955 that "a few doughty souls there were indeed who soon began to question many of [Goddard's] basic assumptions" (p. 113). Although the criticisms were for a time persistently ignored, there was soon open disputation of the validity of Goddard's intelligence test.

The deeply flawed roots and use of IQ tests became more apparent to many professionals, and many rejected the earlier touted virtues and sought to make the use and interpretation of the tests more sophisticated and refined. Not all teachers accepted IQ tests as unambiguous instruments, and not all school administrators saw the measures as the revolutionary, educational, and diagnostic tools of the new century (see Raftery, 1988). Elizabeth Farrell, founder of the Council for Exceptional Children, fought the use of intelligence tests as the single measure for placement of children in ungraded classes ("CEC's founder . . . ," 2002). Many educators, however, did not abandon their belief in progress. They saw the testing programs as offering the ultimate in effectiveness and efficiency. Intelligence testing was an objective scientific method for selecting students for instructionally appropriate programs and would solve their problems with new labeling methods and specialized curriculum. Moreover, even though testing proved less efficient than expected, negating its value would be tantamount to refuting the wisdom of university schools of education, a thought repugnant to most (Raftery, 1988).

In the schools, unprecedented numbers of students were subjected to IQ tests, examinations, and medical inspections. Practically, the use of individual tests, developed to be administered to one child at a time, faded under the pressure to assess large numbers quickly. A reliance on measures designed for group testing grew.

SPECIAL EDUCATION IN TRANSIT

In the early 1920s, industrialization, urbanization, and the effects of World War I reshaped public consciousness about education in a variety of areas and engendered a subtly gentler attitude toward students with special needs. The movement for special schools or classes now began to advocate retaining students with disabilities in the local community, within the framework of the public schools. By 1925, the promotion of special classes was so conspicuous that workers called for the training of all exceptional children in the public schools, including the so-called psychopathic, psychoneurotic, and those with behavioral problems.

Edward Johnstone, superintendent of the New Jersey Training School for Feeble Minded Boys and Girls at Vineland, approached institutionalization with caution, cognizant that such a program was "slow, costly, require[d] infinite patience, watchfulness, and constant urging" (The New Jersey Training School, 1904, p. 65). In 1912, Johnstone argued that "the blind, the deaf, the crippled, and the incorrigibles must some day take their place in the life of the commonwealth with normal people." Therefore, "they at least must have training in the public schools to keep them from becoming institutionalized and thus losing touch with normal community life" (The Training School, 1912, p. 22). Others played variations on the new theme of retaining these people in the community. Wolfe (1925) noted that "special schools or classes would enable many defective children now being sent to institutions to remain at home for at least part, if not the whole, of their school life" (p. 125). Wallin (1924) also argued that it was time to stop ignoring and mistreating the handicapped. They needed, he contended, community-based facilities rather than removal to isolated institutions. Only those unable to care for themselves or those who threatened to become a social menace should be institutionalized in custodial settings. "No child," he wrote, "should be excluded from school as untrainable or ineducable without a fair probationary trial, except idiots and the lowest grade of imbeciles" (Wallin, 1934, p. 12).

Researchers and practitioners embraced a nurture-environmental view and now saw people who were disabled as a pool of potentially productive citizens whose problems most often stemmed from neglect, mistreatment, inadequate economic support, and inappropriate schooling. Effective community-based schooling would stem not only the waste of human resources but also the costs of supporting dependent adults who could have become self-supporting with education and training. By attracting and keeping disabled children and youth in school, special education would cut down truancy and neglect and would reduce criminal behavior. Wallin (1938–39) reported that "in San Francisco, only four of 800 children who had been discharged from the special classes for atypical children up to the year 1929 had appeared in the juvenile court" (p. 5).

Segregated classrooms were the most viable option. According to Wallin (1938–39), "Much pupil dissatisfaction with the school is due to the fact that the method and the content of instruction are not adapted to the capabilities and interests of the learner" (p. 4). Very often, children became "misfits through innate ability to successfully participate in the traditional academic curriculum" (Kugler, 1935, p. 128).

Segregation served the particular needs of special children. Without the competition of general classes, they progressed. Promoters observed that once in special classes, deficient pupils began to respond as they had never responded before as they experienced the influence of individual attention and guidance as well as differential training adapted to individual needs. In Massachusetts, for example, Wallin (1934) reported that "instead of a spirit of dejection and indifference, pupils became industrious and enthusiastic, formed habits of successes instead of failure, and become an asset rather than a liability to the community" (p. 56).

The efficiency of noninstitutional care was further bolstered by studies of adults with disabilities. For example, in a preliminary report, published in December 1915, on children discharged from ungraded cases in New York City, Elizabeth Farrell reported on 350 pupils who had been out of school from 1 to 8 years. Of this number, 54.8% were employed for wages; 8.8% were employable but temporarily out of work at the time of the investigation, and 26.6% "were cared for at home and many of these at home had economic value" (Fitts, 1916, pp. 5–6).

Walter Fernald's study of residents who had been discharged or removed from the Waverly Institution for the Feeble-Minded in Massachusetts in the period 1890 to 1914 (see Winzer, 1993b) indicated that the most successful cases were those cared for outside the institution. It showed, said Fernald, "much justice in the plea of the well-behaved adult defective to be given a 'trial outside' for apparently a few defectives do not need or deserve life-long segregation" (1919, p. 7). Continuing work on the same theme (e.g., Channing, 1932; Kennedy, 1948) showed that mildly mentally retarded young adults, once released from the intellectual demands of the school, could be, at the very least, marginally self sufficient in the community through a variety of unskilled, semiskilled, and service positions.

Curriculum

In many facets of life in early 20th-century North America, efficiency was seen as a panacea for the social ills of the day. School curricula reflected the social order, valuing children as productive future members of society. Educators embraced the notion that schools should assume leadership in initiating social change and accept responsibility for dealing realistically with social problems. Students with disabilities advanced from being seen as burdensome and unproductive purveyors of moral failure to a pool of potentially productive citizens who could contribute to the country. In special classrooms, teachers constructed and then reaffirmed the belief that their students were both capable of and deserving of an education. They abandoned the inflexible general education curricula that proved the undoing of children who did not conform to the common notion of normal.

Nevertheless, children with exceptionalities were generally viewed as filling the lowest rungs of the possible occupational ladder, and as a result, manual training became paramount within curriculum. In Boston, for example, Ada Fitts reported in 1916 that "the program is so arranged that each child has one and one-half hours academic, and two hours manual work each day" (p. 2). The girls were taught domestic science, sewing, millinery, embroidery, crocheting, knitting, mending, and preserving. For the boys, there was brush making, boot blacking, word working, serving of luncheons, dish washing, simple tailoring, gardening, assistant janitor work, and other forms of comparatively unskilled labor.

The Progressive Movement

The ideas of the German philosopher Johann Herbart inspired a number of education reforms in the early 20th century that contributed to what generally became known as the New Education or the Progressive Education movement. Among others, American philosopher John Dewey (1859–1952) was a member of the Herbart Society.

Although it questioned the conventional wisdom of the day, Progressive Education entailed more than just curricular and pedagogical changes. It had a distinct philosophy that attempted to adapt education to the rhythms of modern America. John Dewey, the American philosopher most closely identified with Progressive Education, held to an educative ideal that reaffirmed faith in intelligence and in the scientific method as indispensable to moral and social life. Dewey was convinced that the school should lead the way in developing "a larger society which is worthy, lovely, and harmonious" (Dewey, 1897, p. 16). Progressives viewed education as the primary vehicle for preparing students to live in American society. The object of Progressive Education was to provide a link between curriculum and the demands of adult life. Progressive educators called for scientifically validated practices; they sought to eliminate lockstep schooling, to introduce courses to make children more economically self-sufficient, and to provide equity of educational opportunity to all students.

Herbartian discourses placed the child rather than the content to be taught at the center of the educative process. Dewey believed that children learned best when interacting in a rich environment; that children construct meaning from real-life applications of knowledge; and that when various senses are used simultaneously, the probability of learning is greater (Dewey, 1938). Such a model of education required that each teacher had to be reeducated to move them "from an autocratic authoritative individual concerned with a 'wooden curriculum,' routine procedures, grades, external disciplining, formal atmosphere, and preservation of the status quo, to an individual who becomes a guide, having vision, a democratic spirit, and an understanding of the principles of child development" (Guthrie,1937–38, p. 177).

Elements of Progressivism were fused into the special education movement but were far more germane to the education of gifted students than to those below the norm. Despite the efforts expended and the publicity attending it, the acceptance of Progressive Education was hindered by widespread misconceptions about its underlying philosophies as well as its sociological and psychological implications. Indeed, speaking of the child-centered school and the Progressive movement, Reymert (1939–40) chided that "we are apt in this country to live on a fad" (p. 301). As Grave said in 1939, "older teachers were skeptical of the changes from formality to freedom" whereas "the young teachers were easily convinced of the value of progressive education but did not know enough about exceptional children to adapt their techniques wisely."

THE DEPRESSION YEARS

The 1930s brought a period of unparalleled economic dislocation to North America. Unsurprisingly, after the verve and expansion of the 1920s, the next decade of economic ruin witnessed a sharp decline in the special education process. Optimism faded, and special education became one of the better kept secrets within education. Other than the growing numbers of students that made the institutional and special class levels bulge, little happened and the 1930s was a period of pessimism.

Special education may have been a sound economical approach, but educators, legislators, and other professionals turned adamantly away from the venture that had evoked such excitement a decade earlier. Philadelphia, which had featured special education prominently during the 1920s, virtually ceased to acknowledge its existence in the next decade. New Jersey and California, states that passed special education legislation between 1910 and 1929, did almost nothing throughout the 1930s. By 1935, New York City had only 500 teachers, psychologists, and social workers for 11,000 exceptional children (Howard, 1935).

Classes now had the least trained teachers and children with different disabilities all lumped together with no real effort being made to address their needs. Special classes were "so regarded that they cast a stigma on anyone who is assigned to them" (Chicago, 1932, p. 100). Drill became the watchword, and curricula were weakened versions of the general curriculum supplemented with heavy doses of manual training. Practical instruction in trades and agriculture for the boys and in domestic skills for the girls took precedence over the academic program. About half the time was spent on academics; the remainder was on practical handwork, sewing, weaving, knitting, and cooking for the girls, woodwork for the boys (Percival, 1946–47). For example, students in Chicago had manual training shops, a print shop, and an electrical and metal shop as well as reed-weaving and a rug-making room (Stullken, 1935–36).

Not all parents accepted official diagnoses graciously. Some resisted special placements. One mother in Los Angeles cried, "You can't put my Tony in the dumb-bell school" (Wooden, 1937–38, p. 20). At the same time, Wallin spoke of many school administrators who did "not consider that the handicapped child possesses any rights; who tolerates him in school merely because of the mandate of the compulsory attendance statute; and who would exclude him from school altogether if the laws so permitted" (Wallin, 1936–37b, p. 26). Never one to mince words, Wallin wrote that many schools were "too smug and self-satisfied with their glorious traditions and assumed perfection to bestir themselves unless stimulated by the spotlight of unfavorable comparison" (1936–37b, p. 26).

By 1940, the census of the United States showed 5 million children with special needs who were not in school. Even for those attending, few were actually served by special education. Ninety percent of children with exceptional conditions in both the United States and Canada were in general classrooms and did not receive any educational adjustments (Wooden, 1934–35a, p. 20).

During this period of pessimism, the 1930 White House Conference on Child Health and Protection convened by President Herbert Hoover was a significant milestone that marked the first time that special education received national recognition. The first White House Conference on Children and Youth in 1909 began to take stock of children's needs; in 1930, however, an extensive paper on special education became public. The conference gave birth to the Children's Charter, saw the presentation of reports on special education, and made important recommendations for exceptional children. Speakers stressed that special education was not charity. Instead, "it is good economy and sound public policy to provide medical treatment, special education, and rehabilitation for the disabled rather than leave them unemployed and dependent their lifetimes long" (White House Conference Report, 1930, pp. 6–7). Still, even as they fretted that the great majority of children in need did not receive special services, they also believed that opposition to the further extension of special education was strong. So it was that a decade later participants at the 1940 White House Conference noted the critical failures in special programming for mentally retarded pupils and stressed the need for better community services (White House Conference on Children in Democracy, 1940).

THE WAR YEARS

America's entry into World War II saw a massive mobilization of manpower. People with disabilities were drawn into the war efforts. One writer noted that "the current manpower shortage in the midst of a crucial struggle for survival emphasizes, as never before in our national history, how indispensable to the nation's welfare are the skillful fingers and the nimble brains of hitherto unappreciated individuals" (Brown, 1943–44). Said another, "The reservoirs of labor strength latent in those that may be termed 'dumb' or 'stupid' are far greater than any of us have realized" (Miller, 1943, p. 239). By October, 1942, it was estimated that 3 million disabled men and women were engaged in the war industry throughout the country (Miller, 1943).

The performance during the war of people with mental retardation and other disabilities created a new level of confidence and expectancy and justified the notion that special children could learn more than just fundamental skills. In the schools, the war aligned school programs with national defense priorities. Curricula abandoned at least some of the repetitious drill that had characterized earlier classes as well as the simplified curriculum that stressed manual training, sewing, drawing, nature study, and domestic arts. Now curricula were more acutely directed toward the present and future needs of students. To many practitioners, the ultimate goal of special classes was "to provide as many as possible with the means of living as normally as possible and of procuring independent livelihood" (Percival, 1946–47, p. 237).

POSTWAR PERIOD

After World War II, the problems of urban schools were exacerbated by factors such as increasing enrollments, problems of family organization, racial integration, decreasing opportunities for youth to participate in the labor market, and a decline in teaching authority. Immigration, which showed a large drop after 1924, began to accelerate sharply. The number of children with disabilities increased in the postwar baby boom. The polio epidemic of the 1950s and the rubella epidemic of the 1960s created many more disabled individuals.

Opportunities for students with disabilities gained momentum from a variety of activities. For example, professional interest in health and well-being grew; medical discoveries fashioned further change. Efforts to improve the status of injured veterans brought a flurry of major medical and technical breakthroughs. There were marked improvements in the area of new medications and procedures; in the measurement of aptitudes; in improved hearing aids; and in improved methods and aids in teaching, particularly in the auditory and visual fields (Lee, 1944). Dilantin, for the control of epilepsy, was discovered in the 1940s. Hoover developed the white cane. Hearing aids became smaller and more sophisticated. Antibiotics effectively ended the reign of childhood diseases such as whooping cough and diphtheria. Further advances in medical technology kept more children alive and limited the degrees of impairment,

Special classes were again promoted enthusiastically, at least partly because of parent groups who combined to demand special facilities for their disabled children. In tune with parent agitation, postwar reconstruction witnessed the beginnings of strong legislative activity, and the pace of recognizing the rights of students with disabilities accelerated rapidly. State legislation to reimburse school boards for the excess costs of educating some exceptional groups was a necessary stimulus for the establishment of special classes (Turner, 1944). By 1930, 16 states had passed legislation authorizing special education. By 1946, there were well more than a hundred laws dealing with the education of exceptional children. Thirty-three states had legislation for the physically handicapped; 16 passed legislation for the mentally retarded. Twenty-five states had directors of special education programs for mentally retarded children (Martens, 1946a, 1946b).

By 1951, a total of 39 states provided some form of mandatory or permissive legislation that provided subsidies to local districts for the education of children with exceptionalities. The most pronounced increases in the newly developed special education services seemed to be in the field of mental retardation (Hill, 1951). By the 1950s, there was support for better programming by groups such as the newly formed National Association for Retarded Citizens. The long-held resistance of school systems to accepting students categorized as trainable or moderately mentally retarded began to dissipate. In 1951, California, Minnesota, and Wisconsin passed legislation in favor of trainable children. By 1955, 29 states made provisions for these students (Gilmore, 1956).

On the Canadian scene, seven provinces incorporated permissive legislation into their school laws by 1953, authorizing local school systems to establish special classes (Dunn & McNeill, 1953–54). Only Ontario, however, had a branch of special education as part of the department of education.

By 1947, 500,000 American children in 7,000 city school systems were receiving special education services from 1,600 teachers and supervisors. In the period from 1948 until 1953, special education enrollment jumped 47%, the number of districts providing services increased by 83%, and the number of teacher grew by 48% (Hill, 1956). Despite rapid growth, a 1952 U.S. Office of Education release estimated that there existed 5 million school-age exceptional children, with not more than 15% receiving special help (Porter, 1953).

In 1939, there were a reported 450 residential schools for exceptional students (all institutionalized children, not including delinquents or other noneducational options) in the United States. By 1950, they had a much larger place in the total educational structures of the states, and many became integral units within the state education departments. Residential schools were responsible for secondary and elementary education. In local school systems, education for exceptional children was limited to the elementary grades (Martens, 1946b). State legislation began to recognize the special needs of very young children and of those in their adolescent years. In the 10-year period between 1938 and 1948, the number of exceptional pupils who were enrolled for some form of special education in high schools almost doubled (Martens, 1951).

Before the mid-1950s, only occasional concerns were raised about special education, its rationale, its themes, its clientele, and its programs. Generally, questions about what special education did were invariably dominated by the belief that the problems were quantitative, that is, there was simply not enough of it. The 1950s witnessed a far deeper and more probing questioning of special education. Concerns centered on the kind of setup that existed, on children still failing in special classes, and on whether academic skills should serve as the yardstick of the total education and social growth of children. Most critically, the debate on the location of services, which began in earnest in the late 1930s, accelerated.

Without a doubt, special classes had gained almost universal acceptance by the early 1950s. The assumption that such classrooms were necessary was widely held and supported by publications such as the *Forty Ninth Yearbook of the National Society for the Study of Education* (Henry & Kirk, 1950). A panel at the twenty-second meeting of the International Council for Exceptional Children in 1945 debated the issues and concluded that some segregation might be necessary in the early years because the special needs of the retarded child could not be easily met from the beginning in general classrooms. The editor of *Exceptional Children* argued that placing exceptional children in a normal environment "may lead to disastrous educational retardation and emotional and social maladjustment, for the simple reason that physical presence with a normal group is no guarantee against seg-regation. In fact, it often results in segregation in its worst form, namely that of *impossible* intellectual competition and social isolation" (Wooden, 1946, p. 239; original italics). However, the resulting social isolation and discrimination were seen as serious problems in the later school years, and it was generally felt that educably retarded students should be returned to the normal school environment as soon as possible.

Some argument occurred, but it was generally contained and constrained as the segregated classroom remained the unchallenged setting. But, observed Hill (1956), "a new cliché has appeared on the special education horizon. It is now smart to talk about an 'integrated program of special education'" (p. 317). For example, by 1945, Wallin was reporting "a new approach" in small schools that was a com-bination of time with the remedial teacher, time in the opportunity classroom, but most of the day in the general class (Wallin, 1945).

Shattuck (1946) observed that "the extremists on the question of segregation versus non-segregation have, it seems to me, distorted the issues involved, much to the confusion of both educators and the public" (p. 238). A second writer argued that "the question really is not one of physical segregation or non-segregation. It is a question of creating an environment in which an exceptional child can make satisfactory all-round growth and development" (Wooden, 1946, p. 239). Shattuck (1946) proposed "the utilization of whatever environment will provide the most desirable growth" that is "based on a thorough understanding of the particular child involved rather than an administrative expediency of segregation or a blind ideal of non-segregation" (p. 238).

Segregation was not the real problem, however. The quantity of services avail-able was. The impulse, therefore, was not toward making waves; rather, it cen-tered on tinkering with an existing program. Overall, the reform movement, if it could be termed such, developed a patchwork of demands, most of which did not consider radical change to the system. Reconstruction was achieved by way of renovating, refurbishing, and expanding facilities.

Summary and Themes

The special classes that burgeoned at the opening of the 20th century were formulated piecemeal. They were not founded on a cohesive theory; rather, they blended a multiplicity of assumptions and pragmatic considerations. Of the varied reasons that underlay the establishment of special classes, compulsory attendance laws were the most telling. Schools could no longer ignore exceptional students and were challenged to find solutions to their problems within the system. Teachers were generally unwilling to handle these children in general classes; officials, seeking order, discipline, and standards in the schools, were adverse to placing them in general classrooms. Segregated classes were the obvious solution to satisfy the requirements of the law and the wishes of the school. A second major prompt sprang from the rapidly increasing numbers of immigrant children entering neighborhood schools.

The testing and measurement movement was critical. Testing became basic to the sorting and selection function; it helped meet the need for continuous measurement and accountability and stressed the importance of a larger and more orderly educational system and the use of knowledgeable experts from various fields. Simultaneously and importantly, there occurred development of the fields of psychiatry, psychology, social work, and the mental hygiene movement; legislation affecting women, families, and children; new concepts about child normalcy; the lessened participation of youth in the labor market; and slowly changing conceptions of exceptional people that generated altered ways of viewing the disabled population.

Although special classes represented a significant compromise of common school ideology at the elementary level, they were not a sharp break in the logical progression of special education development. Rather, this step was almost inevitable as the concept of specialized programming expanded to embrace a more diverse range of children who exhibited problems that, while usually less devastating than those of the institutionalized clientele, still created insurmountable barriers to learning and behavior in general classrooms.

The decade beginning in 1910 witnessed a huge spurt in special classes. Special education expanded to embrace more children, to redesignate others, to adopt new philosophies, and to implement more sophisticated diagnostic and instructional approaches. As the types and numbers of children assumed by special education increased dramatically, so did the variety of interventions and the locations of services, which remained dual, different, and separate from the regular stream with alternate guidelines for program planning and service provisions.

Increased financial support for special classes and special schools immediately after World War I ushered in a period of rapid growth in services. The social landscapes of people with disabilities remained pathologized and marginalized, surrounded by oppressive terminology, but in the schools, these students advanced from being seen as burdensome and unproductice purveyors of moral failure to being considered a pool of potentially productive citizens who could contribute to the country through the astute application of the principles of special education.

Pessimism characterized the 1930s. The reasons for the period of decline are readily discernible: the retrenchments of the Great Depression and the distractions of World War II occupied everyone. The late 1940s saw a huge expansion of special education and a route cleared for the rewriting of the special script that would begin in earnest in the early 1960s.

Notes

1. Essentially, deprivational studies looked at the effects of nurture on children. For example, Skeels and Dye (1939) took children identified as mentally retarded from an orphanage and placed the youngsters in a home for adult feeble-minded women. Over various periods of retesting, the children showed normal IQs, said to result from the care and attention they received. All the children were adopted, and all but one reported to do well.

2. Edgar Doll (1935, 1936) devised the Vineland Scale of Adaptive Behavior. The scale was initially administered to 620 residents at the New Jersey Training School for Feeble-Minded Boys and Girls at Vineland. On the basis of the results, the scale was modified, a method of administration was verified, and new norms were established. The revised scale was published in March 1936.

3. Brigham also conceived the Scholastic Aptitude Test (SAT) and held that it measured innate ability. In 1994, the College Board organization changed the name to the Scholastic Achievement Test. In 1997, the board decided on SAT, which stands for nothing.

Chapter 5

Turning Points

$\mathbf{I}$t is one of the quirks in the chronological development of special education that certain decades are definable as turning points—benchmarks when an unprecedented array of changes and reforms occur. The 1960s stand out as a beacon of change, an optimistic period of American history, a time when both the desire and the finances existed to promote social and educational changes. Because special education institutions, policies, and practice were always cast in terms of more general issues and processes in society, the multiplicity of complex, interrelated developments that characterized the decade led to a massive remodeling of the field.

During the 1960s, the nation was preoccupied with a group of major issues that included, but were not restricted to, the Vietnam War, the struggle for civil rights, and school desegregation. Other issues affected sexual roles and relationships. Women's participation in the labor force, for example, rose sharply with an expanding economy. There was a new zeal on the part of politicians for humanistic programs such as the Peace Corps together with a new sense of individual rights and the need to assist those traditionally oppressed. Greater openness in public life exposed the frailties of much authority—the law, the church, medicine, and education—and prompted attacks on discriminatory laws, traditions, and customs.

Conflict and confrontation characterized much of the decade. Nevertheless, as changes occurred, whether through debate and negotiation or through acrimony and conflict, each spilled over to special education in some way. As an example, the successful launch of an earth-orbiting satellite by the Soviet Union on October 4, 1957, shocked the United States out of its complacency. To meet a national educational emergency, Congress passed the National Defense Education Act (Pub. L. 85-864) on September 2, 1958. With this legislative advance, the federal government began to move slowly into a supportive role in both finance and research in special education services. Similarly, the 1964 Civil Rights Act spurred a major focus on prohibiting discrimination in education, social services, and other federally sponsored activities on the basis of race and national origin. Educational institutions at all levels began to respond to the civil rights movement in various ways. Parents, consumers, and advocates used the period's increased sensitivity to human and civil rights to promote the normalization philosophy, the "handi-cappism" movement, and to mount a case against special education as it was prac-ticed at that time. In addition, women's increased participation in the labor force and mounting concerns about poverty led to ameliorative programs for young children that inevitably spawned early childhood special education.

Right into the 1960s, institutional settings and segregated classes remained the primary mechanisms for educating students with disabilities. In fact, special classes expanded even more during the late 1960s, in part because of the creation of the category of learning disabilities in 1963 and in part because of the gener-ous funding now provided for training personnel and implementing separate pro-grams. Paradoxically, as the number of classes continued to grow at the local level, the concept of special classes was attacked at the national level.

Questions in the 1960s were far more incisive and demanding than those of earlier periods. Both critics and friends asked What is special about special educa-tion? Are the teaching procedures really different? What are the effects of segre-gation and labeling? Is stigmatization increasing handicap? As issues were con-fronted, the traditional support and demand for institutional settings seriously eroded, and the educational integration of students with disabilities became the central theme of special education. The two movements—(a) normalization and deinstitutionalization in the human service delivery system and (b) mainstream-ing in the educational system—were different movements in different systems, but with a common mission and addressing the same fundamental problems. In both fields, reformers fashioned a critique of existing provisions and practices as well as provided a focus for action and popular expectations for reform.

Sociopolitical pressures rather than pedagogical interests shaped new routes. While the availability of funds for research and special training dramatically changed the focus of the field, it was easy to discern a gradual liberalizing of atti-tudes toward persons with disabilities. The movement toward integration and desegregation that developed in the halcyon days of the 1960s were part of a wider process of liberalization and an emphasis on equity characteristic of the decades following World War II. Questions related to the education of students with spe-cial needs began to be passionately debated through the lenses of morality, equity, and civil rights. In concert, the 1960s provided a dynamic context in which knowl-edge generation in the social sciences was seriously challenged. Vastly different constructions of disability and its social effect emerged.

NORMALIZATION

President Kennedy took office in 1961. The Kennedy era marked a willingness to initiate and support strong legislation for those who were disabled and brought a new awareness and sensitivity to the problems of disabled persons in society. It marked the beginning of a period of considerable federal interest and growth in the field of mental retardation, in special education, in vocational education, and in other programs designed to assist unemployed youth and adults with disabilities.

College and university programs in special education began to grow under the federal legislation and funds of the Kennedy and Johnson administrations, which both required and supported such programs.

In 1961, President Kennedy began a national attack on the causes and consequences of mental retardation. He called the National Panel on Mental Retardation, which sent missions to study programs for the mentally retarded in Russia, the Netherlands, and Scandinavia. Kennedy's 26-member panel included authorities from every field that affected those who were mentally retarded. Their extensive report to the president in 1962, *A Proposed Program for National Action to Combat Mental Retardation* recommended important changes in public support and practices affecting retarded citizens and provided the framework for a nationwide plan.[1]

The committee also issued a monograph (Kugel & Wolfensberger, 1969), which brought to public notice the Scandinavian concept of normalization—the belief that all individuals who are exceptional, no matter what the level and type of disability, should be provided with a living environment and education as close to normal as possible. Neils Erik Bank-Mikkelson (1969) introduced the concept that was later refined by Benge Nirje, secretary general of the Swedish Association for the Retarded and later coordinator of training in the Ontario government's Ministry of Health, as "making available to all mentally retarded people patterns of life and conditions of everyday living which are as close as possible to the regular circumstances of society" (Nirje, 1979, p. 173).

Nirje's (1976, 1979) generic definition emphasized the underlying purpose of all special services for the disabled—to enhance the functions and enjoyments that are normal to human living. It did not entail the meaningless mimicry of conventional activities by those who could not accomplish them. The major goal was for society to regard people with disabilities as individuals and to treat them fairly and humanely. Traditional boundaries created by disabilities were to be broached as people filled a variety of roles in general society and were offered the chances for a normal life routine; normal developmental experiences; independent choices; and the right to live, work, and play in normal surroundings.

An institution is defined as a publicly supported, professionally managed facility for 15 or more people with similar disabilities. Despite increased community services and special education programs, the number of people institutionalized in the 1940s and 1950s continued to grow. Davies (1959) reported that in 1904, there were 17.5 places per 100,000 population. By 1920, the ratio had grown to 22.5; by 1923, 39.3; and by 1956, 66.1. Inevitably, the institutions were overcrowded, with long waiting lists. By 1967, there were approximately 201,000 people living in instituions (Minnesota Governor's Council on Disabilities, 2009).

Deinstitutionalization was the obvious outgrowth of the philosophy of normalization. In the physical sense, it meant moving people from large institutions to community-based living arrangements. In the broader social context, it addressed a return to the community, maintenance in the community, the respect of other citizens, and acceptance by peers and others in the culture.

Institutional settings became the target of serious criticisms in the 1960s. When governments began to explore various options for the care and education of people with significant disabilities, three distinct positions crystallized. Some still claimed that institutions were a desirable setting and that lifelong institutional placement was a viable option. Others preferred community-based settings but felt that institutionalization was suitable for some people with mental retardation (e.g., Nirje, 1976). Other authorities (e.g., Blatt, Ozolins, & McNally, 1979; Wolfensberger, 1975) argued that institution were inherently destructive and fostered deviance. They contended that the institutions were symbolized by barriers to social intercourse and looked askance at the specter of lifelong marginality with all the accompanying burdens for society. Pragmatically, many institutions were characterized by gross overcrowding, lack of privacy, regimentation that demanded and enforced conformity, and inadequate facilities and personnel. Societal movements similarly circumscribed institutionalization for other groups. In 1977, a National Research Council committee recommended that the large custodial institutions that housed emotionally disturbed, physically handicapped, and delinquent children be abolished (see Gaylin, 1977).

Policy analysts recommended alternatives to the cloistered, costly, and segregated residential environments. By the early 1970s, class-action litigation began to demand either institutional reform or the actual closing of institutions. There ensued a continuing movement of residents of institutions to community alternatives such as regional centers, group homes, and foster care. The institutionalized population of people with mental retardation dropped from 174,000 in 1972–73 to 139,000 in 1978–79 (Scheerenberger, 1981).[2]

INTEGRATION TO MAINSTREAMING

The late 1950s and 1960s witnessed cracks in the veneer of segregated education for exceptional students. From many constituencies, the appropriateness of special education as a system, as well as the classification and placement of some students within the system for the majority of their educational experiences, came under heavy attack. Dozens of disintegrating factors were at work. Legislation, litigation, changing societal views and attitudes (particularly in relation to the thorny issue of mental retardation) parent advocacy, and a plethora of research studies on the efficacy of segregated classrooms all contributed.

The Construct of Mild Mental Retardation

As a construct, mild mental retardation (classified as educable mentally retarded, or EMR), was unique among the categories eligible for special services. The genesis of the concept can be traced back to the British construct of moral insanity from the 1850s, the American conception of moral imbecility that emerged in the 1880s, and to Henry Goddard's creation of the moron in 1910. All were medical orientations larded with moral homily (see Chapters 4 and 7).

Goddard's work, which repackaged earlier assumptions about morality and intelligence as well as the putative relationship between the two remained influential in the early decades of the 20th century. One result was the thrust toward institutionalization and sterilization that was so prominent in the first three decades of the century. Another was the advocacy for classes that were special, segregated, and separate from the mainstream.

In the field of special education, policy has generally outpaced research. Plans typically were more often based on ideology or professional consensus rather than empirical verification. As research methodologies and research topics developed in the field, they usually followed rather than created a trend. Research activity often derived from specified new paradigms and were linked to changing beliefs or ideals, new pedagogical initiatives, educational settings, or the clients served. Among other things, this pattern translated into ever-changing prominence being given to various topics over the decades.

When Henry Goddard presented his description of the feebleminded, socially menacing Kallikak family, social research was in its infancy. The methods used for the family pedigree studies had inherent limitations, and the findings had doubtful validity; the results were inconclusive. It was incontrovertible that the children of feebleminded parents often appeared feebleminded or that the children of criminals often drifted into crime. The second step of the equation—that criminals, paupers, drunkards, and other social undesirables arose from the genetic stock of the mentally deficient—made headline news but essentially was unproven and taken on faith. Within their own contemporary frame, the poor or even complete lack of scientific methodology in the family pedigree studies was overlooked, as was the need to capture the nature of class and to conceptualize and study feeblemindedness in terms of social competence as well as environmental and cultural parameters.

By the 1920s, the strong emphasis on nature as the paramount factor in development faded conspicuously. Among legitimate researchers in professional fields such as genetics, psychology, anthropology, and education, the eugenics preoccupation was gradually displaced. A reliance on research findings to settle issues relating to intelligence grew; many studies attempted to clarify the basic concepts, methods, and presuppositions of intelligence and heredity. A tacit assumption of fixed ability and the notion of intelligence as an entity rather than a concept remained, but as methods for studying and understanding human behavior became more sophisticated, it grew clear that both heredity and environment shaped behavior. Changing concepts of disability, intelligence, and degeneracy led inevitably to the realization that mental deficiency was not a clear-cut entity with a single cause, nor was it a condition that could not be determined by anyone with a simple, all inclusive measuring stick.

In the 1930s and 1940s, researchers sought to define various groups in terms of their essential characteristics, the social significance of disability, and the needs of the members. Case studies used to illustrate various disorders and their possible treatments were widely popular (e.g., Rhodes, 1946) as were deprivational studies (e.g., Skeels & Dye, 1939). As this perspective of research in the social sciences developed, people with mental retardation were studied as a separate category of human beings who required specific and different descriptions and different theories to explain what was seen as different behavior.

In general, severe retardation was attributed to central nervous system damage (Goldstein, 1984). People with significant cognitive disabilities were thought unable to develop normally "because of some defect in the brain" (League for Preventative Work, 1916–17). For those considered to be mildly retarded, considerations of etiology and developmental consequences were far murkier; for many decades, mild mental retardation was seen as a behavioral disorder (Goldstein, 1984) and the educational problems of such individuals were regarded as primarily related to low achievement. It follows that much of the research work was essentially atheoretical and focused merely on demonstrating that retarded people did not learn as efficiently as did nonretarded people. Limited utility could be attached to the findings because much of the understanding of the cognitive and learning characteristics of the mentally retarded population was based on investigations where the sample had mean IQs close to, or exceeding, the current upper limit for defining mental retardation (Grossman, 1983).

Goddard's classification system persisted into the 1950s. In 1941, however, Edgar Doll provided what became the standard definition of mental retardation. Doll's criteria, considered essential to an adequate definition and concept, focused on "poverty in social competence due to mental abnormality which was developmentally arrested; and which obtained at maturity or was of constitutional origin, and was essentially incurable" (Doll, 1941a, p. 215). So widely accepted were Doll's premises that a contemporary commentator noted that "the matter of definition has been pretty well settled by universal agreement" (Ontario School Inspectors' Association, 1958, p. ix). Consistency, however, was never a characteristic of the field, and the 1960s represented a turning point for the field in terms of research, funding, and teacher training as well as more enlightened views of intellectual disability.

Pragmatically, one of the most significant events was the 1959 *Manual of Terminology and Classification of Mental Retardation* (American Association of Mental Deficiency, 1959). The American Association of Mental Deficiency departed from Doll's traditional definition by no longer considering the condition as an incurable trait. Mild intellectual disability, especially, no longer fulfilled the expectation of biologically based, permanent, and comprehensive incompetence. Once the criteria of permanence was abandoned, an optimistic shift occurred.

The paradigm shift that took root in the field of mental retardation quickly spilled over to affect all special populations. Broadly construed, a paradigm is a set of explicit or implicit presuppositions or basic beliefs that provide coherence to a picture of the world and how it works. As a particular lens—a way of seeing things— paradigms provide the route to understanding particular phenomena and the relationship between elements that uniquely define particular segments. Thomas Kuhn (1970) argued that scientific paradigms survive despite mounting internal contradictions until a superior replacement is available. Then a new paradigm sweeps aside the old and the process of seeing the world through the new frame begins.

The paradigm shift provided a new lens for seeing mental retardation and the services provided. Notions about segregation that had appeared so logical, connected, and obvious a decade earlier were quite rapidly replaced with new conceptions and constructions of disability and its meaning. Although the process of negotiating new understandings was contentious, even precarious, there occurred a movement among professionals toward new delivery models that was less representative of changes in the effectiveness of educational methods and in the educational system than it was of new educational and social philosophies.

Until the 1960s, disability was a poorly theorized concept in sociology, law, and politics. New ideas of social justice, individual rights, as well as oppression and marginalization wrought indelible changes. For many, the problems of the special education system extended far beyond empirical research findings—a view that led them to discard the traditional medical orientations that bounded and described disability and moved instead to embrace sociocultural theories. Parties questioned the notion that disability was an inherent personal trait and looked to society to locate and transform the sources of inequality.

Disability as a social construct was stylized from the 1950s onward (e.g., Barker & Wright, 1952; Goffman, 1961; Hanks & Hanks, 1948). In essence, the social model offered a sociopolitical analysis that described disability as an ideological construction rather than a reflection of personal defects as identified in the medical model. Social models challenged the oppressive binary assumptions of normal versus pathological, autonomous versus dependent, competent versus retarded, and integrated versus segregated. Having made clear that direct responsibility for educational or social failure could not be assigned to an individual factor, the questions for inquiry therefore involved considering how multiple factors such as social, economic, and political structures, along with educational systems influenced failure.

As cultural perspectives opposed the more inviolable and narrow subtexts of medical interpretations, a new way of conceptualizing disability was created. By the close of the 1960s, a clearly formulated philosophy informed by a sociological understanding of mental retardation and other disabilities had emerged. Of the many variables that affected change in the decade, the social construction proved one of the most influential in policymaking and legislation, particularly in developing legislation based on arguments about rights. It both fed on and fed into nascent changes in research methodologies and shepherded the birth of the disability rights movement and the field of disability studies.[3]

Constructed and Contested Truths: The Efficacy Studies

Although the EMR category was the core concern of special education, it increasingly garnered more dissatisfaction than any other exceptionality. This trend occurred in part because of the issue of placement in segregated settings and the increasing numbers of such placements and in part because of the concern expressed for the hypothesized, though rarely demonstrated, effects of the EMR label.

The 1950s and 1960s spawned an emphasis on so-called efficacy studies that were devoted chiefly to students within the category of mildly mentally retarded and that focused on determining where such students were best served—in general education or in special programs. The efficacy studies did not trigger the far-reaching controversy about students' school addresses. Rather, they stimulated interest, sensitized many to the vicissitudes of the situation, and melded with calls for reform to become one more focus and justification of discontent. Importantly, although the central and chief concern of the efficacy studies was classes for students determined to be mildly mentally retarded, the results spilled over to influence other special class programs, albeit somewhat glacially.

Any and all of the studies on the merits of special versus regular and integrated versus segregated programs for EMR students were vulnerable to criticism with respect to methodology (for discussions, see e.g., Gardner, 1966; Keogh & Levitt, 1976; Kirk, 1964; Robinson & Robinson, 1976; Spicker & Bartel, 1968). Major issues related to the ethics of data collection and uncertainty about the sample as well as the authenticity, credibility, and trustworthiness of the findings. Flaws existed in the inadequately described and defined samples, students were not in many instances assigned randomly to different treatments, and the researchers used tests of questionable technical adequacy. Nor were the results used for their original intent. The plethora of efficacy studies were not formulated to challenge the effectiveness of special education for EMR pupils, although they were used for that purpose.

Although no solid results could be claimed, the studies did present two major conclusions. First, the academic benefits of special classes were sparse. There were few significant differences between disabled children in special classes and those in general classrooms; the evidence could not confirm whether special services enhanced the academic competencies of children beyond what might have been expected in the general classroom (Blatt, 1960). Second, placement alone was not sufficient. Many retarded pupils in general classes were uniformly labeled. They were isolated or rejected in general classroom settings by their normal peers, and were not more accepted by their peers than segregated children (Gottleib & Budoff, 1973; Johnson, 1950; Johnson & Kirk, 1958; Jones; 1977). Special children in special classrooms appeared to have better social maturity and emotional adjustment—possibly because the teacher in special classrooms showed greater acceptance of the special child (Blatt, 1960). The paradoxical nature of the findings and the sense of frustration with the ability of the data to settle the location controversy was epitomized by Johnson (1962). "The regular classroom does not provide a social climate conducive to healthy behavioral development," he wrote, "but the basic question concerning the best placement remains unanswered" (p. 3).

Research findings in the literature must be interpreted within their time frame and the period within which the sample was secured and must give sufficient consideration to the social and political context in which the ideas developed. Interpretations of the results of the efficacy studies, therefore, suggest much about the changing character of social concern for children with exceptionalities. They foreground the changing nature of pedagogical thought and practice as well as the changing influence and scope of social influences.

The intensification of the trend away from special classes answered not the educational decision-making process but, rather, noneducational influences. Disability was always situated and mediated within the larger sociocultural framework.

During the 1960s, the sociopsychological variables that determined attitudes to exceptionality changed as there was a gradual (though not uniform) progress in public sentiment. "More and more," observed one commentator, the exceptional child "is being considered a positive national asset, with potential that must be mobilized, rather than a liability that must be tolerated for sentimental reasons" (Krugman, 1962, p. 245).

Education has a long history of adopting new ideologies, curricula, and teaching methods with little or no empirical evidence of effectiveness. In special education, public policy changes clearly have always been driven by beliefs with respect to what is considered best for people with disabilities, not by scientific data (Bryan, 1999). Emphasis on a research base for program decisions was not a primary feature of the 1960s and 1970s. Although the efficacy studies showed generally superior achievement for students in regular classroom environments but better social adjustment for those in sheltered special classrooms, the complex array of tangible and elusive properties of the research allowed the center to shift. Discussions of the results of studies of the comparative effect of special as opposed to regular class placement began to show a greater bent to look at evidence in favor of the latter. The overt and unconscious assumptions of professionals changed, and tentative, fallible theories began to mutate into fact.

Some professionals questioned the merits of sweeping condemnations of special classes and expressed alarm at the trend away from special settings, particularly for those designated as EMR. Holders of the status quo continued to cite the effectiveness of special settings and concluded that administrative practices and curriculum deficiencies, rather than the classes, represented the major drawbacks (e.g., Kolstoe, 1972). They contended that all attacks on special classes were really against a straw man and that the ideal class had to be set up and researched before the question could be answered. Further, a number of post-school studies (e.g., Porter & Milazzo, 1958) were said to confirm the effectiveness of special education. One study related to mild mental retardation (Dinger, 1961) found that 83.2% of former students were employed, housewives, or in school; of those working, 42% were earning more than their former teachers.

However, the set of values that underlay segregated classes in general and particularly those for EMR pupils was on the wane and champions of services for the disabled assiduously promoted alternate placements. Agents of change challenged the persistence of traditional attitudes and saw benefits deriving from general classroom placements. Segregated classes, they argued, were often more benefit to the people who did not attend them than to the people who did. Lloyd Dunn is credited with sounding the loudest of the many death knells for special classes (Polloway, 1984). Although Dunn had "loyally supported and promoted special classes for the educable mentally retarded for most of the last 20 years," he felt that "much of our past and present practices are morally and educationally wrong" (1968, p. 5). To Dunn, "a large proportion of this so-called special education in its present form is obsolete and unjustifiable from the point of view of the pupils so placed" (p. 6). He urged educators to stop "a continuing and expanding special education program that we know now to be undesirable for many of the children we are dedicated to serve" (p. 5).

Dunn shored up his arguments against special education classrooms by citing the effects of classification and labeling on the attitudes and expectations of teachers as well as the effect of labeling and special class placement on children's self concept and adjustment to their peers. He further observed that 60% to 80% of children taught by teachers of the retarded were "children from low status backgrounds—including Afro-Americans, American Indians, Mexicans, and Puerto Rican Americans; those from nonstandard English speaking, broken, disorganized, and inadequate homes; and children from other non-middle class environments" (Dunn, 1968, p. 6).

Dunn did not call for the abolition of special classes. Even 5 years later, he stated that the trend of the time was to neither "uncritically sponsor special classes nor to abandon them completely." He felt that "a consensus appears to be emerging that special class placement makes sense for selected pupils at certain stages in their school career" (Dunn, 1973, p. 162).

Although Dunn was cautious and focused on socioculturally deprived students labeled as EMR, other observers clearly felt license to broaden his refutation of educational practices and extend his premises far beyond his stated intent. As the 1970s got underway, the justification of special education came under heavier attack, with most of the verbal criticism of special classes coming out of higher education (Vergason, 1972). After Dunn, Mercer's 1973 classic, *Labeling the Mentally Retarded*, emerged as one of the most important empirical studies on the misdiagnosis of ethnic pupils in special education.

Other critics claimed that special classes were too often used as dumping grounds for students viewed as the detritus of the social landscape. Echoing Dunn and Mercer, they castigated special education for the disproportionate number of ethnic and minority children found in special classes. Schools institutionalized different treatment for students on the basis of culture, race, and class through placement, testing, and instructional practices. For many students, low achievement, attrition, and school failure were the rule, not the exception.

Special education was often exclusionary rather than remedial and did not appear to be returning a significant number of children with EMR or other mild disabilities to the general classrooms (Gallagher, 1972). Special classes provided low-quality education and were often allotted inferior facilities and untrained teachers. Many of the conditions that were assumed to exist in such programs in fact did not exist, including reduced ratio, individualization, and programs matched to the students' needs. Ethically, critics pointed to the inherent discrimination they saw in providing separate schooling for children based on presumed mental, physical, or behavioral incapacities. They deplored labeling children and separating them from their normally developing peers. Special classes cast a stigma on children with disabilities; they were barely tolerated by regular classroom teachers and administrators.

The Issue of Labels

Over the decades, a plethora of labels emerged to define and classify children with exceptionalities. The framework in which labeling occurred was not isolated and self-contained: the messages made sense in their own time and space. Often, fresh labels came into existence as a result of paradigm shifts and were seen as offering more differential, benign, and enlightened views. Just as often, however, the constructs and metaphors used to evoke understanding were misleading or incomplete: they inhabited the territory of loose terminology and, lacking precision, created boundary conditions.

Children's characteristics were expressed in a framework of words and ideas freely borrowed from medicine. When educators operationalized the medical model, they assumed that disorders had distinct patterns of symptoms and signs that resulted from different disease entities and causes and that responded to different treatments. Children were classified within this medical knowledge, labeled with a particular disability designation, viewed as deviant, and propelled toward certain institutions, special classes, and pedagogical practices.

Increasingly, the labeling of deviance presented fundamental problems for the helping professions. The most fervid objections equated labeling with stigmatization. Advocates juxtaposed the capricious labeling and stigmatization of children with images of rights without labels (see Kauffman, 1993b).

The long-standing distrust of labels and the effectiveness of the discrete compartmentalization that permeated special education became acute in tune with the movement toward greater integration of children with exceptionalities. Nicholas Hobbs of Vanderbilt University, for example, saw the classification system for exceptional children as a major barrier that impeded the efficient and effective delivery of services (Hobbs, 1975a, 1975b). As part of the Project on the Classification of Exceptional Children, a task force headed by Hobbs studied and analyzed the benefits and detriments of labeling. The researchers, for example, looked at labeling bias—the expectations that others may develop for a person with a certain label—but could not determine the effect. The conclusions were ambiguous and inconclusive: although there was always the potential for labeled individuals to suffer deleterious effects, in some cases, the practice of labeling could prove advantageous.

LEGISLATION

The United States has a long history of placing great faith in law and legislation as the palliative to discrimination and prejudice. It relies on legislative and judicial remedies for social issues, including special education, which is prescribed and supported by legal leverage. Laws provide the general framework. Amendments add, delete, or change the emphasis of legislation. Once laws are passed, at least three sets of regulations typically follow, which describe the processes necessary to comply with the laws. The first regulations determine local education agencies' provision of programs and services for exceptional students. The second set is state laws and the regulations. The third set comprises the various local educational agency policies and regulations.[4]

State Legislation

In the United States, school law has had a state and local district emphasis from the early days. The original federal constitution did not assume responsibility for this governmental function and hence delegated all school matters to the states. Subsequent amendments to the U.S. constitution also avoided any direct federal assumption of school authority or responsibility. The privilege and obligation was left to the states and whatever school entities they chose to provide free public education (Melcher, 1976).

Constitutions in each of the states provide the general mechanisms under which free public education can or must be provided. Each of the 50 states has its own system for financing schools; most use some combination of local property taxes and general state support. These state constitutions vary markedly in the manner in which they carry out their prerogatives (Melcher, 1976). The delivery of special education services is governed primarily by state laws; each state has additional laws that clarify special education practices and procedures.

Throughout the 20th century, enabling legislation for special education became increasingly specific and mandatory, although the focus was largely on the three traditional groups: deaf children, blind children, and mentally retarded children. No group was as favored by special legislation as the legally blind. Their benefits encompassed areas as diverse as tax exemptions or deductions, the privilege of being the operators of vending machines in federal buildings, reduced postage rates for reading and writing materials, special appropriations for books and for social security, rehabilitation centers, and well-staffed and well-financed welfare agencies, both governmental and voluntary (Kim, 1970).

Legislation was either mandatory or permissive. Mandatory legislation dealt primarily with setting minimum standards. Permissive legislation centered on provisions for facilities operating beyond the minimum standards undertaken under local initiatives. For children who were exceptional, the bulk of legislation was permissive.

State statuatory legislation began with New Jersey in 1911; Minnesota in 1915; and Wisconsin, New York, and Illinois in 1917. By 1930, 16 states had passed mandatory or permissive legislation in special education. The Depression slowed the process. Legislative activity accelerated again in the 1940s. By then, many states had now passed basic special education laws or had widened their existing laws. Residential school facilities for deaf children and for blind children were universally provided by all the states. By 1946, there were more than a hundred laws dealing with the education of exceptional children (Martens, 1946b).

By 1950, 34 states had enacted laws that would provide direct subsidies for special education programs in most cases for all or most categories of children and youth with disabilities (Martens, 1951). Resolutions in the 1950s placed the responsibility for education squarely on the state departments of education and local school districts and specified both the quality and extent of intervention (Mackie, 1951). During the 1960s and early 1970s, most states enacted legislation mandating that schools provide special education services to all school-age children and youth.

Federal Legislation

Before World War II, few federal laws existed. The first federal laws directed at people with disabilities can be traced to 1798 when Congress authorized a Marine Hospital Service to provide medical care for sick and disabled seamen. In 1912, that service became the Public Health Service (Kaplan, 1996).

Public concern for the ability of individuals with disabilities to pursue employment arose during World War I when thousands of American veterans who were physically disabled required assistance in returning to the work force. Legislation in favor of veterans as well as programs designed to serve the uenemployed in the 1920s and the 1930s, including the Civilian Conservation Corps, benefited some youth with disabilities. For example, in 1918, Congress enacted the first Vocational Rehabilitation Act to serve veterans. Further federal funding was allowed with Woodrow Wilson's signing of the Federal Civilian Rehabilitation Act on April 8, 1920, which provided training to veterans and all disabled citizens. The later Smith-Fess Act authorized the expenditure of $75,000 for a joint federal-state program for the physically disabled. The 1943 Amendments to the Vocational Rehabilitation Act expanded services, including rehabilitation counseling for people with mental disabilities (Rusch & Phelps, 1987).

By 1948, the U.S. Office of Education had only two professional staff members who devoted time to special education for all groups of exceptional children (Ingram, 1948). Federal legislation passed in the 1940s and 1950s was modest, although this period did educate legislators to the needs of children with disabilities and to the problems involved in making adequate provisions for them. For example, the 1939 Pepper-Boland bill, sponsored by all the leading special education organizations of the United States through the initiative of the National Society for Crippled Children and under its leadership, enabled each state to establish services for educating children with physical handicaps—those who were crippled, blind, partially seeing, deaf, hard of hearing, defective in speech, "cardiopathic," diagnosed with tuberculosis, or otherwise disabled.

The October 4, 1957, launching of Sputnik, the world's first artificial satellite, by the Soviet Union was construed as a major technological fear with strong military, national defense, and industrial significance. Its advent created an almost hysterical condition in the nation and had direct consequences for both general and special education. The year 1958, immediately following the Russian launch of Sputnik, signaled an unprecedented flurry of activity in Congress and marked the federal government's greater involvement in education. The National Defense Education Act (Pub. L. 85-926) provided funds to encourage school districts to provide better programs in mathematics and science as well as money for universities to train teachers, including those destined for special education.

The 1960s witnessed the federal government's giant step into educational matters. In 1965, the administration of President Lyndon B. Johnson, beseiged by urban riots, sought to direct federal funds to the poor in American cities. Congress brought the federal government squarely into education through the passage of a series of laws designed to benefit those who were economically and educationally disadvantaged. With the passage of the Elementary and Secondary School Education Act of 1965, Johnson succeeded not only in directing money to the poor but also in overcoming historical opposition to federal aid in education (Casanova & Chavez, 1992).

The barrage of federal legislation from the 1960s on affected every aspect of special education as well as the care, the training, and the vocational routes of people with special needs. A sampling of critical federal laws is shown in Appendix B.

Public Law 94-142 (Education for All Handicapped Children Act)

During the early years of the public school integration movement, legal provisions were made on an individual basis and as needs became apparent. The major characteristics of federal legislative proposals consisted of unilateral activity by each exceptional group for a desirable objective or an improvement in already existing programs. And, although much federal legislation for the handicapped was passed between 1959 and 1967 (Chaves, 1977), none of it dealt with mainstreaming or the compulsory attendance of disabled children in local school systems (Sigmon, 1982–83).

The political movement for federal legislation to aid students with special needs followed a path similar to the rest of the civil rights movement. Finding themselves unable to change educational institutions by pressuring local and state governments, organized groups interested in improving educational opportunities for students with special needs turned to the courts. From the mid-1960s on, a series of court cases attacked special education on various fronts. The series of court decisions that reaffirmed the states' responsibilities to provide education for all children with exceptionalities caused great dismay among many state executive and legislative leaders who wondered where the funds would be found. Inevitably, they increased pressure on Congress to pass legislation that would compel the federal government to assist in funding.

State pressure was one prompt toward comprehensive federal legislation. Another influence was a focus on what was wrong with education, or on the lack of education, for those with exceptional conditions. A complementary theme spoke to the estimate that "one-half the estimated 7,000,000 handicapped children in our nation are still not receiving special education services in our schools" (Gallagher, 1970, p. 712). Similarly, the influence of lobbying activities and pressure from parent associations, often in uneasy alliance with professional groups, should not be overlooked.

The Education for All Handicapped Children Act, more commonly referred to as Public Law 94-142, was signed into law by President Gerald Ford in November 1975. It stood as the most significant bill in a chain of federal enactments. The law emerged primarily from civil rights: it had a constitutional rather than an empirical foundation.

As a legislative remedy to some of the past failures of school systems to provide appropriate education, Public Law 94-142 had a massive effect on the provision of services to children who were exceptional. The law defined the requirements needed to reach and enrich the lives of individuals not adequately served by traditional educational means. It contained four major provisions: it guaranteed the availability of free special education to children who needed it; it assured that decisions about special education would be fair and appropriate in the least restrictive environment; it required clear management procedures for special education at all levels; and it provided federal funds to supplement the costs of state and local governments special education programs. Under the legislation, exceptional children were, for the first time, ceded the rights to a free and appropriate education in the least restrictive environment. It was, however, procedural rights that were granted, not those related to specific curricula or services.

The drafters of Public Law 94-142 imposed numerous conditions on state and local school systems. As of September 1, 1978, all educators became subject to the national policy put forth in the legislation. After that date, it was no longer permissible for school administrators or others to exclude handicapped children on the grounds that they could not learn, that their handicaps were too severe, or that there were no programs for the problems in question. Systems could not exclude students with physical or intellectual disabilities, nor could they doom students to inappropriate placements and inadequate curriculum. Participating states had to establish priorities that first concerned children who were not receiving an education and then those with the most severe disabilities who were inadequately served. Parents or guardians were given right of due process and confidentiality, and school boards were mandated to provide a continuum of educational services, an individual education plan for each student, and culture-fair testing. Personnel preparation needs were extraordinary. There were mandates to restructure university and college training programs, to give vocational and career education added emphasis, and to train personnel to work with children with low-incidence disabilities.

The advent of Public Law 94-142 and the concept and practice of the least restrictive environment demanded a redistribution of resources in favor of those labeled as different. The state formula grant program that arose from the legislation was the cornerstone of national policy in instructing children with disabilities. The landmark legislation set forth a federal-state partnership in which the federal government committed itself to allocating financial support and toward helping state governments fulfill their responsibilities for educational programming. When Congress passed Public Law 94-142, many legislators and lobbyists believed that the federal government would chip in the excess costs for the new mandate on states. But even as a federal law, the major expenditures for Public Law 94-142 came from state and local expenditures. Children with disabilities also received support through other federal programs, although Public Law 94-142 represented the major fiscal commitment.[5]

The legislation had many faces, both positive and problematic. It had the positive effect, for example, of immediately generating an expansion of the number of students receiving special education services. In 1940, 1.2% of children with special needs from kindergarten to Grade 12 were enrolled in special education (Carrier, 1986b). Rates were identical in 1948. Ten years later, the numbers had grown to 2.1%. By 1968, there were 4.4% of school-aged children in special education, approximately 38% of the nation's children with disabilities. In 1978, 8.2% of school-aged children were in special education (Carrier, 1986b). Public Law 94-142 made education possible for 500,000 previously unserved, seriously disabled children (Will, 1986).

However, Public Law 94-142 was never intended to guarantee every child with a disability a place in the general classroom (Abeson & Zettel, 1977). A new and critical term, *least restrictive environment*, surrounded by contention and debate, was added to the special education lexicon and was interpreted as *mainstreaming*. The principle was established through several landmark decisions by the courts that children had the right to an appropriate education.

Resource rooms staffed by specialized teachers became popular under the influence of serious questioning with respect to the effect of segregation on students, professional criticism of existing services, parental pressure, and the implementation of the least restrictive environment clause in Public Law 94-142.[6] Moreover, paraeducators (variously titled paraprofessionals, teacher aides, and learning assistants) began to flow into the schools. The use of these personnel began in the 1950s both to counter a severe teacher shortage and to assist in bilingual education. There was a dramatic increase in numbers in concert with President Johnson's War on Poverty initiatives and the development of early childhood programs. With the passage of Public Law 94-142, paraeducators began to serve the needs of children with significant disabilities in neighborhood schools (Winzer, 2005b).

The legislation confirmed a paradigm shift in special education. Yet the substitution of one paradigm for another was not as easy as erasing a chalkboard, especially when the "chalkboard" was a system already in motion. The expansion of educational responsibility for those with special needs was a complex process that involved many different legal, economic, political, social, and technical issues.

Despite the radical structural changes that accompanied the intervention of the federal government, the legislative mandates and public expectations in many ways exceeded not only the technical capacity of professionals to deliver but also the service delivery system to respond effectively. With the elaboration of legislation, an already burdened education system with inadequate resources was now forced into new channels. Systems and teachers were not necessarily prepared to implement mainstreaming and other aspects of the legislation. As Samuel Kirk (1984) chided, "Our mistake, as usual, was to launch a program without adequate preparation and without really training the classroom teacher" (p. 47).

The study of problems associated with the implementation of Public Law 94-142 was a major concern for special education policy analysts and researchers. Much of the inquiry and critique dealt with inconsistencies among local education agencies with respect to the process of determining the eligibility of students for special education services. Other studies examined the cascade or continuum of services that provided a model for supports for students with disabilities. Still others attempted to determine whether the actual treatment provided underwent transformations comparable to that of the legislation.

One of the issues confronting Congress during the debates over the legislation was that of increased federal control over local school systems. One way that Congress decided to resolve this issue was to require than an Individual Education Plan

(IEP) be written for each student with special needs. This approach avoided direct federal control by requiring that each child's IEP be developed at the local level. The federal role was primarily coercive. Of all the aspects of the legislation, therefore, no document was more significant to districts, agencies, administrators, parents, educational advocates, and students than the IEP. As the sine qua non of Public Law 94-142, the necessary cornerstone of the legislation, and the critical point from which to monitor and enforce the law, it is hardly surprising that Rinaldi (1976) observed that "just about everyone is scared of the provision" (p. 151).

Nevertheless, reviews of the implementation of the IEP questioned whether it actually improved education and whether it reflected actual practice. Analyses of team meetings were dismal and concluded that parent participation was more fiction than fact. Simply because children were in general classes and file cabinets were stuffed with IEPs did not mean that they were being taught more effectively.

Advocates of change failed to confront the proposition that they were calling for the general education system to assume rsponsibility for students it had historically failed. In perhaps a timeless tension, teachers' responses to the reform were varied. Some teachers pushed or sustained reform efforts; others actively resisted or subverted them. Promoters recognized that the beliefs of school personnel were a conservative force that could impede or obstruct change. Melcher (1971), for example, cautioned against assuming that general classroom teachers would embrace the new paradigms. Many doubted (and research on teacher attitudes confirmed) whether regular classroom teachers in general were enthused about the return of hard to teach children or mildly handicapped learners, were prepared to meet the learning needs of these children, or were willing to make the pilgrimage to do so.

Litigation

In 1954, the Supreme Court, in its decision on *Brown v. Board of Education*, held that separate facilities by race was unconstitutional. Chief Justice Earl Warren stated the opinion of the Supreme Court that education that was separate was not equal, the first official step toward the vision of education as a vehicle of equity. Although *Brown* demanded "all deliberate speed," it took more than 15 years before the standard was fully addressed. Unsurprisingly, the implications for disabled children of the Supreme Court decision in *Brown* were not seriously considered until more than 10 years later, during the mid-1960s. It was then that parents in substantial numbers began to take their cases to the courts.

During the 1970s, a growing feeling of urgency developed among parents and others who refused to let a good idea such as mainstreaming walk rather than run (Melcher, 1976). The decade saw a sharp increase in litigation calling states and school districts to task for violating statutes, constitutions, and the rights of children. In fact, after the passage of Public Law 94-142, special education became one of the most litigated areas in school law (Zirkel & Osborne, 1987). By the 1980s, there was a steady stream of suits involving the rights of disabled children; it represented 30% of all school litigation by 1988 (Zirkel, 1990).

A set of basic arguments were presented in early court cases. One set surrounded issues on appropriate education, the inadequacy of special education, the stigmatization inherent in special placements, the classification of students, and lack of parental involvement. For example, *Wolf v. the Legislature of Utah* (1969) concerned whether children labeled as trainable mentally retarded were receiving a suitable education.

Leader reported that in Pennsylvania in 1957, there were four residential schools for mentally retarded students that provided an "inadequate sort of institutional care, with occupancy rates running around 129 percent" and further, that "waiting to join these 9,000 children were thousands more. Children who registered in 1955 for admission to one particular institution faced a waiting period of 20 years before they could expect to get in at the prevailing rate of discharge" (Leader, 1957, p. 68).

In January, 1971, the Pennsylvania Association for Retarded Children (PARC) objected to conditions in the Pennhurst State School and Hospital and filed a class action suit against the Commonwealth of Pennsylvania for failing to provide free and appropriate public education for all mentally retarded citizens residing in the state. The plaintiffs in PARC were 13 retarded school-aged children and all the other school-aged children of their classification in Pennsylvania. The lawyers for PARC focused on the legal right to an education for children with special needs and overwhelmed the court with evidence on the educability of such children. They simultaneously argued on the Fifth Amendment (not been given due process before being denied life, liberty, and property) and the Fourteenth (not afforded equal protection under the law). The case was settled through a consent agreement, resulting in an overwhelming victory for PARC.

PARC was as important for the rights of disabled children as *Brown* was for African Americans. The ruling provided the leverage that opened school doors to children with severe and profound disabilities and provided an explicit groundwork for the adoption of the least restrictive environment provision in later legislation. In 1972, *Mills v. Board of Education of the District of Columbia* reinforced and extended the rights afforded in PARC. Together, the PARC and Mills lawsuits served as an impetus for subsequent litigation designed to confirm the educational rights of children with disabilities.

Wyatt v. Stickney (1971) was on the issue of whether handicapped children committed to state institutions must be provided a meaningful education in that setting or whether their incarceration could be condisidered unlawful detention. *Lau v. Nichols* (1974) concerned whether non-English speaking students were entitled to bilingual special education. After *Lau*, bilingual education grew within the context of compensatory education.[7]

In the initial wave of legislation after Public Law 94-142, the courts were unsympathetic when school districts claimed lack of funds as the rationale for denying appropriate programs. *Board of Education of Hendrick Hudson Central School District v. Rowley* (1982) was the first case on Public Law 94-142 to reach the U.S. Supreme Court. The parents of a hearing impaired child filed suit, requesting an interpreter. The court overturned all previous rulings and stated that Public Law 94-142 required schools to provide an appropriate education for students with disabilities, not an educational program to maximize education for the student. The U.S. Supreme Court stated that Public Law 94-142 was intended more to open the door of public education to handicapped children by means of specialized educational services than to guarantee any particular substantive level of education once inside. An appropriate program was one reasonably calculated to enable the child to receive educational benefits. However, the 1992 court decision in *Oberti v. Board of Education of the Borough of Clementon School District* involved an 8 year old classified as educable mentally retarded. The Court decided that Rafael Oberti could manage in a general classroom with special aides and a special curriculum and wrote that "inclusion is a right, not a privilege for a select few."

Another set of litigative activity concerned due process requirements. *Lessard v. Schmidt* (1972) declared that anyone deemed in need of residential treatment had the right to a trial at which time the person's interests would be represented, witnesses could be called, and the need for institutionalization could be challenged.

In early 20th-century special education, IQ as a construct achieved an almost sacred inviolablility. Severe and substantive critiques from the 1930s onward dimmed the gloss, although the tests remained a backbone of special education assessment, eligibility, and planning. In the mid-1960s, President Johnson's War on Poverty, which directed funds to the underprivileged, saw the nature-nurture question flare again. Arthur Jensen reopened a series of social and political arguments on the inheritance of intelligence and fueled massive controversy by suggesting that differences in intellectual ability could be traced to racial inheritance (Jensen, 1968, 1969). The furor over the articles spawned dozens more articles in the popular and academic press in the next 5 years (Haney, 1981).

Contemporaneously, a third set of legislative activity focused on inappropriate tests and incompetent test administration. The passing of the IQ dominance was fought in the courts more than in the educational arena. Because selected populations were disproportionately removed from the general classroom, many school systems were challenged legally from the 1960s on, chiefly on the basis of the presence of lower-class and non-White pupils in special programs.

IQ tests assumed a reasonably common experience base for most White Anglo-Saxon children, not necessarily others. It was argued with increasing success before the courts that children of non-White, lower-economic backgrounds were being misplaced into stigmatizing and educationally inferior tracks for the mentally retarded or emotionally disturbed. As examples, *Hobson v. Hanson* (1967) ruled that students could not be inappropriately evaluated with tests reflecting cultural bias and subsequently placed in special classes. *Diana v. State Board of Education* in California (1970) was on the issue of whether Mexican-American children were being inappropriately placed in classes for mental retardation. Diana led to the decertification of between 11,000 and 14,000 children labeled as mildly mentally retarded in California and ushered in a decade of strong judicial scrutiny and intervention on the misdiagnosis of minority children in special education. *Larry P. v. Riles* (1972), one of the longest running cases, essentially ruled that no Black student could be placed in a class for mentally retarded children solely on the basis of an IQ test (see Winzer & Mazurek, 1998).

EARLY CHILDHOOD SPECIAL EDUCATION

In the middle decades of the 19th century, state officials, medical spokesmen, and schoolmen discouraged the attendance of very young children at school (Finkelstein, 1985). This view was revised in the latter decades of the century as an offshoot of the new child study movement and the development of the field of psychology. Kindergarten care, together with day care and nursery education (but with a widening of the original mission) became a feature of American education in the 1880s (Taylor Allen, 1986). One of the most significant innovators was William Torrey Harris who, while superintendent of the St. Louis Public Schools, incorporated the kindergarten into his school system in 1873.

Kindergartens were initially designed for poor and immigrant children in urban centers, one piece in larger reform efforts of moral reform through education. Programs differed from other forms of school offerings in several ways: they were directed toward children below compulsory school age; the development tended to be independent of the public schools; and the programs relied in specific pedagogical models and assumptions such as Froebelian kindergartens in which notions of mother love were critical. Many preschool initiatives arose from the work of individual teachers, mostly women (Hewes, 1989).

As women's roles in the work force expanded dramatically after World War II, so did the need for day care and preschool programming. By 1952, there was a 55% increase in the number of children in kindergarten compared with 1932 ("The Sixty-Second . . .", 1952).

Special education for young children with disabilities can be dated from the 1880s when schools for the deaf and the blind initiated programs. Programs and instructional procedures were developed for use by parents with their young children, and the professional journals were replete with suggestions for parents. By the 1930s, preschool special education was very much alive. By the middle of the 1940s, state legislators began to recognize the needs of adolescent students as well as those of young children, particularly those needing long years of special training techniques such as deaf students or blind students (Martens, 1946b).

The federal government began its support of early childhood special education in 1968 with a series of acts designed to provide grants and contracts. The Handicapped Children's Early Education program supported demonstration and dissemination programs as well as research in the area. Public Law 94-142 carried a special incentive grant designed to encourage the states to provide special education and related services to its preschool disabled children.

Project Head Start came into being as the nation's premier public policy effort, attempting to eliminate poverty and promote social equality. Head Start legislation was passed in 1964 as part of the Economic Opportunity Act; programs were established the following year. Each program was required to include the six components of early childhood education: health screening and referral, mental health services, nutrition education and hot meals, social services for the children and their families, and parent involvement. A 1972 mandate that required Head Start programs to serve children with special needs focused on integrating these children in normalized environments.[8] In doing so, it merged ameliorative programs with special education, thus creating the groundwork for the emergence of a new discrete area of early childhood special education.

PARENT ASSOCIATIONS

According to Cain (1976), parent groups have been part of U.S. educational history since the establishment of the colonies. The first national parent group in the United States was the National Society for Crippled Children founded in 1921. The Cuyahoga County (Ohio) Council for the Retarded Child, established in 1933, operated and financed the first parent-supported community class for the "gravely" retarded (Wallin, 1962). In 1936, the Washington Association for Retarded Children was organized, followed shortly afterward by the Welfare League for Retarded Children in New York. The National Association of Retarded Citizens was founded in 1950 as the National Association of Parents and Friends of Mentally Retarded Children. (Over time, it transmuted to the National Association for Retarded Children, the National Association for Retarded Citizens, the Association for Retarded Citizens of the United States, and now the ARC of the United States). By 1950, 88 parent groups were operating in 19 states (Hay, 1952). By 1954, more than 30,000 people were actively involved in groups for retarded children (Stevens, 1954).

It is difficult to overestimate the effect of parent organizations on special education in the 1950s and 1960s. Once united, parents formed strong organizations and developed considerable local, state, and national prestige. Parents set out to educate and sensitize legislators to the needs of exceptional children. They added their voices to the calls for carrying out constitutional mandates, promoted and advocated policies that would increase their involvement in the education of their children, and encouraged school boards to provide programs or banded together to begin their own programs. Through the development of national coordinating groups, parent groups forced the transfer of larger portions of educational funds to special education. Groups and associations were concerned with state laws that excluded children with significant disabilities and campaigned to eliminate discriminatory laws and demonstrate the educability of all children. Professionals serving the disabled began to amalgamate their efforts and activities in both scholarly and political forces and reinforced parental demands for services (see Melcher, 1976).

Elizabeth Boggs (1966, 1971, 1972) observed that parents were very active in the legislative branch of government in the 1950s, with the executive branch of government in the 1960s, and with the judicial branch of government in the 1970s. Groups such as the National Association for Retarded Citizens and the United Cerebral Palsy Association became powerful lobbying bodies and had much effect on federal legislation. With these, groups such as the Pennsylvania Association for Retarded Children (PARC) sought relief in the judicial system.

SUMMARY AND THEMES

During the 1950s and 1960s, the professional arena witnessed a heated debate on special education as detrimental or beneficial. Occasional questions about what special education was and what it actually did, articulated during the 1950s, amplified in the next decade.

A spirit of optimism characterized the 1960s, with successful court battles for the rights of children with disabilities; federal enabling legislation; and freely flowing funds for research, training, and program development. Enormous changes resulted from enabling legislation in both the United States and Canada. The dual philosophies of normalization and mainstreaming emerged and impelled children with mild to severe disabilities into the orbit of the public schools.

From 1960 on, there was a significant movement to normalize, through integration, the education of children who were exceptional. The chief impetus cannot be attributed to the laboratories of the public schools nor to a compelling research base. Rather, cumulative dissatisfaction with the old paradigm made the new ideas seem particularly attractive, even if their validity was not well supported. It was novel egalitarian and humanistic tendencies, aroused so strongly in the 1960s, that created the propitious climate that advanced the philosophy. Ideas about dealing with people with disabilities changed from those of socially responsible custodial care to those of social integration. Change stemmed from the social and political context of the 1960s and was based on mounting concerns about social justice, equity, and individual civil rights in education and economic opportunity. A social construction of disability was adopted by increasing numbers of social scientists who showed that disability was profoundly shaped by contextual conditions and meanings and by human purposes and interests.

There was also a series of exposés about society's treatment of disabled persons, and there was growing professional and community interest into the problems of social disadvantage. The deprived and the oppressed as well as those who saw themselves that way, gained in militancy; the civil rights movement translated into decisive action to improve the lot of African Americans, of Chicanos, of women, and of those with disabilities. It manifested as legislation, action by the courts, and pressure from interest groups and professional organizations, which in turn brought about the initiation of programs to integrate children with disabilities for education in general classrooms.

Of primary importance in the 1950s and 1960s were efficacy studies that stressed the academic progress and social adjustment of students with disabilities in special classes as contrasted against those in general classrooms. All of the studies had methodological weaknesses to the extent that generalizing conclusions from this body of work was problematic at best. Nevertheless, most of the research, conducted on students with mild mental retardation, stressed that children performed no better in special classes than regular classrooms. Other studies, however, supported the advantages and the effectiveness of special classes for post-school success. Grave dissatisfaction with segregated classes, numerous efficacy studies, and a rapidly liberalizing social climate were further bolstered when Lloyd Dunn authored a paper that can best be described as a catalyst for change.

Throughout the early 1970s, vexatious questions about segregated instruction mounted, chiefly on the basis of efficacy studies on pupil outcomes. Many professionals, parents, and legislators questioned the progress and structure of special education. Central to the issue was the relative value of segregated and integrated settings and whether such separate or integrated classes offered qualitatively different educational ecologies. Many saw segregated classes as inherently discriminatory and unequal, and they expressed concerns about the stigmatization of children identified for special education.

The 1970s saw a torrent of mandatory legislation at the state level. In 1975, the federal government of the United States led the world in writing and enacting a comprehensive law that guaranteed an appropriate education to children with disabilities. Public Law 94-142 (Education for All Handicapped Children Act) brought all of the legal principles and philosophies of the courts into a single instrument of law. The design and implementation of the legislation reflected a significant departure from traditional community attitudes about people with disabilities. It represented official recognition by the U.S. Congress of a growing dissatisfaction with placing students with disabilities in separate settings and provided the impetus for dramatic changes in the ways that students with disabilities were served in the public schools. Several features of Public Law 94-142 structured the way that educators identified, diagnosed, placed, and taught students with disabilities. It led to the establishment of individualized instruction and increased the role of parents in the special education process. Few aspects received more attention than the development of the IEP.

Effective parent organizations existed in the United States only from the 1950s. Once underway, parents' associations formed and spearheaded a social movement to extend educational and treatment services to the more severely disabled children. In state after state, lobbying organizations convinced key legislators to support more special education, fought apathy or hostility in departments of education, and often assisted in writing the legislation itself.

NOTES

1. The report of President Kennedy's Panel on Mental Retardation in the early 1960s detailed the need for each state to establish a protective service for retarded individuals in an appropriate state agency. Guardianship of the property of the retarded person was to be clearly differentiated from guardianship of the person, while the court was to have at its command a comprehensive clinical evaluation by appropriate personnel drawn from the professions of medicine, psychology, education, and social work. There was to be a judicial review every 2 years with respect to the need for continued institutional care for all retarded adults, whatever their type of admission. Further, the whole body of the law related to mental retardation was to be reviewed periodically in each jurisdiction (Melcher, 1976).

2. A body of important literature surrounds the deinstitutionalization movement. Relevant examples are Bruininks, Meyers, Sigford, and Lakin (1981), Goffman (1961), Meyers (1978), and Wolfensberger (1975).

3. One outcome of the tumultuous social movements of the late 1960s was the birth of the disability rights movement and the advent of a new field of disability studies. Disability studies grew as an area of research that offered a fresh lens through which to analyze social relations. Work areas that developed from this area are linked to the interpretation of the disabilities themselves, with an emphasis on understanding what it means to be disabled in society and on listening to the voices of those served. The work does not deny that there are real physiological characteristics; what it does deny is the oppressive meanings attached to labels. The notion of disability as a characteristic intrinsic to the individual is aberrant. Disability, a social construction that varies in eras and cultures, cannot be abstracted from the social world that produces it. Therefore, disability is conceived as a failure of society.

4. Regulations are not an actual part of the legislation but rather guidelines for the implementation spelled out by members of the executive branch of the federal government and published in the *Federal Register*. Today, an administrative agency writes detailed regulations to guide implementation that are founded on the *Code of Federal Regulations*.

5. Besides special education, most school districts conduct other categorical programs such as Chapter 1 for students who are economically disadvantaged, migrant education for children of migrant farm workers, immigrant assistance programs for recent immigrant children, and limited-English-proficiency programs for children whose primary language is other than English. In addition, dozens of other kinds of categorical programs are offered in various school districts throughout the United States (Reynolds, Zetlin, & Wang, 1993).

6. The concept of resource rooms was not new. They began for children with visual impairments in 1913 and, soon after, for those who were hard of hearing. During the 1950s and 1960s, many schools implemented resource programs specifically to help children overcome difficulties in reading, math, and speech (Wiederholt & Chamberlain, 1989).

7. The first references to bilingual special education appeared in the 1970s. It is defined as "use of the home language and the home culture, along with English, in an individually designed program of special instruction" (Baca & Cervantes, 1984, p. 18).

8. Although currently all Head Start programs must include a minimum of 10% children with disabilities, the Head Start definitions of disabilities differ from those used by the Department of Education and the Individuals With Disabilities Education Act legislation.

Chapter 6

Handling "the Holdbacks and the Drags"

Children and youth with behavioral disorders are not a product only of modernized social, economic, and educational systems. Recalcitrant, difficult, and disruptive young people have long and consistently challenged society and school systems. In the schools, behavior has been a constant issue—always there, always a matter of degree, and almost always a transaction between an individual pupil and the teacher or system (see Clough, Garner, Pardeck, & Yeun, 2005).

Whether viewed through a social, educational, legal, or correctional lens, the dominant orientation to defining and meeting the needs of behaviorally deviant children and youth has always been a paradox. Definitions, classifications, treatment regimes, and educational interventions have been bounded and constrained by a matrix of interlocking factors. Further, a century and a half of applying various models of intervention have met with only the most limited success, and the picture of how these students fare in the school remains bleak. James Kauffman (1976) pointed out that the steady stream of psychological, educational, social, and legal changes and events that developed throughout the late 19th and all of the 20th century have simply left a storehouse of unresolved issues and lasting puzzles facing policy makers and practitioners. Few critical issues in the field have been resolved in the past hundred years or so, and "current issues and trends seem only to be a recycling of those that have been with us for well over a century" (Kauffman, 2001, p. 96). Whether the persistance of the issues rests on the intractibility of the sociopsychological problems they represent, the ineptness with which potential solutions have been implemented, or the injudicious use of teaching interventions is open for extended debate.

The complexities and range of deviant behaviors themselves assume primary importance in compounding the matrix of surrounding problems. In general, deviant behavior has always referred to differences of a specific nature: they are unacceptable, they cross the line into emotional or mental illness, or they are illegal. Yet interested parties find it notoriously difficult to arrive at a concensus as to what particular behaviors delineate deviancy.

The areas of juvenile misbehavior and offending have been "the subject of study by all of the social sciences" (Rothstein, 1954, p. 42); they constitute "one of the most researched and theorized topics in criminology" (O'Mahoney, 2005, p. 167). In both the historical and contemporary literature, child malfeasance and delinquency has been explicitly examined through varied lenses—sociological (e.g., Hagan & Leon, 1977); legal (e.g., Platt, 1969); historical (e.g., Houston, 1982); cross-cultural (e.g., Winzer, 2005c) and educational (e.g., Kauffman, 1976; Robinson, 1936; Wallin, 1938–39). Academics and professionals have mulled over the problems, and the popular press as well as local and federal investigative bodies have probed into the causes, prevention, and treatment of juvenile delinquency. Yet the areas of behavioral disorders and juvenile offending remain an enigma; researchers cannot logically isolate one single cause, and the relative weight of theorized factors is difficult to determine.

Moreover, questions about how to identify and define social deviance have always been perplexing. Unlike overt and visible disabilities, disordered behavior cannot be detached from the observer. Rather, it is a subjective reality constructed on the basis of a judgment as to what is tolerable, appropriate, and acceptable. Differing moral codes in different times and places have defined and condemned different behaviors as aberrant. Changing definitions of crime and growing police activity may also account for some of the ebbs and apparent rises in crime and juvenile delinquency.

Further, mental retardation and behavioral disorders are inextricably intermeshed. For many decades, mild mental retardation was seen, among other things, as a behavioral disorder (Goldstein, 1984). Wyatt (1919) observed that "mental deficiency in varying degrees and the lack of proper facilities for treating those who are thus handicapped, are responsible for no small number of young offenders" (p. 10). Some students would rather be thought bad than dull. As a 1939 commentator put it, "There is a certain amount of glory in badness." If the child "cannot shine in the classroom, by means of his intellectual achievement, he can at least be very noticeable by his superiority in non-conformity" (Farson, 1939–40, p. 139).

Finally, the area is confounded by the number of agencies and professionals involved. Systems did not succeed in creating unambiguous missions and goals. Conflicting views of the problems as well as conflicting goals, needs, and objectives of correctional and special education were propounded by diverse wings of the correctional, welfare, and educational bureaucracies as well as various areas of mental health, social work, and psychology. These agencies, though united in pursuit of major strategies to control behavior, showed a lack of comprehensive planning and interagency cooperation and often followed somewhat different routes.

In the first half of the 20th century, confrontations with nonconforming children and youth played out in multiple variations. The legal system established juvenile and family courts; the correctional arm used a wide variety of dispositions; psychiatric and psychological clinics, together with testing and assessment regimes, arose from psychology. Social workers intervened with dysfunctional families. School systems provided visiting teachers, special schools, and special classes, although they simultaneously displayed an enduring reluctance to confront and handle recalcitrant, rambuncious, and disturbed children and youth. The latter half of the century witnessed far greater public school involvement with more special classes and programs and a plethora of behavioral regimes and practices.

No other group in special education has been, and is, more confusing and more challenging than that area broadly categorized as juvenile delinquent in the opening half of the 20th century and, more recently, as emotionally and behaviorally disordered. Early 20th-century commentators were provoked and dismayed by delinquency. The war years saw rises in delinquency, often attributed to mothers now working outside the home. During the 1940s and 1950s, there was massive research directed toward the area. In the 1960s, workers characterized delinquency as "unquestionably one of the most serious social problems in the United States" (Quay & Peterson, 1960, p. 472). Current writers observe that educating students with behavior problems will continue to be one of the most stressful, complex, and difficult challenges facing public education today. Students have high dropout rates, high rates of academic failure, poor achievement, low graduation rates, high numbers of institutional placements, and poor post-school adjustment (Eber, Nelson, & Miles, 1997). In many instances, intervention remains dual, different, and separate from the regular stream, with alternate guidelines for program planning and service provisions.

The common theme among children and youth in the encompassing category of emotional and behavioral disorders is the demonstration of maladaptive behaviors that seriously impair the individual's ability to work, live, and function successfully in society. A wide variety of services evolved to deal with these behaviors. This chapter is devoted to examining the various interventions and dispositions that emerged for children with deviant behavior, generally viewed historically as delinquent or pre-delinquent children. Attention is first directed toward disorders that garnered social and educational sanctions. Today's ubiquitous category of attention deficit hyperactivity disorder (ADHD) is also discussed, albeit briefly. The extreme of the spectrum includes mental illness. Children with psychoneurotic traits—severe emotional disorders—are treated separately. Autism Spectrum Disorders were traditionally (although not currently) treated as an emotional disorder. That category is also addressed along with severe emotional disorders.

DEFINING AND PINPOINTING DEVIANCE

During the middle decades of the 19th century, children who behaved badly were slotted into categories of matchless elasticity, commonly dubbed as neglected, vagrant, and delinquent. The formation of juvenile courts in the 1890s allowed for more comprehensive labeling of delinquent and neglected children. Still, efforts to sweep away strict divisions between normality and abnormality, and responsibility and irresponsibility, did little to add clarity. No clear demarcation existed between neglect and delinquency and between obstreperous and recalcitrant pupils and defective learners. Robert Yerkes (1917) noted that "we have no suitable term for this class of unfortunates." These "instinctively, emotionally, or morally peculiar or defective children," he said, "are quite commonly described as queer, uncontrollable, or even lacking moral judgment" (p. 293).

As descriptive terms, *neglected, vagrant,* and *delinquent* persisted in the legal system until the 1950s. Characteristically, educators were driven more by a search for specificity. The need to understand deviance led to a parsing of complex actions. As special educators broke diffuse generic concepts into specific categories, the terms for categorical definitions of exactly who was behaviorally disordered constantly expanded, collapsed, and were reenvisioned. Descriptors and classification systems generally showed a murkiness that reflected both changing public morality and the subjective offerings of observers. In fact, the terminology used by the educational, legal, and correctional systems became so unclear and overlapping that a 1959 writer chided that "all of these categories, supposedly separate and distinct, represent a paragon of confusion since they may very well describe similar facts" (Clayton, 1959, p. 207).

The problem of deviant child behavior was most often approached by describing behaviors and citing examples. Throughout the 19th century, a variety of titles were heaped on these children. Many revolved around their street culture or lifestyle. Kinder elements referred to children as waifs and strays, uncared for, friendless children, or ragged children. More pointed labels included gutter snipes, young blackguards, reprobates, urchins, and street Arabs. Others spoke of the perishing and dangerous classes and viewed such youngsters as dirty, verminous, slovenly urchins, semi-barbarians, incorrigibles, and backward and ill-favored.

Informal 20th-century descriptors were no more generous than those of the earlier era. Juvenile delinquency remained an enigma, a grave social problem that was disturbingly persistent and provokingly resistant to understanding. Yerkes (1917) described "affective deviates," a group that included "juvenile delinquents, the uncontrollable or incorrigible" and "in general those individuals who tend to become social derelicts and menaces" (p. 294). Wallin (1938–39) pointed to the truant child as an "infant fugitive" and "village urchin" who came from "the hazards of slums, alleys, and dens of vice" (pp. 1, 2). A 1959 writer was led to descriptors such as the "black sheep of the family," juvenile gangsters, or neighborhood hoodlums (Clayton, 1959).

Certainly, more precise specifications were available from the 1930s on. The most popular term was *behavior problem cases* with the two categories of conduct problems: (a) delinquent or pre-delinquent children and youth and (b) personality disorders, or maladjustment of children with psychoneurotic traits (Baker & Stullken, 1938). Other terminology included socially handicapped children, behavior children, socially unadjusted, extremely aggressive pre-delinquents, nervous or emotionally unstable, and the withdrawing and highly introverted individual.

A behavior problem referred to "a child who exhibited characteristics that were so noticeable and undesirable that they were not acceptable to society and also one that exhibited emotional traits that caused maladjustment to school" (Porter, 1944–45, p. 110). Williams (1943–44) characterized the delinquent child as "a social rebel. Being unable, or unwilling, to develop action patterns which are made normal by convention and majority acceptance, he makes patterns of his own, often to the distress and inconvenience of his chronological superiors" (p. 195). Serious personality problems, according to teachers, were those in which aggressive or troublesome behavior made life uncomfortable for the teacher (Snyder, 1947–48). Unacceptable traits included sexual behavior, masturbation, smoking, drawing obscene pictures, cheating, and profanity (Snyder, 1947–48).

The term *emotional disturbance* appeared in the literature in 1900, but without being defined (Reinert, 1980). In fact, it is not possible to find a definition of this term, which subtly crept into the field, until the 1950s. The emotionally disturbed child, said Edgar Doll in 1952, "is most simply interpreted as one who is confused and bewildered. He does not understand his own social stresses, and he feels unaccepted in his efforts to resolve them" (p. 105). Another writer observed that "The pathologically acting out boy has little ability to deal with reality without severely distorting it" (Newman, 1956, p. 188).

During the 1940s, attempts were made to generate sets of typological categories by the use of factor analysis and other related procedures. In a series of studies, researchers defined three types: unsocialized aggressive, socialized delinquent, and overinhibited (Hart, Jenkins, Axelrad, & Sperling, 1943; Hewitt & Jenkins, 1946; Jenkins & Hewitt, 1944).

Until the late 1950s, the legal system relied on the primary categories of delinquent, neglected, and dependent. Other terms crept in for children subject to juvenile court jurisdiction, including the miscreant and the wayward (Kansas); the abandoned, destitute, physically handicapped, and crippled (New York); the feebleminded (Maryland); defective (Nebraska); abandoned (North Carolina and Tennnessee); destitute (South Carolina); and uncared for child and defective delinquent (Connecticut) (Clayton, 1959, p. 207).

Definitions in the first half of the 20th century did not seriously attempt to discriminate emotional from behavioral disorders, or conduct disorders from social maladjustment. It was not until 1975 that a legal definition of emotional disturbance appeared in Public Law 94-142. It described the child as showing an inability to learn and to relate to peers and adults, inappropriate reactions, and pervasive unhappiness as well as the development of physical symptoms as a reaction to stress. Until 1997, the condition was defined as *seriously emotionally disturbed*, which made it the only federal category to include an indication of severity level. The broader term *emotional or behavioral disorders* was adopted in the late 1980s by the National Mental Health and Special Education Coalition and, by 1991, was well accepted (Kauffman, 1993a). The Individuals With Disabilities Act (IDEA) of 1990 specified *emotional or behavioral disorder*, although the 1990s saw a continuation of debate on the term largely based on the contention that neither logical argument nor empirical studies supported a distinction between social maladjustment and emotional disturbance (see Kauffman, 1993a).

Even though numerous ways to define behavioral disorders emerged over the decades, there still remains a struggle to arrive at a common understanding. A universally accepted definition remains extremely problematic. The many attempts to define disturbed child populations and to define aberrant behavior have had only varying degrees of success, and no single definition of behavioral disorders exists.

Educators disagree over what constitutes a severe behavior disorder; whether the use of the term is even justifiable; and whether to call these children emotionally disturbed, behaviorally disordered, socially maladjusted, deviant, psychologically impaired, educationally handicapped, character disordered, children in conflict, delinquent, or some other descriptor. In addition, children in the area are being labeled with an inordinate amount of detail based on the close alliance forged between the field of behavioral disorders and the *Diagnostic and Statistical Manual* of the American Psychiatric Association (1994, 2000).

NEGLECTED, VAGRANT, AND DELINQUENT CHILDREN

Emerging industrialized society was particularly pernicious to children; they were often caught in the contradictions between the profit-making adult society and the claims of childhood. In the middle decades of the 19th century, social unrest, economic vicissitudes, and migratory habits caused an apparent upsurge in the numbers of children on the streets. Many of them roved the public thoroughfares in gangs. The instability in the lives of these groups was a thorn in the eye of communal law and order: their perceived unending assault on the rest of the population was seen as a direct threat to social order. In addition, the presence of delinquent and neglected children pointed to an apparent breakdown of families' childrearing responsibilities. Together, these caused the authorities serious concern.

Just being on the streets, particularly in gangs, was offensive and enough to damn children. For boys, callings such as "newsboy, errand boy, driver and helper on wagons, and workers in stores and markets" were suspect (Social Survey Commission of Toronto, 1915). Of these, newsboy was far and away the most commonly cited occupation associated with youthful crime (Bench, 1919).

Selling newspapers or visiting poolrooms were almost natural precursors of poor behavior. Even worse was smoking tobacco ("Juvenile Courts," 1921). It was estimated that among children deemed troublesome, "Eighty-five per cent smoke cigarettes" (Henderson, 1919, p. 16). Susan Houston (1982) noted further crimes and misdemeanors. She observed that "youngsters who drank, swore, pilfered orchards, played with catapults, harassed Salvation Army cadets, lit bonfires, stole newspapers, or broke into letter boxes were routinely disciplined" (p. 134).

Female delinquency, because of its sexual nature, was treated as behavior that was dangerous and potentially contaminating, with enormous long-term consequences (Sedlak, 1983). J. J. Kelso, Ontario's superintendent of Neglected and Dependent Children, wrote that "with the girl, the downward course is somewhat different, though the result is essentially the same. Escape from the family quarrels and squalor is sought on the streets, where vice is easily learned, and the road to comfort and luxury made to appear comparatively easy, until by stages she sinks into a common outcast, unpitied and unloved" (Kelso, 1893–94, p. 214). Domestic service was "the commonest occupation of girls who go wrong" (Whitton, 1919, p. 142).

Intervention With Neglected, Vagrant, and Delinquent Children

Early measures to control children and youth who matched the broad category of neglected, vagrant, and delinquent assumed only punitive and aversive dimensions. Until the end of the 18th century, American and British courts meted out corporal punishment, from whipping to execution, far more often than imprisonment (Achenbach, 1975). Cole and Visser (1999) wrote that "in 1785, in keeping with a long Puritan influence that suggested that some children were born bad and the world might be a better place without them, 90% of the so-called criminals executed were under 21 years of age" (p. 57). The humanitarian spirit of the late 18th century brought a reduction of the number of crimes punishable by death. Imprisonment was seen as a more humane alternative to execution and severe corporal punishment (Achenbach, 1975).

In the early decades of the 19th century, children were routinely sent to common gaols (jails), Houses of Correction, juvenile detention homes, and prisons. The first major attempt to improve the treatment of delinquents appears to have been the establishment of the New York House of Refuge in 1825. It became the model for the enlightened treatment of delinquent and destitute children, and similar institutions were founded in other American cities (Achenbach, 1975). The Boston Disciplinary Day School for truant and emotionally disturbed clients, for example, opened in 1830.

Reformatories emerged, which fused the care of vagrant children with the discipline of youths convicted of crimes by catering to a clientele of neglected and vagrant children as well as confirmed delinquents. Critics vehemently denounced such facilities that may have sufficed to "reform a boy who has become criminal" but were decidedly unable to "train and instruct a pauper boy while yet innocent of crime" (Meredith, 1862/1975, p. 271). When the practiced criminal and the neglected child came together, it was feared that the more experienced in crime would recruit relatively untried accomplices.

Industrial Schools

By the middle decades of the 19th century, the laissez-faire credo that had characterized early 19th-century American society faded conspicuously. The emerging tendency was for society to widen and multiply its grip on human affairs and to enlarge its rights to intervene with children and their families. Reformers also began to recognize that the problems of juvenile crime and neglect were not apt to be resolved simply or primarily through the work of the reform schools or prisons, but required other and more basic approaches. What was needed was a link between the common schools and the reformatories—institutions free from the opprobrium attached to the name *reform school* and designed to serve young potentially delinquent children.

Just as Americans had adopted European models for the earlier institutional settings, for normal schools, as well as for the ungraded classes and classes for unruly students, so, too, had they imported European notions of industrial education. The idea of industrial schools (sometimes referred to as parental schools) as closed institutions began in 1833 when Wiuchwem founded his Rauhe Hause (Rough House) near Hamburg, Germany (see Goffman, 1961). The organization of the schools was based on the family plan or cottage system. This design also originated in Germany when Gustav Werner founded Gotthilf (God's help) in Reutingen in 1836. The boys lived in cottages of about 40 boys, each house under the care of a matron and a guard who acted as mother and father of the so-called family.[1]

The late 19th century saw the United States and Canada found industrial schools for relatively young dependent and semidependent children. By 1918, the United States had 149 schools designated as state industrial schools (although some were privately operated). These schools were described as "reformatory institutions for delinquents receiving inmates committed by juvenile or other court decision" (Bonner, 1920, p. 8). Schools showed an average enrollment of 493 children of ages between 5 and 19 years taught by an estimated 1,137 teachers (Bonner, 1920). Child savers viewed these industrial schools as highly significant advances in children's institutions, representing the most modern thinking and practice (Jones, 1978). The attempt to combat and control pauperism and crime among urban children was simply "defensive foresight of the citizens who would protect the future of the state" (Bryce, 1920, p. 256). Such schools would serve as a triple rescue from parental ineptitude and viciousness, from child immorality, and from future incompetence.

A primary cornerstone of the reforming philosophy that underlay the industrial schools was that delinquent children were victims of environments in which vicious adults crippled the plastic natures of children. Parents faced the official reproach of ineffeciency. Parental neglect, cried J. J. Kelso, "is the cause of seventy-five percent of juvenile delinquency" (Kelso, 1910, p. 18).

Because reformers interpreted delinquency as the product of pathological, crime-breeding homes, they saw their mission chiefly in terms of removing the child from a pernicious environment. Children could be taken if the parents were contributing directly or indirectly to dereliction and criminality. The separation was often executed with righteous zeal. The interpretation of reasonable citizens was all that was necessary to unmask a delinquency-generating environment.

Occasionally, harassed parents committed their own child. Of the first 50 boys admitted to the Victoria Industrial School in Toronto in 1888, 25 had been sent on the specific request of parents and guardians who said that the children were uncontrollable or drifting toward crime (Morrison, 1974). Mrs. W. G. wrote in 1912 to the director of the Victoria Industrial School that "I have a Boy who will be 13 years old Next Month which I can Not controle at all and his father being dead. Makes it Much harder for Me. I Can Not Keep him out of Pool Rooms and playing Pool and I have just been told today that he even plays' Poker. I want him in a good Strict School."[2]

Once rescued from dangerous environments before they became truly criminal, children's incipient immorality was stemmed and they were set on the paths of righteousness, subjected to rigorous discipline and appropriate education. Child savers held the laudatory belief that "bad boys are merely good boys who have strayed into side paths and who may, in nearly every instance, be guided back into the main road if only the right person is leading" (Kelso, 1910, p. 4).

Industrial schools saw the marriage of industrial education and cherished social values. In theory, the type of education supplied was broad-based moral, social, and vocational training—a judicious mixture of humane amelioration and the pursuit of rational objectives. The schools attempted to prepare the inmates for an eventual return to American society. Programs were designed to prevent and control incipient social disorder by diminishing the urban nuisance of beggars and paupers and to ensure the regulation and use of unused labor capacity by providing more skilled workers. Boys were taught shoemaking, printing, tailoring, carpentry, baking, and laboring (British Columbia Provincial Industrial School for Boys, 1903; Victoria Industrial School, 1896). Supervisors in the industrial schools for girls held that "marriage is the greatest trade open to women." Therefore, household training was her greatest necessity. The 1927 report of the British Columbia Provincial Industrial School for Girls pointed out that "in home-like surroundings of scrupulous cleanliness the girls are given a training in home efficiency, in the preparation and value of plain wholesome food, in household cleanliness, the use of soap" and "the cultivation of pleasures of simple tastes, and the value of moral and spiritual behaviour" (p. R7).

Whether viewed as ameliorative or correctional education, the process became rapidly plagued by a range of philosophical and programmatic concerns. In many industrial schools, the professional allegiance was to reactive discipline and to the mechanisms of control. Many succumbed to punitive institutionalization.[3] At the Victoria Industrial School, a lad by the name of Wilfred Fletcher narrated to the newspapers how the principal "stripped me and thrashed me with a thick rubber strap." He was "placed on a bread and water diet for two months. I had to stand at every meal and in the playground."[4] A visitor to an American institution for juvenile delinquents told the story of the boys given a break in their work schedule. "Two by two they marched in and stood to attention," he explained. Then "one by one they were dismissed to go to the lavatory and allowed sixty seconds for the trip; as they came back they took their places at the other end of the line and stood stiffly to attention." The boys were not allowed to talk at work or at the table, and they only had a Saturday afternoon every third or fourth week for play" (Barss, 1920, p. 210).

During the 1930s, the industrial school designation faded. Some schools closed; others were reinvented as closed dispositions and training schools for delinquent youth who were committed by order of the courts. The chief purpose of training schools, reform schools, parental schools, protectories, junior republics, houses of the Good Shepherd, and so on was to reform the inmates and protect society (Best, 1930). By 1945, approximately 30,000 delinquent youth were in residential schools in the United States (Ingram, Martens, & Cook, 1945).

Alternate Placements and Dispositions

In the closing decades of the 19th century, a reformist faction waxed tenacious in the pursuit of alternate child-saving models. Although reformatories and industrial schools continued to serve a discrete clientele, many child savers viewed institutional means as suspect unless they assimilated family life structure when claiming to rehabilitate. Increasingly, more advanced social thinkers and those in the new profession of social work condemned large aggregations of children as injurious and harmful in the long run to child, family, and community. The mother, not the matron, was the best employee for which the state could hope.

The emphasis on the reconstruction of the nuclear family as the unequaled environment for optimal child development entailed a significant break with much of what had been practiced previously. Now, children within family units were seen in an enhanced way as a community resource, and a certain value was attributed to having children raised by their own mother, even if government funds were required to make it possible. Tanenhaus (2004) observes that the mother's pension law, established in 1911, influenced dispositions. Overall, fatherless children were most often allowed to remain in their homes; motherless children were more often sent to institutions.

A complementary prong of the family care paradigm centered on placing children in foster care in hopes of reducing public expenditures and preventing the creation of future criminals. Beginning in 1853, the New York Children's Aid Society specialized in placing city children with families in distant parts of the country. By 1879, the society had placed 48,000 children outside New York (Achenbach, 1975). From this beginning, foster care was practiced by a number of public authorities and private societies in the United States from the 1870s.

The family care paradigm, together with the care of recalcitrant children, related intimately to the development of the court system and to the enhancement of the social welfare system, particularly the new profession of social work, which was a well established and growing profession by 1920.

THE JUVENILE COURT SYSTEM

A rising crescendo of the rhetoric of socialized justice from the 1880s onward brought about the establishment of special procedures and personnel for children. In most jurisdictions, the reordering of summary justice entailed the establishment of children's courts and the adaptation of other courts for the hearing of domestic problems.

During the 1850s, child savers became concerned about the brutalization of youth by the criminal justice process and sought to change the notion that children were criminals who deserved the moral condemnation of the community. Instead, these reformers contended, children needed care, education, and protection (Orlando & Black, 1975). Even so, the juvenile court was one of the last institutions to be created in establishing the American juvenile justice system.

It was not until 1899 that a reform movement gained sufficient impetus to achieve unanimous approval of a state law for the establishment of a court whose sole function would be to act as a chancery court—one charged with the responsibility of ensuring the welfare of those in its charge as opposed to one adjudicating criminal responsibility. The rigid set of definitions that distinguished delinquency from crime and affected subsequent legislation throughout North America was formulated by Harvey B. Hurd (who became the first judge) in the state of Illinois in 1899. In the same year, Denver passed a law to establish juvenile courts; other states soon followed suit (Addams, 1925) and produced legislative systems and procedures to keep youngsters from entering the criminal court system.

The Illinois Juvenile Court was designed to regulate the treatment and control of dependent, neglected, and delinquent children (McGrath, 1965). However, many of the basic principles of the court had long been implicit in judicial proceedings concerning children. Juvenile courts and their counterparts, family courts, were in most cases extensions of magistrate or police courts. However, they did represent a landmark in that the state no longer engaged in punishing antisocial behavior but, instead, sought to assist wayward children. At the same time, the courts brought a new party into the basic relationship of parent and child. Now the state could intervene.

The advent of juvenile courts separated delinquency from adult crime for the first time and gave it its own philosophy, its own legislation, and its own treatment services (McGrath, 1962). A fundamental principle was that the role of the court should be to protect the child from further bad influences to prevent him or her from becoming a hardened criminal. The court's responsibility was to assess the child physically, mentally, and morally and "then if it learns that he is treading the path that leads to criminality, to take him in charge not so much to punish as to reform, not to degrade but to uplift, not to crush but to develop, not to make him a criminal but a worthy citizen" (Mack, 1909, p. 107).

A second principle was that the child did not need to be convicted of any crime to be placed under the court's jurisdiction. The only requirement was that the child be neglected or otherwise in apparent danger of becoming a criminal (Achenbach, 1975). Juvenile courts were not designed to determine the guilt or innocence of youngsters; they were a "first attempt by the state to make the aim of the law a protective rather than a punitive member of the body patriotic" (Henderson, 1919, p. 16).

The third principle was that the court should be free to arrange for the juvenile's protection in a relatively informal manner. Courts were designed to oversee children's welfare by placing them under the supervision of the courts, in foster homes, in reform institutions, or in the custody of welfare agencies or church groups. By the 1930s, the juvenile courts were experimenting with other options such as community organizations and neighborhood leadership for supervising delinquent youth (Tanenhaus, 2004). Dispositions were for indeterminate periods rather than specific sentences for specific crimes. Placing children in jails was now forbidden; probation became a legally defined option and treatment strategy.

For the first time, the disposition of children to private welfare organizations was explicitly sanctioned, even if the child had committed criminal acts (Achenbach, 1975). However, Wallin (1938–1939) noted that a youngster "may become guilty of a round of offenses that bring him to the juvenile court followed by terms in the detention home, the industrial school, the workhouse, and even in prison"

(p. 3). Large numbers of children were still confined with adult offenders. In one unnamed state, 400 children younger than the age of 16 were in jail, 84 of them younger than the age of 12 years ("Proposals for Extending . . .", 1945–46).

A new terminology was used, which was free from the odium of penal tradition and emphasized the nature of the juvenile court proceedings. The actual term, *juvenile delinquent*, became ensconced in law and provided an operational definition shared by a range of professionals. The term *petition* was substituted for *complaint*; *hearing* for *arraignment*; *adjudication of involvement in delinquency* for *conviction*; and *disposition* for *sentencing* (Achenbach, 1975).

A long and varied list of misdemeanors propelled boys to the courts and earned official reproaches. These acts included robberies and breaking and entering; arson; assault with a dangerous weapon; begging; carnal knowledge; carrying concealed weapons; disorderly conduct; drunkenness; forgery; jumping on moving trains; reckless driving; placing obstructions on railway tracks; trespass; truancy; violating bicycle, curfew, or firearms ordinances; violating the tobacco law; and violating the poolroom law (see Bench, 1919, p. 126). For girls, they included vagrancy or wandering abroad; frequenting a common bawdy house; theft and shoplifting; and sex offenses. Because of the danger of pregnancy, society considered that the girl must be protected more than the boy. Therefore she was more likely to be brought into court for a sex offense, or a suspicion of it, than was a boy (Warner, 1940–41).

By the mid-20th century, juvenile court jurisdiction was broad and extensive. In all states in 1959, the juvenile courts had jurisdiction over delinquent, neglected, and dependent children (Clayton, 1959). With the exception of delinquents, children in the latter two groups either were offenders or in danger of becoming so.

SOCIAL WORK

Child saving was one of the staples of 19th-century reform. During the century, the penetrating and monitoring of family life took place through an alliance of philanthropy and the state. Much of what became the profession of social work had been carried out on a volunteer basis by women's groups. By about 1910, the traditional modes of social welfare organization were under attack from the next generation of child savers—the professionals. The interests of these ambitious and social-scientifically oriented practitioners lay in the coordination of child rescue agencies under central voluntary and government-assisted structures headed by trained personnel. The 1920s saw the professionalization of social welfare services. Social work professionals now secularized the discourse of child rescue formerly couched in humanitarian and even evangelical terms (see Cahan, 1989).

Following the Great Depression of the 1930s and the social welfare programs that emerged during that period, there was a heightened sensitivity to the needs of those less able to thrive and a significant extension of governmental responsibilities in meeting the needs of such individuals. The state was beneficent; its agents, experts. When families were neglectful or simply overwhelmed, then the state had an obligation to respond. The piecemeal voluntary approach to social services, already under attack by about 1910, gave way fully to a comprehensive, government-supported system. This development led inevitably to the reformulation of services under a comprehensive body of laws and a routinization of procedures for the bestowal of benefits.

In concert with juvenile courts, the United States and Canada effected a major reorganization of family law, particularly in relation to the dependent poor. A proliferation of legislation arose dealing with women, children, their labor, and the family. Family courts shifted the focus from the removal of the child from a pernicious environment to reconstruction of the nuclear family. As one worker observed, "it is the wrong conditions that should be dealt with, rather than the unfortunate victim" (Kelso, 1910, p. 15). Improving conditions in the child's own family would render arbitrary removal unnecessary; once a delinquency-generating environment was unmasked by the state's agents, the task of the family courts was to enforce conformity to middle-class standards of morality, hygiene, and education.

The new tribunals, characterized as they were by their adherence to the best interests of children and their families, stressed the existence of a specialized apparatus that was peopled by specialized workers. Social workers emerged as the party that focused on the reconstruction of the nuclear family. Workers intervened in the tension between preserving family unity and the realities of dysfunctional families and stressed the need to assist dependent people in their homes.

Social work stood at the juncture point between the family and different practices—education, medical-hygienic, judicial, and penal. In the period from 1910 to 1920, the piecemeal voluntary approach to social services began to give way to a more comprehensive, government-supported system. The changes in methods of delivery developed under pressure. The experiences of World War I and its aftermath—a serious economic depression, the problems of providing relief to soldiers' families, and the effect of the devastating postwar Spanish influenza epidemic—strengthened calls for child and family welfare. During the 1920s and the 1930s, family case work became the leitmotif of social work. Social work gained added stature: social workers were one of the few groups to experience 100% employment during the Depression (Struthers, 1981).

EDUCATIONAL CONSIDERATIONS

The discovery of children who displayed conduct and personality traits beyond those considered normal severely tested the principles and practices of common school ideology almost from the beginning. Behavioral abnormality served as a plausible excuse for exclusion from the general classroom and led to the formation of classes for unruly students.

In the middle of the 19th century, despite the formation of classes for unruly students and similar placements for disruptive children, few of that group took advantage of schooling. When they did attend, schools juxtaposed recalcitrance, rudeness, truancy, and rule infractions with the schools' need for order and compliance. School systems tended to preserve the rights of the majority: disruptive children could be excluded for the sake of preserving order, protecting the teacher's time from excessive demands, and sparing normal children the pain of seeing others who were disabled. Early public school special education just as often served as a transmission belt to move those displaying behavior problems beyond the schools through the mechanisms of expulsion and suspension.

Court decisions and legislation typically showed the belief that school attendance was a privilege to be awarded or withheld at the discretion of the school authorities. Throughout the 19th century, the preponderance of decisions upheld and thereby strengthened a board's right to reject and expel deviate children whose presence in the school was presumed to "impair the efficiency or interfere with the rights of other pupils" (Zelder, 1953, p. 187).

In the first half of the 20th century, the special education literature allowed significant emphasis on behavioral disorders. For example, a study of all doctoral and master's theses in special education in 1938 showed that more than 41% dealt with problem cases, delinquency, and social maladjustment. Only 13% were devoted to children with intellectual disabilities and less than 9% to the gifted (Good, 1938). Rhetoric and research far outweighed practice; educational progress was stilted, and a dismal probability existed for students with emotional or behavioral disorders.

Compulsory school laws propelled these children, however unwilling, into education. The schools, equally reluctant to handle rambunctious students, created a range of alternate placements. Because "serious malconduct cases" were unamenable to general classrooms, educators set up special schools and classes to care for this type of problem. Placements were given various names—adjustment centers, social adjustment classes, welfare classes for the maladjusted, and truant and disciplinary classes.

Special Schools and Special Classes

By the 1930s, early notions of hereditary degeneracy faded; the common view now affirmed the notion that delinquencies were learned. Orthodox thinking looked to environmental causes for crime and delinquency. Problems were seen as "the result of economic conditions of home and neighborhood, the product of the influence of the personalities with whom the child comes in contact, the effect of cheap movies and the places of recreation he attends" (Postel, 1937, p. 18).

Most educators agreed that children had to be educated and led to civility. Paradoxically, school systems were less ready to accommodate uncivil students. In educational circles, screening for and pinpointing the child with behavioral disorders, still referred to as juvenile delinquency, remained haphazard and scattered until the 1950s (Dupont, 1957). Even with the pressure of compulsory school laws, rhetoric and research outstripped intervention, and school system intervention was relatively sparse. By 1954, for example, 122 teacher training programs had sequences in one or more of the areas of exceptionality; fewer than 14 had specialized work for teachers of children with emotional or behavioral disorders (Mackie & Dunn, 1954). In the same year, reports indicated that only 17 out of 88 school systems in Canada provided special classes for students with behavioral disorders (Dunn & McNeill, 1953–54). It was not until the 1960s that children with emotional and behavioral disorders were viewed as rightful recipients of education in North American public schools. Federally funded specialized teacher training originated in 1963.

A 1927 writer observed that "sentimentality, hysteria, blind rage or drastic punishment will not cure youthful delinquency" (Cooley, 1927, p. 23). Children with deviant behaviors were "frequently the result of conflict between themselves and the regular type of school organization" (Postel, 1937, p. 12), but there existed "no panacea or general rule for solving behavior problems" (Beaman, 1948, p. 84).

Special placements were avidly promoted as allowing more freedom in adjusting to individual cases. Wallin (1938–39) argued that "the best method of supplying suitable, vitalized, stimulating instruction as a preventative to truancy is to transfer the more serious types of mental and behavior cases to properly organized and conducted special classes having an enrollment small enough to permit personal contacts between the teacher and pupil" (Wallin, 1938–39, p. 6). Lacking such specialized intervention, "socially handicapped children are those likely to build up behavior problems that finally culminate in more serious crimes" ("Convention Study-Section Reports," 1942–43, p. 49).

A few thoughtful commentators recognized that "some stigma may attach itself to pupils transferred to special schools and classes and there may be some hazard in the mutual association of a large number of delinquents" ("Notes From the 22nd Annual Meeting," 1946–47, p. 49). General classroom tranquility far outbalanced the specter of stigma. The infrastructure of segregated special classes remained the most important vehicle for providing services to students with behavioral disorders right into the 1960s.

The Mental Hygiene Movement

The moral therapy of the 19th century broadened to mental hygiene under the leadership of Clifford Beers, a Yale graduate and author of *A Mind That Found Itself* (1908). Along with Adolf Heyer and William James, Beers founded the National Committee for Mental Hygiene in 1900. The goals were to educate the public, raise the standards for the care of mental illness, promote detection and prevention of mental illness, and establish child guidance clinics.

The mental hygiene movement was one of the social uplift movements designed "to improve the brains of people" (Hincks, 1919, p. 130). At the end of World War I, mental retardation constituted the central work and worry of mental hygienists. Concern about abnormal and social pathology gradually ceded to attention to the principles of mental health and the prevention of mental illness and social deviance. By the 1930s, mental hygiene was generally seen in terms of preventive and remedial work with at-risk students.

As the mental hygiene movement spread quickly, it soon included an emphasis on early detection and treatment of childhood disorders. The efforts then created the need for diagnostic and treatment facilities and fed directly into the birth of child guidance clinics. Simultaneously, it elevated the role of psychologists in treatment and prevention.

Psychological Clinics

Various educational and auxiliary social service programs and institutions adopted sophisticated diagnostic machinery with which to scientifically screen potentially troubled children and efficiently provide them with effective individual therapeutic services. Earlier forms of clinics had opened as private enterprises, sometimes associated with universities. At the University of Pennsylvania, Lightner Witmer marked the beginning of clinical psychology when he founded what may have been the first psychological clinic in 1896. Witmer studied parental neglect, environmental deprivation, physical disorders and defects, aphasia, disturbed laterality, word blindness, post-encephalitic behavioral difficulties, and other causes of educational and mental retardation (see Witmer, 1907).

In 1909, Chicago's model juvenile court was further enhanced by the adoption of a quasi-clinical approach with the establishment of the Juvenile Psychopathic Institute (later the Institute for Juvenile Research) for the clinical evaluation of delinquents established under the aegis of reformers of the Hull House Settlement. The Illinois clinic was directed by psychiatrist William Healy (1869–1963) assisted by Grace Fernald (1879–1950), the first psychologist to work in a child guidance clinic. In turn, the Juvenile Psychopathic Institute became the model for future clinics.

Many clinics were independent agencies operating under community chest or other philanthropic support. Others were founded in public school systems and in private schools. For example, a clinic in St. Louis following Healy's model opened in 1921. Healy's clinic looked at delinquency as a behavior problem of a neurotic nature (Healy, 1915a, 1915b; Healy & Bronner, 1969/1926). Future guidance clinics came to take a focus on delinquent and pre-delinquent or problem children (Cohen, 1983). They concerned themselves chiefly with emotional problems and behavior disorders in children.

Eight clinics opened across the country in the period 1922 to 1927 under the Program for the Prevention of Delinquency, which was begun in 1922 and financed by the Commonwealth Fund, a private foundation. This effort "greatly stimulated the school social work or visiting teacher movement as well as the development of child psychiatry and psychiatric social work" (Cohen, 1983, p. 198) and became the fulcrum for mental hygiene in the schools.

By 1930, both permanent and traveling child guidance clinics were a frequent sight, and child psychiatry was emerging as an established discipline. Variable as the services were, they created a trend. Children with emotional or behavioral disorders belonged to mental health professionals who fixed them and then sent them back to school (see Whelan & Kauffman, 1999).

Educational Considerations Today

Over a 150-year period, a wide array of supports, services, treatments, and interventions evolved to confront children who did not conform to the school's or to society's views of acceptable behavior. In general, continued failure appears to characterize the enterprise of assisting students with emotional and behavioral disorders. Programs have not been associated with generally positive outcomes (Eber, Nelson, & Miles, 1997), and this area is "perhaps one of our greatest failures' (Osher, Osher, & Smith, 1994, p. 7).

Moreover, the frequency and intensity of students' behavioral disorders have increased, and contemporary teachers in many industrial nations are facing far more challenging behaviors than did their predecessors (Gulchak & Lopes, 2007; Sutherland, Wehby, & Copeland, 2000). Some researchers (e.g., Larrivee, 2005) maintain that teachers will continue to face greater instructional, behavioral, and classroom management challenges as they strive to accommodate the increasing diversity of student learning styles and behavioral needs.

Students with emotional and behavioral disorders are the most underserved in the population. They are rated the least accepted and the most negatively stereotyped of all exceptionalities. This group is often the last group considered when inclusive options are available (Eber, Nelson, & Miles, 1997): those with serious behavioral disorders are often cited as exemplars of the times when inclusion is not appropriate. As compared with the total of all students with disabilities in the United States, almost four times as many students with behavioral disorders are educated in segregated settings and only half as many in general classrooms (Cheney & Muscott, 1996).

In the classroom, students with behavioral disorders are noted for their academic underachievement. Their levels of functioning are, on average, a year or more below grade level in all content areas (Reid, Gonzales, Nordness, Trout, & Epstein, 2004). Reading problems are rampant (Benner, Nelson, & Epstein, 2002; Glassberg, Hooper, & Mattison, 1999). Evidence also suggests that academic deficits actually worsen over time (Mattison, Hooper, & Glassberg, 2002; Nelson, Benner, Lane, & Smith, 2004). Less than 50% of these students graduate from high school (see Maag & Katsiyannis, 1998; Rylance, 1997). Few continue education after leaving high school and most do not link with services from community-based agencies, entering what "truly is an unwelcoming and cold world as adults" (Bullis & Cheney, 1999, p. 2). Their experiences are likely to be early school exit, unemployment, perhaps incarceration, and significant interpersonal problems.

Of the many behavior management strategies that have been available, rigorous empirical research has shown few to be effective. Newly touted interventions, often old wine in new bottles, consistently appear. The preferred "vintages" for the opening of the new millennium are behavioral regimes such as Functional Behavior Analysis, Positive Behavior Supports, and other science-based methods derived from behavioral psychology.

Motor Excess (Attention Deficit Hyperactivity Disorder)

A historical survey of the field of behavior disorders cannot ignore ADHD, which has become one of the most popular disabilities. Writers observe that "not since the establishment of learning disabilities as a special education category has a condition so captivated both the professional community and general public as has attention deficit hyperactivity disorder" (Reid, Maag, & Vasa, 1993, p. 198).

The terms used to classify ADHD have passed through several changes. Henrich Hoffman, a German physician, first spoke to hyperactivity in 1845; he willed to future workers the descriptor, "Fidgety Phil."[5] In a series of lectures presented to the Royal College of Physicians in England in 1902, Dr. Richard Still described 20 children he had seen in his practice. He characterized them as excessively emotional, defiant, aggressive, resistant to discipline, overtly active, and inattentive. On the other side of the Atlantic, an outbreak of encephalitis in North America from 1917 to 1918 left many children with "post-encephalitic disorder" characterized by impairments in attention, impulse control, and activity level, with memory and social problems (Barclay, 1990).

Brain pathology was posited as the likely etiology of such problems. Unsurprisingly, by the 1930s, children with the characteristics were referred to as brain injured or brain damaged. Some teachers talked about the runabout child; others described restlessness, which was shown through squirming in the chair, playing with the pencil, tapping with the feet, and the like (Challman, 1939). By the 1950, a group of terms was in use—*hyperkinetic impulse disorder, hyperactive child syndrome,* and *learning disability*. The acceptance that minimal brain damage was involved became common as professionals realized that many children who showed these behaviors had no history of brain trauma (Barclay, 1990).

The *Diagnostic and Statistical Manual*, second edition (DSM II; American Psychiatric Association, 1968) first categorized the syndrome as *hyperkinetic reaction of childhood*. In 1979, psychologist Robert Spitzer proposed the phrase *attention deficit disorder* and created a list of specific symptoms to make the diagnosis in children (Sanghavi, 2005). The American Psychiatric Association (APA), which adopted the term *attention deficit disorder* in the *DSM-III* in 1980, listed the behavioral symptoms of each feature separately and specified two primary subtypes based on the presence or absence of hyperactivity.

After 1980, every new version of *DSM* presented a revision of the criteria. In *DSM-III* (American Psychiatric Association, 1980), the APA changed the conceptualization of the disorder from one that was defined primarily as the presence of hyperactive-impulsive behaviors to one that reflected developmentally inappropriate levels of inattention, impulsivity, and hyperactivity. The revised APA edition, *DSM-III-R* (American Psychiatric Association, 1987), maintained the three features of inattention, impulsivity, and hyperactivity but listed three types of symptoms together in a composite syndrome called Attention Deficit Hyperactivity Disorder.

Between 1987 and 1994, the research data necessary to document the existence of a subtype of attention deficit without hyperactivity emerged. Using the markers of inattention, impulsivity, and hyperactivity, the *DSM-IV-TR* (American Psychological Association, 2000) described the subtypes—ADHD, predominantly inattentive; ADHD, predominantly hyperactive/impulsive type; ADHD, combined type; and ADHD, not otherwise specified .

The entire concept of ADHD has been challenged on a number of fronts (Winzer, 2007b). To some commentators, the diagnosis is more a function of political pressure and professional fad than student reality. They note that a clinical diagnosis of ADHD does not lead to special placement and does not predict responses to instruction. ADHD is not included among the 13 categories in the *IDEA of 1997*, and many hold that adding ADHD as a disability category is unnecessary because students who manifest symptoms severe enough to impair educational performance are currently eligible for educational services under existing categories such as learning disabilities or behavioral disorders (e.g., Ysseldyke, Algozzine, & Thurlow, 2000). Others object to ADHD because it may divert resources away from children with serious disabilities and because it is difficult to define and identify (Aleman, 1991).

Many of the drugs used to treat ADHD have been around for decades; the treatment was available long before the disorder was clearly conceptualized (Conrad, 2004). The story begins with Charles Bradley, a Rhode Island psychiatrist who in 1937 gave a stimulant drug, Benzedrine, to 30 children who were having various problems in school. Bradley noticed an overall improvement in the children's mood, activity level, and educational achievement. He noted that 14 of his patients showed a great increase in interest in school material (Bradley, 1937).

Ritalin was originally patented in 1950 by the CIBA Pharmaceutical Company and was promoted as an amphetamine without the more undesirable side effects. Ritalin was approved by the FDA in 1955; in 1961, it was approved for use with children. Since then, the use of the drug has increased dramatically and synthetic compounds have rendered more predictable effects of the drug. By 1996, American youngsters were consuming 90% of the world's Ritalin (Will, 1999). By 2002, data from the U.S. Drug Enforcement Agency showed an increase in the production of methylphenidate (Ritalin), 90% of which was consumed for treatment of ADHD (Snider, Busch, & Arrowood, 2003). Samuels (2006) reported that 2.5 million children in the United States from ages 4 to 17 were receiving medication for ADHD in 2003.

SERIOUS EMOTIONAL DISTURBANCE AND AUTISM SPECTRUM DISORDERS

References to children exhibiting serous emotional disorders tended to be brief and fleeting before the opening of the 19th century. The recognition of insanity in children seems to have been delayed until the various early training centers for mentally defective children were established.

In the first part of the 19th century, the psychotic child was an object of study, and a substantial body of knowledge on the subject was accumulated in that period (see Kanner, 1962; MacMillan, 1960). Esquirol (1845) demonstrated some concerns for emotionally disturbed children and documented aberrant behavior. Maudsley (1867, 1868), an authoritative writer on the subject of the psychotic child, offered a classification system. He described sensory-motor insanities such as epilepsies and choreic movements (such as toe walking) associated with hallucinations and delusions (Hare, 1962).

In the latter decades of the century, most practitioners disparaged the notion that emotional disturbance could affect children. They held that "insanity is rare in childhood, arising from the same sources whence it comes in the adult" (The New Jersey Training School, 1894, p. 37). Because it was commonly assumed that insanity was an adult disorder, childhood manifestations were either defined as illness and primarily dealt with by physicians or were presumed to be mental deficiency.

During the late 1880s, the mental health revolutions in America and Europe began to encompass the study of disturbed children. By 1910, it was no longer legitimate to ascribe insanity solely to the adult population or as only a subtheme of mental retardation. A clear demarcation emerged between the defective child—the "child who is suffering from a defect of the brain which is congenital or inherited, or caused by some serious illness such as meningitis or poliomyelitis"—and the child characterized as "mentally unbalanced or insane" (Mundie, 1919, p. 5).

Kraepelin (1896) outlined the disorder of dementia praecox, which included two clusters of symptoms—manic depressive psychoses and schizophrenia. Sancte de Sanctis applied concepts from adult psychopathology to children when he described the entity of dementia praecoxissima (dementia of childhood) (de Sanctis, 1908). His work, along with that of Eugen Blueler and others, contributed to the identification of schizophrenia as a distinct condition. By the 1930s, a number of researchers were working in the general area of childhood schizophrenia, and the loose strands of their efforts led Potter (1933) to describe the syndrome more carefully.

Credit for first identifying autistic behaviors in children and adults goes to Eugene Blueler (1857–1939), a Swiss psychiatrist, who in 1906 isolated specific nonverbal and nonrelating behaviors. Blueler used the word autistic as an adjective; it was not until Leo Kanner's major study in 1943 that an autistic syndrome, with autism as a noun, was identified in children (Blueler, 1911/1950; Kanner, 1943).

During this period, childhood schizophrenia and autism were often discussed in one breath. As a term, *schizophrenia* was used to classify all presumed childhood psychoses even though the extant research actually explored autism and other psychiatric disorders as well as schizophrenia. A disproportionate number of studies focused on infantile autism; research into the area of childhood and early adolescent schizophrenia was limited. However, the same researchers worked on both topics and often simply generalized the research, although much of the data had little direct relevance to the schizophrenic group.

Leo Kanner, a child psychiatrist at Johns Hopkins University, used the phrase "early infantile autism" to describe a set of symptoms he observed among a group of 11 children. In particular, he stressed the subjects' profound withdrawal from human contact and their obsessive desire for sameness in their environments. Kanner found the parents to all be highly intelligent and unusually high achievers, but also emotionally cold, aloof, and reserved in their interactions with their children. After Kanner, Mahler (1952) described "symbiotic infantile psychosis (overattachment to the mother). Others described children with "unusual sensitivity to sensory stimulation" (Kanner, 1962).

In 1944, Hans Asperger, a Viennese pediatrician, published "Die 'Autistischen Psychopathen' im Kindesalter." But Asperger's keen insights languished in Europe's postwar turmoil. Although his syndrome eventually became a popular research topic in Europe, it was not until 1981 that British psychiatrist, Lorna Wing, reintroduced Asperger's findings. In 1994, the *DSM-IV* (American Psychiatric Association, 1994) acknowledged Asperger's syndrome.

Following Kanner, many researchers agreed that parents created a climate that contributed to autism, although few attributed the condition solely to parent behavior. Kanner himself did not reject biological factors as contributory causes of autism but spoke to genetic footprints. Bruno Bettelheim, who established the Sonja Shankman Orthogenic School for severely emotionally disturbed children in 1944, did not deny the possibility of genetic or organic causes. But he chose to focus almost exclusively on psychogenic properties and speculated that that lack of adequate parenting was the primary factor in the onset of autism. Bettelheim (1967) used the term "refrigerator mother" to characterize the mothers of autistic children. An even more devastating term, "the schizophregenic mother" laid direct responsibility for the child's condition on the mother's failure to provide love and nurturance.

After World War II, the stress on studying pathology or psychopathology moved to studying practices for treating it. Within treatment regimes, a therapeutic mind-set dominated: it sanctified therapy, clinicalized behavior, and centered problems exclusively within the child. The preferred treatment was psychiatric in nature, based on the development of a therapeutic relationship between child and therapist. Treatment also required a change in the child's total living environment, usually placement in a residential setting.

During the 1970s, environmental theories were largely abandoned as emerging evidence indicated that children from emotionally deprived settings were not at higher risk for autism and that mothers of children with autism also had nondisabled offspring. With little to support environmental theories, autism emerged as an ideal candidate for biological study. Researchers turned their attention to investigating a range of biochemical, sensorimotor, neurological, and cognitive defects.

Educational Intervention

The first psychiatric hospital for children in the United States was established in Rhode Island in the 1930s. In the same decade, Lauretta Bender organized a children's ward at Bellevue Psychiatric Hospital in New York. She then convinced the New York Board of Education to provide two teachers for the classrooms she set up (Kauffman, 1981). Bellevue became a model for other psychiatric hospital schools.

By the late 1950s, many states had legislation pending relating to the education of emotionally disturbed children. Most states, however, saw the first step in providing services as one of legal exclusion. In most cases, "such legislation consisted of provisions for the exclusion of emotionally handicapped children from school, and educating them in their homes" (Bower, 1959–60, p. 183). It was not until the 1960s that public and professional concerns about emotionally and socially maladjusted children and about special provisions for them in the public schools were aired. Several factors intertwined. First, there was the general paradigm shift that characterized all interventions for people with special needs. Joined to this shift were strong attacks from both within and without psychiatry on the legitimacy of the medical paradigm of sickness when applied to the problems of children labeled as emotionally disturbed. Szatz (1961), one of the leading proponents within psychiatry for redefining both the conditions and the treatment regimes, viewed the problem more as a deficiency in adapting or an inability to cope than as mental illness.

Another salient factor sprang from the crisis in mental health manpower and in the time and resources required to train traditional mental health specialists in an interdisciplinary health model, a crisis brought to focus by the Albee studies in the late 1950s (Albee, 1959). From this starting point, Nicholas Hobbs (1966), one of the few scholars to recognize the dimensions of providing adequate services to emotionally disturbed children, developed models that saw mental health specialists replaced by educators. In addition, the passage of the Comprehensive Community Mental Health Centers Act (Pub. L. 88-164) in 1963 prompted the movement to develop community services. Finally, improving services for disturbed children became one of the original seven priorities of the U.S. Bureau of Education for the Handicapped (Moss, 1968).

Current Views on Autism Spectrum Disorders

Autism was long conceptualized as a severe emotional disturbance—a childhood psychosis. Ongoing etiological research in the 1970s showed autism to be a developmental disability, not an emotional disturbance. In 1978, under the Developmental Disabilities Act (Pub. L. 95-602), autism was removed from the federal list as a discrete category of exceptionality within the area of emotional disturbance. It was replaced, first, as "other health impaired" and then as a separate category in 1990.

Despite being the subject of massive research efforts, the entire area referred to as Autism Spectrum Disorders remains difficult to understand. A precise definition does not exist and the boundaries remain vague and undifferentiated. The enigmatic nature of autism perhaps explains why so many advocacy groups and societies have on their logos some depiction of a puzzle with a piece missing (Smulker, 2005).

In the past, Autism Spectrum Disorders were assumed to be comparatively rare. Initial surveys in 1966 estimated that the condition was found in about 4 to 5 people per 10,000. With troubling increases seen recently in the number of affected children worldwide, autism "has moved from being a relatively unrecognized disability to having a position of notoriety" (Simpson, 2001, p. 137). In the United States, estimates vary, but the federal government estimates that the risk for autism spectrum disorders is about 3.4 for every 1,000 children between the ages of 3 and 10 (Vedantam, 2006). In Canada, about 3,000 new cases are identified each year (Autism Society Canada, 2004). Asperger's syndrome is known as a relatively common developmental disorder; it is estimated that as many as 48 to 70 per 10,000 children could have Asperger's (Kadesjo, Gillberg, & Nagberg, 1999).

Some researchers (e.g., Fombonne, 2003; National Research Council, 2001) think that concern for the apparent increases in autism and related disorders can probably be accounted for by better diagnoses and a broader definition, not by dramatic changes in occurrence. Other epidemiologists see a real surge in absolute numbers. A study in California found an increase of 273% in the number of children with profound autism from 1987 to 1998, a number that continues to grow (Gross, 2003). In the California study, the increasing numbers could not be attributed to loosening diagnostic criteria, a rise in the number of children with cognitive impairments misdiagnosed as autistic, or a migration of children with autism to the state (Bird, 2002).

Given the multiple facets of the condition, intervention with children with Autism Spectrum Disorders is complex and not marked with enduring or consistent success. Applied Behavior Analysis (ABA), defined as "the study of behavior and the manipulation of contingencies and setting events to increase or decrease specific behaviors" (Choutka, Doloughty, & Zirkel, 2004, p. 96), appears to be a promising practice. The regime includes predictable routines, supportive teaching arrangements, an intensive structured program that breaks down lessons into small elements, planned transitions, and family involvement. The ABA program is intense—6 or more hours a day. Success is mediated by four variables: the age when treatment begins; the quantity of the therapy; the quality of therapy; and the intellectual potential of the child, for example, whether autism is coupled with intellectual disability. The earlier treatments are started, the better the chances that a child attains normal functioning levels (Dawson & Osterling, 1997).

The mounting optimism engendered by the ABA approach has brought its own set of effects. The pronounced emphasis on using the power of the courts to settle disputes of an educational nature was stimulated by ABA and by its general application to only preschool-aged children (see Nelson & Huefner, 2003).

SUMMARY AND THEMES

The historical literature surrounding social deviance belongs to many disciplines. Its varied facets suggest the disruptive social forces at work in rapid urbanization, the hierarchal nature of social organization, the ideology of child savers and reformers, the enduring enigma of youthful misconduct and delinquency, the development of the juvenile justice system, the evolving nature of social welfare, and the reluctance of school systems to confront difficult and recalcitrant youngsters. More broadly, the literature speaks to the responses to deviant behavior that have been proposed and propounded by legal, correctional, and educational agencies as well as to the manner in which interagency cooperation and planning were hampered by conflicting philosophies and goals. Most critically, the historical record addresses the essential dichotomy between the best interests of the school and the best interests of learners with behavioral and emotional problems, a dilemma that has plagued special education from the outset.

Four distinct stages in the treatment of juvenile malfeasance can be identified. In the era of vengeance or retribution, children were severely punished and were incarcerated with adult offenders. During the period of repression, lengthy stays in reformatories replaced sentences in the jails. Reform schools catered to a clientele of neglected and vagrant children as well as confirmed delinquents.

In the mid-19th century, recalcitrant and rambunctious children were loosely grouped within the labels of neglected, vagrant, and delinquent, primary categories that persisted in legal circles into the late 1950s. The 1870s saw a further shift in popular and philanthropic opinion that conceded to new theories about the rehabilitation of young people. Prevention overrode incarceration as reformers sought to alter the dangerous attitudes of confirmed delinquents and to halt the slide of problematic children. Attempted reformation or rehabilitation was the focus. Reformers who articulated the duty of the government to intervene in the lives of all children who might become a community crime problem often did not share delicate feelings about family integrity in their efforts to rescue children from pauperism and immorality. The rescue mission was accomplished in two ways: by removing the child or improving the family.

Industrial schools combined humanitarian concerns for children with coercive practices to control deviant behavior. Institutionalization served to sanction and hinder youthful crime and was a response to the highly visible evidence of need, destitution, and dependence. Faulty nurture was the fundamental assumption; prevention the basic credo; reintegration the chief goal. By the close of the 19th century, altered perceptions of child rearing and child saving saw the family again applauded as the most natural setting to develop proper moral and social values.

When the common schools were born, school systems, lacking compulsory attendance laws, did not force children to attend. Indeed, nonattendance was tolerated, even celebrated, as an informal means by which to exclude children who did not fit expected characteristics of pupils. By the opening decades of the 20th century, compulsory laws were supplemented by juvenile courts, a social welfare system, and an increasing array of supports, services, treatment regimes, and interventions.

Juvenile legislation represented a critical stage in the history of child welfare. The concrete origin of special court procedures for children is often dated from the establishment of the Chicago Children's Court in 1899. The juvenile court nestled comfortably with the progressive reforms of child labor laws and other welfare policies and was widely publicized as a breakthrough in the prevention of delinquency. The creation of a separate court explicitly distinguished between the juvenile and the adult justice systems. Juvenile law provided for suspended sentences, probation with public and private agencies, and separate detention and trial.

Educational intervention to confront the educational needs of behaviorally and emotionally maladjusted children proved glacially slow. Schools were often antagonized by, and resisted providing services for, recalcitrant and rambunctious students. Educational wariness was even more pronounced for severe emotional disturbance, a condition that was not a concern of the courts and, largely ignored by the schools, was left chiefly as the responsibility of medicine and psychology.

It was not until the 1960s that special education for disturbed children was on the way to becoming an established discipline.

NOTES

1. The first historical evidence of a reformatory comes from the Hospital of St. Michael in Rome in 1586, which was designed for destitute and runaway boys. The next advance was made by Pestalozzi who tried to establish a home school with industrial training for endangered children (Barnard, 1857). The history of "ragged schools" in Great Britain shows that some of them evolved from industrial day schools in the 1830s and 1840s to closed residential industrial schools in the 1850s. The first Industrial School Act was passed by the British Parliament in 1857.

2. Letter to Victoria Industrial School, 1912, original punctuation. The Victoria Industrial School files are located in the Ontario Archives.

3. Brenzel (1980) describes separate state-funded reform institutions for girls that were originally designed to provide family training. Over the course of the 19th century, the institutional mode shifted to custodial care and harsh disciplne.

4. From a 1912 *Toronto World* newspaper clipping located with Victoria Industrial School files, Ontario Archives. Although the focus of this section is on industrial schools for dependent and delinquent children, other institutions with similar designations existed. For example, both the United States and Canada established industrial schools for Indian children. Schools that stressed manual training, often for children with physical disabilities, were occasionally designated as industrial schools, for example, Boston's Industrial School for Crippled and Deformed Children (see Chapter 7).

5. In 1845, Hoffman wrote a children's book—*Der Struwwelpeter (Slovenly Peter)*—with several stories about children with behavior problems. "Die Geschichte vom Zappel-Phillip" (The Story of Fidgety Phillip) is the story that characterizes "Fidgety Phil."

Chapter 7

Going to Public School

$\mathbf{A}$s the 20th century opened, large institutional settings such as the American Asylum (American School for the Deaf) continued to thrive. Special classes and alternate programs and schools sprang up. The special segregated classes, destined to become the backbone and the chief bone of contention in special education for almost all of the next century, arrived largely unheralded. Once in place after about 1910, however, growth was dramatic and sustained. The most heavily funded programs in both the United States and Canada addressed mild mental retardation.

Intervention for children with exceptionalities assumes a certain systemic approach and a particular conceptual framework concerning origins and causes. But the systems and structures of early special education were not fixed; rather, they were constantly shifting. Moreover, research and writing on the nature, etiology, and epidemiology of disabilities in children as well as the types and breadth of intervention was extremely uneven. The literature shows many instances of key silences or omissions. History also provides much speculation and personal opinion as well as much less of the research necessary for understanding exceptional children and for theorizing about curricula and behavioral interventions. As Samuel Kirk noted in 1950, "What we know about exceptional children is a by product of research from the basic sciences. There is very little educational research pointed toward the solution of problems in the education of exceptional children" (p. 233).

Even when research findings were available, the traditions of education research were not themselves strongly aligned with effective models linking research and practice. "When it comes to its consumers," observed a 1937 author, "Special Education research" was "a complicated and sometimes conflicted, and always challenging task" (Marinies, 1937, p. 9; original punctuation). Teachers, chiefly women, often found the findings of the mainly male cadre of researchers irrelevant to daily classroom functioning, and a glaring disconnect between research and practice began to develop (see Chapter 9).

The period from 1910 to 1960 is the most informative with respect to special classes and the students served. Examination of the early developments suggests

a number of points. For one thing, the lack of an overarching theoretical framework or theoretical base made the development and growth of segregated classes
a vulnerable and shaky proposition. This observation is not to dispute the fact that
special classes became the unchallenged settings for students identified as having
special needs. Rather, it points out that uncritical applications of constructs meant
that as the labels used to identify special classes grew, they tended to reflect the ad
hoc nature of the movement as well as stunted and incomplete knowledge about
the clients. Teachers were often innovative and creative in their interventions, but
little existed in the way of consistent and universal curriculum.

Much attention was directed toward some groups, particularly those with
mild mental retardation, while others are largely ignored or subsumed within
larger categories, such as children who were hard of hearing. Similarly, spurts in
interest characterized the field, and the literature shows many peaks and valleys
in the foci on particular groups. In the first half of the century, for example, mild
mental retardation attracted considerable interest. During the 1970s, the problems
of learning disabilities became increasingly engrossing. As this change occurred,
the relative high attention to mental retardation shifted to relative neglect to the
extent that Haywood (1979) was led to ask, "What happened to mild and moderate mental retardation?" Autism gained special favor during the 1980s; the next
decade witnessed broad interest in ADHD.

Research, special classes, curriculum, and disability itself, cannot be separated
from the social context. For some groups—most specifically those who were deaf,
those in the ever flexible category of mild mental retardation, and later, those
deemed to be learning disabled—the word *education* extended far beyond the
boundaries of classroom and school, although in quite different ways. In the area
of hearing impairment, distinct and opposing views of deafness surfaced in different periods. A change in conceptual construction signaled a change in legitimate
authority: the prevailing construction of deafness determined the responses of the
hearing world, status or marginalization of those who were deaf, and the influence
of the deaf community. Mild mental retardation, with its fluctuating definitions
and changing IQ cutoff levels, was a socially constructed category that incorporated children affected as much by environmental variables as by cognitive dysfunction. When the field of learning disabilities was formed, the projected clientele
were White middle-class children who were failing in school for no immediately
discernable reasons.

It is not possible to discuss the range of special settings and programs that
extended from steamer classes for immigrant children to Opportunity A classes
for those who were gifted, nor can every disability category eventually subsumed under the special education banner be fully addressed here. The following
discourse is essentially a simple version of a complex context—unavoidably a syn-
opsis of interventions for various groups identified as requiring special education services. This chapter consciously eschews any sustained examination of the
literature; the mapping of such diverse and complex territory is only partial, the
historical data abbreviated, and only the most critical facets addressed. Historical
circumstances and professional issues involved in the assumption of educational

responsibility for children with special needs are singled out in the discussion that follows for the purpose of providing the spirit and sense of the developments. The chapter is structured around some of the different categories that were served in the first half of the 20th century.

DEAF STUDENTS GO TO SCHOOL

The experiences of those who were deaf is far more complex than a mere educational journey. For this group, the persistence of the interplay between residential schools, the deaf community, and education reform movements is striking throughout different eras.

Deaf students were the first to be offered intervention within the evolving practice of special education. From the outset, the traditions of the education of the deaf were set and remained directly within residential contexts. Once in institutional settings, deaf people rapidly began to identify deafness as a personal and primary trait that propelled them into an identifiable culture. As the residential institutions became cradles of deaf culture, they stimulated the formation of the American Deaf community, making the deaf population the only so-called disabled group to form into a discrete, identifiable, and politically viable cultural group.

Few areas within the total educational structure manifested so marked a shift in philosophy, models, and techniques as did the education of deaf students. Beginning in the 1860s, the notion of sign as the natural language of deaf people came under heavy attack by advocates of oral modes of instruction. After this widespread and rapid philosophical shift, not only the hearing establishment serving deaf people but also deaf people themselves developed two different points of view, two different conceptions of deafness and the roles of deaf people, and two radically different agendas.

Alexander Graham Bell, one of the most critical players, derided deafness as culture founded on community and communication. Instead, he assumed an audiological construction and viewed deafness as a handicap to be overcome. Bell similarly disparaged the consequences of methodologies founded on sign language. He sought to unmake the deaf community and eliminate deaf culture through the medium of oralism.

According to W. W. Turner (1848), the vast majority of deaf people were uneducated and unmarried until about 1840. Once they became segregated into institutions for schooling, most of them married, and the majority chose deaf partners (Tinkle, 1933). "The constant selection of the deaf in marriage," Bell cried, "is fraught with dangers to the community" (Bell 1884b, p. 74). The best way to prevent such marriages was to teach deaf children orally so that they would be made as like their hearing counterparts as possible. Again and again, Bell repeated the call, "Let us banish the sign-language from our schools" (Bell, 1884b, p. 58).[1]

It is hardly surprising that many deaf people found Bell's philosophy and pedagogy inimical to their best interests. Adult deaf people saw oralism as an implausible ideology; they rejected its faddisms and idealism. In a meeting of deaf people in 1900, the group resolved that "oralism, exclusive of any other methods for the deaf of different mental capacities, be condemned" (Ontario Institution for the Education and Instruction of the Deaf and Dumb, 1900, p. 9). Bell's mission patronized deaf people; under his audiological construction, they were unable to uphold their own views and owned fewer rights. The values of those with the power established the system; those organizing it reiterated the values and translated them into practical instructional approaches. Those being served had little input. Hearing teachers reserved for themselves the seat of enlightenment, although they differed in how much potential and innate intelligence the deaf possessed and how fixed the traits were. Deaf people were allowed "practically no voice in directing matters" (Tillinghast, 1906, p. 466). The interests and aspirations of deaf people, when accounted for at all, were weighed against the perspective of more powerful groups of educators and oral advocates and backed eventually by the power and authority of the state.

As the controversy on communication raged from about 1870 on, the continued commitment of many institutional instructors, administrators, and deaf adults to enforce sign language as the fundamental solution to deafness defiantly opposed the oral contentions—to little avail. The first decade of the new century witnessed a rapid conversion to oralism. In 1907, the Ontario school's annual report noted that "among educators of the deaf the preponderance of opinion and of observed results is in favor of oralism, so far at any rate, as related to the large proportion of the pupils" (Ontario Department of Education, 1907, p. 510). In the same year, 96% of American schools for the deaf were designated as oral schools under oral methods of training (Crouter, 1907). It was reported that students "receive all instruction, of whatever character, by and through speech and lip-reading, and not through the medium of the sign-language or the manual alphabet" (de Land, 1919, p. 665). By 1919, there were 66 schools for the deaf in North America, of which all but six taught some speech (Numbers, 1974).

As an educational policy and approach, oralism reigned for the next half century. The model viewed deafness from the perspective of pathology—abnormality of structure and function characteristic of disease. The field, in its efforts to handle pathology, became populated by the "troubled-persons industries" (Lane, 1997, p. 157) with the mission to prevent, compensate for, or cure deafness. It was legitimized by the invention of hearing aids in the 1920s and by the growth of the fields of otology, microsurgery, and audiology. Educators sought to normalize deaf children by eradicating sign language and stressing speech, speechreading, and auditory training. The major criterion for success was intelligible speech (Miller & Moores, 2000). The orthodoxy of sign, the "beloved language" of the deaf (Schein, 1989, p. 29), became the new heresy. Sign language faced a barrage of hostility, ridicule, and oppression, relegated to the status of a ghetto slang. Together with the culture of deafness, it was driven underground.

A brief excursion into the world of deaf teachers illustrates with some precision the changing ideologies in deaf education. In 1852, deaf males formed about 40% of the teaching staff; by 1870, deaf teachers were about 42% of the teaching personnel in North American schools for the deaf (Jones, 1918). As oral advocates seized dominance of the profession, deaf teachers were jostled to the side. In the oral-ists' eagerness to obtain intellectual results and prove the validity of their mode, they made it one of the tenets of their philosophy that no deaf person should be employed in any school for the deaf in any capacity whatsoever (Draper, 1889). Deaf people who wanted to teach were not admitted into the graduate program at Gallaudet College for teachers. Hearing applicants could practice teach at the Kendall Demonstration School on Gallaudet's campus. Deaf candidates could not practice at all; they could do only individual tutoring.

The late 1950s witnessed a retransformation of deaf education that began with generous federal funding together with enabling legislation. Between 1954 and 1970, more than 100 projects relating directly or indirectly to the rehabilitation of deaf people were funded (Adler, 1991). In 1964, the federal government commis-sioned a report on the status of services to deaf students (Babbidge, 1965). The Bab-bidge report pointed to multiple problems and, joined to a later report, deemed the education of deaf and hard of hearing students as unsatisfactory (Easterbrooks, 1999). For example, pupils ages 6 to 20 attending schools and programs for the hearing impaired in the United States were surveyed, and even by age 16, many were found to have achieved a reading age of only about 5.0 and a vocabulary level of 3.7 at age 16 (Gentile, 1969).

Until the 1960s, American Sign Language (ASL) was viewed as an invented language somewhat in the vein of the later fictional or artificial language systems associated with the Klingons in Star Trek (see Davis, 1997). In the decade of the 1960s, a veritable explosion of research from the fields of linguistics, psycholinguis-tics, and sociolinguistics created new conceptions about language for both hearing and deaf children. The work of William Stokoe (1960) demonstrated that ASL was indeed a language with its own set of syntactic, semantic, and pragmatic rules that often include aspects of processing that have no analogy in spoken English and do not conform in many cases with rules of spoken English.[2]

New humanitarian movements in the 1960s played a significant role in chang-ing the attitudes and perceptions of society toward disability. Deaf people tuned in: they inserted their own perspectives and began to stress their own charac-teristics, status, and image. In 1972, they organized Deaf Pride, which sought to counter years of self deprecation, shame, isolation, and passivity among members of the Deaf community, which they now referred to with a capital *D*. Colorado began Deaf Awareness Week, and many other states followed suit (Gannon, 1991). Organizations such as the National Association for the Deaf became increasingly more vocal about the rights of deaf people. Public attention focused on Gallaudet University in March 1988 when students protested to demand that the board of trustees appoint the first deaf president in the school's history.

Coming full circle from the 1850s, it was accepted that deaf people "constitute a legitimate cultural and linguistic group" (Reagan, 1988, p. 1). The Deaf com-munity was not a claim about hearing status: it was an expression of the self-recognition that is defining for all minority or ethnic groups. Within the cultural framework, what educators called disability, the Deaf community called ability. To label deaf people as disabled demonstrated a failure to understand that such people were not disabled in any way within their own community. Instead, it is an asset in the Deaf community to be deaf in behavior, values, knowledge, and fluency in ASL (Lane, 1993).

Throughout the 1980s, educational programs changed and expanded, communication modes became more flexible, and the skills and competencies required by teachers broadened. Teachers of "hearing impaired" students required not only the same repertoire of skills as all teachers but also a considerable number of techniques peculiar to the education of hearing impaired students, specifically in the areas of speech, audition, and particular communication modes that required using manual methods such as ASL or Total Communication.

It must not be assumed that once the long battle concerning oralism and manualism ended that educators of the deaf reached consensus. Rather, a debate on communication modes persists, although the arena has changed to a struggle between (a) advocates of ASL and bilingual-bicultural education (see later discussion) and (b) proponents of various manually coded communication approaches such as Signing Essential English, etc. At the same time, the deaf community battles specific types of educational and medical interventions.

Cochlear implants—audiological surgical techniques designed to dramatically improve the hearing status of an individual—"have met tremendous opposition from the Deaf community" (McKinley & Warren, 2000, p. 252). Founded on the belief that children's birthright of silence should not be violated, many deaf advocates consider the devices as genocidal to deaf culture (Lane & Bahan, 1998). They argue that the implantation of children conflicts with the right of the deaf cultural minority to exist and flourish.

The reform movement of inclusive education, so dear to many educators and parents of children with disabilities, is viewed by the Deaf community as a brutal type of assimilation that is inimical to their strength and propagation. They describe inclusive schooling as "forced assimilation"—an "unnatural attempt to make deaf persons hearing" (Elliott, 1993, p. 11). Centrally concerned with the problem of intergenerational renewal, the Deaf community supports a strong separate special education system in which residential schools serve as the primary and sustaining factor in the Deaf community.[3] Further, they assert, because deaf people constitute a legitimate cultural and linguistic group, "they are entitled to educational programs which take this into account" (Reagan, 1988, p. 1). Within the residential framework, bilingual-bicultural education (bi-bi) is promoted.

The bi-bi approach, first explored at Gallaudet University in the 1970s (Swanwick, 1998), allows deaf children to mingle daily within a sign environment. ASL is the major medium of instruction in preschool through the primary grades, with a focus on sign production and comprehension of signs and written English (bilingual). Advocates also see the world of deafness as distinctive, rewarding, and worth preserving, and they focus on exposing pupils not only to the standard cultures of the spoken word but also to the rich heritage of folklore, literature, customs, and values found within the signing world (bicultural). Bi-bi, therefore, stresses immersion in a program where many of a child's experiences are couched within deaf culture, and the interaction with deaf peers and role models both in and outside the classroom provide "for the self-esteem and emotional well-being of [the] deaf child" (Gallimore & Woodruff, 1996, p. 93). Today, an increasing number of schools for the deaf are using the practices of bi-bi education. Miller and Moores (2000) present data to indicate that bi-bi education is already a reality in 75% of the largest programs for deaf students.

A clear picture of inclusion for students with severe hearing losses in general classrooms has not yet emerged. Experts contend that "deafness is arguably, . . . the most difficult [impairment] for teachers to deal with, since in its severe form it is not so much the deprivation of sound but the deprivation of language which creates a barrier to learning" (Palmer & Sellars, 1993, p. 37). Many general classroom teachers are not very knowledgeable about hearing impairment and it is not unusual for teachers to express anxiety about working with a student with a hearing impairment in a general setting, especially if adequate communication and social supports are lacking (see Jones, Clark, & Soltz, 1997). In general, what is seen as the most effective educational setting for a specific child is determined by (a) linguistic needs; (b) the severity of the loss and the potential for using residual hearing with or without amplification; (c) academic level; (d) social, emotional, and cultural needs, including appropriate interaction and communication with peers; and (e) communication needs, including the child and the family's preferred mode of communication (Marschark, 1993).

Almost all of the concern in the area of hearing impairment was devoted to deaf people. The phrase *hard of hearing* entered the lexicon after 1867 and came into common use after World War II. A true audiometer, providing accurate parameters of loss across frequencies and intensity levels did not emerge until the 1920s, at about the same time as the first mechanical hearing aids. With technological advances, consistent definitions emerged. Generally, hard of hearing people were described as those who could obtain information through auditory means; deaf individuals were unable to use the auditory channel with or without a hearing aid. Special classes for hard of hearing children emerged in the 1920s. By 1936, reports noted that efforts on behalf of hard of hearing children "have risen from a state of chaos to a workable program" (Peck & Samuelson, 1936, p. 116).

CHILDREN WITH VISUAL IMPAIRMENTS GO TO SCHOOL

People who were blind did not form identifiable communities as did their deaf counterparts. Their tale is focused far more on solely education. Three points stand out in the history of education services for the blind population: the myriad agencies and legislation devoted to serving the group, the relative ease with which integration into general classrooms was accomplished, and the fruitful relationship with technology.

A major spurt in interest and intervention occurred when soldiers affected or blinded by mustard gas returned from World War I. Guide dogs were introduced in 1928, new agencies such as the American Foundation for the Blind formed, and federal legislation promoted braille as a reading aid. Similar advances ensued after World War II. Hoover introduced the white cane, and the term *low vision* was introduced when a distinction from totally blind was necessary to tailor specific rehabilitation services for veterans returning to the work force (Goodrich & Bailey, 2000).

Throughout the 19th century, the segregation of those who were blind in institutions was the common educational mode. However, the trend in America toward loosening the institutional element in the education of blind students arrived early. By 1900, the practice of institutionalization came to be seen as only a step toward integration with the seeing community (Best, 1934).

Screening programs for visual impairment began in 1899 when Connecticut used the Snellen chart as a measure of visual acuity. Accurate screening and the relative ease with which children who were blind and visually impaired could be accommodated in the public schools contributed to the early establishment of special classes, which were designated as braille classes or, more commonly, sight saving classes. Day classes for visually impaired students opened in Cincinnati (1905), Milwaukee (1907), Boise (1909), Cleveland (1909), New York (1909), and Boston (1909). Classes grew quickly, from 260 in 1925 to 476 in 1935 (Wooden, 1936–37). After this period of initial growth, the number of public school classes and the number of children attending them reached a plateau that lasted until about 1948 (Lowenfeld, 1956). Need exceeded supply, however, and by 1940, it was estimated that one in every 500 children needed sight saving classes and that one in every 2,000 needed to learn braille (Frampton & Rowell, 1940). Until the 1960s, it was believed that visually impaired children should conserve their vision so as not to "wear it out"; the need for sight saving was primary.

By 1910, 4.5% of children who were blind were in public school programs. By 1913, students who were visually impaired were beginning to be cooperatively caught by specialists and general classroom teachers. Students spent part of the day in general classrooms and part in sight saving classes (Abraham, 1976; Kirk & Gallagher, 1979; Lowenfeld, 1956). Before 1949, however, less than 10% of all blind children in the United States attended public school classes. From 1949 on—the year when the first retrolental fibroplasia (retinopathy of prematurity)[4] cases reached school age—the total number of children who were blind in the United States began to increase, and public school classes and their populations grew much faster than residential schools. By 1956, about 25% of blind children attended their local public schools (Lowenfeld, 1956).

Meyer (1934) observed that "there is no clear cut and well defined philosophy underlying the education of the blind child" (p. 44). Commonalities were found in the use of braille as a critical reading aid and in a stress on orientation and mobility. Until the 1960s, there was consensus with respect to the need for sight saving measures.

The education of children with visual impairments embarked early on its fruitful relationship with technology. In the 1930s, there appeared "certain new devices in the field of the education of the blind; such as the talking book, the printing visagraph and the dictaphone" (Bryne, 1934, p. 44). By the 1970s, some researchers felt that high-tech advances would eliminate the need for braille completely.

Despite contentious debate, braille emerged as traditional medium of literacy for those who were blind. After its acceptance in North America in the 1890s, braille was widely used. During the 1960s, the orthodoxy altered its approach from saving sight to a strong emphasis on the use of residual vision. The number of braille users declined dramatically. In 1955, more than 50% of all people with severe visual impairments used braille. In 1963, about 55% of legally blind children were using braille. By 1978, the rate dropped to 18%, and in 1989, only 12% used braille. By 1994, only 9.45% were braille users; in 1995, the number was 9.62% (De Witt, 1991; Schroeder, 1996).

Contemporary scenarios find an increased emphasis on braille. Both educators and adults who are blind recognize that it is important to have more than one literacy medium, and they acknowledge that the ability to read and write braille maximizes students' chances of educational and vocational success and lays the foundation they need to benefit from many new technological advances (Stephens, 1989). Data also suggest that braille is not only a tool of literacy but also an identity mechanism for adults who are blind, a symbol of independence and competence, even group identity (Schroeder, 1996).

There is not another field that has benefited as much from technological advances as has that of visual impairment. More than 2,000 technical aids, accessories, and devices exist for reading, mobility and orientation, and magnification. In the classroom, a student may use adaptive computer peripherals such as a voice output system, a specialized keyboard, a screen-enlarging device, a four-track tape recorder/player, a laptop braille computer, a print enlarger machine, a talking calculator, and various types of reading aids (Winzer, 2007b).

CHILDREN WITH INTELLECTUAL DISABILITIES GO TO SCHOOL

A redefinition and reorientation of intellectual disability began in the 1880s on a number of fronts: use of the new term, *feeble mindedness*; the discovery of the construct of moral imbecile and the parallel concept of degeneracy; the admission into the institutions of people with greater disabilities; state intervention into admission policies; and the support of lifelong segregation. From that time on, psychologists, educators, and sociologists expended great energy on issues relating to intellectual disability, and the population of so-called mentally subnormal people in North America grew to prodigious proportions (Penrose, 1949/1966).

Even though special classes for children with intellectual disabilities were central in special education, the broader field of mental retardation in many ways ultimately and critically retained its affiliation with the institutional side. Segregation was a lifelong enterprise. On a poignant note, a teacher from the New Jersey Training School at Vineland in 1942 narrated how "Henry Koenig was our first pupil—a tiny boy about five years old. After all these years [54 years] Henry is still at the Training School" (Vernon, 1942, p. 22).

The custodial nature persisted right into the 1960s, although the idea of the institution as a conveyor belt back to the community was partially resurrected. A 1940 observer wrote that

> [t]he population of an institution for the mentally handicapped and epileptics (not insane) may be classified as 1. Permanent custodial cases; 2. Permanent cases trainable for institutional maintenance duties; 3. Alternating parole and institutional cases of unstable physical and emotional equipment; 4. Temporary cases trainable for gainful employment, and 5. Temporary cases not trainable for public employment, but returnable to their families. (Springsteen, 1940, p. 54)

During the period of special class ascendancy, which began in about 1910, mild mental retardation was positioned in a central place. The category absorbed more classes and more teachers, and attracted more funding and legislation, than did any other group. Much of special education curriculum and methodology was designed for students in the category.

Simple statistics clearly spell out the manner in which mild mental retardation was the center of attention for years. In 1919, there were 75 classes; by 1941, there were 141 classes with an enrollment of more than 22,000 pupils (Johnson, 1962). In 1946, 13 states had legislation concerning special education opportunities for children deemed mentally retarded; by 1955, 40 states had some form of legislation pertaining to the education of this group. Between 1948 and 1966, the number of students with retardation served in the public schools increased by 400% (all but 10% of those provided services in 1963 were taught essentially in full-time classes). By 1966, 89.5% of school districts provided programs, with the great majority in the form of self-contained classes (see Polloway, 1984). Teacher training programs directed most attention toward those who were labeled educably mentally retarded (EMR). When Blackman (1958) undertook a study of postsecondary survey courses of exceptional children, 26 schools responded to his questionnaire. In those schools, the topic of mental retardation topped the list in terms of (a) the number of courses taught at the undergraduate and graduate levels, (b) the frequency of journal use with respect to particular topic, and (c) the settings for field trips related to a topic.

From the time of the establishment of the field of mental retardation, the key problem was accurately identifying the clientele. Descriptions were never straightforward but always beset by ambiguities, particularly at the upper end of the spectrum of cognitive dysfunction. Much vacillation existed in the setting of criteria for defining children with low academic functioning as opposed to those with poor performance that was a result of general intellectual disability. The contradiction is intriguing. Attempts at understanding mental retardation were thwarted, on the one hand, by arbitrary statements and, on the other, by the fluid nature of the concept.

When the first systematic attempts to help those who were retarded were made in the mid-19th century, the label "feeble minded" replaced "fool" and "idiot." Nineteenth-century ideas were then quickly elaborated into a series of categories of mental defect. People were variously described as idiots, morally insane, moral idiots, moral imbeciles, feeble minded, and morons. By 1912, the term *mental sub-normality* had surfaced in the United Kingdom, soon matched by the category of mental retardation in the United States. After that, the construct and the definitions of mental retardation were periodically revised by the American Association on Mental Retardation (AAMR). The 1921 definition of mental retardation has been revised nine times (Scruggs & Mastroprieri, 2002).

Goddard's "feeble mindedness" and its subcategories persisted into the late 1940s. Alternate terminology in the 20th century included terms such as *backward, laggards, mentally deficient, mentally defective,* and *mentally retarded.* Edgar Doll, who provided what became accepted as the standard definition of mental retardation in the 1940s (see Chapter 5) placed the burden of retardation on the constitutional nature of the individual. Such individuals, said Doll, showed "the inherent incapacity for managing themselves independently beyond the marginal level of subsistence" (Doll, 1941a, p. 218). In 1955, Sloan and Birch offered the severity levels of mild, moderate, severe, and profound in relation to mental retardation; this hierarchy was adopted in 1959 by the American Association on Mental Deficiency and formally accepted in 1961. The criterion of immutability of functioning was abandoned; adaptive behavior was formally added to the construct of mental retardation in 1961.

Before 1962, the IQ level determining mental retardation was variable, a potent indicator of the socially constructed nature of EMR. Generally, children who fell between one and two standard deviations below the norm (IQ 85 and below) were included in the EMR category. The definition adopted by the American Association on Mental Deficiency in 1973 limited the category to those with an IQ of 70 or less. With this change, 80% of the defined population was eliminated (Zetlin & Murtaugh, 1990).

Language, terms, and definitions are powerful tools that gird the formation of concepts and notions about persons who are exceptional (Winzer, 2007b). The problem of terminology, while most acute in the field of intellectual disabilities, was not restricted to this area, however. All the classification systems used by special educators evolved gradually, haphazardly, and inconsistently, and a single universally accepted method of describing and grouping different groups of children with certain exceptional conditions did not, and does not, exist. Almost every category in special education displayed marked changes in descriptors as more was learned about exceptionalities and as special classes expanded. Some of the terms had relatively short-lived but headline-making histories; others persisted for decades. Different terms are shown in Table 7.1.

Most of the curriculum that was developed and implemented for special classes focused on children labeled as mildly mentally retarded. As discussed in Chapter 4, curriculum was often of uncertain validity and muddled meaning. Special education was "a cottage industry" where teachers generally cobbled together programs for those who were mentally retarded (Goldstein, 1984, p. 59). Relatively little continuity existed over the 12 to 20 years of schooling guaranteed most children, although they could remain with the same teacher for 4 years (Goldstein, 1984).

Table 7–1

Constructions and Terminology of Disability

Area of Exceptionality	Historical Terms	Contemporary Terms

Attention-Deficit-Hyperactivity Disorder	Hyperactive
	Fidgety Phils
	   (Hoffman, 1845)
	Post-encephalitic disorder
	Runabout children
	Restless children
	Hyperkinetic disorder
	   (American Psychiatric
	   Association, 1968)
		Attention Deficit
		   Disorder
		Attention Deficit-
		   Hyperactivity
		   Disorder

Autism Spectrum Disorders	Juvenile insane
	Autistic behavior
	   (Blueler, 1911/1950)
	Infantile autism
	   (Kanner, 1943)
	Symbiotic infantile psychosis
	   (Mahler, 1952)
		Autism
		Asperger's syndrome

Behavioral Disorders	Neglected, vagrant, and
	   delinquent
	Waifs and strays
	Friendless or uncared for
	   children
	Ragged urchins, guttersnipes,
	   blackguards, reprobates,
	   street Arabs
	Incorrigibles
	Aggressive pre-delinquents,
	   socially handicapped
	Unsocialized aggressive,
	   socialized delinquent,
	   over-inhibited
		Behavioral-emotional
		   disorders

Deafness	Deaf and dumb Deaf mute	Deaf Hearing impaired Hard of hearing

Emotional Disturbance	Ideational insanity, amentia,
	   simulative idiocy
	   (Howe, 1848)
	Sensory motor insanities
	   (Maudsley, 1867, 1868)
	Juvenile insane
	Dementia praecox
	   (Kraepelin, 1896)
	Dementia praecoxissima
	   (de Sanctis, 1908)
	Mentally unbalanced, insane
	   (Mundie, 1919)
		Emotionally disturbed
		Psychotic
		Childhood
		   schizophrenia

Gifted, Creative, and Talented	Genius More than average ability Brilliant children Pupils of supernormal ability	Gifted, creative, and talented Creative and talented

Table 7–1 (*continued*)

Constructions and Terminology of Disability

Area of Exceptionality	Historical Terms	Contemporary Terms
Intellectual Disability	Idiots, imbeciles (Esquirol, 1838, 1845) Low grade, or idiots; middle grade, or fools; high grade, or simpletons (Howe, 1848) Congenital, accidental, or developmental feeble minded, idiots (Down, 1866) Moral imbeciles, feeble minded, imbeciles, idiots (Kerlin, 1879, 1887) Backward, feebly gifted (Barr, 1904a) De debile, imbeciles, idiots (Binet & Simon, 1908) Backward, morons, imbeciles, idiots (Goddard, 1910) Laggards (Ayres, 1909) Mild, moderate, severe, profound (Sloan & Birch, 1955) Slow learners, educable mentally retarded, trainable mentally retarded, custodial mentally retarded (Davitz, Davitz, & Lorge, 1964)	Mild, moderate, severe, profound Needs-intermittent, limited, pervasive, extensive Multiply disabled, pervasive developmental disability
Learning Disabilities	Congenitally word blind (Hinshelwood, 1917) Strephosymbolia (Orton, 1927) Brain crippled, brain injured, minimal brain dysfunction (Strauss, 1939, 1941a, 1941b) Neurophrenia (Doll, 1951) Pseudo mentally retarded (Burks, 1957) Strauss syndrome (Stevens & Birch, 1957) The other child (Lewis, 1951, 1960)	Learning disabilities Specific learning disabilities
Physical Disabilities	Brain injured, brain injured child, brain crippled, Little's disease, cerebral palsy	Physically disabled, orthopedically disabled, cerebral palsy, specific conditions such as muscular dystrophy, spina bifida

The amazing growth of the field of learning disabilities and the altered IQ cut-off levels for mild retardation in 1973 brought a significant change in the population served under the EMR label. A kind of tension developed, with increasing prevalence rates of learning disabilities and interest in that field weaning consideration with respect to the altered IQ criteria.

During the 1960s and early 1970s, mild intellectual disability and learning disabilities were central foci. Studies comparing EMR samples with samples of those who were not retarded—referred to as the development-difference controversy—abounded, particularly in efforts to understand differences in attention, verbal learning, memory processes, use of mnemonics, and the like (see Ellis, 1963; Zigler & Balla, 1982). The research focus that emerged on intraindividual differences in mental retardation spilled over to learning disabilities. Similarly, much research focused on the functional similarities of learning disabilities and mental retardation (e.g., Neisworth & Greer, 1975).

In the 1980s, many students who had previously been labeled mildly mentally retarded were propelled into the classification criteria of learning disabilities. School personnel often bent the rules and applied the label of learning disabilities rather than the more stigmatizing mental retardation (MacMillan & Siperstein, 2001). This flexibility meant that students in the learning disabilities category now had a range of IQs that extended lower (see e.g., Gottlieb, Alter, Gottlieb, & Wishner, 1994; Gresham, MacMillan, & Bocian, 1996). At the same time, pupils identified as mildly intellectually disabled tended to have greater disabilities than those of previous years; included were children with Down syndrome and those previously classified as trainable mentally retarded (Robinson, Palton, Polloway, & Sargent, 1989).

Although the term *mental retardation* remains important in clinical definitions, many educators and advocacy groups strongly discourage its use. For years, the AAMR has engaged in much soul searching about the term. It knows that risks accrue to the traditional designations, and yet they remain simply because there does not seem to be a better alternative. As one forward step in 1992, the AAMR introduced a new set of qualifiers that focus on needs and supports. Within the needs classification, the stress is on an individual's future potential rather than intellectual limitations; the focus changes from the effect of an individual's disability to the needs of "people who have a life and need support" (Butterworth, 2002, p. 85).

SPEECH CORRECTION CLASSES

Although the data is somewhat muddied, contemporary reports noted that New York City began a program for children with defective speech in 1908. The first formal school programs for speech disorders began in 1910 when 10 speech correction teachers were hired in both the Chicago and Detroit systems (Paden, 1970). The first statutes in the United States addressing special services for speech defects were enacted by Wisconsin in 1913. In 1914, Dr. Smiley Blanton established the first university clinic for speech problems at the University of Wisconsin (Irwin, 1955).

By 1925, there were programs throughout the United States for children with speech defects, lisping, stammering, and stuttering. Remediation efforts were focused on treating stuttering, lisping, infantile speech, and foreign accent as well as children who were tongue-tied or had clefts and other physical disabilities. Speech improvement work addressed the physiological and mechanical problems associated with speech pathology as well as the psychological and behavioral problems that teachers believed accompanied speech disorders. "A speech defect should be handled as a symptom of some underlying emotional difficulty," observed one worker. "To correct the defect the whole personality of the child must be studied and readjusted" (Zerler, 1938, p. 85). She went on to say that "Thumb sucking, masturbation, biting of nails, tics, irregular habits of living are all studied and suggestions offered for readjustment" (Zerler, 1938, p. 87).

In this period, the terms *alexia, dyslexia,* or *word blindness* were used to distinguish a special type of speech difficulty or aphasia. The earliest organized methods for teaching affected learners began sometime between 1900 and 1920. In the schools, "dyslexias" were "called to the attention of the speech worker with increasing frequency. Children who are slow in learning to read, learning to spell, and learning to talk, present a special educational problem for the teacher of remedial reading" (Hawk, 1934, p. 44). Children were usually taught to master the technique of reading through the alphabetic method, letter by letter, syllable by syllable, and sound unit by sound unit. "The modern rapid, flash-card system is too difficult for them. They must also employ kinesthetic and muscular impressions of the words, through tracing and writing frequently, to strengthen the weak auditory and visual images" (Hawk, 1934, p. 44).

By 1944, speech programs were "no longer considered frills or fads," but were "a basic part of the education scheme" (Morris, Ainsworth, & Pauls, 1944, p. 213). The first teachers were called speech improvement teachers or speech correctionalists. After World War II, the preferred title was speech therapist. Speech therapy, per se, was not considered a regular part of special education programs until the 1950s, and practitioners evolved as professionals separate from special education teachers.

HEALTH DISORDERS

Educational services for children with chronic illnesses were developed to address specific diseases such as polio and tuberculosis. Programs, referred to as open-air or open-windows schools or classes, typically followed a medical model. They were generally offered in special schools or centers, although some were located within public schools. Programs are reported from Boston (1908), Buffalo, Chicago, and New York (1910), and Michigan (1911).

Open-air schools were for "children of lowered vitality, undernourished, or with incipient tuberculosis tendencies" (Stullken, 1935–36, p. 74). Within the classes, children were provided a school program that included fresh air—a temperature of not more than 68 degrees. They were "supplied with Eskimo suits to wear in the lowered room temperature, and with comfortable cots and wool blankets for rest periods" (Stullken, 1935–36). The classes avoided too much homework and the strain of too long classes; they provided rest periods, extra nourishment, and other necessities for health building.

CHILDREN WITH PHYSICAL DISABILITIES

Crippled referred to individuals with mobility impairments and included many of those first labeled as birth injured; later, brain-injured children. *Birth injured* was recognized as a medical classification in the first decades of the 19th century when researchers suggested a relationship between intracranial hemorrhage at birth and the later development of cerebral spastic paralysis (Miller, 1940). From the outset, the lives of crippled children were dominated by the medical profession (Enns, 1981; Stone, 1984). Credit for the first real study of the condition is given to Dr. William Little (1810–1894), an English orthopedist, who published *On the Influence of Abnormal Parturition, Difficult Labours, Premature birth and Asphyxia Neonatorum on the Mental and Physical Condition of the Child, Especially in Relation to Deformities* in 1862. Little described children who walked with a scissors gait, grimaced, drooled, and were mentally retarded (Miller, 1940). After Little's work, no further distinguished efforts were forthcoming on brain-injured children until about 1930 when pioneering research on intellectual and motor difficulties emerged along with a series of studies on the social maturity of brain-injured children (Block, 1954). The term *cerebral palsied* came into use at this time.

During the Civil War, the New York Hospital for the Ruptured and Crippled became the first institution to address the problem of the crippled child (Bryam, 2004). Dr. James Knight, superintendent of the hospital, decried the number of crippled beggars on the streets and sought to relieve them of the need to beg alms (Bryam, 2004). In concert, philanthropists along with a number of organizations (most notably fraternal groups such as the Shriners and Rotarians) began working to create institutions that they believed would greatly improve the lives of crippled children. The first institutions, referred to as hospital schools, emerged, as did the first programs for the vocational training of cripples, an approach that came to be known as rehabilitation (Bryam, 2004). In Boston, for example, the Industrial School for Crippled and Deformed Children (also known as the Industrial School for Crippled Children and as Cotting School for Handicapped Children) was founded in 1893 (Manzo & Peters, 2008).

Home-visiting programs in the United States created to support the development of children in disadvantaged families, date back to the late 1800s when visiting teachers worked with children in immigrant and other settlement communities (Halpern, 1999). For children with exceptionalities, the visiting teacher movement began in Boston and Hartford in 1906. Home instruction in New York City was originated in 1913 by Adela Smith and 125 volunteer teachers. After a polio epidemic in 1916 and 1917, increasing numbers of crippled children resulted in the New York board of superintendents recommending that home training be a part of organized schooling for homebound crippled children. Rochester, New York, was the first district to join visiting teachers to its school board (Howard, 1935).

Classes for physically disabled children—those with crippling conditions, heart defects, and asthma—developed in various centers. As examples, Cleveland set up classes for epileptic children in 1906. In the same year, New York initiated classes for "cardiopathics." For crippled children, educational programs were organized in the form of decentralized, hospital-based facilities, diagnostic centers, and local clinics (Cruickshank, 1967). By 1944, 21 states had legislation to aid crippled children (Turner, 1944). By 1950, special instruction for homebound and hospitalized children was in most cases an accepted part of the state legislative program (Martens, 1951).

Special facilities for the education of crippled children expanded side by side with medical programs on their behalf. The numbers of orthopedic surgeons and physiotherapists grew (Turner, 1944). Winthrop Phelps championed the cause of cerebral palsied children and was the first medical specialist to deal directly with an educational as well as a physical problem. He operated a private school in Baltimore and spent his professional life explaining the nature of the disability as well as training hundreds of people to work as therapists and teachers for cerebral palsied children (Aiello, 1975).

Hanes (1995) notes that many of the orthopedic surgeons involved with crippled children took the work beyond the borders of medical intervention and became involved in reconstructive and rehabilitative treatments and educational programs. The Industrial School for Crippled and Deformed Children in Boston, for instance, was founded by two orthopedic surgeons from Children's Hospital Boston (Manzo & Peters, 2008).

At the same time, many of those involved with crippled children referred to the psychological characteristics as a "mental warp" (e.g., Davis, 1914, p. 2). Given their dubious mental qualities, the education of such children foregrounded character development and the instillation of moral values. Schooling sought "to educate them in the habits of industry, order, cleanliness, self respect, and self reliance and to apply such mental, moral, and religious training as would render them true, honorable, and useful citizens" (Willard, 1909, p. 780).

The history of another entire field feeds into the development of education for students with physical disabilities. Prosthetics is the field of science concerned with the artificial replacement of body parts and includes designing, manufacturing, and fitting artificial limbs (Tiessen, 1996).

Prostheses have been used probably since the beginning of humankind: artificial limbs and braces appear in ancient frescoes, mosaics, and pottery. The first written account is 2,200 years old and concerns one Marcus Sergius, a Roman general who lost his right hand in battle and had it replaced with a metal one. Ambroise Pare (1982), the surgeon general from the French army in the 16th century, is considered to be the modern father of prosthetics and orthotics. He advanced surgical techniques and made many devices for wounded soldiers. Many other people, from pirates to panhandlers, were leg amputees who used crude peg legs fashioned out of forked sticks or tree branches (Tiessen, 1996).

GIFTED CHILDREN

"Genius" was the traditional designation of outstanding individuals. As a descriptive term, *gifted* was first used in the educational literature by Guy Henry in 1920. Throughout the 20th century, a group of other descriptors emerged—pupils of more than average ability, brilliant children, or pupils of supernormal ability (Passow, 1990). It was not until the 1960s that the constructs of creative and talented came into being within the giftedness mind-set.

A dynamic interplay of social and historical forces shaped the conceptualization and nurturing of those who were gifted. Similarly, educational provisions were always subject to the prevailing attitudes in society toward high achievers. In general, Americans have had a love-hate relationship with gifted education. The tradition of egalitarianism has frequently denied the presence of extreme individual differences, and many concerned parties have seemed unwilling to make any judgments that might reveal an elite by creating an overadvantaged meritocracy within the school population.

The scientific investigation of giftedness can be readily traced to Francis Galton whose most memorable work began when he authored a two-part series for *MacMillans Magazine* (1865) followed by a report (1870) on his genetic and statistical studies. Often considered the father of gifted education, Galton forwarded two enduring and dangerous myths that recur in the field. First, Galton (1870) proposed that motivation to achieve was innate and inborn and claimed that genius would actualize itself despite external circumstances. Galton believed that the "true genius rises despite all obstacles while no amount of family pull will succeed in making a mediocrity into a genius" ("Nature or Nurture?", 1915, p. 235). His position that the cream would rise to the top regardless of difficulties or lack of environmental support led to "a general assumption in society that genius will find itself and will fight its way to expression by its very nature" (Munson, 1944, p. 3).

Galton, sickly himself, also posited a link between genius and insanity. "Men who leave their mark on the world," he said, "are very often those who, being gifted and full of nervous power, are at the same time haunted and driven by a dominant idea, and are therefore within a measurable distance of insanity" (Galton, cited by Pearson, 1914, p. 32).

Francis Galton created a climate of acceptance for persons who were gifted. However, it was Lewis Terman who developed much of the knowledge base for the study of giftedness. In 1921, armed with the Stanford-Binet Intelligence Test and a single-measure concept of intelligence, Terman embarked on a massive longitudinal study of giftedness among California school children, which he later believed was his greatest achievement (Sokal, 1984). The study, which included 1,528 children (856 males and 672 females), "was designed to discover what physical, mental, and personality traits are characteristic of gifted children as a class, and what sort of adult the typical gifted child becomes" (Terman & Oden, 1951, p. 21). The sample came to be nicknamed "the Terman kids," sometimes "the termites."

Terman's study dispelled many myths about gifted children, while creating a new one. He stressed the centrality of IQ and a unidimensional conception of intelligence manifested as "school house giftedness." Terman set the IQ level as 140 for his study, although he admitted some children with IQs of 135. To Terman, intelligence was manifested essentially in the ability to acquire and manipulate concepts. He defined those who were gifted as students who scored in the top 1% of general intellectual ability as measured by the Stanford-Binet Scale or a comparable instrument (Terman, 1926a, 1926b). After Terman's study, the earliest definitions of giftedness in the United States were tied to IQ scores, particularly the scores of the Stanford-Binet.

Echoing Francis Galton, Terman viewed giftedness as an already developed capacity that did not require nurturing and support. However, Terman's studies dispelled the myth of the sickly egghead. "Children above 140 IQ are not as a group characterized by intellectual one-sidedness, emotional instability, lack of sociability, or of social adaptability, or other types of maladjusted personality," he found. "Indeed in practically every personality and character trait such children average much better than the general school population. In social intelligence ratings, social interest and play activities, gifted children as a group are either normal or superior" (Terman, 1926b, p. 473).

Terman's student, Leta Hollingworth, a clinical psychologist and chief of the psychological laboratory at Bellevue Hospital, was actively involved in studying the nature and needs of gifted students in New York City at the same time that Terman was initiating his longitudinal study of gifted students in California. Hollingworth (1931) also asserted that the IQ was the only way to identify gifted children with certainty.

Despite the efforts of those involved, no premium attached to giftedness. Throughout the decades, gifted education was generally unfunded and ignored. Workers complained that "a great deal more study has been devoted to the dull than to the gifted" (Ontario School Inspectors' Association, 1958, p. x) and it was "the more dramatic and more socially acceptable deviates" who were rewarded with "an indisputable monopoly" (Kvaraceus, 1955–56, p. 329). Accommodating the needs of students with disabilities sapped almost all energy, funding, and research. For gifted children, programs were "poorly conceived, short lived, and of little consequence" (Cruickshank, 1950–51, p. 235). Many clung to the myth that the cream would rise to the top. As a 1943 writer chided, "We have been shamefully prodigal of our gifted children on the assumption that 'they can take care of themselves'" (Brown, 1943–44, p. 5).

A few brave souls recognized early that "the social importance of specialized treatment, both intellectual and manual, for this group of children is incalculably great" (Yerkes, 1917, p. 293). But the ambivalence that characterized attitudes toward giftedness meant that the idea of special programming won both staunch supporters and bitter critics.

The campaign for gifted learners was chiefly oriented along the lines of saving talent—preparing the human resources of the nation. Proponents further argued that the "provision of such specialized help is the school's attempt to meet one of the basic principles of our democracy—the right of every child to the kind of education through which he can reach his potential and become, within his capacities, a useful member of society" (Poole, 1955–56, p. 20). Critics juxtaposed the opportunity for advanced work with exclusiveness and privilege. They alleged that special classes "breed only snobs" (Percival, 1946–47, p. 241) and were inappropriate for schools, parents, and gifted pupils themselves. They held that the child is sometimes "made offensively boastful and conceited through exaggerated attention from doting parents and proud teachers" (Ontario School Inspectors' Association, 1958, p. xii) and that "in some cases the constant cheap triumphs over slower children lead to the development of an exaggerated ego with a concomitant expectation that all life situations can be overcome without intellectual exertion" (Brown, 1943–1944 p. 5).

Rapid advancement classes for exceptionally bright children started in New York in 1900. By 1915, what eventually came to be known as "SP classes" (which could mean either special placements or special programs) were designed to hasten the progress of bright children by enabling them to complete seventh, eighth, and ninth grades in 2 years (Henry, 1920). In 1922, the Teachers College in New York received a grant from the Carnegie Corporation to establish experimental classes for gifted students. In the same year, Hollingworth formed two special opportunity classes, one for children with IQs higher than 150 and one for those with IQs between 134 and 154. In 1936, Hollingworth established the Speyer School in New York City, which focused on this group of students (Passow, 1990).

The 75 classrooms serving 1,834 gifted children in the United States in 1934 grew to 93 classrooms serving 3,255 pupils by 1940 (Froelich, McNealy, Nelson, & Norris, 1944). By 1948 in city school systems in the United States, there were 87,142 students in special classes for the mentally retarded and only 20,712 in classes for the gifted (Ontario School Inspectors' Association, 1958). As late as 1946, only a handful of states had any laws or legislation dealing with gifted students. By 1952, Kansas was the only state that named those who were gifted among its exceptional population.

Right from the start, class designation proved difficult. Hollingworth observed that "to label it 'special Opportunity Class for Superior Children' would be a good way to arouse hatred and envy among those not included" (Hollingworth, 1926, p. 304). In an effort to shed the elitist attitudes associated with the terms *gifted* and *giftedness*, those working in this arena used "Special Opportunity" class as a common designation. Later, some settings were referred to as "Terman classes."

As work proceeded to meet the needs of gifted students, "first one plan then another was formulated" (Froelich et al., 1944, p. 207). Acceleration models were the first form of curriculum differentiation used, based on the flexible promotion model established in schools in St. Louis as early as 1868. By 1934, special classes, enrichment, and acceleration approaches were in vogue, with acceleration remaining the most popular. By 1956, the same three avenues existed (Kvaraceus, 1956).

The concurrent reaction to traditional school practices, encapsulated as Progressive Education, was readily embraced in classrooms for gifted children. Teachers, said Rutherford (1939–1940) had "swung our emphases from the curriculum to the child, demanding freedom for individual growth, the elimination of lockstep education, and the opportunity for untrammeled development and maturation" (p. 33). As curriculum began to take the shape of Progressive reforms, instruction became more child centered and more practical, seen as providing the link between curriculum and adult life. For example, Howard Rudd's Project Method was adopted, sometimes renamed the Enterprise Method. The Major Work Program, developed in Cleveland for students with IQs of 125 plus, offered intellectual and creative stimulation (Bain, 1980).

In the late 1950s, the Russian development of space technology and the launching of Sputnik caused panic among American legislators and policymakers. Schools were blamed for what was perceived as the second-rate technological status of the nation. Concerned about losing its unchallenged preeminence in commerce, industry, science, and technological innovation to international competitors, the United States responded with the passage of federal legislation that led to reevaluating and revamping educational programs, particularly in the areas of math and science (Bruner, 1960). The period witnessed a "gifted children mania" (Ontario School Inspectors' Association, 1958, p. 151) with gifted and talented programs at an all-time high. Generous funding allowed schools to implement a variety of progressive programs and strategies such as honor classes, innovative math and science curricula, early admissions to college, and enrichment courses. As an example, the National Merit Scholarship Corporation was established in 1955 to identify and honor high school students "who rank at the uppermost end of the academic ability scale" (Haney, 1981, p. 1024).

The gifted and talented movement that started in the late 1950s ended abruptly in the 1960s. As the initial shock of Sputnik paled, Congressional interest in the gifted and talented began to recede. At the same time, the climate of the 1960s meant that concern for excellence was replaced by concerns for equity. The public and the government directed their attention to those who were educationally disadvantaged and economically deprived (Zettel, 1982). Many of the statutes, regulations, and policies concerning gifted education that had been fought for and won at the state and local levels during the late 1950s never became truly institutionalized. A substantial portion of federal expenditures intended for the development of gifted programs were now spent on services that would also benefit other students (Zettel, 1982). By 1969, only 17 states had within their education code a term that could be construed to apply to the clinical entity known as the gifted child. Only 10 of these states provided any legal guidelines or definitions for determining the type of child to be served ("Summary Analysis . . . ," 1969).

The 1970s witnessed a short period of talent mobilization. One spur developed as North American educators saw their school outcomes drop below those of the Japanese and Europeans. Linked to this development were international reports criticizing American education and, particularly, the ignoring of gifted children. Another was an offshoot of the women's movement that began to open avenues to females to enter less traditional roles.

A compelling call to action arrived in October 1971 when Sidney Marland, the U.S. commissioner of education, reported to Congress on the status of gifted and talented education and dispensed with "the comfortable notion that a bright mind will make its own way" (U.S. Office of Education, 1972, p. 1). Congress responded with a new method of federal assistance (Sisk, 1982) and the beginning of a broad-based interest in developing educational programs for gifted learners. From 1972 to 1981, the federal government provided direct support to the education of gifted learners. Congress passed Public Law 93-380, an amendment to the Elementary and Secondary Education Act, which was the first law to provide direct assistance to "gifted and talented children at the elementary and secondary educational levels, not postsecondary students or specific programs" (Zentel, 1982, p. 61). State and local educational agencies were able to plan, develop, operate, and improve programs for gifted and talented children at all levels.

During the 1980s, the public airing of *A Nation at Risk* (National Commission on Excellence in Education, 1983) engendered a flurry of concern and reform proposals (see Chapter 9) markedly similar to those that multiplied after the launching of Sputnik. Among other things, the National Commission on Excellence in Education accumulated evidence that many gifted students were bored with the lockstep of mass education and were turning into chronic underachievers and dropouts. It gave the startling estimate that 50% of gifted students were failing or failing to achieve at their potential.

Nevertheless, the social climate had changed and a declining economy quenched the thirst for innovation. The 1980s witnessed another sharp drop in gifted programs. There was not a national legislative mandate for special programs for gifted and talented students. Indeed, attempts to enlarge the educational entitlement of gifted students through litigation based on the federal constitution and federal legislation were consistently unsuccessful (Zirkel & Stevens, 1987). Excellence and equity became competing issues: excellence required focusing support on the most capable learners; equity required the opposite (Kauffman, 1989). On the balance scales, it was equity that suited the tenor of the times. The notions were in concordance with wider social notions and chimed with the philosophy of a liberal political system and pluralistic culture (see Thomas, 1997). The gifted field was subject to "virulent attack" (Pfeiffer, 2003, p. 161). The zeal for equity meant that programs for the gifted were terminated because they were not politically correct. Many educators contended that because gifted children were already advantaged, programs for the gifted made as much sense as welfare payments for the rich.

In 1993, the U.S. Office of Education released *National Excellence: A Case for Developing America's Talent*. It signaled that problems abounded in educating learners who were gifted and talented, that policies alone had not been adequate to meet the learning needs of youngsters in this group. Yet by 1998, Gallagher was led to describe gifted education as in a state of "quiet crisis."

CREATING THE FIELD OF LEARNING DISABILITIES

The term *learning disabilities* was part of the educational lexicon in the opening half of the 19th century, although it was applied inconsistently and only occasionally to various manifestations of learning and behavioral problems. In an attempt to generate more stable and consistent terminology within a fragmented field, the term was introduced again in 1963 when a small group of concerned parents and educators involved with the Fund for Perceptually Handicapped Children met in Chicago. To describe the target population, each parent group had used a different name such as perceptually handicapped, brain injured, or neurologically impaired. In fact, Clements (1966) identified some 38 labels that were used interchangeably and applied to this group of children. The Chicago meeting aspired to organize a cohesive entity from the separate and isolated parent groups that had formed throughout the country.

The creation of the new area evolved during the 1930s out of the confluence of two research mainstreams. First were studies of the brain from the mid-18th century on. Second were educational and psychological investigations into specific cases that began in the 1850s.

The field of brain research belongs to early physicians who examined victims of stroke, accident, or disease. One of the first explorers of the brain was Franz Joseph Gall (1758–1826) a Viennese physician and anatomist, best remembered for his detour into the world of phrenology. The French scientist and anthropologist, Paul Broca (1824–1880), further explored the brain as he searched for the roots of aphasia. After conducting postmortem examinations on four stroke victims, Broca identified the left temporal lobe as primary in speech production; he identified the speech center (Broca's area) in 1861 (see Hilgard, 1987; Sagan, 1979).

The development of scientific neurology during the 2 decades after 1850 led to a detailed system of classification of brain pathology and to examination methods for assessing the integrity of the nervous system (Blanton, 1976). After World War I, the evidence of the ravages of shell shock sensitized many to the realities of psychological complaints. Kurt Goldstein, among others, observed the behavior of soldiers who had sustained head wounds (Goldstein, 1940).

As neurology and ophthalmology developed as medical specialties, physicians began to describe problems in understanding and using spoken and written language that were associated with damage to specific areas of the brain. The early research on manifested behaviors emphasized clinical investigation rather than practical application in the schools and focused primarily on three areas of disorder—(a) spoken language, (b) written language and reading, and (c) motor and perceptual problems.

The pioneering case studies, generally centered on middle-class intelligent children who were incapable of learning to read, concerned two distinct entities; word-blindness and word-deafness. Congenital word-deafness was first pinpointed by Dr. James Kerr in Bradford, England. Word-blindness was far more widely described (e.g., Hinshelwood, 1900; Kassmaul, 1859/1877; Tredgold, 1929).

The term *word-blindness* was used for the first time by Kassmaul (1859–1877). Parallel terms included *imperception, agnosia, alexia, mind-blindness,* and *aphasia.* The term *dyslexia* was introduced by the German ophthalmologist, Rudolf Berlin (1872) as an alternative to word-blindness. Dyslexia referred to extraordinary difficulty experienced by otherwise normal children in learning to identify the printed word.

The first individual case of word-blindness was described by Broadbent in 1872; W. Pringle Morgan in 1896 described the first congenital case (see Thomson, 1984). In *Congenital Word-Blindness* (1917), Scottish physician and eye surgeon James Hinshelwood defined word-blindness as a congenital defect occurring in children, with otherwise normal and undamaged brains, who could not learn to read through conventional methods. Later, Tredgold (1929), an English neurologist, explained that in word–blindness, the problems concerned only the printed word: either children were totally unable to learn to read or they read with the greatest difficulty. More boys than girls were affected. Tredgold felt that although some children were of average intelligence, the majority were seen to be of lower intellectual functioning. They also often suffered emotional and social difficulties such as lack of interest, lack of initiative, impulsive behavior, and incapacity for sustained mental application.

The two strands of study—brain research and case studies—joined in the last decades of the 19th century. Dejerine (1871) attributed loss of reading comprehension to a left unilateral lesion. Kassmaul (1877/1859) saw the difficulties arising from injuries to the left or dominant hemisphere of the brain controlling speech.

During the 1920s, great emphasis was placed on brain theory and its relationship to aberrations in behavior and traits such as mirror writing and left-handedness. In this period, Samuel Torrey Orton, an American psychiatrist, began to theorize about the neurological components of dyslexia after he organized an experimental mobile mental hygiene clinic in outlying communities in 1925 and met a 16 year old of average intelligence who could not read. Orton discarded the common theory that many of the problems were caused by emotional maladjustment and instead focused on the mixed laterality he observed. Orton (1937) perceived the defect as lying in the visual system: he suggested that one hemisphere of the brain failed to become dominant and that this condition caused the apparent dysfunction in visual perception and visual memory as well as the tendency to see letters and words in reverse. Orton coined the term *strephosymbolia* to describe individuals who saw mixed symbols when they tried to read (Orton, 1925). His publications on the matter attracted considerable attention; they seemed to offer a starting point to learn more about these human differences.

Although early researchers made some provocative and relevant findings, the field that evolved as learning disabilities was most cogently encapsulated in the work of Alfred Strauss (1897–1957). Strauss trained in Germany as a pupil of Kurt Goldstein. It was Goldstein's work with brain damaged soldiers in the 1920s and 1930s that provided the backdrop for the work of Strauss and his associate Heinz Werner (1890–1964), a developmental psychologist.

Both Strauss and Werner fled Germany in the 1930s.[5] They were eventually hired by the Wayne County Training School, a facility for mentally retarded children, especially those with disciplinary problems, in Northville, Michigan. Robert Haskell, director of the school, aspired to make it a stronger research institution than the New Jersey Training School (see Stogdell, 1938). He also hired Samuel Kirk in 1931. When he hired Strauss as a research psychiatrist, the work with brain-injured children during the 1930s and 1940s became the basis for the continued development of learning disabilities as a field of study (Lerner, 1981).

At the same time, the preponderance of studies of learning disabilities in the United States established that condition as an essentially American disability. After Strauss, the bulk of descriptions of programs, practices, policies, and research were published in the United States (Moats & Lyon, 1993).

As Strauss implemented the contemporary concepts of German psychology, specifically the work of Kurt Goldstein, he sought medical causes for behavioral characteristics. His initial work introduced a new term, the *brain-injured child*, which alerted physicians to events that could be related to injury of the brain. Strauss developed tests to diagnose brain injury in children and demonstrated the differences in mental organization between the brain-injured, mentally retarded child (exogeneous) and the familial mentally retarded child (endogeneous). Because the behaviors of distractibility, perseveration, and inattention in the brain-injured group seemed essentially different from the behavioral correlates of other groups, Strauss's work led to a refinement in the differential diagnosis of the brain-injured, neurotic, and psychotic child (Gardiner, 1958; Strauss, 1939, 1941a, 1941b). Strauss then crystallized an organic behavior syndrome that was diagnosable even in children where residual isolated signs of brain damage were absent. He outlined a behavioral syndrome that characterized the minimally brain-damaged child, later known as the Strauss syndrome. The five principal components—hyperactivity, hyperemotionalism, impulsivity, distractibility, and perseveration—have been expanded, subdivided, and made more specific over the years but still describe the core characteristics of children with learning disabilities.

Strauss developed procedures for educational programs based on his own theories of cortical functioning. Because the brain damage itself could not be treated, he attempted to control the environment. His approach gave rise to individual and analytical approaches in teaching the brain-injured child (Strauss, 1939). With Laura Lehtinen, Strauss was responsible for some of the first meaningful educational programs for learning disabled children (Strauss & Lehtinen, 1947).

After Strauss and Werner, the focus of research gradually shifted to encompass seemingly normal children who were achieving poorly in school. The neurological explanation for learning disabilities was expanded by researchers who claimed to have identified a similar pattern of neurologically based learning and behavior problems in children of average or above average intelligence (Mann, 1970, 1971).

The field began with a strong focus on perceptual-motor theories that maintained that motor development was a necessary requisite for perceptual development. The majority of the major approaches that emerged therefore were related to perceptual-motor theory and stressed the remediation of visual or auditory processing disorders. As examples, beginning in the 1930s, Newell Kephart began to develop and refine the concept of perceptual-motor training (Kephart, 1968). Bryant Cratty became interested in perceptual-motor training through his interest in kinesiology oriented toward physical education (Cratty, 1969). Marianne Frostig, a psychiatric social worker and rehabilitation therapist in Austria and Poland, came to the United States in 1938 and trained as a psychologist. Her training programs were widely used (Frostig, 1961). Jean Ayres, who became involved with neu-rologically disabled children as an occupational therapist, is credited with first describing the theory of sensory integration (Ayres, 1972). Grace Fernald (1943) popularized multisensory approaches.

Strauss paid scant attention to linguistic deficits in his characterization of the brain-injured child. The psycholinguistic stance that viewed remediation as a linguistic problem was confronted by Henry Bastian, Charles Osgood, Joseph Wepman, and others who developed models that, they believed, explained the process of communication through speech (see Wiederholt, 1978). Kirk, McCarthy, and Kirk (1968), for example, used a modification of the Osgood model in the development of the Illinois Test of Psycholinguistic Abilities; Wepman developed the Language Modalities Test for Aphasia (Wepman & Jones, 1961). Tests and pro-grams focusing on written language came from Grace Fernald, Samuel Kirk, Anna Gillingham, Bessie Stillman, and Samuel Orton.

Minimal brain dysfunction became the common concept by which to iden-tify within a single psychology those children with learning problems, clumsiness, hyperactivity, and attention problems. Lewis (1951) described the uninhibited, fre-quently hyperactive, brain-injured child. Burks (1957) observed that such a child "most often demonstrates severe academic deficiencies particularly in reading. He can be shown to possess a general intelligence rating above that accepted as a cri-terion for placement in a mentally retarded class" (p. 169).

Although children were identified primarily in reference to, and classified in terms of, the presumed etiology of brain damage, central nervous system dysfunc-tion, or cerebral dysfunction, brain injury was a difficult concept and one that was excessively condemning on a child's school record. To create consistency and overcome stigma, Samuel Kirk proposed an encompassing term at the Chicago parents' meeting in 1963. Kirk forwarded the term *learning disabilities* as a standard description of children of normal intelligence with learning problems. He defined his term carefully:

> Recently, I have used the term "learning disabilities" to describe a group of children who have disorders in development in language, speech, reading, and associated communication skills needed for social interaction. In this group, I do not include children who have sensory handicaps, such as blindness and deafness, because we have methods of managing and training the deaf and the blind. I also exclude from this group children who have generalized mental retardation. (Kirk, 1963, p. 3)

Kirk's speech had a number of major effects. First, it isolated the general char-acteristics of the population to be subsumed under the label of learning disabili-ties. Second, it stimulated the growth of the Association for Children with Learn-ing Disabilities (ACLD), renamed the Learning Disabilities Association in 1989. Primarily a forum for parents of learning-disabled children, the ACLD expanded rapidly and became a powerful lobby group in Canada and the United States. It also cemented Samuel Kirk's leading role in the new field of learning disabilities as it emerged from its roots in language disorders, reading, and brain injury. Finally, the creation of a new term served as a catalyst to generate interest in the field (Winzer, 2007b).

The new field's terms and principles met with favor. It became a socially constructed category in the sense that learning disabilities applied to children from middle-class backgrounds who had no discernible mental or physical anomalies but who were nevertheless failing in school (see e.g., Sleeter, 1986). Parents found the term *learning disabilities* more palatable than mild mental retardation; apparently, a label that specified a particular problem was less stigmatizing than one that implied a global developmental impairment.

During the late 1960s, pioneering professionals and parents worked arduously to educate the public and generate political support at local, state, and national levels to establish the field of learning disabilities. A federally sponsored study provided a better description and an acceptable definition, the term *learning disabilities* was coined, and the Division for Children with Learning Disabilities was organized within the Council for Exceptional Children. In 1968, the newly formed National Advisory Committee on Handicapped Children recommended that high priority be given to the development of programs for those with learning disabilities. The Children with Special Learning Disabilities Act of 1969 was passed.[6] Most states passed legislation and established school programs specifically for learning disabled children. Colleges and universities developed program to prepare teachers.

Kirk's conception created an entirely new area of special education and set it on the road to an astonishing expansion (Winzer, 2007b). Research, professional interest, and the number of students served under the label grew dramatically. The field of mild mental retardation shrunk accordingly. Perhaps because of its rapid and unprecedented expansion, no other area in special education has been as open to challenges, controversy, misunderstandings, fads, and questionable interventions as has been learning disabilities.

Psycholinguistic and process training dominated the 1970s. The stress on visual perceptual motor areas gradually gave way to the behaviorally rooted ideas of Direct Instruction. A hallmark of the 1980s and 1990s was the considerable progress made in designing, implementing, and evaluating effective and well-validated methodologies. The field was transformed with an emphasis on internal cognitive processes and learning strategies. Affective factors then received focus. Response to instruction is a recent innovation. Not to be forgotten, however, are "a myriad of slippery interventions" (Vaughn, Gersten, & Chard, 2000, p. 100). More problematic regimes included, but were not restricted to, multivitamin therapy, special diets, patterning, and colored lenses.

Two additional issues have consistently challenged the field of learning disabilities—an appropriate definition and the criteria to identify students within the definition. Establishing a comprehensive and pertinent definition has been a central focus since the birth of the field. The failure to produce a unified definition "has meant that LD [learning disabilities] lacks two critical elements: understanding—a clear and unobscured sense of LD—and explanation—a rational exposition of the reasons why a particular student is LD" (Kavale & Forness, 2000, p. 240).

By the late 1990s, the blurring among the categories of mild disability and unclear identification muddied definitions and rendered rates so unstable that some researchers were led to question learning disabilities as a disability at all (see Lyon, 1996). Others saw learning disabilities as increasingly unrecognizable as a discrete category and used terms such as "myth" or "questionable construct" or "imaginary disease" (Kavale, Holdnack, & Mostert, 2005).

The lack of a clear process of identification stems from the definitional dilemma. Typically, identification involved a convoluted set of criteria, often based on the logic of default. The regulations accompanying Public Law 94-142 in 1975 attempted to separate learning disabilities from intellectual disabilities by stating that learning disabilities were present when "a severe discrepancy between achievement and intellectual ability" was demonstrated. The Individuals With Disabilities Act of 1997 reiterated discrepancy as the primary criterion in identifying learning disabilities. In the United States, about 98% of states use a discrepancy criterion in their definitions (Gresham, 1997).

The lack of standardization and misinterpretation of the discrepancy are blamed for the high rates of students identified as learning disabled. Many researchers now argue that assessment should begin with a controlled trial of intervention strategies to see how a child responds to both scientific-based instruction and a sound program of early intervention (Case & Taylor, 2005; Mahoney, 2002). Supporting that approach, the Individuals With Disabilities Education Improvements Act of 2004 removed the discrepancy criterion and allowed responses to intervention as part of the learning disabilities assessment process (Kavale, Holdnack, & Mostert, 2005).

SUMMARY AND THEMES

The period from 1910 to 1970 saw special segregated classes rise to become the unchallenged leaders for the education of children and youth with exceptional conditions. Over the decades, a greater number of children with a greater variety of conditions were propelled toward an increasing variety of segregated classes, surrounded by more and more specialists. New categories of exceptionality emerged—most particularly and critically, the field of learning disabilities.

Institutional settings continued to thrive, particularly for students within the traditional categories. Schooling for blind children followed educational routes in both residential and segregated class settings. Mental retardation retained its affiliation with the institutional element for people with more severe disabilities. In the schools, programs for those with mild mental retardation absorbed more commitment, funding, and research than did any other area of exceptionality. Because of the nebulous, fluid, and socially constructed nature of the category, mild mental retardation also generated the major portion of discussion and controversy, mainly in relation to terminology and stigma.

The evolution and formation of the deaf community resulting from institutionalization in the first half of the 19th century is more than an isolated and autonomous historical event. In both historical and contemporary contexts, deaf people have adhered to a cultural or social view of deafness. Many characterize themselves as a linguistic minority group in society defined by their own unique culture and language, not as a group bounded by the categories of disability.

The unusual influence of Alexander Graham Bell on the lives of deaf people was of singular quality and broad scope. Bell patrolled the deaf community. He probed, and then deplored, the cohesive institutional settings and the nature of the relationships formed: relations to sign as the natural language of the deaf; to the culture of deafness and the deaf community; and to the inevitable friendships and marriages that ensued. Oralism was elevated to the dominant ideology by the opening decades of the 20th century. Manualism was put to rout and the course of the education of deaf students was altered for almost 100 years.

Socially and politically, deafness is not on the defensive as it once was. It is accepted that being deaf is a social role as well as linguistic difference, a cultural construction as well as a matter of audiology. Deaf people today lay claim to make decisions about their own lives, their own mode of communication, their own schools, and the curriculum presented therein. Many deaf people and professionals working in the field of deafness do not accept today's educational integration; they see the residential schools as a cultural component that is vital in creating group solidarity.

Throughout the century, the gifted child suffered from neglect and suspicion. The area of gifted education witnessed large ebbs and flows of support, commitment, and funding. Perceived crises in U.S. education and in society stimulated by the Soviet launch of the first earth orbiting satellite increased funding and interest but did not spawn permanent legislative activity. The 1972 Marland Report signaled changes in commitment and funding for programs supporting gifted children, but the egalitarian climate of the 1980s saw many of those special programs abandoned in favor of calls for equity.

In the field of learning disabilities, many individuals generated concepts that advanced the thinking in the field. Beginning with Strauss and Werner, other pioneers in the field include William Cruickshank, Ray Barsch, Marianne Frostig, Newell Kephart, Samuel Kirk, and Grace Fernald. After the official launching of the field in 1963, the ensuing massive interest in the area, the number of students identified and served as learning disabled, the development of parent and professional organizations, and the contributions of allied disciplines was little short of phenomenal. Today, learning disabilities is the largest single focus of special education in many school districts. However, it is under pressure to articulate a more exact definition of learning disabilities and to specify clear criteria for the various subgroups within it.

NOTES

1. Speaking to a deaf audience at Gallaudet College in 1891, Bell denied "that I want to prevent you from marrying as you choose, and that I have tried to pass a law to interfere with your marriages" (1898, p. 3). However, he continued by saying that "I think, however, that it is the duty of every good man and every good woman to remember that children follow

marriage, and I am sure that there is no one among the deaf who desires to have his affliction handed down to his children" (Bell, 1898, p. 4). Many deaf persons heeded Bell and either did not marry or sought sterilization for themselves or their children voluntarily.

2. ASL is founded on a combination of symbolic gestures produced by the shape, the location, and the movement of the hands. Many of the signs symbolize concepts rather than individual words. Most have an arbitrary tie to the referent. Some are iconic in that they represent an object or action for which they stand; some are metonymic—taking a relatively small aspect or feature of the referent and using that as the basis of the sign. For example, the sign for *dog* combines tapping the thigh and snapping the fingers, as if calling a dog. ASL has no signs for the grammatical markers such as -ed or -ing endings that express verb tense and condition. Rather, users depend on spatial location of signs, facial expressions, and body language to articulate tense and speaker and to replace voice intonation and enhance meaning (Meadow, 1980).

3. Institutional completeness, a concept often applied to ethnic groups, asserts that groups determine their own destinies through institutional control. They develop a sufficiently broad and deep institutional structure that allows members of a community to fulfill their basic and social needs without moving beyond the perimeters of the community. Institutional completeness is a critical goal among today's deaf community within North American residential schools for the deaf, which serve the same function in instilling culture and language today as they did in the past. They are, in a sense, the homeland of the deaf, cultural sites where advocates have structured a hidden curriculum—the reproduction of the deaf community. Mandel (2005) reported on a new town in South Dakota being built for individuals who communicate using sign language. Named for Laurent Clerc, the town will be home to as many as 2,500 people, both deaf and hearing.

4. Retinopathy of prematurity (ROP), until recently referred to as retrolental fibroplasia, was first described in 1942 in Australia. The retinas and vitreous humour of low-birth-weight babies was damaged by the high levels of oxygen in incubators, resulting in serious levels of visual impairment and blindness. Although it is now known that other factors besides incubators play into ROP, about 20% of incubator-bound, low-birth-weight babies continue to be affected (see Winzer, 2007a).

5. Strauss was a neurologist who received his medical training in neuropsychiatry, psychopathology, and special education at the University of Heidelberg in Germany. He filled a number of prestigious positions, including assistant professor of neuropsychiatry at the University of Heidelberg, guest professor at the University of Barcelona, and head of the Governmental Child Guidance Clinic in Barcelona. Strauss emigrated to the United States before 1937 and joined the staff of the Wayne County Training School. In 1947, Strauss founded the Cove schools at Racine. In 1945, Werner joined the faculty at Clark University to resume his earlier career in developmental psychology.

6. In 1970, The Children With Specific Learning Disabilities Act legislation was incorporated into the Education of the Handicapped Act of 1970 (Pub. L. 91-230).

Chapter 8

The Professionalization
of Special Education

The development of teaching as a distinct profession in the 19th century was neither clear cut nor simple. In the opening decades, elementary teaching was a virtually unskilled and temporary job (Herbst, 1988), not viewed as a profession for either men or women. By the 1820s, a few private academies in the United States began to offer a modicum of teacher education (Woodring, 1975). Few candidates were accommodated; even up to the time of the Civil War, many elementary teachers had little or no training.

Massachusetts opened the first normal school in Lexington in 1839. Horace Mann, the founder, first consulted with Thomas Hopkins Gallaudet in Hartford with respect to the original plan (Steiner, 1919). Following Mann's Massachusetts enterprise, normal schools opened in Connecticut, New York, Rhode Island, Pennsylvania, Michigan, Illinois, and Minnesota. In 1860, there were 11 normal schools in the United States; by 1874, 67 state and 54 private normal schools were serving prospective teachers. By 1898, the number had risen to 166 and 165, respectively (Connor, 1951; Kelly, 1946). In Canada, the province of Ontario had 8 normal schools by 1921.

The model for normal schools was European, linking them with primary and secondary schools rather than with universities. Together with public and private normal schools, there were well more than 100 colleges and universities by 1900 that offered courses designed to prepare secondary teachers, administrators, normal school instructors, and college faculty in education (Osgood, 1997).

SPECIAL EDUCATION

The term *special education* arose from initiatives taken in 1884. Alexander Graham Bell was probably the first to use the phrase at a meeting of the National Education Association (NEA) in Madison, Wisconsin, in that year. The term emerged as Bell, with the assistance of Joseph Gordon of Gallaudet College, was attemping to form a new professional group. Bell's proposal was "primarily intended for educators of the deaf" but "soon came to include the educators of the blind, and afterwards took in those who are interested in the education of backward and feeble-minded children" (National Education Association, 1898, pp. 1031–1033). The attempt to organize into a multidisciplinary organization failed because there were not 20 qualified NEA members petitioning for the department (Geer, 1977). Bell further discussed the term and usage at the NEA meeting in Milwaukee in 1897. Another petition was presented, and the new NEA department was accepted. Although Bell specifically requested that the new organization be named the "Department of the education of classes requiring special methods of instruction," the NEA board of directors named it the "Department of education of the deaf, blind, and feebleminded" (Geer, 1977).

When the new department held its first meeting in 1898, Bell seized the opportunity to stress integration and the necessity for day schools. At the closing session of the NEA's national convention in 1898, he recommended that children with disabilities should become "an annex to the public school system, receiving special instruction from special teachers, who shall be able to give instruction to little children who are either deaf, blind, or mentally deficient, without sending them away from their homes or from the ordinary companions with whom they are associated" (cited in Gearheart, Mullen, & Gearheart, 1993, p. 7). Bell and William Torrey Harris spoke of the issue again to the NEA in 1902 when they called for closer contact and affiliation between special and regular educators.

The group was firmly established within the NEA in 1902. Over the years, the name changed to the Department of Special Education. It existed until 1918 when it disintegrated as a result of lack of publications, meager committee work, and limited funds (Kode, 2002). Although no trace of the department remained, the phrase special education joined the lexicon of educators.

At the opening of the 19th century, the notion of women as professionals was rarely entertained. During the 19th century, women's work in the classroom became deeply entrenched. Beginning in the 1830s, women began to move into teaching, particularly in the elementary schools and within special education. Many young women viewed teaching as "one means of providing a respectable and useful occupation" ("Seminary for Female Teachers," 1831, p. 341). When, as part of his reorganization of the Massachusetts school system, Horace Mann founded the first normal school in Lexington, Massachusetts, in 1839, he found that men were abandoning teaching for more lucrative opportunities. Young women formed the bulk of candidates.

By the middle decades of the century, there was an influx of women to the extent that teaching developed as the province of married men and single women. The acceptance of women as teachers in the common schools was so universal, in fact, that they dominated the profession in numbers. As examples, by 1837, 60% of all Massachusetts teachers were women; the number rose to 88% by 1870 (Herbst, 1988). Approximately one in every five white women in pre–Civil War Massachusetts was a teacher at some time in her life (Bernard & Vinvovskis, 1977). By 1886,

63% of American teachers were women, 90% in the cities (Sklar, 1973). In the Philadelphia school system, 93% of the teachers were women by 1903 ("Wanted—Men in the School System," 1903, p. 81). At no time between 1870 and 1970 did teaching fall below fifth place on the list of the 10 leading occupations of all women in the labor force (Clifford, 1991).

Much has been made of the two main factors accounting for women's numerical dominance in teaching. One is the ideology of women's sphere as teachers, including the rhetoric of woman's natural mission as teacher. Edouard Seguin, for example, applauded American education as "feminine—that is to say, gentle, breeding more gentleness in pupils" (1866/1907, p. 88). Second was the economic necessity that determined the entry of women into all areas of the teaching profession in the early decades of the 19th century. The common schools, supported by taxes, were forced into thrifty housekeeping. School promoters, avidly seeking means to lessen expenditures and assuming that economy and improvement went hand in hand, hired women at about one-third the cost of male teachers. For example, in 1868–69, men teachers earned an average of $111.23 a month; women $80.12 (Berkeley, 1984). Lower salaries for women were justified on the basis that females did not have families to support; women were not expected to have job-related aspirations, but were to look to eventual marriage; and the increased costs concomitant with the expanding school systems simply determined the lower rates for women. In addition, the limited purposes to be achieved in the school led to lower pay.

Women had been excluded from institutional settings at the dawn of North American special education. Parallel with their counterparts in the general system, women moved into teaching in the 1840s, first in schools for the deaf and then in broader contexts. Once women entered the institutional settings and special classes, they were assigned roles that perpetuated a differential status; salaries and advancement opportunities were unequal to those available to male educators. In many ways, the systems functioned as did specific types of traditional households—largely dependent on male leadership and female domestic employment, with administrative structures carefully designed to direct females into employment vacancies that were suitable but in which they were subordinate to male bosses. As examples, in 1893, the annual report of the Iowa Institution for the Feeble-Minded showed a staff of 14–13 females and 1 male. In 1892, the New Jersey Training School for Feeble-Minded Boys and Girls at Vineland was staffed by five female teachers and a male superintendent.

Throughout the 19th century, the women's lot was so small that men rarely cast envious glances at it. The traditionally high value attached to male labor blinded many to the worth of women as teachers. Indeed, to be female was to be dependent and powerless; to be male ensured power, independence, and opportunities for professional and social mobility. Women had their proper sphere and faced differential treatment with respect to responsibility, occupational mobility, and economic remuneration.

By the early 20th century, the ease with which school systems filled their classrooms with women belied the strains articulated by male educators. Gradually, male teachers discovered that "men and women are in active competition" (Taylor, 1900, p. 237). The increasing numerical dominance of women in the schools developed as an area of grave concern to male teachers. Many male teachers disapproved "of the preponderance of female teachers" (Ontario Department of Education, 1904, p. 37) and declared that "the women are forcing them out of many positions that they formerly considered their indisputable right" (Balis, 1901, p. 311). Men argued that it was unjust of women to crowd them out. Men had families to support and it was impossible for them to live on what a woman would accept as remuneration for her labor (Taylor, 1900).

Progress was linked to male superiority and patriarchal processes over female independence. Educational background was critical in deciding who was to become a professional, and women were often hindered by their lack of education when they competed with men to professionalize an occupation. Women teachers ran afoul of men who viewed them not only as inadequately educated and improperly socialized but also as carriers of an unfortunate professional ideal and as threats to the gender order. Male teachers contended that women undermined males' most important professional quest and clearly identified connections between femininity and failure (Winzer, 2007b).

In the special education arena, men cited both the arduous nature of the work—too trying for frail women—and the pernicious effects of boys. Because of the "essential differences between the mind of man and the mind of woman," it was argued that extended exposure to women teachers would "simply develop the female mind in the male body" (Howard, 1902, p. 279). Young men required "daily contact with the sterner attributes of human nature, the more logical faculties, and the stricter sense of justice that are masculine characteristics" (Draper, 1904, p. 359).

TRAINING SPECIAL TEACHERS

The founding profession of special education, which had been largely an enterprise for the clergy, was characterized by two basic qualities: a highly progressive and reformist zeal among the leaders and the need to train its own for the profession. Hence, an important goal of 19th-century education for deaf and blind students was teacher training, which included preparing a very few of the most promising pupils for roles in the teaching profession.

With the growth of special classes in the early 20th century, systems initially employed general education teachers. Sometimes, they turned to the institutions for their staffing needs. The Boston school system, for example, sought teachers with some experience at the Barre Institution in Massachusetts or at Seguin's schools. Other teachers opting to work in the field were sent to the Elwyn Institution to study for a period of 3 months. As the normal schools expanded, it became common practice to recruit teachers from among those trained in either kindergarten (preferred) or primary education.

The profession soon passed the point when it could simply pluck somebody out of a general classroom. College and university programs began to parallel the growth of day schools and day classes. Training special education teachers for the general schools began at Michigan State Normal College at Ypislanti in 1924 (Lee, 1936). Subsequently, special education departments opened in 12 institutions, 3 teachers' colleges, 3 normal schools, and 6 universities and colleges (Scheier, 1931). In addition, 18 institutions had courses on physical handicaps, including 10 on speech defects, 4 on sight saving, 3 on the hearing impaired, 2 on the crippled, and 2 on the blind (Scheier, 1931). At the same time, college and in-house training melded; for example, Smith College with the Clarke School for the Deaf, Harvard University with the Perkins School for the Blind, and George Peabody College for Teachers with the Tennessee School for the Blind (Martens, 1936). By mid-century, at least 65 colleges were offering a year-round curriculum or sequence of courses in one or more specialized areas. Fifteen institutions had well-defined departments or divisions of special education within the administrative organization of the college (Martens, 1951). From the mid-1960s, normal schools and training colleges were increasingly incorporated into faculties of colleges of education.

Certification standards kept pace. Illinois in 1929 required specific certificates of qualifications from teachers of the deaf and the blind (Wallin, 1936–37a). By 1930, 16 states had passed legislation authorizing special education. Of these, 10 also set forth legal requirements for teacher certification, which, in most instances, was limited to an elementary degree plus supplemental training (see Haines, 1925; New Jersey Commissioner, 1965; Scheier, 1931).

Teachers of the Deaf

From the earliest days of the American Asylum, Thomas Hopkins Gallaudet undertook the training of teachers. He used the resources of the Hartford institution to train young hearing and deaf men to enter the profession of the education of the deaf. His school became, in a sense, "a normal school in which teachers were trained for his and other institutions" (Clarke, 1900, p. 346). From 1817 on, prospective teachers from all of the United States and Canada applied, almost exclusively, to the American Asylum for training.

Typically, institutions for the deaf using manual pedagogy, and later those for the blind and the mentally retarded in the United States and Canada, adopted the apprentice-type in-house teacher training model developed by Gallaudet. Practitioners of the oral persuasion in deaf education followed suit. The first formal programs held in schools for the deaf and led by master teachers emerged in 1889 at the Clarke School (Clarke, 1900; Gallaudet, 1907). The principal, Carolyn Yale, established the normal training class (which apparently received only ladies) "in order more adequately to equip the teachers in her own school" (Moore, 1934, p. 194). In 1892, the Clarke School began to train teachers for other schools. Training followed at the North Carolina School for the Deaf in 1894 and at the Central Institute for the Deaf in St. Louis in 1914. Beginning with Gallaudet's program,

Canadian teachers trained in the United States. It was not until 1924 that the Ontario Institution began a 3-year, in-house training program (Ontario Department of Education 1925).

By 1929, 30 schools for the deaf in the United States trained teachers. Right into the 1940s, preparation programs remained almost exclusively in teacher training departments of schools for the deaf (Lane, 1952). The enduring popularity of in-house programs rested on a number of facets. First, the training class was a decided asset to the school in which it was conducted. Candidates were provided a practical knowledge of the methods and practices geared to a specific program and situation so that an individual school's on-site training produced a tailor-made product, patterned after its own ideals (Numbers, 1927, p. 346). Knowledge was transmitted to the next generation. As young teacher candidates observed and practiced, "the 'teaching skill' of the master teacher was passed on to the neophyte as an art" (Withrow, 1967, p. 656). Upcoming professionals not only attained methodological expertise but also performed a service to the school by helping the teacher in the classroom or the houseparent in the dormitory (Withrow, 1967).

Programs hoped to acquire the service of college graduates; more often, they recruited from high schools. Fred Numbers (1927) chided that most candidates could not teach arithmetic to the upper grades. "Algebra," he said, "is entirely out of the question" (Numbers, 1927, p. 343). With tongue in cheek, Numbers further observed that "oftentimes girls just out of high school don't know how to discipline themselves. Springtime, a moonlight night, and a 1927-model sport roadster, with the accent on 'sport'—and most normal students forget the technical differences between a consonant and a vowel" (Numbers, 1927, p. 345).

College-based training for teachers of the deaf began in 1864 at the National Deaf Mute College. By 1920, a small number of programs were offered in colleges and universities. The earliest university-based program for teachers of the deaf was founded at the University of Wisconsin in Milwaukee in 1913. Programs began at New York University and San Francisco State College in 1934. However, critics carped that "there is no uniformity of procedures at all, and . . . there is no uniformity in the purpose for which the training classes are formed" ("The Training and Certification of Teachers," 1929, p. 247). Programs lacked cohesion and pattern in method, purpose, or standards, and varied from a few months to 2 years.

Immediately after World War II, a number of new training programs developed. Frequently, these new programs differed from their earlier counterparts in that a full-time staff was created at the college or university, but there still remained a close administrative tie with the practicum facility.

In 1950, there were 18 training centers in the United States; 47 by 1963 (Lane, 1952; Streng, 1964). A trainee in the field of teaching the deaf was now defined "as an individual who is engaged in a program of study which consists of a planned sequence of courses in the education of deaf children which leads to certification in the field. We do not refer to those who may be enrolled merely for certain courses dealing with deafness" ("The Sixty-Second Summer Meeting," 1952, p. 492).

At no time was there a surplus of skilled teachers of the deaf (Craig, 1946). Helen Lane, principal of the Central Institute for the Deaf observed that "Unemployment has never been a worry of a well-trained oral teacher of the deaf" (1946, p. 704). Before World War II, the number of teachers being trained approximately offset the numbers of those who retired or left the profession (Craig, 1946). After the war, the shortage was acute; recruitment became a pressing issue. By the 1950s, "the most discussed topic in educational circles" was "the critical shortage of qualified teachers" (Flint, 1957, p. 66). Compounding the problem was the fact that, in some schools, marriage automatically cancelled a woman's contract (Lane, 1946).

Teachers of the Blind

As part of his campaign for the betterment of blind people, Samuel Gridley Howe assiduously promoted in-service teacher training for some of his most promising pupils. He cited "the superiority of blind to seeing persons as teachers of the blind" and viewed "a school for the blind without blind teachers as necessarily imperfect" (Dunscombe, 1836, p. 108). By 1861, the Perkins institution employed four blind teachers (Perkins Institution for the Blind, 1861). Ten schools for the blind in the United States were initiated by blind individuals (Best, 1934). However, apart from schools for the blind, few graduates got jobs as teachers: blind teachers were unable to teach in the common schools because they could not supervise (Perkins Institution for the Blind, 1851, 1856).

In-house training was as popular for teachers of the blind as it was in deaf education, and the previous discussion on the deaf can be generalized to training programs for teachers of the visually impaired. However, although Samuel Gridley Howe agitated for a college for the blind along the lines of Gallaudet College, he was unsuccessful. For those involved with the blind, college training began in 1884 at the Teachers College of Columbia.

Teachers of Students With Intellectual Disabilities

In-house teacher training for candidates preparing to work with those with intellectual disabilities was first established at the New Jersey Training School for Feeble-Minded Boys and Girls at Vineland on an internship basis in the 1890s. The programs were taught and supervised by superintendent E. R. Johnstone and psychologist Henry Goddard. The formal program that was established later became the prototype for professional training programs that were introduced into other institutions in the following decades. In 1902, the Vineland institution announced the first formal 6-week summer seminar training program for public school teachers and first offered summer training for American and Canadian teachers of mentally retarded children in 1904 (Johnstone, 1914).

In the final decades of the 19th century, normal schools, colleges, and universities began to recognize the mentally retarded student. Beginning in 1897, the University of Pennsylvania offered a three-course sequence on mental retardation (Wallin, 1914). By 1929, 37 teachers' colleges and 8 normal schools in 22 states and an additional 4 colleges and universities in 38 states and Washington, DC offered one to twelve courses for the preparation of teachers and supervisors of mentally retarded children (Scheier, 1931). The programs generally included curriculum and methods, practicum as well as industrial, manual, and domestic training.

By 1941, elementary teachers could take an extra 24 semester hours of approved courses to be certified to teach mentally retarded children ("Pennsylvania Certification of Teachers . . . ," 1941). Still, by April, 1957, only 40 colleges and universities reported course work on mental retardation, and at these schools, there were only 28 full-time and 64 part-time instructors. Only 15 universities had capacity for doctoral training in mental retardation (Burke, 1976).

Recruitment and Salary

Throughout the history of special education, recruiting enough teachers formed a central theme. Problems ebbed and flowed. For example, the acute teacher shortage of the years during World War II stretched on into the postwar era because young people did not prepare for teaching during the war (Lord, 1947). In deaf education, for example, the number of trainees in 1946 was only about 48% of those trained in 1940 (Craig, 1946). Training centers either were not at full capacity or were shut down entirely (Craig, 1946). By 1952, six of twenty centers in one study reported no trainees completing the training program ("The Sixty-Second Summer Meeting," 1952).

Of the multiple factors contributing to teacher shortages, one of the most telling was the wage differential as compared with salaries in other professions. During the years of World War II, wages and salaries in general increased much faster and advanced much higher than prices. Teachers' salaries did not keep pace. By 1947, a teacher's wage was about $2,000 or less; the wage of an employee in the federal government averaged $4,150 (Lord, 1947, p. 182).

Salary, which offered no great inducement to any teacher, was contentious in the field of special education with respect to differences between day schools and institutional settings and along gender lines. An institutional teacher trainer from Michigan pointed out in 1927 that "the maximum salary is less than the minimum paid to teachers in the city of Detroit, and I dare say this condition exists in most states" (Numbers, 1927, p. 346). Another administrator complained that "the conflict between the state schools and the day schools in some states is quite fierce," with "much opportunity for rivalry and jealousy and things of that kind" ("The Training and Certification of Teachers," 1929, p. 312). In-house programs lost graduates to the higher-paying school systems. Said one administrator, "When I had my teachers trained, the day-schools snapped them up just as fast as they got a little experience" ("The Training and Certification of Teachers," 1929, p. 268).

Equal pay for men and women was discussed, and placing salaries on a par was a constant cry of residential school principals determined to bolster recruitment and halt attrition to the day schools. For example, at the Missouri School for the Deaf in 1929, men earned $2,000; women $1,500. Men received one-third more than women although some of the women were doing "incomparably better work than the men" ("The Salary Question," 1929, p. 262). Women contended that female teachers should receive the same pay as the man doing work of the same nature (Taylor, 1900). The issue was unresolved.

In the late 1950s, the federal government stepped into teacher training with an ongoing commitment to fund the preparation of teachers of students with disabilities (see Chapter 5). After 1958, a boom in legislation and generous funding provided for training personnel and implementing programs. Still, from the 1970s on, there was a decline in the number of special educators graduating from teacher preparation programs. Attrition rates climbed to 15% (Singer, 1993). Although the schools were increasingly multicultural, members of minority groups were not entering the profession. By 1986, minority teachers were described as "an endangered species." Only 6.9% of the teaching corps were people of color (Lytle, 1987).

In the reform climate of the 1980s, teacher education received enormous attention (see Chapter 9). The spirit of reform, restructure, and reinvent brought a torrent of reports critical of teacher education (e.g., Carnegie Forum, 1986; Holmes Group, 1986) and a matching avalanche of reform avenues. Recommendations included placing greater emphasis on subject-area training for teachers, placing professional education courses in a fifth or graduate year, and increasing standards for entry into the teaching profession. The No Child Left Behind Act (NCLB) of 2001 brought another wrinkle to teacher requirements. The NCLB was the first federal education policy establishing teacher requirements. It introduced the phrase "high quality teacher" (but did not define high quality teacher) and mandated that all teachers meet this requirement by the end of the 2005–2006 school year.

Although faculty personnel are critical to teacher preparation programs, qualified personnel are not available today. Doctoral programs are producing 30% fewer graduates than 2 decades ago (Smith, 2003). Moreover, there is barely any sign of sustained growth in the number of new graduates moving into faculty positions. It is estimated that for every faculty position left unfilled, 25 special education teachers go untrained and 400 students with special needs go unserved, or underserved (Smith, Pion, Tyler, Sindelar, & Rosenberg, 2001).

FROM ARTISAN TO PROFESSIONAL

An occupation becomes professionalized when people systemize the knowledge needed to perform it. Members develop shared beliefs about the mission of the profession; how it should be carried out; what preparation and credentials members should possess; and the status and power of the profession in relation to its clients, to other professionals, and to the world at large (Achenbach, 1975).

Within the general public school system, teacher professionalism was enhanced through the development of professional associations, journals, and conventions. In 1818, the first educational journal addressed to education professionals was founded in the United States. Thomas Hopkins Gallaudet was prominent in the organization of the first teachers convention, held in Hartford in October 1830, presided over by Noah Webster. The National Teachers Association (later the National Education

Association, NEA) was formed in 1857 by 43 educators from a dozen states and the District of Columbia "to elevate the character and advance the interests of the profession of teaching, and to promote the cause of popular education in the United States" (West, 1984).

One of the first professional groups dealing with a disabled population was the Association of Medical Superintendents of American Institutions for the Insane, created in 1844 (McGovern, 1986). At the same time, the *American Journal for Insanity* was founded to provide a forum for scientific discussions and an impetus for scientific research (Goodenough, 1949). The Association evolved into the American Medico-Psychological Association from 1892 until 1921 when it was succeeded by the American Psychiatric Association. The official publication became the *American Journal of Psychiatry* in that same year.

Teachers of the deaf were early in asserting a sense of unique professional identity; the process of professionalization began during the 1840s when various professional organizations emerged within the field. The Convention of American Instructors of the Deaf, founded in 1850, was the first national conference of special education teachers to be held in the world.

As workers adhering to an oral philosophy battled relentlessly to achieve a radical new vision of the role in society of deaf people, they absorbed, to a marked degree, the question of professionalism. Oral teachers held that the course of pure oralism could be more effective in independent organizations; they created a parallel profession, almost entirely the domain of females. Journals and conventions served to foster the oralists' conception of themselves as a group separate from the manualists. Associations promoted the development of members as a social group with a distinctive style and distinctive values. For example, the American Association to Promote the Teaching of Speech to the Deaf (AAPTSD), established in 1891 for the dissemination of the oral creed, was an effective forum. The AAPTSD allowed the public advocacy of pedagogical philosophy and enabled the oral teachers to see themselves as a special group of experts with their own professional ideals and values. It became the Alexander Graham Bell Association for the Deaf in 1953. In 1917, Max Goldstein began the Society for Progressive Oral Advocates in St. Louis, which continued to meet annually until 1952. The official publication was *Oralism and Auralism* (Goldstein, 1919, 1976).

Edouard Seguin encouraged the establishment of the first American association devoted solely to people with mental retardation. He called on his fellow superintendents to meet annually to share their experiences and lent his influence to form the Association of Medical Officers of American Institutions for Idiots and Feeble-Minded Persons. Dr. Isaac Kerlin, prominent in the foundation of the new group, advocated an abbreviated title—the American Association for the Study of the Feeble-Minded—in 1907. In 1933, the group became the American Association of Mental Deficiency; in 1988, the American Association of Mental Retardation.

As teachers established their professional legitimacy, they developed an infatuation with professional status. Treading the paths of other occupational groups seeking to transform work into profession, they developed a professional mien manifested by participation in associations, conferences, and journals. Professional allegiance emphasized the importance of a specific body of knowledge and the development of a unique technical expertise, all with a separate lexicon. Teachers' unions, associations, or federations slowly developed from the benevolent associations of the 19th century that served to assist teachers in lean times.

Specialized training defined the parameters of the work and the uniqueness of particular pedagogical and intellectual concerns. Such training generated the perception that the knowledge and pedagogy related to the education of students with disabilities constituted a unique body of information while the nature and language of special education practices communicated a message that the endeavor was somehow very different from the work of other educational professionals. This perception not only baffled consumers and nonspecial colleagues alike but also distanced special educators from their general education peers, setting them apart in terms of what they knew and how they saw themselves (see Osgood, 1999).

People who taught in institutional settings and special classes required indispensible qualifications above those of general teachers. Teachers in programs for students with disabilities not only met the standard academic qualifications but also satisfied additional ones related to their specific work. Just as critically, unique personal attributes attached to special education teachers. Teachers were expected to respond to the complex interrelationships of social, emotional, and intellectual traits brought to school by "pupils with dull minds, crippled bodies, speech defects, deafness, or twisted emotions" (Laycock, 1937–38, p. 108). "The special class teacher," observed one writer, "must be an artist. She must forever work with the stones rejected by the builders, and though she may never cause them to be elevated to the head of the corner yet she must search for the hidden possibilities they possess and make the most of them" ("Michigan Loses a Pioneer," 1942, p. 123). Teachers of special children were not only required to achieve additional qualifications but also were selected on the basis of personality qualifications (Font, 1944–45). Samuel Laycock (1940–41) warned that a teacher of special classes should be "emotionally mature and have a wholesome emotional life of her own" (p. 5). She could not be irritable or bad tempered, fussy or coddling, self-pitying, nor starved in her emotional life. Rather, she should be grown up in her sex life and free from frustration and conflict in her own life.

Teachers of the deaf claimed, based on their own beliefs and the apparent belief of others, that "teaching the deaf child is the most difficult job in the whole field of education" (Lane, 1952, p. 497). Teachers were said to have "as many anxieties as teachers of the hearing, perhaps more," so that "a high-strung nervous person, one who is not thoroughly self-possessed or does not make proper distribution of her time, will sooner or later break down at it" (Ontario Department of Education, 1906, p. 451). Those in the profession required "natural qualifications" such as "an attractive personal appearance, a cheerful disposition, good health, and an active, energetic temperament" (Crouter, 1907, pp. 293–294) together with "tact, ability, patience and love for the work" (Ontario Institution for the Education and Instruction of the Deaf and Dumb, 1891, p. 12). "Acquired advantages" included "a good education and a cultivated mind" (Crouter, 1907, pp. 293–294).

Council for Exceptional Children

The formation of the Council for Exceptional Children (CEC) in 1922 filled the void left by the defunct federal Department of Special Education. It created an association that could comfortably encompass all special education personnel but still allow very specialized groups their own foci. The CEC eventually came to be accepted "as the defining and controlling agency for special education" (Blake, 2005, p. 419).

The CEC evolved from two courses at Columbia Teachers College, one on methods and one on the organization of special classes, taught by Elizabeth Farrell (1870–1932), a supervisor of ungraded classes in New York City.[1] Eleven members of the class met at a dinner and discussed the possibilities of forming a national association for people interested in the care and treatment of exceptional children (Warner, 1942, 1944). Elizabeth Farrell was unanimously elected as the first president for 4 years.

At the first annual meeting in February 1923, Farrell addressed herself to the needs of the embryonic organization and the children and teachers it would serve. The clientele included "the gifted, dull and defective, deaf, blind, feeble-minded, tubercular, undernourished, cardiac, idiot, dull normal, and anti-social" (Abraham, 1976, p. 331). One goal of the council was "to have all children classified and educated according to their ability, the gifted as well as the dull." Another purpose was "the establishment of standards for classes of all types of exceptional children" (Sargeant, 1935, p. 32). For educators, Farrell hoped that the organization would be a clearinghouse of knowledge useful to teachers in their special fields; would promote the ideas of special education and professional training; would become the authoritative body on questions of subject matter, method, and school and class organization; and would sponsor conventions and journals (Geer, 1977).

During the first year, a constitution was drawn up; by-laws were put into action by 1924. Membership was to be open to all people interested in the education of special children. The movement spread rapidly. In 1923, the organization held its first convention in Cleveland; 50 people attended, and the secretary reported a membership of 389. By 1944, there were 4,134 members; by 1950, 6,500 members; by 1977, the membership had expanded to 67,000 (Geer, 1977).

The original name selected was the International Council for the Education of Exceptional Children. At the Minneapolis meeting in 1933, the word *education* was dropped, and the name changed to the International Council for Exceptional Children to reflect the notion that the problems of exceptional children were broader than just education alone. In 1958, *international* was dropped because the council was by then a unit of the NEA and because the U.S. Congress was confused by the fact that an international organization was striving to deal with national problems (Kirk & Lord, 1974).

At the outset, the new group did not have an official publication. A section of the magazine *Ungraded*, a journal published by the Ungraded Class Teachers' Association, was subsidized as the official organ of the council. This publication was followed by the *Council News Letter* in 1923. It became the official *Council Review* in 1934 and was renamed the *Journal of Exceptional Children* in the same year. At first, the journal was privately owned but was bought by the CEC in 1942. In 1954, it became simply *Exceptional Children*.

The acceptance of the CEC as a participating educational organization came rather slowly. In the first few years of its existence, Farrell was unable to convince the federal Department of Superintendents to include the new association as a section at its annual meeting. Farrell said later that "the Department of Superintendents felt that we were the *baby* of the public school system, and they could not accommodate babies at a meeting of superintendents" (cited in Sargeant, 1935, p. 33, original italics). In 1937, the National Society for the Study of Education did not approve the suggestion of a yearbook on exceptional children because it was believed that the field was not sufficiently structured or of sufficient interest to educators (Kirk, 1950). In 1933, the CEC voted against becoming a department of special education within the NEA but did become one in 1942. From 1941 on, the CEC was affiliated with the NEA. Affiliation was withdrawn in 1977.

SUMMARY AND THEMES

For those aspiring to the specialized fields of teaching deaf, blind, or mentally retarded students, in-house training was the most plausible process. Once established by Thomas Hopkins Gallaudet at the opening of the 19th century, this teacher-training mode retained an enduring popularity. By the close of the 19th century, however, an increasing commitment to specialization and certification saw three major models of teacher training in place—the apprenticeship or internship model, the normal school plus in-house training model, and a novel departure in which universities and colleges established programs and courses directed toward special education.

Although new visions of teacher training emerged, no clearly conceived pattern for training existed. A major commonality lay in the arrangements made by programs to provide advanced training that was not available to the general corps of teachers and that was above and beyond that asked of teachers in the standard streams. Another was founded on the careful selection of teachers. Unique attributes attached to potential special education teachers and the expectations with respect to their superior teaching skills and personal characters were set high.

Teachers of students with special needs assiduously developed their own sense of professionalism and authority. Increasingly, they developed a belief about their mission, how it should be carried out, and the credentials that qualified a person to enter the profession. In doing so, they generated new beliefs about educators' status and power in relation to the clients, to parents, to allied disciplines, and to the world at large. Professional affiliation was concretely manifested in new and more encompassing professional associations, journals, conventions, and meetings.

NOTE

1. CEC founder Elizabeth Farrell was born in Utica, New York. Her teaching and university training were done in her native state. Her first teaching position was in an ungraded class in Oneida, New York (see Kode, 2002). In 1900, she accepted a position as a grade teacher in the New York City Public Schools. Farrell taught a class of 18 to 20 boys, ages 8 to 16, who had been failing in general education. Her students were incorrigible, truant, unable to read or count, and retarded in their grades; many had health problems. Farrell later became the first inspector of ungraded classes in New York City. She held that students who did not fit into standard educational practices should be educated differently and decided that the curriculum needed overhauling to meet the needs of the child. She developed a curricular model that was individualized and pragmatic. During the last few years of her work as inspector of ungraded classes, Farrell laid the foundation for an important extension of the work. In 1928, she founded classes for students who had IQs lower than 50. In 1924, she cooperated with the Manhattan Trade School in the establishment of trade classes for older girls with mental retardation (Warner, 1944). She was one of the founders of the Association of Consulting Psychologists in 1921 and a member of the White House Committee on the Mentally Retarded in 1929 (Warner, 1944).

Chapter 9

The Era of Inclusion

Complexity and contradiction characterized the reforms and paradigm shifts of the 1960s and 1970s. The next decade was perhaps more contemplative in that it witnessed much education debate that manifested as a fervent reexamination of schooling and of school systems as well as a re-imagining of the philosophy and practice of special education. A broad swath of social, demographic, economic, and educational factors contributed. These included dissatisfaction with the current educational system, public concern over the costs and outcomes of education, changing lifestyles and family structures, new and diverse needs in the marketplace, and changing demographics in North America. As mirrors and microcosms of society, the public schools experienced dramatic population shifts: school communities were increasingly composed of students from a wide variety of ethnic groups.

A general school reform movement emerged strikingly in the United States and other Western nations during the 1980s. In the United States, it brought a swell of indignation at the lack of educational accountability, which led to an unrelenting assault on the content, processes, and results of schooling and to a plethora of educational policies proposed, passed, reviewed, and eventually evaluated. One school of reform thinking called for greater accountability in academic outcomes and standards to ensure world-class standards in education. An equally compelling strand argued that the United States had become a polycultural society with monocultural schools. Reformers juxtaposed changing demographics with concerns about equity. It was imperative in any effort to confront the new social demands on education that reforms should change the schools, not the students. This reform demanded reconstruction of the entire education system as the solution for preparing at-risk children, culturally and linguistically diverse students, and other young people for a global and technological society. If structural processes created inequality, then restructured schools would counter long-standing patterns of unequal access to the outcomes of educational programs and would pave a route to guarantee equity and equal opportunity. Terms that became proxies for restructuring included *inclusive schooling*, *inclusive education*, or simply *inclusion*.

Special education readily and rapidly co-opted the voice of general education reform. Inclusive schooling for students with disabilities was elevated to the dominant ideology. In essence, inclusion as interpreted by special education implied a fundamental conceptual shift that involved the way in which people with disabilities and their place in society were seen and how educational rights were provided. In concert with the general education realm, inclusive schooling was equated with school restructuring; reformers called for melding practices from general, compensatory, and special education to create an inclusive educational system (Will, 1986). Location—the specific educational setting where services were provided—became the central motif of the inclusion movement.

For many educators, advocacy groups, and parents, inclusion was a clarion call to reshape the field and discard many of the traditional rubrics for organizing efforts. For others, inclusion defied educational orthodoxy and was viewed as a radical reform to be approached cautiously. Unsurprisingly, few issues received the attention or generated the polarization of perspectives and controversy as did the movement toward the inclusion of students with disabilities. Although the philosophy of inclusion was well operationalized within the special education arena by the early 1990s, the entire decade saw open and hostile turbulence within the profession. Rather than reasoned debate, unproductive disputation surrounded the reform movement.

Inclusion was promoted and advanced primarily on the basis of social policy considerations that addressed fundamental assumptions such as social justice, individual rights, the right to equal access, nondiscrimination, social opportunity, and so forth. The reform movement was not founded on scientifically supported practice; the efficacy of inclusion as a treatment variable was unknown. Research activity had not halted, however. Rather, the political environment that shaped the discourses about philosophical preferences and promoted an inclusive climate both fed into and fed off of a rapidly changing culture of research and an altered research slant. Ethical arguments about serving the needs of all students in a culturally diverse society, including those with disabilities, played into epistemological arguments framing the traditional logical positivism that characterized special education research in opposition to alternate paradigms.

Researchers are used to scholarly quarrels: positions advanced by some players are almost invariably attacked and contradicted by others. Without doubt, undercurrents of discontent with the use of natural science methods were not born in the 1970s. As early as 1941, for example, Merle Frampton wrote, "I see a battle between the quantitative and qualitative approach in our field" (p. 144). The continuing epistemological debate accelerated in the 1980s: it saw a widening dichotomy between approaches grouped broadly as empirical-quantitative and interpretative-qualitative. But while new surveys of the intellectual terrain resulted in different maps being drawn, they also eroded the common understanding that facilitated cooperative work between groups. Glaring gaps developed among researchers who dedicated their work to one or the other views of educational reality.

This chapter discusses the inclusive reform efforts and the factors that influenced or were influenced by the movement. Knowledge generation through varied research methodologies is addressed, as is the disconnect between research and practice. Two caveats are in order. First, it is recognized that the philosophy of inclusion and the fundamental propositions and dimensions of the current status and direction of special education are resilient and advocated unequivocally. Currently, diversity, equality, and inclusion are critical principles not only in legislation but also in social and educational policy, and inclusive schooling is fairly standard practice. However, the chapter is focused on the historical development of the inclusive movement. The discussion here essentially ends with the passage of the No Child Left Behind Act in early 2001, which is an arbitrary end point. Second, the ultimate goal of including all students may be straightforward, but it is larded with concepts that are ambiguous, complex, and value laden. Although many themes have taken their flavor from the inclusive paradigm, only a restricted sample of the multiple changes wrought by the movement can be discussed.

REFORMS IN EDUCATION

During the 1980s, the outcomes of education became a key concern of reform. An alarming critique of the American education system was issued in *A Nation at Risk: The Imperative for Educational Reform*, which was released in 1983 by the U.S. Department of Education (National Commission on Excellence in Education, 1983). The 18-member commission of university presidents, eminent scientists, policymakers, and educators used combative language to indict education leaders, school officials, and the American public for complacency. They portrayed high school diplomas as meaningless, presented to barely literate students, and they cited the loss of accomplishments of gifted students. The commission deplored the smorgasbord of electives that pervaded American schools, and they called for an upgrading of standards, a return to basic academic subjects, and substantial improvement in teacher preparation programs. Further comprehensive reports such as John Goodlad's *A Place Called School* (1984) and *Barriers to Excellence: Our Children at Risk* (National Coalition of Advocates for Students, 1985) followed.

Failure in schools is a familiar story in American history. But as parents, legislators, the general public, and educators themselves pointed to the gaps and deficiencies in the educational system, many were unwilling to accept the grim statistics on school failure and dropouts. *A Nation at Risk* became an unrestricted enterprise, distinguished by the intensity of debate and the range of instructional, social, and political issues addressed. It shook loose an avalanche of education reforms inspired by the spate of national reports and manifestos generated by individuals, foundations, associations, governmental agencies, university boards of regents, state boards of education, and local school boards.

Two main threads could be discerned in the fabric of the multiple reforms that were proposed. One thread sought to restore educational productivity and develop world-class standards. Education would serve to prepare workers and citizens in ways that were relevant to emerging labor markets in an increasingly globalized world. Reformers called for greater accountability from schools and teachers; advanced academic achievement from students, especially in mathematics and science; higher academic standards; an emphasis on competition; stricter discipline; ways to improve literacy skills; and ways to halt dropout rates. Ideas to bring about education reform ranged from administrative practices such as lengthening the school day to full-scale restructuring of educational systems such as plans to provide open enrollment options.

A quite separate reform strand conceptualized a complete and complex plan for reforming education to better accommodate culturally different and other marginalized learners. Problems were viewed as institutional, within the culture of schools; therefore, the major focus lay in modifying the norms, rules, policies, procedures, and arrangements of the traditional system. Reformers set out to create socially just and democratic communities by transforming schools into places where all students belonged and learned together. They focused on ways to incorporate multiethnic and multicultural perspectives into classrooms and schools, ways to promote bilingualism and to teach students with limited English proficiency, and ways to ensure educational equality and opportunity for all students. The term that emerged to describe educational systems where equity was in place for all students was *inclusion* or *inclusive schooling* (Dei, James, James-Wilson, Karumanchery, & Zine, 2000).

REFORMING SPECIAL EDUCATION

A reform stance in the field of special education can be traced to the 1960s. In that decade, a fervent egalitarianism brought large-scale political, social, and economic change in the context of many disenfranchised and marginalized groups and created a wholly new climate for exceptionality. The period witnessed a marked change in attitude toward special education, people with disabilities in general, and exceptional children in particular. Arguments held that people with disabilities had a civil right to live, attend school, and work in the same environment as others. Traditional support and demand for the separate institutions seriously eroded; critics advocated closing all residential institutions and moving toward smaller, community-based facilities. Although the decade closed with continued growth in the number of special classes and with the consensus position among practitioners and researchers that such settings were the most suitable for disabled children, educational integration became the central theme of special education. Change was imminent.

By the 1970s, a more humanistic movement was well developed, representing a gradual but positive change in society's attitudes toward people with exceptionalities. Two basic ideologies—normalization and mainstreaming—took root and flowered. The special education script was rewritten, and the profession came of age. Overarching and prescriptive federal legislation in the form of Public Law 94-142 brought the concept of the least restrictive environment, interpreted as mainstreaming. The field continued to adjust and readjust its priorities, particularly its obligations to children and youth who had often been excluded from education, and a genuine and sustained movement toward integration and desegregation emerged.

Although general education was seeking reform in the 1980s, special education passed through a crisis of confidence and embarked on a period of self-flagellation. The suspected ills were many, although there were some primary ones. Concerns about the mainstreaming movement were legion. Only a small number of children were being mainstreamed, resource rooms were not functioning as effectively as they should, and the promises of the Individual Education Plan (IEP) were not being met. Regular education and special education still functioned in the traditional way—as dual and parallel rather than integrated enterprises.

Critics raised questions that had been resonating since the late 1950s, now grounded in quite specific conceptions of social justice, ethics, and civil and individual rights. They searched for the meaning of disability and considered the purpose and effectiveness of special education. Many expressed concerns about the stigmatization of children labeled as exceptional. They viewed special classes as inherently discriminatory and unequal, not a fulfillment of the right to education but a denial of the right by virtue of exclusionary practices.

Although legislation had diminished the line between the systems of general and special education, many decried the persistence of a dual system of education and looked askance at the high proportion of funding—about 10% to 20% of education funds directed toward 10% of the school population (Greer, 1992). They were similarly critical about the fragmentary nature of services that should have been supplementary and correlative but were often duplicative and competitive. The multiplicity of specialists undermined the ability of systems to meet the individual needs of students because every specialist hired not only reduced a school district's ability to provide lower student-teacher ratios but also perpetuated teachers' dependence on specialists (Pugach & Sapon-Shavin, 1987). Critics further suggested that the identification of students for categorical placements was unclear. They complained about the reliability of instruction for children with disabilities, the efficacy of pull-out programs, and curriculum misalignment (Manset & Semmel, 1997). The manner in which special education classes could be made more effective was not solved, and the outcomes for youth who were exiting special education had not improved.

As a reform movement honed the demand for special education change, agents drew energy from negative research findings and marshaled evidence of the failure of special education. "Unless major structural changes are made" they cried, "the field of special education is destined to become more of a problem, and less of a solution in providing education for children who have special needs" (Reynolds, Wang, & Walberg, 1987, p. 391). The urgent need for fundamental change could be met only through revolutionary processes rooted in a wholesale revision of the field. Rhetoric called for special education to "break the mold" as well as for "revolution," a "paradigm shift," "fundamental reconceptualization," and "radical restructuring" (Kauffman, 1993b, p. 10).

The Regular Education Initiative

The Regular Education Initiative (REI) was proposed in 1986 by Madeline Will, then assistant secretary for the Office of Special Education and Rehabilitative Services of the Department of Education. Will called for new partnerships in education—partnerships between states and federal government, between regular and special educators, and between educators and parents.

The REI surfaced in a period that saw the resurgence of political conservatism following 2 decades of rapid expansion. Policy was undergoing substantial alteration, epitomized by the *A Nation at Risk* report (National Commission on Excellence in Education, 1983), which was essentially born out of a conviction of the failing performance of public education. Therefore, federal deinvestment in education and deregulation of special education were hallmarks of the Reagan administration.

President Reagan vowed to reduce the growing federal role in domestic affairs, particularly in education. His New Federalism was intended to reverse the shift of educational power away from the states and local agencies and onto the federal government, which had began during the Johnson presidency. Proposals by the Reagan-Bush administration saw attempts to reduce federal expenditures for social programs, including decreases in federal requirements, consolidation of federal education programs, and reductions in the amount of federal money appropriated for education. The result was declining federal support for programs designed to ensure equity in education for those who were disadvantaged or disabled.

The full federal funding for Public Law 94-142 had not been phased in when the Reagan administration had legislation introduced that was designed to replace the law. Reagan further moved to eliminate the categorical funding for special education, which guaranteed federal support for both local and state level programs. President Reagan made efforts to dismantle the newly formed U.S. Department of Education and, through Public Law 97-35, the Education Consolidation and Improvement Act of 1981, to create block grants from a number of previously discretionary education programs to states. Those efforts ushered in widespread concern that both the hard-won rights and federal fiscal support for the education of students with disabilities would be lost.

Will's proposals for the REI were consistent with the Reagan policy objectives to consolidate strategies to reduce federal influence and expenditures for education. Costs were to be lowered by the elimination of special budget and administrative categories, and the federal regulations were withdrawn in favor of local control (see Kauffman, 1989). In its concrete form, the REI consisted of a varied set of reform proposals sharing a common theme—the need to remove the barriers that excluded students with special needs from full integration into the life of the school and the larger society (Will, 1986). It had several distinguishable goals that involved a number of fundamental changes in the way in which special education would be provided.

Will (1986) did not argue for a consolidation of general and special education but did propose restructuring education to more closely merge general and special education and thereby allow students with learning problems to receive more instruction in general as opposed to special education settings. The merger focused on excellence for all; that is, all students with disabilities would be best served by the improvement of education for all students. Hence, the REI would bring about a system of education in which children with quite diverse, heterogeneous needs were educated in the same classroom. General, compensatory, and special education teachers would work collaboratively, and their collective skills and resources would be used to meet the needs of all students. Regular educators were to assume the responsibility for exceptional children in general classrooms; special educators could serve as consultants and provide support to general educators. All instructional resources—financial, educational, and human—would be pooled under a single administrator. Will advocated not categorizing and labeling students. She spoke primarily to the needs of students with mild disabilities but also promoted the integration of students with low-incidence and severe disabilities into the general education system.

Advocates of the REI claimed that a merged system would better meet the needs of all children. Opponents expressed concerns that the merger would do harm, particularly to those children who lacked adequate support services, and that an adequate research base was not in place to underline such a drastic change in system design. Despite critiques, mainstreaming was reinterpreted under the REI. More critically, questions raised by advocates of the REI soon co-opted the voice of general education reform that spoke to equity and specific versions of social justice. The rallying cry of mainstreaming was replaced by calls for full access to a restructured mainstream, encapsulated as inclusive schooling.

The Movement to Inclusion

The general school reform movement that engulfed the United States and many Western nations during the 1980s lent significant strength and credibility to the calls by people with disabilities and their advocates for increased participation. As special education became rapidly immersed in a reform agenda, it borrowed and adapted the dialogue of general education reform.

The reform strand that endorsed the accountability dynamic of education and that equated efficiency with outcomes was not the priority of special educators. How could this perspective be true when students with special needs were often viewed as poor risks in upwardly aspiring school communities? In general, students with special needs were ignored in the accountability or outcomes oriented models of the 1980s. Even the *Barriers to Excellence* report (National Coalition of Advocates for Students, 1985) that was most critical of policies toward students with disabilities did not question the underlying separateness of general and special education systems.

The specific aspect of the reform conversation that was so appealing to special education centered on social transformation ideals made concrete through school restructuring. In its philosophical guise, the concept of inclusion was egalitarian, affirming, and key in eliminating social injustices. It reflected a large-scale political and social change in attitudes toward disenfranchised and oppressed groups. Ulti-mately, as Len Barton observed, inclusion was "about the transformation of a soci-ety and its formal arrangements, such as education. This means changes in the values, priorities and policies that support and perpetuate practices of exclusion and discrimination" (1999, p. 68).

Proponents of inclusive schooling strived to rid education of stubborn, long-standing inequalities through a revisualization of the organizational structures of schools. As a proxy for school restructuring, inclusion was not merely minor tin-kering done to improve basic educational structures; it was a major reform that was designed to transform and alter permanently the structure and organization of schooling. Those seeking change posited that rather than perpetuating special education, reform needed to change general education fundamentally in terms of its teaching and learning processes to fashion school programs that would be respon-sive to the needs of all learners. The goal was "an educational model for all stu-dents—supple, variegated, and individualized—in an integrated setting" (Gartner & Lipsky, 1987, p. 368). In this sense, inclusion advanced the field from redefining special education to reforming general education: the special education conundrum collapsed into the general mission of school improvement (Slee, 1997).

Operationalized, the advent of inclusive schooling reversed the field and rejected many of the practices that had been carried out in special education. Of the many discernable trends, one of the most important advanced the concept of dis-ability as diversity. Chiefly, however, that trend led to students' schools addresses became the primary focus and the major hub of controversy.

Disability as Diversity

It was during the 1970s and 1980s that enormous changes in the demograph-ics of the United States (and Canada) took hold. Once countries with populations predominantly of European ancestry, they now had absorbed a large number of people who belonged to mostly identifiable racial minorities and who came from traditions and cultures little known to Americans (or Canadians). According to the 1990 U.S. Census, the total number of people from outside the U.S. increased 40% between 1980 and 1990. Only 10% of those who arrived in the 1980s were European (Lustig & Koestner, 1996). Most were from Latin America and Asia. Mexico provided the greatest number, followed by the Philippines, China, Korea, and Vietnam (Figueroa & Garcia, 1994). Projections for the year 2020 indicate that Hispanic Americans will be the largest ethnic minority group in the United States and that students of color will make up 46% of the nation's school-aged youth (Piirto, 1994).

Special education has not been traditionally noted for its responsiveness to cultural differences; there has existed little understanding or recognition of the variables that occurred among diverse populations. Inevitably, ignoring cultural and linguistic differences created one of the most troubling and enduring issues in the field—the overrepresentation of minority and economically disadvantaged populations. Persistent overrepresentation occurred as the membership of certain groups in special programs was larger than the percentage of that group in the educational system or within a certain disability category.

As special educators coopted the voice of education reform, a minority group perspective subtly emerged without significant opposition. Researchers and practitioners connected the trend toward inclusive education with the broader diversity goal: there was an increasing tendency to locate special education under the umbrella of diversity. Disability was constructed and described through discourses similar to the discourses on other forms of discrimination and marginalization that was based on race, class, gender, sexual orientation, primary language spoken, age, religion, and immigration status.

Theorizing on multicultural education began in earnest in the 1980s (see Winzer & Mazurek, 1998). By the mid-1990s, questions of equity raised diversity to the status of a critical educational variable. The arena for serving culturally different students in special education expanded dramatically. Many educators scrutinized and assessed the changed societal and educational context in which all students develop. They internalized the tenets of cultural pluralism, which encouraged and fostered differences in the belief that society is strengthened and enriched by the contributions of different cultural groups. As a result, they committed to education that supported racially, ethnically, linguistically, and economically diverse children.

Although the language of diversity was easy to find in special education, the conceptual base was more problematic. The relationship between disability and diversity is far more complicated than merely viewing disability as another parallel "ism" among the many "isms" that today are located under the general term "diversity" (Pugach & Seidl, 1996, 1998). Despite the obvious parallel with respect to access and civil rights, differences exist between the needs of students with disabilities and the demands of a multicultural society. Arguments held that calling special education cultural diversity was a denial tactic. Differences are important, remarked Kauffman (2003), but "the differences that are called disabilities require different responses than do differences in color or ethnic origin or gender or many other forms or marks of distinction" (p. 207). Pragmatically, however, diversity is a critical issue in the classroom. Teaching students from diverse backgrounds and with diverse needs is one of the most compelling challenges that teachers face (Futrell, Gomez, & Bedden, 2003).

The Inclusive Agenda

Discussions of inclusive schooling first appeared in the special education literature in the mid-1980s. Immediately, the basic constructs of individual rights and equity translated into sameness of treatment that rapidly mutated into sameness of experience. Inclusive education identified with a much deeper philosophical ideal than did integration, the least restrictive environment, and mainstreaming. Advocates argued that the social-cultural realities of mainstreaming and integration saw one group viewed as the mainstream and the other group as not mainstream. Hence, one group was not made up of fully fledged members of a class but had to push into the activities and settings occupied by the other (see Salisbury, 1991). Under the principles of inclusion, children did not push into the mainstream because an underlying supposition of inclusive programs was that all children would be based in the classrooms they would attend if they did not have a disability.

When the philosophy and principles of inclusive education were first foregrounded in the 1980s, the commentaries surrounding the reform were often fervent and thoughtful—and just as often, clamorous. Then, as a cluster of underlying arguments and positions emerged, the values of inclusion were masked and attenuated by internal conflicts. Contentions that emerged aspired to usurp the credibility of ideological rivals for the purpose of leadership and dominance of the profession were a driving force.

The field of social antagonisms had two main sets of players, variously termed "abolitionists and conservationists" (Fuchs & Fuchs, 1992), "inclusionists and traditionalists" (Brantlinger, 1997), "full inclusionists and selective inclusionists" (Winzer, 2005a), or "the right thinking, politically correct 'good guys'" and those "on the wrong side of the fence" (Bricker, 1995, p, 180). Depending on their own ideological predispositions, commentators and practitioners operated with different concepts and different scripts as they provided evidence in support of their own positions. Of all issues, that of the location for the delivery of services was most critical: it became the podium for value-laden stances and much emotional moralizing (see Kauffman, 1993b).

Often, different perspectives reflected the working agenda of people within discrete areas so that the rifts that developed over perceptions and educational issues were a function of disability boundaries (see Fuchs & Fuchs, 1994). Full inclusionists, primarily in the areas of mental retardation and severe and profound disabilities, challenged the location where supports were provided to students with disabilities and posed inclusion as a contrast to providing a continuum of services. They held that the desirability of placement options, as represented by a continuum, had outlived its usefulness and that no meaningful transformation could occur unless special education and its cascade of placements were eliminated altogether. In contrast, selective inclusionists, primarily from the fields of learning disabilities and behavior disorders, supported a continuum of services within the least restrictive environment.

At the dawn of the inclusion movement, full inclusionists seized the moral and ideological high ground. They re-imagined special education by suggesting new assumptions, systems, and procedures, and produced boundless propositions, images, key words, phrases, and metaphors. But they also attempted to foreclose debate and tended to use the inclusive reform as an instrument of ideological intimidation. Their rhetoric often held much angry righteousness, the tone of exasperated evangelists in fury against those who were heretics and nonbelievers. This approach was not accidental. Those seeking full inclusion soon became a cast of people who demanded final and virtually infallible authority with respect to inclusive matters. These promoters focused primarily on what was wrong with special education, on moral imperatives, on value-laden stances, and on civil rights and social justice arguments.

The notion of egalitarianism was so entrancing that it pulled many workers into an abyss of emotionality. Full inclusionists often used the language of oppression, which made an indelible effect when inclusion was used in counterpoint to its evil opposite, exclusion. Children with special needs were described as segregated, "humiliated, cast out, or neglected" (Befring, 1997, p. 185). In stressing the dynamics of oppression and domination, some of the more forceful advocates drew parallels between labeling and segregation in special classes and negative connotations in society and history. Some writers compared special education with South Africa's policy of apartheid (Lipsky & Gartner, 1987) and with slavery (Stainback & Stainback, 1988). Forest and Pearpoint (1992) linked the label "disabled" to the "yellow star pinned on people labeled Jewish, and the pink triangle pinned on people labeled homosexual during World War II" (p. 81).

Scientific evidence was displaced by subjective interests and perspectives. Some reform advocates (e.g., Biklen, 1985; Lipsky & Gartner, 1987, 1998; Stainback & Stainback, 1988) trivialized or disparaged experimental trials and empirical data. They found challenges to be unnecessary distractions and often rejected the need to empirically test the effects, arguing that restructuring the system was a moral imperative and the weight of ethical arguments outbalanced the necessity for data. Because the issue of the best education could be answered only, in their opinion, by moral enquiry, questions of location and equal rights were elevated above scientific authority. Inclusion was not a matter of scientific study but should be promoted on the basis of moral and ethical considerations. Science, wrote Biklen (1985) "cannot tell us that integration is right. We can answer it only by determining what we believe, what we consider important" (pp. 183–184).

The torrent of rhetoric did not pass unscathed by those supporting selective inclusion. Many found the new breed of moral entrepreneurs more accomplished at ideological posturing than at presenting substance. They viewed the extreme rhetoric as the front line in defense of frail logic and "fixed on their adversaries' unrealistic remedies and intemperate rhetoric to portray them as out-of-touch ideologues" (Fuchs & Fuchs, 1992, p. 413).

Others with more conservative voices did not argue that inclusion in itself was inherently moral or correct. Nor did they accept any blanket policy. They held that a child's right to an appropriate education overshadowed any ideology so that broad, sweeping generalizations about the ethics of segregation versus integration were fruitless and unnecessary polemics. A more productive and rational approach was to consider the appropriateness of placement for each student identified as disabled. Rather than automatically integrate all children with special needs into general classrooms, those in the field should clarify a range of options founded on student needs and should carefully assess the capacity of individual school systems to educate all children.

By the latter years of the 1990s, the cautious countermovement began to create an intense undercurrent. As conservative voices gained in volume, the hysteria and fervor of the inclusive reform was replaced by more sober reflections.

The rhetoric of full inclusion was challenged and deconstructed. The liberal trappings and emancipatory dialogue came under heavy attack, dismissed by many thoughtful commentators as utopian and impractical.

Nevertheless, services were popularized based on arguments that all students were best served in general education classrooms rather than in segregated classes where a disability classification formed the common denominator. Webb (1994) reported that "by the fall of 1993 almost every state was implementing inclusion at some level" (p. 2). After that, the rates increased substantially and consistently. Almost 96% of students with disabilities in the United States were served in general school buildings (Olson, 2004) although the degree to which students were taught in general classrooms varied greatly across states and districts. Children and youth with mild disabilities were more likely to be in general classrooms; those with significant disabilities in special classes, schools, or facilities. Students who were deaf and blind, who had multiple disabilities, or who had serious emotional disorders made up the largest proportion of those in separate schools (McLeskey, Henry, & Hodges, 1999).

Legislation

Legislative and judicial remedies for social issues, including special education, emerged persuasively from the 1950s on. Public Law 94-142 was first amended in 1986 through Public Law 99-457. The amended legislation divided the preschool population into two groups—infants and toddlers (birth to 3 years, Part H) and preschoolers (3 to 6 years, Part B). The law first provided full services for 3 year olds and dramatically increased funding for preschool programs.

The Individuals with Disabilities Education Act (IDEA; Pub. L. 101-476) again amended Public Law 94-142 in 1990. The IDEA retained all the basic provisions of the original legislation but expanded to include 13 types of disability when it added autism and traumatic brain injury as categories. The title of the law was also changed to stress people-first terminology—that is, to say "a child with a disability," rather than "a handicapped child."

The IDEA was amended in June 4, 1997 (Pub. L. 105-17). This amendment refined the basics and addressed the issues of school discipline and the authority of school personnel to handle children who could be a danger to themselves and others. It put new discipline provisions in place, strengthened the role of parents, required that the general education curriculum be a starting place for all students, and required that outcome measures on IEPs (goals and objectives) be tied directly to the general education curriculum goals and objectives. The Individuals With Disabilities Education Improvement Act of 2004 (Pub. L. 108-446) passed into law on June 19, 2004.

Inclusion is a state-of-the art term; it is not mentioned in federal law or in state statutes. The IDEA of 1990 stipulated that children with disabilities be provided with a free, appropriate public education in the least restrictive environment. The 1997 amendments did not mandate inclusion but strongly encouraged consideration of educational placements in general classrooms. Federal rulings about inclusion also determined that the focus of an intervention should be on where a child can receive an appropriate education that meets his or her needs and that this setting may be a segregated or a regular setting (see McLaughlin & Henderson, 2000). These rulings further stipulated that students can be placed in special settings only when the use of supplementary aids and services in the general classroom cannot achieve a satisfactory education (Culross, 1997).

Canada and the United States hold to a shared purpose when it comes to the inclusion of students with disabilities. Since at least 1987, each jurisdiction has modernized its laws to reflect inclusive education tenets, and the movement to integrate students with exceptionalities into neighborhood schools and general classrooms has progressed rapidly. However, the decentralized nature of the Canadian system of education has shaped inclusive schooling into distinct configurations: much diversity exists in the momentum and the actual enactment is quite different from province to province. In addition, the lack of prescriptive legislation means that Canada tells a rather different story than does the United States.[1]

Much of the sentimental egalitarianism of the early inclusive movement was designed to affect parents. The most vocal and partisan were parents and groups lobbying for children with significant disabilities, those most intimately concerned with participation and acceptance. The parent base, however, eroded: the inclusion movement eventually lacked support from "a critical mass of parents whose children with severe disabilities would be directly affected by the agenda" (Palmer, Fuller, Arora, & Nelson, 2001). Parents of preschool children became the group most likely to support inclusive options (Soodak, 1998). Many parents of school-aged children seemed confident about the social goals of inclusion—more opportunities for children with disabilities to be exposed to the real world and to be accepted by their communities—but were apprehensive about the approach's effect on the quality of services their children received (Green & Stoneman, 1989; Palmer, Borthwick-Duffy, & Widaman, 1998). Regularly, parents voiced concerns about lack of support shown by children's teachers, about teachers and administrators who dismissed their points of view, and about those educators who did little to involve parents in the children's education beyond pro forma correspondence (see Hanson et al., 2001; Heinze & Leyser, 1990; Schuller & O'Reilly, 2003).

It is hardly surprising that litigation activity mounted. Although education litigation generally declined in the 1980s and 1990s, special education litigation increased dramatically (Zirkel, 1997). The 613 published court decisions during the 1990s represented an almost tenfold increase from the total of the 1970s. In a study limited specifically to special education litigation, Maloney (1995) found that more than 60% of the pertinent 1,200 court decisions since 1978 had been decided since 1989.

No Child Left Behind Act

It is now very generally agreed that people with disabilities have a natural and rightful place in society and that schools should mirror this broader commitment. The reforms have made significant political progress, and there was a general acceptance of the need for affiliation opportunities for students with disabilities and their typical peers as a basic human right.

Contemporary educators confront the increasingly high expectations for students with disabilities. For example, the No Child Left Behind Act (NCLB), an amendment of the Elementary and Secondary Education Act; the Good Start, Grow Smart initiative of 2000[2]; and the corresponding Reading First initiative (2002) were all designed to improve access to quality education programs and to provide an ever-improving education for all American children. The NCLB took the notion of accountability to a new level. It requires all students to be proficient in core school subjects by 2014.

The law increased the responsibility of both states and schools to ensure that programs are effective in helping children learn and grow (Rous, 2004). It required state officials to monitor improvement by measuring outputs—progress on content and achievement—through state and district assessments derived from standardized achievement tests of their own choosing (high-stakes testing). States were required to use any of five options (including restructuring and takeovers) for intervening in schools that fail to meet annual performance targets for 5 consecutive years. The NCLB contains an explicit policy commitment to ensure that all students, including those with disabilities, have a fair and equal opportunity to meet state standards, thus melding the requirements of the NCLB with the IDEA of 2004. States, districts, and schools had to test 95% of all students, including those with disabilities, in Grades 3 through 8 in reading and math.

Both supporters and critics alike credit the NCLB for forcing attention to the needs of underperforming children. Advocates see the inclusion of special education students in state testing as an important step in ensuring that every child receives a high-quality education and note that collecting achievement data is the only way to determine whether students are progressing and whether schools are doing their job. Critics contend that the law is not flexible enough to take into account the individual needs of students with disabilities. There is also the often-cited lack of incentives to boost advanced students. In addition, the "highly qualified teacher" specified in the act has not yet been defined.

RESEARCH, KNOWLEDGE, AND INQUIRY IN SPECIAL EDUCATION

Many observers take educational research to task and hold that it is not impressively effective and is accorded little respect (e.g., Greenwood, 2001). Similarly, the field of special education cannot construct a distinguished history. There has not been a strong research commitment in special education. The area has not produced its own research methodology but has borrowed instead from a host of other disciplines.

Traditionally, positivism served as the research framework and as the dominant discourse in understanding and treating disability (Kliewer & Drake, 1998). The historical antecedents of positivism can be traced back to the much broader social movement of the Enlightenment. The modernist theories influenced by

Enlightenment rationalism promoted the notion that prediction and control of human conditions is possible. Scientific explanations were advanced as the principal tool for reaching these ends. Thinkers held the ideal of "a unified epistemology that discovers the foundational truths of physical and biological phenomena and unites them with an accurate understanding of humanity in its psychological, social, political, and aesthetic aspects" (Sasso, 2001, p. 179). In the context of the Enlightenment, positivism acted as a liberation philosophy: it liberated education from the traditional authority of the state, the prince, and the Pope. The French philosophers such as Diderot, Voltaire, Rousseau, Condillac, and many others, questioned the legal, moral, and religious foundations of the French state. They believed in the concept of progress through science and reason, the perfectability of humans, individual freedom, and the efficacy of empiricism (Winzer, 1986).

Later, what followed constituted legitimate research focused on logical positivism, which favored predictability and logical sequencing of events and viewed human conditions as manageable and predictable. Ideas were not to be trusted unless they could pass the stringent test of consistency and could demonstrate validity. The principles of objective knowledge and analysis of phenomena therefore relied on empirical verification.

The predominant positivist empirical set of assumptions that traditionally underlay most theories in the social sciences had an enormous influence on special education. Nevertheless, from the beginning, researchers were the stepchildren of the natural and biological sciences, including philosophy, anthropology, sociology, literary criticism, history, and especially, natural science. The first research methods used in special education derived from medicine and then from the fledgling discipline of psychology. Francis Galton and Karl Pearson, for example, developed the field of biometrics, including most of the methods of modern statistical analysis. (see Chapter 3). As psychology, anthropology, and sociology became academic disciplines, they provided further methodological modes for research in special education. William Wundt was the architect of methodological research in psychology, the field closest to educational research. The development of scientific research methods in the closely allied field of educational psychology can be attributed to Edward Lee Thorndike who began his work in the 1920s.

After World War II, the standards of research and problem analysis continually progressed. A range of conceptual and theoretical tools developed for the study of special education. Researchers devoted to special education were most often trained in the tradition of the scientific method. The primary and preferred mode was process-product research that adhered to the tenets of the scientific method used extensively in the natural sciences. From this paradigm, research was conceived as a universal activity that was quantifiable, objective, disinterested, and aseptic. Knowledge could be gained in a methodological and repeatedly verifiable way uncontaminated by the researcher's values, beliefs, assumptions, prejudices, knowledge, and passions and without reliance on guessing, superstition, or coincidence. Educational situations were perceived as a set of variables to be controlled, manipulated, and understood following a prescribed, replicable methodology. The researcher separated from the research setting, made observations, manipulated variables, and documented the results of the experimental condition. Research goals included discrete descriptions of the research setting, lucid articulation of the research process, and generalizibility to other educational settings.

A growing disenchantment and frustration with the use of traditional methods for the study of human behavior gained enormous momentum in the 1970s. Psychologists and educators raised new questions about the type of research appropriate for a science of human behavior and the practice of education. Discussions revolved around whether there was a better strategy than the traditional empirical models by which to study teaching and learning and to examine the variables that may eventually enter into the general laws governing the enterprise.

The various dissenting voices were characterized as the "family of discontent" (Gergen & Gergen, 1982). The chosen targets of the family's philosophical assaults were the prevailing ideologies of positivism. They held that the dominant positivistic and empiricist traditions were profoundly inadequate, standing in the way of a fuller and more accurate understanding of human behavior (Heshusius, 1986). When pointed toward special education, many parties felt that progress was stalled. Positivist research was one of the structures that perpetuated the medical model, and research activities that consisted of a single paradigm and a small handful of psychological theories served to limit vision.

The severe challenges to the persistence of logical empiricism led to fundamental reappraisals of research theory and methodology that were very much at odds with the positivist research tradition as well as with the metaphysical and methodological assumptions of special education researchers. Critiques challenged the theoretical and pragmatic pillars of the positivist-empiricist tenets—specifically, that fact could be separated from value, that only what could be readily observed could reach the status of scientific knowledge, that quantitative measurement was necessary to be able to know, and that the use of an unambiguous set of rules was the privileged way to knowledge (Heshusius, 1986). On a more pragmatic plane, a growing number of special education researchers became interested in studying topics that did not translate into designs that were experimental in nature. Those dealing with special education increasingly pursued a variety of theoretical approaches and adopted the tools of qualitative-interpretative research.[3]

Compared with the relatively narrow and one-dimensional quantitative methodologies, the body of work broadly labeled qualitative is richly variegated. The qualitative field is filled with varied dimensions, nuances, theoretical foundations, differences, and contradictions; the theories and methods are "diverse to the point of disorderliness" (Smith, 1989, p. 173). The traditions of qualitative inquiry practiced in the social sciences uses blurred categories variously described as interpretive, naturalistic, inductive, ethnographical, symbolic, biographical, phenomenological, grounded theory, oral history, narrative, descriptive, anthropological, hermeneutic, field study, case study, or some combination of these. Each area has a different focus and emerges from a different tradition and perspective. Some qualitative-interpretative research brings a change in model. A more persuasive change is postmodernism—a distinct source of theoretical argumentation.

To be sure, some commonalities exist among the wide palette of quantitative methodologies. Critical among them is the underlying belief that knowledge is shaped by contextual conditions and meanings; that is, research activity is inevitably influenced by the social, political, and economic context: behavior cannot be validly studied apart from its natural context. A second powerful theme of qualitative methodology is the attempt to provide a platform for hearing the voices of those who have been traditionally muted or silenced. In addition, advocates contend that alternative, qualitative approaches to research are more grounded in trying to understand classroom culture than the fractionalized and directionless empirical variety that investigates possibly hundreds of different variables. They argue that qualitative methodology is particularly well suited for evaluating program goals and outcomes, for identifying their effects on individuals, and for facilitating positive change (Bogdan & Biklen, 1982). Within the qualitative genre, there is no requirement that the assertions be subjected to empirical testing. Tests of quality include plausibility, internal consistency, knowledge and understanding, and fits to prevailing wisdom.

Given its mounting popularity, a proliferation of research studies and results have arisen from the interpretative approach. By 2005, experimental designs appeared to represent less than one in every eight projects funded; the remainder were correlational or qualitative studies (Forness, 2005).

Postmodern Themes

The modern era is said to have ended near the middle of the 20th century (Smith, 1989) followed, obviously, by the postmodern era. In academic life, postmodernism is an intellectual current that attacks both the core and the margins of the modernist system. Postmodernism more or less negates the themes and the rationalist tradition of the Enlightenment (see Sasso, 2001). Adherents respond askance at the possibility of an all-encompassing theory, and therefore, there exists no single postmodernist theory. However, the current can be organized around several pertinent frames of thought.

Postmodern skepticism rejects the possibility of enduring universal knowledge in any areas (Koertge, 1998). It denies rationalist explanations, questions the possibility of encompassing theoretical arguments, and rejects predictability as a goal of theory. Skrtic (1991), for example, adopts a postmodernist framework and claims that knowledge is antifoundational (i.e., it does not have fixed foundations) and that it is reliant on community dialogue and discourse. All knowledge is local, the product of a social class, rigidly circumscribed by its interests and prejudices that interact with the historical conditions of its experience (Sasso, 2001).

A basic tenet of postmodern thought holds that basic social values should not be subjected to investigations or reviews of research to determine their efficiency or popularity. Rather, they should be evaluated according to what is right, just, and desirable. Allowing the central postmodernist claim that there are other ways of knowing, it follows that advocates believe that truth can be determined through other means than logical, rational inquiry. The postmodernist stance eschews hard boundaries between belief and evidence. Science is nothing more than a narration, a myth, or a social construction among many others (Sokal & Bricmont, 1998). "The scientific goal of progressively finding and describing truth," said Danforth (1997), "is thus replaced by the moral and political goals of supporting human freedom and community" (p. 120). He speaks to "a place of many legitimate stories," describing these as an arena of dialogue and possibility, "allowing individuals and groups to claim their voices, call out their own identities, and forge paths of action that need not comply with the scientific dictates of truth" (p. 120).

The ideological themes of postmodernism that are related to special education are located within discourses generally founded on social-ethical considerations that are strongly centered on values. Notions are grounded in democratic themes, an outgrowth of the social philosophy about individual civil rights framed in terms of equality of opportunity and intimately connected to common, but very specific, conceptions of social justice. Under the strict rules of the agenda, full inclusion is valorized as the norm or the baseline—the sole route to addressing social and educational issues.

When the ideas are translated into the worlds of children and classrooms, a postmodern philosophy of special education often dispenses with the common governing story. Postmodernist writers assert that special education as it is commonly practiced does not provide a reasonable basis for educating students with exceptionalities. Because there does not exist a single and knowable truth, postmodernists have attacked the traditional scientific bases of special education; they take the field to task for relying on practices established through the tenets of Western science. Postmodernism espouses theoretical discourses disconnected from any empirical test, and hence, there exists a general tendency to view the evidence base in favor of special education as irrelevant (Forness, 2005).

Postmodernism embraces forms of cultural relativism, a stance that recognizes and promotes the position that humanity is better characterized as displaying a range of differences and variations, not binary divisions. It espouses the belief that all humans are neither abled nor disabled but, instead, can be located somewhere along a continuum of differences and are therefore differently abled rather than disabled. Just as critically, disability is socially constructed: disability is identified not as physical status but as deviation from social norms or as the interactions of differences with society.

Whereas positivism is driven to compare people with a standardized norm, relativism sees society creating deviants by selecting certain attributes as norms and calling them desirable. It disdains the evils of a single medical model and argues that disability represents much more than the identifiable and measurable biological impairment of an individual. Founded on the critical assumption that disability is a social construct, deviance is not seen as an inherent and fixed feature of a person. Instead, it is the surrounding social, legal, political, and economic climate that manifests in the problematic beliefs, patterns, and rules of the normative system (see e.g., Albrecht & Levy, 1982; Finkelstein, 1981; Friedson, 1965; Gliedman & Roth, 1980). When bases of substantiation are addressed, relativists assert that logical enquiry is just a matter of social practice because of social constructs that surround disability. Another scenario views the problem of deviation as a problem in the school culture. The child is special and has difficulties that call attention to him or her because the culture of the institutional setting defines the disabled child as being outside the boundaries of the normative system.

Differences between modern and postmodern views are strongly held. They emanate from different epistemological and ontological positions and from opposing sides of an ideological fault line. Some commentators have suggested that "the development of postmodern epistemologies could promote a fusion of conceptual perspectives and allow for the development of new discourses" (O'Brien & Gurney, 2005, p. 145). Others take the view that the paradigms are irreconcible and that adherence to one or the other not only precludes the values and beliefs associated with the other but also is a rejection of the methods and the knowledge generated (Tashakkori & Teddlie, 1998).

There is little doubt that as the inclusive reform in special education accelerated during the 1980s, postmodernism became a powerful faction in the ongoing reform dialogue that expanded theoretical discourse and inspired key philosophical changes. But inclusive philosophies and research paradigms were mutually reinforcing. As the concepts and practices of the inclusive reform mutated and changed, the antidote of postmodern thought to redress the alleged failures of special education was similarly deconstructed, scrutinized, and challenged. Doubts of the pontifications mounted, and thoughtful expositions illustrated the shortcomings of postmodernism as the sole way of understanding special needs and special schooling.

Some critics simply dismissed the ideas of the entire movement as mischievous. More forceful commentators held that "the displacement of the idea that facts and evidence matter by the idea that everything boils down to subjective interests and perspectives is the most prominent and pernicious manifestation of anti-intellectualism in our time" (Laudan, 1990, p. x).

Taking potshots at postmodernist writers became a popular sport among critics from the discrete field of special education. They variously contended that it was difficult to negotiate the maze created by postmodern deconstructivism and that postmodernism negated the ideals that have been at the forefront of liberal intellectual life in the West. Postmodernism lacked a well-defined theoretical position; moreover, the very term *postmodern* suffered from a lack of coherence (e.g., Kauffman, 2002; Sasso, 2001). Perplexed by the strange things that postmodern thinkers said, reviewers critiqued the trendy rhetoric of postmodernism and the vague and often banal pronouncements couched in strings of nebulous words and obscurantist language. James Kauffman (2002) portrayed most postmodern thinking and writing as fraught with "obfuscations, self-contradiction, denial of what one just said, and unintelligibility" (p. 13).

Conclusions grounded in a postmodernist stance were seen as holding limited significance and functionality for special education. Postmodernists, for example, tended to view disability primarily as society's failure to accept individual differences and argued that acceptance, inclusion, and school restructuring would overcome the limitations of any disability (Forness, 2005; Mostert, Kauffman, & Kavale,

2003). Detractors contended that neither deconstructing the traditional sociopolitical view of exceptionality nor changing social group membership would eliminate the real challenges that students with disabilities experience. Postmodern criticism similarly claimed that specialized intervention was essentially a failure of the schools to fully accept the limitations of a child with a disability; research suggesting that certain interventions could be considered effective was seen as inconsequential (Forness, 2005). Although specific interventions were not in accord with the postmodern vision of social justice, many in the field argued that children would fail under regimes that obviated the need for classification or distinguishably different instruction designed to serve their special needs (see Fuchs & Fuchs, 1995; Sugai, 1998).

The standard postmodernist claim—that values supply the foundation or truth for decision making—was increasingly challenged. Many became alert to the deceptiveness of outward show and found that postmodernism offered flawed methods of inquiry and knowledge creation. Writers of reform literature often ignored major limitations, assumptions, and omissions. Critics contended that key outcomes should be more than assertions. Dispensing with empirical data in favor of assertions, narratives, and moral theorizing was not favorable to the progress of special education or its clients. Personal testimony, anecdote, travelers' tales, or "primitive 'craft knowledge'" could not carry the burden of truth (Kauffman, 2002, p. 233).

Others saw the postmodernist disdain of science-based research as attempts "to undermine the epistemic authority of a science of disability, and to valorize 'ways of knowing' incompatible with it" (Sasso, 2001, p. 185). They found the postmodernist view of empirical evidence "so patently out of touch with reality" that it "simply cannot be taken as serious criticism" (Forness, 2005, p. 311). They decried the contention that the new paradigms outdated the scientific study of education and criticized postmodernists who rejected adherence to the limits of logical empiricism as a criterion for scientific responsibility (e.g., Mostert, Kauffman, & Kavale, 2003; Sasso, 2001).

A strong counter movement posited that progress in education depended on a body of reliable research-based information, that research on teaching and learning should follow the canons of science, and that the philosophical attraction of inclusive schooling carried with it the responsibility to measure that it worked. Reform initiatives demanded empirical analyses of policy change: to be effective, efforts to change schools had to be based on knowledge generated by research rather than unsubstantiated beliefs or feelings. Doubts about reform would be removed only in direct proportion to the demonstration that reform worked.

The Research-to-Practice Gap

Epistemological frameworks hold little joy for practitioners in the field. No matter the dominant research ideology, the drift of findings into classrooms and programs is small. Researchers and practitioners operate in vastly different worlds; they ask different questions about instruction and learning, and they speak different languages. A great many teachers, administrators, and policymakers believe that the research is irrelevant and unimportant. Instead of informing practice, large chunks of the research findings lie dormant in the literary museums called journals. Even when research practices are implemented in schools, they may not be sustained over time. Nor does education research keep pace with educational reform: policy often outruns the research base.

The glaring disconnect in special education between research findings, research-based methods, and classroom practice has long formed a central theme in special education dialogue. The dilemma has generated untold revisitations by workers in the field. Of the many reasons underlying the gap, the traditional gender bias is worth mention.

From the outset, men dominated the research world. Charles Judd (1918) viewed research as male work because of the scientific and analytic nature of the endeavor. Teaching was more suitable to the nurturing qualities of women. Thus, ideally, male researchers would transmit new knowledge about teaching and learning to teachers who would, in turn, teach in different ways after they adopted the new knowledge specified by the research findings. Teachers, although often studied, were at best peripheral to the conduct of educational research.

LOOKING FORWARD

The first volume of this history came with the subtitle, "From Segregation to Integration," and chiefly concentrated on developments in the 19th and early 20th centuries. This book, *From Integration to Inclusion*, extends the time line and covers developments, movements, and trends throughout the 20th century. Any relevant subtitles for future books would be risky to pinpoint. With the rapid change and reform movements so characteristic of the field of special education, prediction is tricky. Although inclusive schooling remains at the forefront of educational dialogue and practice, it is not possible to chart future directions. To be sure, it is tempting, but erroneous, to judge what is occurring at the present time as a great deal better than what was practiced in the past. It is equally tempting to adopt a positive bias toward the future and believe that "we are finally emerging into an era of enlightenment in which progress will be coherent, dramatic, and sustained" (Kauffman, 2001, p. 86).

As special education enters the new millenium, the profession must specifically confront a plethora of unresolved and new problems. The varied issues include, but are not restricted to providing effective teacher training and preventing teacher attrition; attracting teachers from groups representative of the population; mediating research practices; resolving the research to practice disconnect; solving the dilemma of universally accepted definitions; finding appropriate and nonstigmatizing terminology; discovering ways to accommodate culturally and linguistically different special learners; responding to the needs for clearer identification and assesment processes; managing the increasing role of instructional and assistive technology; practicing early identification and early intervention; improving transition programs for adolescents; providing access to the general curricula for students with special needs; assessing accountability and high-stakes testing; and understanding globalization and the philosophy of inclusion (for discussions see Cronis & Ellis, 2000; Winzer & Mazurek, 2001, 2005). Scientific advances and the new role of biology are similarly pressing and worthy of highlight.

Throughout the 20th century, the role of biology came full circle. Educational discourses are beginning to acknowledge the relevance of biology in new ways (Geake & Cooper, 2003). After researchers announced that the Human Genome Project was complete on April 14, 2003, the often dizzying pace of the genetic research that followed accelerated advances in a number of domains (Anderson & Nickerson, 2005). Biology and neurosocience are now seen to play a critical role in the understanding of human thought and behavioral processes. New genetic syndromes were discovered rapidly, and understanding of the known causes of disabilities grew. Monolithic and one-dimensional conceptions of intellectual disability crumbled as different genetic syndromes were shown to possess specific behavioral phenotypes—certain behaviors, psychopathology, cognition, language, and developmental sequelae (see Dykens, 2001).

Optimistic views of medical advances must be tempered by more pragmatic reflections on the possible darker aspects. As one example, the bogey of eugenics haunts special education. Many would assume that the pseudoscience that was eugenics is now dead. But it is not clear whether the issues or the solutions raised in the eugenics dialogue have passed totally from the public forum. Some see the resurgence of the notions in the debate over *The Bell Curve* (Tyor, 1977). Others point to fallout from the Human Genome Project (Kevles & Hood, 1992). Add to these concerns the sophisticated genetic counseling that identifies many likely forms of disability, which suggests that a nondisabled child is far more valued than one with potential disabilities.

The continued persistence of the inclusive ideology and its accompanying notions are anything but ensured. The heated discourses about inclusive schooling, the flux and change, the challenges, and the desconstruction underscore the manner in which a common understanding of special education has eroded. The practical issues have both riven and riveted the field and demonstrated an inability on the part of special educators to reach consensus on various aspects of the reform agenda.

Arguments about how to educate students with special needs should be more compelling than those that focus solely on placement options. A location-dominant perspective obscures critical pedagogical dilemmas. By framing inclusion and segregation as mutually exclusive, and general and special classrooms as fundamentally different ecologies, it misrepresents their relationships. In addition, it is ludicrous to assume that all students be placed in general classrooms as a matter of policy. Inclusion should be regarded as an organizational rather than an educational intervention: it is not a place where student with disabilities receive services but a way to deliver services effectively. The opportunities made available by the setting, not the setting itself, are important.

The goals, process, and outcomes associated with inclusion have historically not been perceived by many professional, parents, and policymakers as empirical or scientific issues. Typically, inclusion has been theory rich, data poor. The space for inclusive reform was constructed before any knowledge about its real functioning. Yet it seems clear that policies and decisions connected to whether children and youth with disabilities should be educated in general settings would be better made on research that is data based and replicated over time. Whether practices are, in fact, effective, can be answered only on a reliable basis and with empirical grounding. Thoughtful commentators contend that "special education needs clear direction towards its historic purpose and refueling of its commitment to reliable data with respect to the link between instruction and learning" (Kauffman, 1996, p. 206). Progress should follow from the application of the scientific method and on the systematic collection of data. Empirical research based on the scientific method offers by far the greatest opportunity to establish intervention efficacy for people with disabilities.

Inclusion does not arise from a well-defined, static corpus of information that is accepted by the profession. One of the defining and enduring characteristics of the inclusive reform lies in its ultimate mutability. Inclusion means different things to different people, and the definitions are continually reinterpreted by professionals and advocacy groups to fit the needs of a particular constituency. The many interpretations are evidenced by "the steady stream of administrative complaints, mediation, due process hearings, and litigation regarding special education issues where opposing lawyers and dueling 'experts' argue over their interpretations of the law" (Giangreco, 2001, p. 341).

Reform is passed off in so many guises that many writers no longer speak to inclusion, but to inclusions (e.g., Dyson, 1999; Odom et al., 1999). The shifting landscapes and continuing fluidity and flux beg two overlapping questions. First, will inclusion as a reform share a similar fate and the same unhappy ending as have a string of earlier reforms in the field? Second, into how many guises can inclusion be transmuted and still remain true to its original conception and purpose?

Feeding into the dilemma are the paradigm wars that seek to establish a single theoretical perspective or methodology as superior. It is important to acknowledge the limitations of one methodological orientation or the other for inquiring into particular issues. No single research paradigm can identify all of the questions that need to be asked, nor can a single view provide methods by which all questions can be answered. Analysis techniques are not the property of the approaches, but are at their service. The research objectives and the data themselves are what will determine usage of one technique or the other.

There seems to be a natural tendency for researchers to work mainly within a given category of models to make a world view and to look at all educational problems from that perspective. Nevertheless, it is essential that the field reach some level of agreement on the central tenets of knowledge production through the research process and acknowledge that many alternative research traditions with contradictory assumptions and world views can legitimately co-exist and contribute to the advancement of educational knowledge. A discernable trend toward the use of mixed-method approaches in educational evaluation and research perhaps reflects a new conceptualization of the relationship between opposing objectivist and interpretist paradigms.

Even if researchers move in the direction of greater tolerance for different perspectives, however, there are still practical functions of the perspectives that need to be examined. For those in the special education field, research has never held a central place. A key goal of research is to add to the extant knowledge by formulating, expanding, or evaluating a theory that will lead ultimately to the improvement of practice. Findings and speculations from research that should play a pivotal role in special education are often perceived as irrelevant by practitioners in the field. Many parties advocate changing education "to make it an evidence-based field" (U.S. Department of Education, 2002, p. 48). School professionals are increasingly being urged, and even required, to base their practices on scientifically based methods and to use practices that have the highest possibility of yielding the desired outcomes.

SUMMARY AND THEMES

It is a truism that every time a report is published on the deficiencies of public education, a flurry of new reform directions emerge. The devastating findings of the National Commission's *A Nation at Risk* elevated school reform to a dominant ideology and process. Reform, restructure, and reinvent became the rallying cries of reform in general education, and the literature was replete with a myriad of initiatives to change the structure and culture of schools. Studies and reports outlined the major thrust of the new reform movement.

One strand of reform sought higher standards, increased accountability, effective schools, and responsibility based on outcomes. A second and more dominant group fused their ideals with the changing demographics of American society. They rejected the traditional notions of schooling that seemed to simply reproduce societal inequalities and instead argued that schools should become inclusive to best serve the needs and create equity for the increasingly diverse school population. Reform centered on reconstructing the entire system as the solution to eliminating segregation and on building classroom cultures according to the multiple identities of users.

Following the mainstreaming movement of the 1970s, the Regular Education Initiative (REI) represented policy objectives for reducing expenditures for education. One of the primary hypotheses of the REI was that students with disabilities would be best served by the improvement of education for all students. It recommended a restructuring of the relationship between general and special education. The principles did not seek to achieve full integration but to restructure mainstreaming.

During the 1980s, special educators willingly and readily co-opted the voice of general education reform. As the thought of many was increasingly located within the dominant sensibility, advocates presented arguments in favor of creating a single system of education for all children. One strand led to conceptualizations of disability as examples of diversity equivalent to linguistic, ethnic, racial, and economic diversity. A parallel strand embraced the notion of inclusive schooling and school restructuring as relevant to the education of students with special needs. The fixity of basic assumptions that underlay inclusion, concepts such as social justice, civil rights, and equity, were fundamentally different from traditional conceptions of disablement. However, the philosophical paradigm shift rapidly mutated into a heated debate about students' school addresses.

Full inclusionists were adept in taking out the adoption papers on reform; they valorized inclusion as the single route to addressing disability. Promoters were extreme rather than unique: they erected their logic on the ills of special education that had been the center of dialogue at least from the 1960s. Not to be inclusive was soon to be out of educational fashion. Sober and cautious voices were drowned in a tide of rationales that were essentially value oriented, philosophical, and conceptual. Theories were reduced to assertions, the language was saturated with slogans, the paradigms were simplified. Inclusion rested on moral righteousness rather than on what was empirically sustainable. The layer upon layer of rhetoric and argument was appealing not only because it advanced solutions to the dilemma of special needs and special education but also by virtue of its conjunction with reigning conceptions of equity and social justice.

The advocacy for full inclusion began with a priori moral and desirable premises (ending discrimination and segregation) but moved from there to unsustainable assumptions and prescriptions. Eventually, however, even the cascade of allures could not counterbalance sober reflections. By the mid-1990s, the fervor of the reform movement muted, and research was moved to the forefront. The more conservative viewpoint, which argued for selective inclusion founded on the particular needs of individual students, prevailed.

In the latter part of the 19th century, social science research, which includes educational research, patterned itself after the physical sciences. After that, special education set on a pedestal certain kinds of theoretical and empirical knowledge and favored particular methodological avenues as routes to such knowledge. By far the most widespread type of models in educational research consisted of those that used some algebraic combination of a number of independent variables to predict one or more dependent variables. A paradigm dialogue that began in the late 1950s grew increasingly strident to reach contentious proportions by the 1990s. Questioning of the value-free traditional empirical research led to the emergence of alternative, qualitative approaches.

NOTES

1. By 1969, all of the Canadian provinces and territories had legislation guaranteeing education to all children, including those who were exceptional. In the following 2 decades, most jurisdictions moved to seriously assess their special education offerings. Often with the American model as a touchstone and the Canadian Charter of Rights and Freedoms as a guide, they acted to form the policy and statutory and operational frameworks to define and facilitate special services for students with exceptionalities. For example, Ontario's

Education Amendment Act of 1980 was fully implemented in 1985 after a phase-in period, concurrent with the repatriation of the Canadian Constitution to Ottawa from Westminster and the establishment of the Canadian Charter of Rights and Freedoms. In Nova Scotia, Bill 85, which passed into law in 1986, requires the inclusion of all children with disabilities within general classrooms. British Columbia saw the development of special education policy take place against the backdrop of international discourse and attempts to clarify the extent to which the Canadian Charter had implications for education.

2. Good Start, Grow Smart is the Bush administration early childhood initiative that was announced April 2002.

3. For analyses of research in special education see the whole issue of *Exceptional Children* (Graham, 2005).

References

Abeson, A., & Zettel, J. (1977). The end of the quiet revolution: The Education for All Handicapped Children Act of 1975. *Exceptional Children, 44,* 114–128.

Abraham, W. (1976). The early years: Prologue to tomorrow. *Exceptional Children, 42,* 330–335.

Achenbach, T. M. (1975). The historical context of treatment for delinquent and maladjusted children: Past, present, and future. *Behavior Disorders, 1,* 3–14.

Addams, J. (Ed.). (1925). *The child, the clinic, and the court.* New York: New Republic.

Adler, E. (1991, June). *History of rehabilitation research.* Paper presented at the First International Conference on Deaf History, Washington, DC.

Aiello, B. (1975). *Making it work: Practical ideas for integrating exceptional children into regular classes.* Reston, VA: Council for Exceptional Children.

Albee, G. W. (1959). *Mental health manpower trends.* New York: Basic Books.

Albrecht, G., & Levy, J. (1982). Constructing disabilities as social problems. In G. Albrecht (Ed.), *Cross national rehabilitation policies: A sociological perspective* (pp. 11–33). London: Sage.

Aleman, S. R. (1991). *CRS report for Congress: Special education for children with attention deficit disorders: Current issues.* Washington, DC: Congressional Research Services.

American Association of Mental Deficiency. (1959). *A manual of terminology and classification in mental retardation.* Washington, DC: Author.

American Association to Promote the Teaching of Speech to the Deaf. (1899). Proceedings (except papers and lectures) of the Sixth Summer Meeting of the AAPTSD, held at Clarke School for the Deaf, Northampton, Mass., June 22–28, 1899. *Association Review, 1,* 53–106, 162–176.

American Asylum for the Deaf and Dumb. (1826). *American Journal of Education, 1*(10), 631.

American Psychiatric Association (APA. (1968). *Diagnostic and statistical manual of mental disorders* (2nd ed.). Washington, DC: Author.

American Psychiatric Association (APA). (1980). *Diagnostic and statistical manual of mental disorders* (3rd ed.). Washington, DC: Author.

American Psychiatric Association (APA). (1987). *Diagnostic and statistical manual of mental disorders* (3rd Rev. ed.). Washington, DC: Author.

American Psychiatric Association (APA). (1994). *Diagnostic and statistical manual of mental disorders* (4th ed.). Washington, DC: Author.

American Psychiatric Association (APA). (2000). *Diagnostic and statistical manual of mental disorders*. (4th ed., text revision). Washington, DC: Author.

Americans With Disabilities Act of 1990, Pub. L. No. 101-336, 42 U.S.C. 12101 *et seq.*

Anderson, N. B., & Nickerson, K. J. (2005). Genes, race, and psychology in the genome era: An introduction. *American Psychologist, 60,* 5–8.

Asperger, H. (1944). Die "Autistischen Psychopathen im Kindesalter." *Archiv für Psychiatrie und Nervenkrankheiten, 17,* 76–136.

Autism Society Canada. (2004, March). *Canadian autism research agenda and Canadian autism strategy: A white paper*. Ottawa, ON: Author. Retrieved April 23, 2009, from http://www.autismsocietycanada.ca/pdf_word/finalwhite-eng.pdf

Ayres, A. J. (1972). *Southern California Sensory Integration Tests*. Los Angeles, CA: Western Psychological Services.

Ayres, L. (1909). *Laggards in our schools: A study of retardation and elimination in city school systems*. New York: Charities Publications Committee.

Ayres, L. (1915). *Child accounting in the public schools*. Cleveland, OH: Cleveland Education Survey.

Babbidge, J. (1965). *The Babbidge Committee report*. Washington, DC: Department of Health, Education and Welfare. (ERIC Document Reproduction Service No.ED014188)

Baca, L. M., & Cervantes, H. T. (1984). *The bilingual special education interface*. New York: Merrill.

Bain, D. A. (1980). Gifted and enriched education in Canada. In M. Csapo & L. Goguen (Eds.), *Special education across Canada: Issues and concerns for the '80s*. Vancouver: Centre for Human Development and Research.

Baker, E. M., & Stullken, E. H. (1938). American research studies concerning the 'behavior' type of exceptional children. *Journal of Exceptional Children, 4,* 36–45.

Baker, H. J. (1949–50). Significance of individual items in case work. *Journal of Exceptional Children, 16,* 203–206.

Balch, W. M. (1926). Is the race going downhill? *American Mercury, 8,* 432–438.

Balis, S. C. (1901). A woman's view. *American Annals of the Deaf, 45,* 310–316.

Ball, T. S. (1971). *Itard, Seguin, and Kephart: Sensory education—a learning interpretation*. Columbus, OH: Merrill.

Bank-Mikkelson, N. E. (1969). A metropolitan area in Denmark: Copenhagen. In R. Kugel & W. Wolfsenberger (Eds.), *Changing patterns in residential services for the mentally retarded* (pp. 227–254). Washington, DC: President's Committee on Mental Retardation.

Barclay, R. A. (1990). *Attention-deficit hyperactivity disorder: A handbook for diagnosis and treatment*. New York: Guilford Press.

Barker, R. G., & Wright, B. A. (1952). The social psychology of adjustment to physical disability. In J. R. Garrens (Ed.), *Psychological aspects of physical disability* (pp. 18–22). Rehabilitation Service Series No. 210. Washington, DC: Federal Security Agency, Office of Vocational Rehabilitation.

Barnard, H. (1852). Eulogy. *American Annals of the Deaf and Dumb, 4*, 81–136.

Barnard, H. (1857). *Reformatory education: Papers on preventative, correctional and reformatory institutions and agencies in different countries.* Hartford: F. C. Brownell.

Barr, M. W. (1899). Mental defectives and the social welfare. *Popular Science, 54*, 747–754.

Barr, M. W. (1902). The imbecile and epileptic versus the tax-payer and the community. In I. C. Barrows (Ed.), *Proceedings of the National Conference of Charities and Corrections, 1902* (pp. 161–165). Boston: Ellis.

Barr, M. W. (1904a). Classification of mental defectives. *Journal of Psycho-Asthenics, 9*, 29–38.

Barr, M. W. (1904b). *Mental defectives: Their history, treatment and training.* Philadelphia, PA: Blakiston's.

Barr, M. W. (1913). *Mental defectives: Their history, treatment and training.* Philadelphia, PA: Blakiston's.

Barss, J. N. (1920). The treatment of the delinquent as social service. *Social Welfare, 2*, 188–190, 210–213.

Barton, L. (1999). Market ideologies, education and the challenge. In H. Daniels & P. Garner (Eds.), *World yearbook of education: Inclusive education* (pp. 54–62). London: Kogan Page.

Baynton, D. C. (1991, June). *Sign language.* Paper presented at the First International Conference on the History of Deafness, Washington, DC.

Baynton, D. C. (1993). "Savages and deaf mutes": Evolutionary theory and the campaign against sign language in the nineteenth century. In J. V. Van Cleve (Ed.), *Deaf history unveiled: Interpretations of the new scholarship* (pp. 92–112). Washington, DC: Gallaudet University Press.

Baynton, D. C. (1997). "A silent exile on this earth": The metaphorical construction of deafness in the nineteenth century. In L. Davis (Ed.), *The disabilities study reader* (pp. 128–150). New York: Routledge.

Beaman, F. N. (1948). Present day thinking in relation to behavior problems. *Journal of Exceptional Children, 15*, 81–84.

Beck, T. R. (1834). *An inaugural dissertation on insanity.* New York: J. Seymour. (Original work published 1811)

Beecher, C. E. (1835). *An essay on the education of female teachers.* New York: Ford.

Beers, C. W. (1908). *A mind that found itself.* New York: Longmans, Green.

Befring, E. (1997). The enrichment perspective: A special educational approach to an inclusive school. *Remedial and Special Education, 18*, 182–187.

Bell, A. G. (1884a). Deaf mute instruction in relation to the work in public schools. *In National Education Report: Addresses and discussions relating to the education of the deaf, Madison, Wisconsin, 1884* (pp. 8–18). Washington, DC: Gibson Brothers.

Bell, A. G. (1884b). Fallacies concerning the deaf. *American Annals of the Deaf and Dumb, 29*, 32–69.

Bell, A. G. (1884c). Memoir upon the formation of a deaf variety of the human race. In *Memoirs of the National Academy of Sciences* (Vol. 2, Part 4, pp. 179–262). Washington, DC: Government Printing Office

Bell, A. G. (1888). *Facts and opinions relating to the deaf from America*. London: Spottiswoode and Co.

Bell, A. G. (1891). Visible speech as taught to the deaf: An address delivered Tuesday, July 7th., 1891, at the First Summer meeting of the American Association to Promote the Teaching of speech to the Deaf. Washington, DC: Mentor Print.

Bell, A. G. (1898). *Marriage: An address delivered to members of the Literary Society of Kendall Green. Wash., DC March 16th., 1891, with an appendix on consanguineous marriages*. Washington, DC: Sanders Printing Office.

Bell, A. G. (1908a). A few thoughts concerning eugenics. *National Geographic, 19*, 119–123.

Bell, A. G. (1908b). The twelfth census. *Association Review, 10*, 138–147, 240–255, 349–364, 455–464.

Bell, A. G. (1914). How to improve the race. *Journal of Heredity, 5*, 1–7.

Bell, A. G. (1920). Is race suicide possible? *Journal of Heredity, 11*, 339–341.

Bell, A. G., & Gillett, J. L. (1884). *Deaf classes in connection with the work in public schools*. Washington, DC: Gibson Brothers.

Belmessous, S. (2005). Assimilation and racialism in seventeenth and eighteenth-century French colonial policy. *American Historical Review, 110*, 322–349.

Bench, P. J. (1919). Juvenile delinquency–its causes. *Social Welfare, 1*, 126–127.

Benner, G. J., Nelson, J. R., & Epstein, M. H. (2002). Language skills of children with EBD: A literature review. *Journal of Emotional and Behavioral Disorders, 10*, 43–59.

Berkeley, K. C. (1984). "The ladies want to bring about reform in the public schools": Public education and women's rights in the post-civil war South. *History of Education Quarterly, 24*, 45–58.

Berlin, R. (1887). *Eine besondere Art der Wortblindheit (Dyslexie)* [A specific kind of word blindness (dyslexia)]. Weisbaden: J. F. Bergmann.

Bernard, R. M., & Vinvovskis, M. A. (1977). The female school teacher in antebellum Massachusetts. *Journal of Social History, 10*, 332–345.

Best, H. (1930). *Crime and criminal law in the United States: Considered primarily in their present day social aspects*. New York: Macmillan.

Best, H. (1934). *Blindness and the blind in the United States*. New York: Macmillan.

Bettelheim, B. (1967). *The empty fortress: Infantile autism and the birth of self*. New York: Free Press.

Biklen, D. (1985). *Achieving the complete school: Strategies to effective mainstreaming*. New York: Teachers College Press.

Binet, A. (1898). La mesure en psychologie individuelle. *Revue Philosophique, 46*, 113–123.

Binet, A., & Simon, T. (1908). Le development de l'intelligence chez les enfants. *L'Anee Psychologique, 14*, 1–94.

Binet, A., & Simon, T. (1916). *The development of intelligence in children*. Baltimore, MD: Williams and Wilkins.

Bird, R. (2002). *Report to the Legislature on the principal findings from an epidemiological study of autism in California: A comprehensive pilot study*. California: University of California at Davis.

Black, E. (2003). *War against the weak: Eugenics and America's campaign to create a master race*. New York: Four Walls Eight Windows.

Blackman, L. S. (1958). A study of survey courses on the exceptional child. *Exceptional Children, 24*, 194–197.

Blake, C. (2005). Do teacher training courses prepare us for the challenge of students experiencing EBD? In P. Clough, P. Garner, J. T. Pardeck, & F. Yuen (Eds.), *Handbook of emotional and behavioural difficulties* (pp. 417–427). London: Sage.

Blanton, R. L. (1976). Historical perspectives on classification of mental retardation. In N. Hobbs (Ed.), *Issues in the classification of children* (Vol. 1, pp. 164–193). San Francisco: Jossey-Bass.

Blatt, B. (1960). Some persistently recurring assumptions concerning the mentally subnormal. *Training School Bulletin, 57*, 49–59.

Blatt, B. (1975). Toward an understanding of people with special needs. In J. M. Kauffman & J. S. Payne (Eds.), *Mental retardation: Introduction and personal perspectives* (pp. 388–427). Columbus, OH: Merrill.

Blatt, B., Ozolins, A., & McNally, J. (1979). *The family papers: A return to purgatory*. New York: Longman.

Block, W. E. (1954). Personality of the brain injured child. *Exceptional Children, 21*, 91–100.

Blueler, E. (1950). *Dementia praecox, or the group of schizophrenias* (J. Zinkin, Trans.). New York: International Universities Press. (Original work published 1911)

Board of Education of Hendrick Hudson Central School District v. Rowley (1982) 458 US, 176; 102S. Ct. 3034; 73 L. Ed. 2d 690.

Bockoven, J. S. (1956). Moral treatment in American psychiatry. *Nervous and Mental Disease, 124*, 167–194, 292–321.

Bogdan, R. C., & Biklen, S. K. (1982). *Qualitative research for education: An introduction to theory and methods*. Boston: Allyn and Bacon.

Boggs, E. (1966). Legal aspects of mental retardation. In I. Philips & M. A. Esser (Eds.), *Prevention and treatment of mental retardaton* (pp. 407–428). New York: Basic Books.

Boggs, E. (1971). Federal legislation affecting the mentally retarded, 1955–1967. In J. Wortis (Ed.), *Mental retardation: An annual review* (Vol. 3, pp. 103–127). New York: Grune and Stratton.

Boggs, E. (1972). Federal legislation affecting the mentally retarded, 1966–1971. In J. Wortis (Ed.), *Mental retardation: An annual review* (Vol. 4, pp. 169–174). New York: Grune and Stratton.

Bonner, H. R. (1920). *Industrial schools for delinquents, 1917–1918*. Washington, DC: Department of the Interior; U.S. Bureau of Education, Statistics Division; Government Print Office.

Boston Council of Social Agencies. (1930). *Report of the Boston mental health survey.* Boston: Author.

Bower, E. M. (1959–60). The emotional handicapped child and the school. *Exceptional Children, 26,* 182–188.

Bowman, K. M. (1944). Guest editorial. *Journal of Exceptional Children, 11,* 33.

Boyer, E. L. (1983). *High school.* New York: Harper and Row.

Bradley, C. (1937). The behavior of children receiving Benzedrine. *American Journal of Psychiatry, 94,* 577–585.

Bradway, K. P. (1937). Social competence and exceptional children. *Journal of Exceptional Children, 4,* 1–8, 18.

Brantlinger, E. (1997). Using ideology: Cases of non-recognition of the politics of research and practice in special education. *Review of Educational Research, 67,* 425–460.

Bremner, R. H. (Ed). (1970). *Children and youth in America: A documentary history: Volume 1, 1600–1865.* Cambridge: Harvard University Press.

Bremner, R. H. (Ed.). (1970–1974). *Children and youth in America: A documentary history* (Vols. 1–3, bound in 5 books). Cambridge: Harvard University Press.

Brenzel, B. (1980). Domestication as reform: A study of the socialization of wayward girls, 1856–1905. *Harvard Educational Review, 50,* 196–213.

Bricker, D. (1995). The challenge of inclusion. *Journal of Early Intervention, 19,* 179–194.

Brigham, A. (1845). Schools in lunatic asylums. *American Journal of Insanity, 2,* 326–340.

Brigham, A. (1847). The moral treatment of insanity. *American Journal of Insanity, 4,* 1–15.

Brigham, C. (1923). *A study of American intelligence.* London: Princeton University Press.

British Columbia Provincial Industrial School for Boys. (1903). *Annual reports.* Victoria, BC: Author.

British Columbia Provincial Industrial School for Girls (1927). *Annual reports.* Victoria, BC: Author.

Brockett, L. P. (1856). Idiots and institutions for their training. *American Journal of Education, 1* (May), 601–603.

Brockett, L. P. (1860). *History and progress of education from the earliest times to the present.* New York: A. S. Barnes and Bun.

Brown, F. (1943–44). A practical program for early detection of atypical children. *Journal of Exceptional Children, 10,* 3–7.

Brown v. Board of Education of Topeka 347 US 483 (1954).

Bruce, H. H. (1936). Sterilization and imbecility. *Social Welfare, 16,* 95–97.

Bruce, R. (1973). *Alexander Graham Bell and the conquest of solitude.* Boston: Little Brown.

Bruininks, R. H., Meyers, C. E., Sigford, B. B., & Lakin, K. C. (1981). (Eds.). *Deinstitutionalization and community adjustment of mentally retarded people.* (AAMD Monograph 4). Washington, DC: American Association of Mental Deficiency.

Bruner, J. (1960). *The process of education.* New York: Vintage.

Bryam, B. (2004). A pupil and a patient: Hospital schools in progressive America. In S. Danforth & S. D. Taff (Eds.), *Crucial readings in special education* (pp. 25–37). Upper Saddle River, NJ: Pearson.

Bryan, T. (1999). Reflections on a research career: It ain't over till it's over. *Exceptional Children, 65,* 438–447.

Bryce, P. (1920). Recent constructive developments in child welfare. *Social Welfare, 2,* 255–256.

Bryne, M. E. (1934). Excerpts from convention addresses. *Council Review/Journal of Exceptional Children, 1,* 44.

Buck v. Bell 274 US 200, 47S C 584 (1927).

Bullis, M., & Cheney, D. (1999). Vocational and transition intervention for adolescents and young adults with emotional or behavioral disorders. *Focus on Exceptional Children, 31,* 1–24.

Burke, P. J. (1976). Personnel preparation: Historical perspectives. *Exceptional Children, 43,* 144–147.

Burks, H. F. (1957). The affect on learning of brain pathology. *Exceptional Children, 24,* 169–172, 174.

Bush, M. G. (1942). The handicapped child helps all children in Wisconsin. *Journal of Exceptional Children, 9,* 153–155.

Butterworth, J. (2002). From programs to supports. In R. L. Schalock, P. C. Baker, & M. D. Croser (Eds.), *Embarking on a new century: Mental retardation at the end of the 20th. century* (pp. 83–100). Washington, DC: American Association of Mental Retardation.

Cahan, E. D. (1989). *Past caring: A history of United States preschool care and education for the poor, 1820–1965.* New York: Center for Children in Poverty.

Cain, L. (1976). Parent groups: Their role in a better life for the handicapped. *Exceptional Children, 42,* 432–437.

Carlson, E. T., & Dain, N. (1960). The psychotherapy that was moral treatment. *American Journal of Psychology, 117,* 519–524.

Carnegie Forum on Education and the Economy. (1986). *A nation prepared: Teachers for the 21st century. The report of the tast force on teaching as a profession.* New York: Carnegie Corporation.

Carrier, J. G. (1986a). *Learning disability: Social class and the construction of inequality in American education.* New York: Greenwood.

Carrier, J. G. (1986b). Sociology and special education: Differentiation and allocation in mass education. *American Journal of Education, 94,* 281–312.

Carr-Saunders, A. M. (1926). *Eugenics.* London: Butterworth.

Casanova, U. & Chavez, S. (1992). Sociopolitical influences on federal government funding of gifted and talented bilingual education programs. *Educational Foundations, 6* (fall), 45–73.

Case, R. E., & Taylor, S. S. (2005). Language difference or learning disability? Answers from a linguistic perspective. *Clearing House, 78,* 127–130.

Cattell, J. M. (1915). Families of American men of science. *Popular Science Monthly, 86,* 505–515.

CEC's founder—One smart lady. (2002). *CEC Today, 9,* 7.

Ceremonies at the completion of the Gallaudet monument. (1854). *American Annals of the Deaf and Dumb, 7*, 19–54.

Challman, R. C. (1939). Personality maladjustments and remedial reading. *Journal of Exceptional Children, 6*, 7–11, 35.

Channing, A. (1932). *Employment of mentally deficient boys and girls* (Department of Labor, Bureau of Publication, No. 210). Washington, DC: U.S. Government Printing Office.

Chapman. P. D. (1979). Schools as sorters: Testing and tracking in California, 1910–1925. (Doctoral dissertation, Stanford University, 1979). *Dissertation Abstracts International, 43*, 3843A.

Chapman, P. D. (1981). Schools as sorters: Testing and tracking in California, 1910–1925. *Journal of Social History, 14*, 701–707.

Chaves, I. M. (1977). Historical overview of special education in the United States. In P. Bates, T. L. West, & R. B. Schmerl (Eds.), *Mainstreaming: Problems, potentials, and perspectives* (pp. 25–41). Minneapolis, MN: National Support Systems Project.

Cheney, D., & Muscott, H. S. (1996). Preventing school failure for students with emotional and behavioral disorders through responsible inclusion. *Preventing School Failure, 40*, 109–116.

Chicago Department of Education. (1932). *Report of the survey of the schools of Chicago*. New York: Teachers College, Columbia University Press.

Choutka, P. M., Doloughty, P. T., & Zirkel, P. A. (2004). The "discrete trials" of applied behavior analysis for children with autism: Outcome-related factors in the case law. *The Journal of Special Education, 38*, 95–103.

Clarke, E. P. (1900). An analysis of the school and instructors of the deaf in the U.S. *American Annals of the Deaf, 45*, 228–236.

Clarke Institution for Deaf Children. (1868). *Annual reports*. Boston: Author.

Clayton, M. P. (1959). Juvenile offenders and the law. *Exceptional Children, 25*, 205–216.

Clements, S. D. (1966). *Minimal brain dysfunction in children: Terminology and classification—Phase 1 of a three phase project* (Health Service Bulletin, No. 1415). Washington, DC: U.S. Department of Health, Education and Welfare.

Clifford, G. J. (1991). "Daughters and teachers:" Educational and demographic influences on the transformation of teaching in America. In A. Prentice & M. Theobald (Eds.), *Women who taught: Perspectives on the history of women and teaching* (pp. 115–135). Toronto: University of Toronto Press.

Clough, P., Garner, P., Pardeck, J. T., & Yuen, F. (2005). Themes and dimensions of EBD: A conceptual overview. In P. Clough, P. Garner, J. T. Pardeck, & F. Yuen (Eds.), *Handbook of emotional and behavioural disorders* (pp. 3–19). London: Sage.

Cobb, J. (1911). The influence of heredity. *American Annals of the Deaf, 56*, 254–255.

Cohen, S. (1983). The mental hygiene movement, the development of personality and the school: The medicalization of American education. *History of Education Quarterly, 23*, 123–149.

Cole, T., & Visser, J. (1999). The history of special provisions for pupils with emotional or behavioral difficulties in England: What had proved effective? *Behavioral Disorders, 25*, 56–64.

Coleman, T. (1973). *Going to America*. New York: Anchor Books.

Committee on Psychological Research. (1901). Report of the Committee on Psychological Research. *Journal of Psycho-Asthenics, 81*, 21–26.

Community Mental Health Centers Act of 1963, Pub. L. No. 88-164, 42 U.S.C. § 2688 (1963).

Connor, L. E. (1951). CEC's federal legislative activity. *Journal of Exceptional Children, 18*, 135–139.

Conrad, P. (2004). The discovery of hyperkinesis: Notes on the medicalization of deviant behavior. In S. Danforth & S. G. Taft (Eds.), *Crucial readings in special education* (pp. 18–24). Upper Saddle River, NJ: Pearson.

Convention study-section reports. (1942–43). *Journal of Exceptional Children, 8*, 46–50, 57.

Cooley, E. J. (1927). Probation and delinquency. *Social Welfare, 10*, 23.

Coveney, K. C. (1942). The growth of special classes in the city of Boston. *Training School Bulletin, 39*, 57–59.

Craig, S. B. (1946). Recruitment of teachers. *Volta Review, 48*, 701–704.

Cratty, B. (1969). *Perceptual-motor behavior and educational processes.* Springfield, IL: Thomas.

Cremin, L. A. (1961). *The transformation of the school.* New York: Alfred A. Knopf.

Cremin, L. A. (1964). *The transformation of the school: Progressivism in American education, 1876–1957.* New York: Alfred A. Knopf.

Crissey, M. S. (1975). Mental retardation: Past, present, and future. *American Psychologist, 30*, 800–808.

Cronis, T., & Ellis, D. (2000). Issues facing special educators in the new millennium. *Education, 120*, 639–648.

Crouter, A. L. E. (1892). The higher education of the deaf. *Science, 19*, 199–200.

Crouter, A. L. E. (1907). The organization and methods of the Pennsylvania Institution for the Deaf and Dumb. In W. H. Addison (Ed.), *Proceedings of the International Conference on the Education of the Deaf held in the Training College buildings, Edinburgh, on 29th., 30th. and 31st. July and 1st. and 2nd. August, 1907* (pp. 125–155). Edinburgh: The Darien Press.

Cruickshank, W. M. (1950–51). Growth in the quality of local services for exceptional children. *Journal of Exceptional Children, 17*, 233–236.

Cruickshank, W. M. (1967). The development of education for exceptional children. In W. M. Cruickshank & G. O. Johnson (Eds.), *Education of exceptional children and youth.* Englewood Cliffs, NJ: Prentice-Hall.

Cubberly, E. P. (1909). *Changing conceptions of education.* Boston: Houghton Mifflin.

Culross, R. D. (1997). Concepts of inclusion in gifted education. *Teaching Exceptional Children, 29*, 24–26.

Danforth, S. (1997). On what basis hope? Modern progress and postmodern possibilities. *Mental Retardation, 35*, 95–106.

Darling-Hammond, L. (1997). *The right to learn: A blueprint for creating schools that work.* San Francisco, CA: Jossey-Bass.

Darwin, C. (1859). *On the origin of the species.* London: Murray.

Darwin, C. (1874). The descent of man and selection in relation to sex (2nd ed.). London: John Murray.

Davenport, C. (1910). Report of the Committee of Eugenics. *American Breeders Magazine, 1*, 126–129.

Davenport, C. B. (1914). The importance to the state of eugenic investigations. In E. F. Robbins (Ed.), *Proceedings of the First National Conference on Race Betterment*. Battle Creek, MI: The Race Betterment Foundation.

Davenport, C. B. (1915a). *The feebly inhibited: Inheritance of temperament*. Washington, DC: Carnegie Institution.

Davenport, C. B. (1915b). The feebly inhibited: Nomadism, or the wandering impulse, with special reference to heredity. Washington, DC: Carnegie Foundation.

Davies, S. P. (1930). *Social control of the feeble-minded*. New York: T.Y. Crowell.

Davies, S. P. (1959). *The mentally retarded in society*. New York: Columbia University Press.

Davis, G. (1914). The education of crippled children. *American Journal of Orthopaedic Surgery, 12*, 1–4.

Davis, L. J. (1997). Universalizing marginality: How Europe became deaf in the eighteenth century. In L. J. Davis (Ed.), *The disability studies reader* (pp. 110–127) New York: Routledge.

Davitz, J. R., Davitz, L. J., & Lorge, I. (1964). *Terminology and concepts in mental retardation*. New York: Columbia University Teachers College.

Dawson, G., & Osterling, J. (1997). Early intervention in autism. In M. J. Guralnick (Ed.), *The effectiveness of early intervention* (pp. 307–326). Baltimore, MD: Paul H. Brookes.

Day, H., Fusfeld, I. S., & Pintner, R. (1928). *A survey of American schools for the deaf*. Washington, DC: National Research Council.

Defective children, their care, occupations and support. (1915). *Canadian Journal of Medicine and Surgery, 38*, 4.

Dei, G. J., James, I. M., James-Wilson, S., Karumanchery, L. L., & Zine, J. (2000). *Removing the margin: The challenges and possibilities of inclusive schooling*. Toronto: Canadian Scholars' Press.

Dejerine, J. (1871). Sur un cas de eccite verbale avec agraphia, suive d'autopsia. *Social Biology, 3*, 197–201.

de Land, F. (1908). The real romance of the telephone. *Association Review, 10*, 1–35, 123–137, 233–239, 343–348, 449–454.

de Land, F. (1919). Some notes about the American Association to Promote the Teaching of Speech to the Deaf. *Volta Review, 21*, 663–669.

de Land, F. (1923). An ever lasting memorial. *Volta Review, 25*, 91–98.

de Land, F. (1925). Hereditary impairment of hearing. *Journal of Heredity, 16*, 141–144.

Delehanty, F. B. (1896). People ex rel. the New York Institution for the Blind v. Ashbel P. Fitch, Comptroller. In *The miscellaneous reports: Cases decided in the courts of record of the State of New York* (pp. 464–470). Albany: James B. Lyon.

de Sanctis, S. (1908). Dementia praecocissima catatonica. *Folio Neurobiology, 2*, 9.

Developmental Disabilities Act of 1978, Pub. L. No. 95-602, 29 U.S.C. § 700 *et seq.*

Dewey, J. (1902). *The school and society.* Carbondale, IL: Southern Illinois University Press.

Dewey, J. (1938). *Logic: The theory of enquiry.* New York: Holt.

Dewey, M. H. (1898). The scope of day nursery work. In *Proceedings of the National Conference of Charities and Corrections* (pp. 105–107). Boston: Ellis.

De Witt, K. (1991, May 12) How best to teach the blind: A growing battle over braille. *New York Times,* pp. 1, 18.

Diana v. State Board of Education. Civil action No. C-7037RFP (N.D. Cal., January 7, 1970).

Dinger, J. (1961). Post school adjustment of former educationally retarded pupils. *Exceptional Children, 27,* 353–360.

DiPaola, M. F., Tschannen-Moran, M., & Walther-Thomas, C. (2004). School principals and special education: Creating the context for academic success. *Focus on Exceptional Children, 37,* 1–12.

Discussion at Chicago concerning day classes in public schools. (1884). *American Annals of the Deaf and Dumb, 29,* 312–325.

Dobson, H. (1919). Illiteracy and retardation. *Social Welfare, 1,* 136–137.

Doermer, K. (1969). *Madmen and the bourgeoisie.* London: Basil Blackwell. (English translation, 1981)

Doll, E. A. (1935). Vineland Social Maturity Scale: Manual of directions. *Training School Bulletin, 32,* 1–7, 25–32, 48–55, 68–74.

Doll, E. A. (1936). *Vineland Social Maturity Scale: Revised condensed manual of directions.* (Department of Research Series 1936, No. 3). Vineland, NJ: Training School at Vineland.

Doll, E. A. (1941a). The essentials of an inclusive concept of mental deficiency. *American Journal of Mental Deficiency, 46,* 214–219.

Doll, E. A. (1941b). Who are the morons? *Journal of Exceptional Children, 7,* 206–207.

Doll, E. A. (1951). Neurophrenia. *American Journal of Psychiatry, 108,* 50–53.

Down, J. L. (1866). Observations on ethnic classification of idiots. *London Hospital Report, 3,* 229–262.

Draper, A. G. (1889). Deaf and hearing teachers. *American Annals of the Deaf, 34,* 158–159.

Draper, A. G. (1904). The education of the deaf in America. *American Annals of the Deaf, 49,* 352–363.

Dugdale, R. L. (1877). *The Jukes: A study in crime, pauperism, disease and heredity.* New York: Putnam.

Dugdale, R. L. (1910). *The Jukes* (4th ed.). New York: Putnam.

Dunn, L. M. (1968). Special education for the mildly retarded Is much of it justifiable? *Exceptional Children, 35,* 5–24.

Dunn, L. M. (1973). *Exceptional children in the schools: Special education in transition.* New York: Holt, Rinehart and Winston.

Dunn, L. M., & McNeill, W. D. D. (1953–54). Special education in Canada as provided by local school systems. *Journal of Exceptional Children, 20,* 209–215.

Dunscombe, C. (1836). *Report upon the subject of education made to the Parliament of Upper Canada 25 February 1836, through the Commissioners, Doctors Morrison and*

*Bruce, appointed by a resolution of the House of Assembly in 1835 to obtain informa-
tion upon the subject of education, etc.* Upper Canada: M.C. Reynolds.

Dupont, H. J. (1957). Emotional maladjustment and special education. *Exceptional
Children, 24,* 10–15.

Dworkin, G. (Ed.). (1976). *The IQ controversy: Critical readings.* New York:
Pantheon.

Dwyer, E. (1987). *Homes for the mad: Life inside two nineteenth century asylums.* New
Jersey: Rutgers University Press.

Dykens, E. (2001). Introduction to the special issue on behavioral phenotypes.
American Journal on Mental Retardation, 106, 1–3.

Dyson, A. (1999). Inclusion and inclusions: Theories and discourses in inclusive
education. In H. Daniels & P. Garner (Eds.), *World yearbook of education, 1999:
Inclusive education* (pp. 36–53). London: Kogan Page.

Dyson, A. (2001). Special needs education as a way to equity: An alternative
approach? *Support for Learning, 16,* 99–104.

East, E. M. (1923). *Mankind at the crossroads.* New York: Scribner and Sons.

East, E. M. (1924). *Heredity and human affairs.* New York: Scribner and Sons.

Easterbrooks, S. (1999). Improving practices for students with hearing impairments. *Exceptional Children, 65,* 537–554.

Eber, L., Nelson, C. M., & Miles, P. (1997). School-based wraparound for students
with emotional and behavioral challenges. *Exceptional Children, 63,* 539–555.

Education for All Handicapped Children Act of 1975, Pub. L. No. 94-142, 20 U.S.C.
§1401 *et seq.*

Elementary and Secondary School Education Act of 1965, Pub. L. No. 89-10, 20
U.S.C. ch. 70.

Elks, M. A. (2005). Visual indictment: A contextual analysis of the Kallikak family
photographs. *Mental Retardation, 43,* 268–280.

Elliott, L. (1993, May 18). Mainstreaming opposed by deaf community. *ATA News,*
p. 11.

Ellis, N. R. (Ed.). (1963). *Handbook of mental deficiency.* New York: McGraw-Hill.

Enns, H. (1981). The historical development of attitudes toward the handicapped:
A framework for change. In D. Freeman & B. Trute (Eds.), *Treating families with
special needs* (pp. 175–185). Ottawa: Alberta Association of Social Workers and
the Canadian Association of Social Workers.

Epée, M. C. de l' (1860). The true method of educating the deaf and dumb, confirmed by long experience. *American Annals of the Deaf and Dumb, 12,* 1–131.

Esquirol, J. E. (1838). *Des maladies mentales.* Paris: Bailliere.

Esquirol, J. E. D. (1845). *A treatise on insanity.* Philadelphia, PA: Lea and
Blanchard.

Estabrook, A. H. (1916). *The Jukes in 1916.* Washington, DC: Carnegie Institution.

A eugenics catechism. (1927). New Haven, CT: American Eugenics Society.

Eugenics section: Its organization. (1910). *American Breeders' Magazine, 1,* 235–236.

Fagan, T. K. (1985). Sources for the delivery of school psychological services during 1890–1930. *School Psychology Review, 14,* 378–382.

Fairchild, D. (1922). Alexander Graham Bell: Some aspects of his greatness. *Journal of Heredity, 13,* 194–200.

Fairchild, H. (1917). The literacy test. *Quarterly Journal of Economics, 31,* 447–460.

Fairchild, H. (1924a). The immigration law of 1924. *Quarterly Journal of Economics, 31,* 447–460.

Fairchild, H. (1924b). The immigration law of 1924. *Quarterly Journal of Economics, 38,* 653–665.

Fancher, R. E. (1987). Henry Goddard and the Kallikak Family photographs: "Conscious skullduggery" or 'Whig history"? *American Psychologist, 42,* 585–590.

Farrell, E. (1908). Special classes in the New York City schools. *Journal of Psycho-Asthenics, 13,* 91–96.

Farrell, G. (1956). *The story of blindness.* Harvard, MA: Harvard University Press.

Farson, M. R. (1939–40). Education of the handicapped child for social competency. *Journal of Exceptional Children, 6,* 138–144, 150.

Fay, E. A. (1883). Review of history of deaf-mute education, with special reference to the development of deaf-mute instruction in Germany. *American Annals of the Deaf and Dumb, 28,* 238.

Fernald, G. M. (1943). *Remedial techniques in basic school subjects.* New York: McGraw-Hill.

Fernald, W. E. (1893). The history of the treatment of the feeble-minded. In *National Conference of Charities and Corrections* (pp. 203–221). Boston: Ellis.

Fernald, W. E. (1903). Mentally defective children in the public schools. *Journal of Psycho-Asthenics, 8,* 25–35.

Fernald, W. E. (1912). *History of the treatment of the feebleminded.* Boston: G. H. Ellis.

Fernald, W. E. (1919). After-care study of the patients discharged from Waverly for a period of twenty-five years. *Ungraded, 2,* 1–7.

Fernald, W. E. (1924). Feeblemindedness. *Mental Hygiene, 8,* 964–971.

Figueroa, R. A., & Garcia, E. (1994). Issues in testing students from culturally and linguistically diverse backgrounds. *Multicultural Education, 2,* 10–19.

Finkelstein, B. (1985). Schooling and the discovery of latency in nineteenth-century America. *Journal of Psycho-History, 13,* 3–12.

Finkelstein, V. (1981). Disability and the helper/helped relationship: An historical view. In A. Brechin, P. Lidiard, & J. Swain (Eds.), *Handicap in a social world* (pp. 58–65). Suffolk, UK: Chaucer Press.

Fitts, A. M. (1916). How to fill the gap between special classes for mentally defective children and institutions. *Ungraded, 11,* 1–8.

Flint, R. W. (1957). Survey shows need for better teacher recruitment programs. *Volta Review, 59,* 66–71.

Flugel, J. C., & West, D. J. (1964). *A hundred years of psychology* (3rd ed.). London: Duckworth.

Fombonne, E. (2003). The prevalence of autism. *Journal of the American Medical Association, 289,* 87–89.

Font, M. M. (1944–45). Who is the exceptional child? *Journal of Exceptional Children, 11,* 19–20.

Forest, M., & Pearpoint, J. (1992). Putting all kids on the MAP. *Educational Leader-ship, 50*, 81–86.

Forness, S. R. (2005). The pursuit of evidence-based practice in special education for children with emotional and behavioral disorders. *Behavioral Disorders, 30*, 311–330.

Foucault, M. (1972). *Madness and civilization: A history of insanity in the age of reason.* New York: Pantheon Books.

Frampton, M. E. (1941). The teacher of the handicapped. *Journal of Exceptional Children, 7*, 143–146.

Frampton, M. E., & Rowell, H. G. (1940). *Education of the handicapped* (Vol. 2). Yonkers, NY: World Book.

Freeberg. E. (1994). "More important than the rabble of common kings": Dr. Howe's education of Laura Bridgman. *History of Education Quarterly, 34*, 305–327.

Freeman, F. N. (1926). *Mental tests: Their history, principles and applications.* Boston: Houghton Mifflin.

French, R. (1932). *From Homer to Helen Keller: A social and educational study of the blind.* New York: American Foundation for the Blind.

Friedson, E. (1965). Disability as social deviance. In M. Sussman (Ed.), *Sociology of rehabilitation* (pp. 71–99). Cleveland, OH: Case Western University Press.

Froelich, C., McNealy, G., Nelson, R., & Norris, D. (1944). Gifted children. *Journal of Exceptional Children, 10*, 207–209.

Frostig, M. (1961). *Frostig Developmental Test of Visual Perception* (3rd ed.). Palo Alto, CA: Consulting Psychologists Press.

Fuchs, D., & Fuchs, L. S. (1994). Inclusive schools movement and radicalization of special education reform. *Exceptional Children, 60*, 294–309.

Fuchs, D., & Fuchs, L. S. (1995). Counterpoint—Special education—Ineffective? Immoral. *Exceptional Children, 61*, 303–305.

Fuchs, L. S., & Fuchs, D. (1992). Special education's wake-up call. *Journal of Special Education, 25*, 413–414.

Futrell, M., Gomez, J., & Bedden, D. (2003). Teaching the children of a new America. *Phi Delta Kappan, 84*, 381–385.

Gallagher, J. J. (1970). Unfinished educational tasks: Thoughts on leaving government service. *Exceptional Children, 36*, 709–716.

Gallagher, J. J. (1972). *The search for an educational system that doesn't exist.* Reston, VA: Council for Exceptional Children.

Gallaudet, E. M. (1888). *Life of Thomas Hopkins Gallaudet, founder of deaf-mute instruction in America.* New York: Henry Holt.

Gallaudet, E. M. (1907). The present state. In W. H. Addison (Ed.), *Proceedings of the International Conference on the education of the deaf held in the Training College buildings, Edinburgh, on 29th., 30th. and 31st. July and 1st. and 2nd. August, 1907* (pp. 18–22). Edinburgh: The Darien Press.

Gallaudet, T. H. (1836). The duty and advantages of affording instruction to the deaf and dumb. In E. J. Mann (Ed.), *The deaf and dumb: Or, a collection of articles relating to the condition of deaf mutes; their education, and the principal asylums devoted to their instruction* (pp. 197–231). Boston: D. K. Hitchcock.

Gallimore, L., & Woodruff, S. (1996). The bilingual-bicultural (bi-bi) approach: A professional point of view. In S. Schwartz (Ed.), *Choices in deafness: A parents' guide to communication options* (2nd ed., chap. 5). Bethesda, MD: Woodbine House.

Galton, F. (1865). Hereditary talent and character. *MacMillans Magazine, 7,* 157–160.

Galton, F. (1870). *Hereditary genius: An enquiry into its laws and consequences.* New York: Appleton.

Galton, F. (1887). Supplementary notes on 'prehension' in idiots. *Mind, 12,* 79–82.

Galton, F. (1904). Eugenics: Its definitions, scope and aims. *American Journal of Sociology, 10,* 1–6.

Galton, F. (1908). *Memories of my life.* London: Methuen.

Gannon, P. M. (1991). The integration of students with disability into regular schools in Australia: Can it be a reality? In A. F. Ashman (Ed.), *Current themes in integration. The Exceptional Child Monograph No 2* (pp. 175–194). St. Lucia, Qld: Fred and Eleanor Schonell Special Education Research Centre.

Gardiner, R. A. (1958). Alfred A. Strauss, 1897–1957. *Exceptional Children, 24,* 373–375.

Gardner, W. (1966). Social and emotional adjustment of mentally retarded children and adolescents: Critical review. *Exceptional Children, 33,* 97–10.

Garis, R. (1927). *Immigration restriction.* New York: Macmillan.

Gartner, A., & Lipsky, D. K. (1987). Beyond special education: Toward a quality system for all students. *Harvard Educational Review, 57,* 367–395.

Gaylin, J. (1977). Our endangered children: It's a matter of money. *Psychology Today, 10,* 94–95.

Geake, J., & Cooper, P. (2003). Implications of cognitive neuroscience for education. *Westminster Studies in Education, 26,* 7–20.

Gearheart, B., Mullen, R. C., & Gearheart, C. J. (1993). *Exceptional individuals: An introduction.* Pacific Grove, CA: Brooks/Cole.

Geer, W. C. (1977). The CEC and its roots. *Exceptional Children, 44,* 82–89.

Gelb, S. A. (1987). Social deviance and the discovery of the moron. *Disability, Handicap and Society, 2,* 247–258.

Gelb, S. A. (1989)."Not simply bad and incorrigible": Science, morality, and intellectual deficiency. *History of Education Quarterly, 29,* 359–380.

Gentile, A. (1969). *Further studies in achievement testing of hearing impaired students, 1971. Annual survey of hearing impaired children and youth* (Gallaudet College Office of Demographic Studies, Series D., No. 13). Washington, DC: Gallaudet College.

Gergen, K., & Gergen, M. (1982). Explaining human conduct: Form and function. In P. Secord (Ed), *Explaining human behavior: Consciousness, human action and social structure* (pp. 127–154). Beverley Hills, CA: Sage.

Giangreco, M. (2001). Interactions among programs, placement, and services in educational planning for students with disabilities. *Mental Retardation, 39,* 341–350.

Gillett, P. (1890). Deaf mutes. *Science, 16,* 248–249.

Gilmore, M. J. (1956). A comparison of selected legislative provisions for special education in local school districts in Illinois with those of other states. *Exceptional Children, 22,* 237–248.

Glassberg, L. A., Hooper, S. R., & Mattison, R. E. (1999). Prevalence of learning disabilities at enrollment in special education students with behavioral disorders. *Behavioral Disorders, 25,* 9–21.

Gliedman, J., & Roth, W. (1980). *The unexpected minority: Handicapped children in America.* New York: Harcourt, Brace and Jovanovich.

Goddard, H. H. (1910). Four hundred feeble-minded children classified by the Binet method. *Journal of Psycho-Asthenics, 15,* 17–30.

Goddard, H. H. (1911). Two thousand normal children measured by the Binet measuring scale of intelligence. *The Pedagogical Seminary, 18,* 232–259.

Goddard, H. H. (1912). *The Kallikak family: A study in the heredity of feeble mindedness.* New York: Macmillan.

Goddard. H. H. (1913a). The Binet tests and the inexperienced teacher. *Training School Bulletin, 9,* 9–11.

Goddard, H. H. (1913b). The Binet tests in relation to immigration. *Journal of Psycho-Asthenics, 18,* 105–110.

Goddard, H. H. (1913c). The reliability of the Binet-Simon Measuring Scale of Intelligence. In T. A. Storey (Ed.), *Transactions of the Fourth International Congress of School Hygiene* (693–699). Buffalo: Author.

Goddard, H. H. (1914). The Binet Measuring Scale of Intelligence: What it is, and how it is to be used. *Training School Bulletin, 10,* 86–91.

Goddard, H. H. (1916a). *Feeblemindedness.* New York: Macmillan.

Goddard, H. H. (1916b). The menace of mental defectives from the standpoint of heredity. *Boston Medical and Surgical Journal, 175* (August), 269–271.

Goddard, H. H. (1917). Mental tests and the immigrant. *Journal of Delinquency, 2,* 243–277.

Goddard, H. H. (1921). *Juvenile delinquency.* New York: Dodd, Mead.

Goddard, H. H. (1928). Feeblemindedness: A question of definition. *Journal of Psycho-Asthenics, 33,* 219–227.

Goddard, H. H. (1976). What it means ... In M. Rosen, G. R. Clarke, & M. S. Kivitz (Eds.), *The history of mental retardation: Collected papers* (Vol. 2). Baltimore. MD: University Park Press. (Original work published 1914)

Goffman, E. (1961). *Asylums: Essays on the social situation of mental patients and other inmates.* Chicago: Aldine.

Goldstein, H. (1984). A search for understanding. In B. Blatt & R. J. Morris (Eds.), *Perspectives in special education: Personal orientations* (pp. 56–100). Glenview, IL: Scott, Foresman.

Goldstein, K. (1940). *Human nature in light of psychopathology.* Cambridge, MA: Harvard University Press.

Goldstein, M. (1919). The meetings of the Convention and the Association. *Volta Review, 64,* 339.

Goldstein, M. (1976). Excerpts from the society of Progressive oral advocates: Its origin and purpose. 1917. *Volta Review, 78,* 140–144.

Good, C. V. (1938). Introduction: Research dealing with exceptional groups. *Journal of Exceptional Children, 4,* 306.

Goodenough, F. (1949). *Mental testing: Its history, principles and applications*. New York: Rinehart.

Goodlad, J. I. (1984). *A place called school*. New York: McGraw-Hill.

Goodrich, C., & Bailey, I. (2000). A history of the field of visual rehabilitation from the perspective of low vision. In B. Silverman, M. Lang, B. Rosenthal, & E. Faye (Eds.), *The Lighthouse handbook on visual impairment and visual rehabilitation* (pp. 675–708). New York: Oxford University Press.

Gorwitz, K. (1974). Census enumeration of the mentally ill and mentally retarded in the nineteenth century. *Health Services Reports, 89*, 181–184.

Gosney, E. S., & Poponoe, P. (1929). *Sterilization for human betterment: A summary of results of 6,000 operations in California, 1909–1929*. Pasadena, CA: Human Betterment Foundation.

Gottlieb, J., Alter, M., Gottlieb, B. W., & Wishner, J. (1994). Special education in urban America: It's not justifiable for many. *Journal of Special Education, 27*, 453–465.

Gottlieb, J., & Budoff, A. (1973). Social acceptability of retarded children in non-graded schools differing in architecture. *American Journal of Mental Deficiency, 78*, 15–19.

Gould, S. (1981) *The mismeasure of man*. New York: W. W. Norton.

Graham, S. (Ed.). (2005). *Exceptional Children, 71*.

Grant, M. (1936). *Passing of a great race*. Of the racial basis of European history. New York: Scribner. (Original work published 1921)

Grave, C. E. (1939). Twenty-five years of progress in education at Woods School. *Exceptional Children, 16*, 83–89.

Green, A. L., & Stoneman, Z. (1989). Attitudes of mothers and fathers of nonhandicapped children. *Journal of Early Intervention, 13*, 292–304.

Greenwood, C. R. (2001). Science and students with learning and behavioral problems. *Behavioral Disorders, 27*, 37–52.

Greer, J. V. (1992). Quality is in the eye of the beholder. *Exceptional Children, 58*, 200–201.

Gresham F. (1997, November/December). We need a better way to identify students with learning disabilities. *CEC Today*, p. 14.

Gresham, F. M., MacMillan, D. L., & Bocian K. M. (1996). Learning disabilities, low achievement, and mild mental retardation: More alike than different? *Journal of Learning Disabilities, 29*, 570–581.

Grinder, R. E. (1967). *A history of genetic psychology: The first science of human development*. New York: Wiley.

Gross, J. (2003, April 13). Nudging toward normal: Step by step, skill by skill, applied behavior analysis taught Ben to talk. *New York Times*, pp. 27–28, 32.

Grossman, H. (Ed.) (1983). *Manual on terminology and classification in mental retardation* (3rd Rev. ed.). Washington, DC: American Association on Mental Deficiency.

Guillie, D. (1817). *Essai sur l'instruction des aveugles ou expose des procedes poiur les instruire*. Paris: Imprime por les aveugles.

Gulchak, D. J. & Lopes, J. A. (2007). Interventions for students with behavior disorders: An international literature review. *Behavior Disorders, 32,* 267–281.

Gulek, G. L. (1988). *Education and schooling in America* (2nd ed.). Englewood Cliffs, NJ: Prentice-Hall.

Gulik, S. (1916). An immigration policy. *Journal of Heredity, 7,* 546–552.

Guthrie, E. (1937–38). The need for knowing the whole child. *Journal of Exceptional Children, 5,* 174–179, 183.

Hagan, J., & Leon, J. (1977). Rediscovering delinquency: Social history, political ideology and the sociology of law. *American Sociological Review, 42,* 587–598.

Haines, T. H. (1925). State laws relating to special classes and schools for mentally handicapped children in the public schools. *Mental Hygiene, 9,* 545–551.

Halifax Institution for the Blind. (1875). *Annual report.* Halifax, NS: Author.

Haller, J. S., Jr. (1971). *Outcasts from evolution: Scientific attitudes of racial inferiority, 1859–1900.* Urbana, IL: University of Illinois Press.

Halpern, R. (1999). *Fragile families, fragile solutions: A history of supportive services for families in poverty.* New York: Columbia University Press.

Hanes, R. (1995). Linking mental defect to physical deformity: The case of crippled children in Ontario, 1890–1940. *Journal of Developmental Disabilities, 4,* 23–40.

Haney, W. (1981). Validity, vaudeville, and values: A short history of social concerns over standardized testing. *American Psychologist, 36,* 1021–1033.

Hanks, J. R., & Hanks, L. (1948). The physically handicapped in non-occidental societies. *Journal of Social Issues, 4,* 11–20.

Hanson, M. J., Horn, E., Sandall, S., Beckman, P., Morgan, M., Marquart, J., et al. (2001). After preschool inclusion: Children's educational pathways over the early school years. *Exceptional Children, 68,* 65–83.

Hare, E. H. (1962). Masturbatory insanity: The history of an idea. *Journal of Mental Science, 108,* 1–25.

Hart, H. H., Jenkins, R. L., Axelrad, S., & Sperling, P. L. (1943). Multiple factor analysis of traits of delinquent boys. *Journal of Social Psychology, 17,* 191–201.

Haskell, T. L. (1985). Capitalism and the origins of the humanitarian sensibility. *American Historical Review, 90,* 339–361, 547–566.

Hawk, S. S. (1934). Excerpts from convention addresses. *Council Review/Journal of Exceptional Children, 1,* 44.

Hay, W. (1952). *Assessment for parents of mentally retarded children.* Arlington, VA: National Association for Retarded Citizens.

Haywood, C. (1979). What happened to mild and moderate retardation? *American Journal of Mental Deficiency, 83,* 429–431.

Healy, W. (1915a). *The individual delinquent.* Boston: Little, Brown.

Healy, W. (1915b). *Mental conflicts and misconduct.* Boston: Little, Brown.

Healy, W., & Bronner, A. F. (1926). *Delinquents and criminals: Their making and unmaking.* Montclair, NJ: Patterson Smith. (Original work published 1926)

Heck, A. O. (1940). *The education of exceptional children.* New York: McGraw-Hill.

Heinze, T., & Leyser, Y. (1998). Variables associated with stress and adaptation on families of children with visual disabilities. *International Journal of Special Education, 13,* 1–17.

Henderson, R. (1919). Child labour, delinquency, and the standards of living. *Social Welfare, 2*, 16–17.

Henry, N. B., & Kirk, S. A. (1950). (Eds.). *The 49th yearbook of the National Society for the Study of Education: The education of exceptional children.* New York: National Society for the Study of Education.

Henry, T. S. (1920). *Classroom problems in the education of gifted children: Nineteenth yearbook, Part 2, National Society for the Study of Education.* Chicago, IL: University of Chicago Press.

Herbst, J. (1988). From citizen teacher to professional. In *Papers of the International Standing Conference on the History of Education* (pp. 143–152). Jounsuu, Finland: International Standing Conference the History of Education.

Here and there at the training school: A straight path. (1943). *Training School Bulletin, 39*, 210–213.

Heshusius, L. (1986). Pedagogy, special education, and the lives of young children: A critical and futuristic perspective. *Journal of Education, 168*, 25–38.

Hewes, D. W. (1989, August). *Entrance age to public education in the United States, 1642 to 1842.* Paper presented at the International Standing Committee on the History of Education, Oslo.

Hewitt, L. E., & Jenkins, M. D. (1946). *Fundamental patterns of maladjustment: The dynamics of their origin.* Springfield, IL: Green.

Higbee, C. E. (1935–36). Sterilization: A brief introduction. *Journal of Exceptional Children, 2*, 10–12.

Hilgard, E. R. (1987). *Psychology in America: A historical survey.* New York: Harcourt Brace Jovanovich.

Hill, A. S. (1951). Legislation affecting special education since 1949. *Journal of Exceptional Children, 18*, 65–67, 90.

Hill, A. S. (1956). A critical glance at special education. *Exceptional Children, 22*, 315–317, 344.

Hincks, C. M. (1918). The need of mental clinics for the diagnosis of feeble-mindedness. *Social Welfare, 1*, 57–58.

Hincks, C. M. (1919). Mental hygiene. *Social Welfare, 1*, 130.

Hines, H. C. (1922). What Los Angeles is doing with the results of testing. *Journal of Educational Research, 5*, 45–47.

Hinshelwood, J. (1900). Congenital word blindness. *Lancet, 1*, 1506–1508.

Hinshelwood, J. (1917). *Congenital word blindness.* London: H. K. Lewis.

Hobbs, N. (1966). Helping disturbed children: Psychological and ecological strategies. *American Psychologist, 21*, 1105–1115.

Hobbs, N. (1975a). *The futures of children: Categories, labels, and their consequences.* San Francisco, CA: Jossey-Bass.

Hobbs, N. (Ed.). (1975b). *Issues in the classification of children: A sourcebook on categories, labels, and their consequences (Vol. 2).* San Francisco: Jossey-Bass.

Hobson v. Hansen, 269 F. Supp. 401 (DDC) (1967).

Hodapp, R. M., & Fidler, D. J. (1999). Special education and genetics: Connections for the 21st. century. *Journal of Special Education, 33*, 130–137.

Hoffman, E. (1972). *The treatment of deviance by the educational system.* Ann Arbor, MI: Institute for the Study of Mental Retardation and Related Disabilities.

Hoffman, E. (1975). The American public school and the deviant child: The origins of their involvement. *Journal of Special Education, 9,* 415–423.

Hollingworth, L. S. (1926). *Gifted children: Their nature and nurture.* New York: Macmillan.

Hollingworth, L. S. (1931). How should gifted children be educated? *Baltimore Bulletin of Education, 50,* 196.

Holman, H. (1914). *Seguin and his physiological method of education.* London: Pitman.

Holmes Group (1986). *Tomorrow's teachers.* East Lansing, MI: Holmes Group.

Hothersall, D. (1984). *History of psychology.* Philadelphia, PA: Temple University Press.

Houston, S. (1982). The 'waifs and strays' of a late Victorian city: Juvenile delinquents in Toronto. In J. Parr (Ed.), *Childhood and family in Canadian history.* Toronto: McClelland and Stewart.

Howard, F. E. (1935). *Mental health: Its principles and practices with emphasis on the treatment of mental deviations.* New York: Harper and Brothers.

Howard, J. C. (1902). Men and women teachers. *American Annals of the Deaf, 47,* 278–281.

Howe, M., & Hall, F. H. (1903). *Laura Bridgman.* Boston: Little, Brown.

Howe, S. G. (1858). *On the causes of idiocy; being the supplement to the report by Dr. S. G. Howe and the other commissioners appointed by the governor of Massachusetts to enquire into the condition of idiots of the Commonwealth, dated February 26, 1848, with an appendix.* Edinburgh: Maclachlan & Stewart.

Howe, S. G. (1866). *Ceremonies on laying the corner-stone of the New York State Institution for the Blind, at Batavia.* New York: Henry Todd.

Howe, S. G. (1871). Education of the blind. In *Annual report of the Perkins Institution for the Blind* (pp. 29–35). Boston: J. T. Buckingham.

Howe, S. G. (1874). The co-education of the deaf and the blind. *American Annals of the Deaf and Dumb, 19,* 162.

Hubbard, G. G. (1876). The origin of the Clarke Institution. *American Annals of the Deaf and Dumb, 21,* 178–183.

Huey, E. (1910). The Binet scale for measuring intelligence and retardation. *Journal of Educational Psychology, 1,* 435–444.

Human Betterment Foundation. (1937). Mental abnormalities. *Journal of Exceptional Children, 4,* 10–19.

Hume, J. (1996, January). *Disability, feminism, and eugenics: Who has the right to decide who should or should not inhabit the world?* Paper presented at the Women's Electoral Lobby National Conference, University of Technology, Sydney.

Hutt, R. B. (1923). The school psychologist. *Psychological Clinic, 15,* 48–51.

Hutton, W. L. (1936). *A brief for sterilization of the feeble-minded. Prepared at the request of the Association of Ontario Mayors at their annual conference, Orillia, June, 1936.* Ontario: Ontario Mayors.

Individuals With Disabilities Education Act of 1990, Pub. L. No. 101-476, 20 U.S.C. §§ 1400–1485.

Ingram, C. P. (1948). Federal legislation and news. *Journal of Exceptional Children, 14,* 154–156.

Ingram, C. P., Martens, E., & Cook, K. (1945). *Education in training schools for delinquent youth* (U.S. Office of Education, Bulletin No. 5). Washington, DC: U.S. Office of Education.

Irwin, R. B. (1955). Speech disorders. In M. Frampton & E. Gall (Eds.), *Special education for the exceptional* (Vol. 2). Boston: Porter Sargent.

Jenkins, R. L., & Hewitt, L. E. (1944). Types of personality structure encountered in child guidance clinics. *American Journal of Orthopsychiatry, 14,* 89–44.

Jenkins, W. G. (1890). The scientific testimony of 'Facts and opinions'. *Science, 16,* 85–88.

Jennings, W. (1930). *The poor law code.* London: Charles Knight.

Jensen, A. R. (1968). Social class, race and genetics: Implications for education. *American Educational Research Journal, 5,* 1–42.

Jensen, A. R. (1969). How much can we boost IQ and scholastic achievement? *Harvard Educational Review, 39,* 1–123.

Johanningmeier, E. V. (1989, August). *Piety and patriotism in 17th and 18th century American education: The foundation for Horace Mann's common school crusade.* Paper presented at the International Standing Committee on the History of Education, Oslo.

Johnson, A. (1900). The self-supporting imbecile. *Journal of Psycho-Asthenics, 4,* 92–97.

Johnson, G. O. (1950). A study of the social position of mentally handicapped children in the regular classes. *American Journal of Mental Deficiency, 55,* 60–90.

Johnson, G. O. (1962). Special education for the mentally handicapped: A paradox. *Exceptional Children, 8,* 62–69.

Johnson, G. O., & Kirk, S. (1958). Are mentally-handicapped children segregated in the regular grades? *Journal of Exceptional Children, 17,* 65–68.

Johnstone, E. R. (1914). The extension of the care of the feeble-minded. *Journal of Psycho-Asthenics, 19,* 3–18.

Jones, A. (1978). Closing Penetanguishine penitentiary: An attempt to deinstitutionalize treatment of juvenile offenders in early twentieth century Ontario. *Ontario History, 70,* 227–244.

Jones, B. E., Clark, G. M., & Soltz, D. F. (1997). Characteristics and practices of sign language interpreters in inclusive education programs. *Exceptional Children, 63,* 257–268.

Jones, J. W. (1918). One hundred years of history. *American Annals of the Deaf, 63,* 1–47.

Jones, K. (1960). *Mental health and social policy, 1845–1959.* London: Routledge and Kegan Paul.

Jones, R. A. (1977). *Self-fulfilling prophecies: Social, psychological, and physiological effects of expectancies.* Hillsdale, NJ: Lawrence Erlbaum.

Jordan, D. S. (1915). *War and the breed.* New York: Beacon Press.

Judd, C. (1918). *Introduction to the scientific study of education*. Boston: Ginn.

Juvenile courts in two Canadian cities. (1921). *Social Welfare, 3*, 238–239.

Kadesjo, B., Gillberg, C., & Nagberg, B. (1999). Autism and Asperger syndrome in seven-year-old children: A total population study. *Journal of Autism and Developmental Disorders, 29*, 327–332.

Kaestle, C. F., & Vinovskis, M. A. (1980.) *Education and social change in nineteenth-century Massachusetts*. Cambridge, MA: Cambridge University Press.

Kamin, S. (1974). *The history and politics of IQ*. Potomac, MD: Lawrence Erlbaum.

Kanner, L. (1943). Autistic disturbances of affective contact. *Nervous Child, 2*, 217–250.

Kanner, L. (1960). Itard, Seguin, Howe—Three pioneers in the education of retarded children. *American Journal of Mental Deficiency, 65*, 2–10.

Kanner, L. (1962). Emotionally disturbed children: A historical review. *Child Development, 33*, 97–102.

Kaplan, P. S. (1996). *Pathways for exceptional children: School, home, and culture*. Minneapolis/St. Paul, MN: West.

Karier, C. J. (1972). Testing for order and control in the corporate liberal state. *Educational Theory, 22*, 154–180.

Kassmaul, A. (1877). *Untersuchungen uber das Sedenleben des neugeborenen Menchen*. Leipzig: C. E. Winter. (Original work published 1859)

Katz, M. (1973). From voluntarism to bureaucracy in American education. In M. Katz (Ed.) *Education in American history: Readings on the social issues*. (pp. 38–50). New York: Praeger.

Kauffman, J. M. (1976). Nineteenth century views of children's behavior disorders: Historic contributions and continuing issues. *Journal of Special Education, 10*, 335–349.

Kauffman, J. M. (1981). *Characteristics of children's behavior disorders* (2nd ed.). Columbus, OH: Merrill.

Kauffman, J. M. (1989). The regular education initiative as Reagan-Bush educational policy: A trickle-down theory of education of the hard-to-teach. *Journal of Special Education, 23*, 256–278.

Kauffman, J. M. (1993a). *Characteristics of children's behavior disorders* (5th ed.). Columbus, OH: Merrill.

Kauffman, J. M. (1993b). How we might achieve the radical reform of special education. *Exceptional Children, 60*, 6–16.

Kauffman, J. M. (1996). The challenge of nihilism. *Teacher Education and Special Education, 19*, 205–206.

Kauffman, J. M. (2001). *Characteristics of emotional and behavior disorders in children and youth* (7th ed.). Upper Saddle River, NJ: Merrill/Prentice Hall.

Kauffman, J. M. (2002). *Education deform: Bright people sometimes say stupid things about education*. Lanham, MD: Scarecrow Education.

Kauffman, J. M. (2003). Reflections on the field. *Behavioral Disorders, 28*, 205–208.

Kavale, K. A., & Forness, S. R. (2000) What definitions of learning disabilities say and don't say: A critical analysis. *Journal of Learning Disabilities, 33*, 239–256.

Kavale, K. A., Holdnack, J. A., & Mostert, M. P. (2005). Responsiveness to intervention and the identification of specific learning disabilities: A critique and alternative proposal. *LD Quarterly, 28*, 2–16.

Kelly, E. (1946). The recruiting of teachers. *Volta Review, 48*, 689–701.

Kelso, J. J. (1893–94). Neglected and friendless children. *The Canadian Magazine, 1*, 213–216.

Kelso, J. J. (1910). *Children: Their care, training and happiness as future citizens.* Toronto: L. K. Cameron, King's Printer.

Kennedy, R. J. (1948). *The social adjustment of morons in a Connecticut city.* Hartford, CT: State Office Building.

Keogh, B. K., & Levitt, M. C. (1976). Special education in the mainstream: A confrontation of limitations. *Focus on Exceptional Children, 8*, 1–11.

Kephart, N. C. (1968). *Learning disabilities: An educational adventure.* West Lafayette, IN: Kappa Delta Pi Press.

Kerlin, I. N. (1879). Juvenile insanity. In I. N. Kerlin (Ed.), *Proceedings of the Association of Medical Officers of American Institutions for Idiotic and Feeble-Minded Persons* (pp. 86–94). Philadelphia, PA: J. B. Lippincott.

Kerlin, I. N. (1887). Moral imbecility. In *Proceedings of the Association of Medical Officers of American Institutions for Idiotic and Feeble-Minded Persons* (pp. 32–37). Philadelphia, PA: J. B. Lippincott.

Kevles, D. J. (1985). *In the name of eugenics: Genetics and the uses of human heredity.* New York: Alfred A. Knopf.

Kevles, D. J., & Hood, L. (1992). *The code of codes: Scientific and social issues in the human genome project.* Cambridge, MA: Harvard University Press.

Kim, Y. H. (1970). *The community of the blind: Applying the theory of community formation.* New York: American Foundation for the Blind.

Kirk, S. A. (1950). Presentation of the 49th yearbook of the National Society for the Study of Education. *Journal of Exceptional Children, 16*, 233–236, 239.

Kirk, S. A. (1963). *Behavioral diagnosis and remediation of learning disabilities. In Proceedings of the conference on exploration into the problems of the perceptually handicapped child: First annual meeting (Vol. 1, pp. 1–7).* Evanston, IL: Fund for Perceptually Handicapped Children.

Kirk, S. A. (1964). Research in education of the mentally retarded. In H. Stevens & R. Heber (Eds.), *Mental retardation: A review of research* (pp. 57–99). Chicago: University of Chicago Press.

Kirk, S. A. (1984). Introspection and prophecy. In B. Blatt & R. J. Morris (Eds.), *Perspectives in special education: Personal orientations* (pp. 25–55) Glenview, IL: Scott, Foresman.

Kirk, S. A., & Gallagher, J. J. (1979). *Educating exceptional children.* Boston: Houghton Mifflin.

Kirk, S. A., & Lord, F. E. (Eds.). (1974). *Exceptional children: Educational resources and perspectives.* Boston: Houghton Mifflin.

Kirk, S. A., McCarthy, J. J., & Kirk, W. D. (1968). *Illinois Test of Psycholinguistic Abilities.* Urbana, IL: University of Illinois Press.

Kliewer, C., & Drake, S. (1998). Disability, eugenics and the current ideology of segregation: A modern moral tale. *Disability and Society, 13,* 95–111.

Knowlson, J. (1965). The idea of gesture as a universal language in the seventeenth and eighteenth centuries. *Journal of the History of Ideas, 26,* 495–508.

Knox, H. A. (1914). A scale based on the work at Ellis Island, for estimating mental defect. *Journal of the American Medical Association, 62,* 741–746.

Kode, K. (2002). *Elizabeth Farrell and the history of special education.* Reston, VA: Council for Exceptional Children.

Koertge, N. (1998). Scrutinizing science studies. In N. Koertge (Ed.), *A house built in sand: Exposing postmodernist myths about science* (pp. 3–6). New York: Oxford University Press.

Koestler, F. (1976). *The unseen minority: A social history of blindness in the United States.* New York: David McKay.

Kolstoe, O. P. (1972). *Mental retardation: An educational viewpoint.* New York: Holt, Rinehart and Winston.

Kraepelin, E. (1896). *Psychiatrie: Ein Lehrbuch fur studirende und Aerzte.* Leipzig: J. A. Barth.

Krugman, M. (1962). Current trends in special education in New York City. *Journal of Exceptional Children, 28,* 245–246.

Kugel, R., & Wolfsenberger, W. (Eds.). (1969). *Changing patterns in residential services for the mentally retarded.* Washington, DC: President's Committee on Mental Retardation.

Kugler, E. M. (1935). Efficient and effective classroom management. *Journal of Exceptional Children, 2,* 128–134, 138.

Kuhn, T.S. (1970). *The structure of scientific revolution* (2nd ed.). Chicago, IL: University of Chicago Press.

Kvaraceus, W. C. (1955–56). Acceptance-rejection and exceptionality. *Exceptional Children, 2,* 328–331.

Lamson, M. S. (1878). *Life and education of Laura Dewey Bridgman: The deaf, dumb and blind girl.* Boston: New England Publishing.

Landman, J. H. (1932). *Human sterilization: The history of the movement.* New York: Macmillan.

Lane, H. (1976). *The wild boy of Aveyron.* Cambridge, MA: Harvard University Press.

Lane, H. (1993). Cochlear implants: Their cultural and historical meaning. In J. V. Van Cleve (Ed.), *Deaf history unveiled: Interpretations from the new scholarship* (pp. 272–292). Washington, DC: Gallaudet University Press.

Lane, H. (1997). Construction of deafness. In L. J. Davis (Ed.), *The disability studies reader* (pp. 153–171). New York: Routledge.

Lane, H., & Bahan, B. (1998). Ethics of cochlear implantation in young children: A review and reply from a Deaf World perspective. *Otolaryngology Head and Neck Surgery, 119,* 297–308.

Lane, H., & Pillard, R. (1978). *The wild boy of Burundi.* New York: Random House.

Lane, H. S. (1946). Recruitment of teachers of the deaf. *Volta Review, 48,* 704–705.

Lane, H. S. (1952). Teacher recruitment and training: A summer meeting panel discussion, June 18, 1952. *Volta Review, 54,* 497–500, 512–513.

Larrivee, B. (2005). *Authentic classroom management: Creating a learning community and building reflective practice*. Boston: Pearson.

Larry P. v. Riles (1979). No. C-71-2270 RFP, U.S. District Court for the Northern District of California.

Lasch, C. (1973). Origins of the asylum. In *The world of nation: Reflections on American history, politics, and culture* (pp. 3–17). New York: Alfred A. Knopf.

Lau v. Nichols, 945 Ct. 786 (1974).

Laudan, L. (1990). *Science and relativism: Some key controversies in the philosophy of science*. Chicago, IL: University of Chicago Press.

Laughlin, H. (1922). *Eugenical sterilization in the United States*. Chicago, IL: Psychopathic Laboratory of the Municipal Court of Chicago.

Laycock, S. R. (1937–38). The whole child comes to school. *Journal of Exceptional Children, 15*, 97–100, 109.

Laycock, S. R. (1940–41). Mental health qualifications for special class teachers. *Journal of Exceptional Children, 7*, 4–8, 23.

Leader, G. M. (1957). The governor reports on Pennsylvania's progress in special education. *Exceptional Children, 24*, 67–68, 76–77.

League for Preventative Work. (1916–17). *The mental defective and the public schools of Massachusetts*. Boston: Author.

Lee, J. L. (1936). Problems in organization of teacher training in special education. *Journal of Exceptional Children, 3*, 142–143.

Lee, J. L. (1944). Editorial. *Journal of Exceptional Children, 11*, 1–2.

Lerner, J. (1981). *Learning disabilities: Theories, diagnosis and teaching strategies* (3rd ed.). Boston: Houghton Mifflin.

Lesperance, J. (1872). The dumb speak. *Canadian Monthly and National Review, 7*, 506–512.

Lessard v. Schmidt (1972) 348 F. Supp. 1078 (E.D. Wis. 972) remanded as 414 U.S. 473 (1974).

Lewis, A. (1960). A study of defect. *American Journal of Psychiatry, 117*, 289–304.

Lewis, R. S. (1951). *The other child*. New York: Grune and Stratton.

Linden, K. W., & Linden, J. D. (1968). *Modern mental measurement: A historical perspective*. New York: Houghton Mifflin.

Lipsky, D., & Gartner, A. (1987). Capable of achievement and worthy of respect: Education for handicapped students as if they were full-fledged human beings. *Exceptional Children, 54*, 69–74.

Lipsky, D., & Gartner A. (1998). Factors for successful inclusion: Learning from the past, looking toward the future. In S. Vitello & D. Mithaug (Eds.), *Inclusive schooling: National and international perspectives* (pp. 98–112). New York: Lawrence Erlbaum.

Little, W. G. (1862). On the influence of abnormal parturition, difficult labor, premature birth, asphyxia neonatorum, on the mental and physical condition of the child, especially in relation to deformities. *Trends, Obstetrical Society, London, 3*, 293–344.

Lord, F. E. (Ed.). (1947). Teachers' pay. *Exceptional Children, 13*, 182.

Lowenfeld, B. (1956). History and development of specialized education for the blind. *Exceptional Children, 23,* 53–56, 90.

Luftig, R. L. (1989). *Assessment of learners with special needs.* Boston: Allyn and Bacon.

Lustig, M. W., & Koestner, J. (1996). *Intercultural competence: Interpersonal communication across cultures* (2nd ed.). New York: Harper Collins.

Lyon, G. R. (1996). Learning disabilities. *The Future of Children, 6,* 54–76.

Lytle, V. (1987). Here's looking at you, teacher! *NEA Today, 6,* 3.

Maag, J. W., & Katsiyannis, A. (1998). Challenges facing successful transition for youths with E/BD. *Behavioral Disorders, 23,* 209–221.

Mack, J. (1909). The juvenile court. *Harvard Law Review, 104,* 107.

Mackie, R. (1951). The mid-century White House conference on exceptional children. *Journal of Exceptional Children, 17,* 129–131, 168.

Mackie, R., & Dunn, L. (1954). *College and university programs for the preparation of teachers of exceptional children* (Bulletin No. 13). Washington, DC: Government Printing Office.

MacDonnell, G. M. (1897). The prevention of crime by the state. *Queen's Quarterly, 4,* 257.

Macmillan, D. J., & Siperstein, G. N. (2001, August). *Learning disabilities as operationally defined by schools.* Paper presented at the LD Summit, Washington, DC.

MacMillan, M. B. (1960). Extra-scientific influences in the history of childhood psychopathology. *American Journal of Psychiatry, 116,* 1091–1096.

MacMurchy, H. (1919). Specialized education of the defective child, part 2. *Social Welfare, 1* (September), 280–281, 299.

MacMurchy, H. (1920). *The almosts: A study of the feeble-minded.* Boston: Houghton Mifflin.

Mahendra, B. (1985). Subnormality revisited in early 19th century France. *Journal of Mental Deficiency Research, 29,* 391–401.

Mahler, M. S. (1952). On child psychosis and schizophrenia. *Psychoanalytic Study of the Child, 7,* 286–305.

Mahoney, J. (2002, July–August). Washington update. *LDA Newsbriefs, 37,* pp. 5–6.

Mandel, C. (2005, November 16). Town for deaf may be modeled after Quebec. *Calgary Herald,* p. A15.

Mann, L. (1970). Perceptual training: Misdirections and redirections. *American Journal of Orthopsychiatry, 40,* 30–38.

Mann, L. (1971). Psychometric phrenology and the new faculty psychology: The case against ability assessment and training. *Journal of Special Education, 5,* 3–65.

Manset, G., & Semmel, M. I. (1997). Are inclusive programs for students with mild disabilities effective? A comparative review of program models. *Journal of Special Education, 31,* 155–180.

Manzo, D., & Peters, E. C. (2008). *Cotting School.* Portsmouth, NH: Arcadia.

Marinies, C. J. (1937). Psychological patterns in school children with endocrine disorders. *Journal of Exceptional Children, 4,* 9–11, 18.

Marschark, M. (1993). *Raising and educating a deaf child: A comprehensive guide to the choices, controversies, and decisions faced by parents and educators.* New York: Oxford University Press.

Martens, E. H. (1936). Present status of opportunities for the preparation of teachers of exceptional children. *Journal of Exceptional Children, 3,* 140–142.

Martens, E. H. (1946a). State directors and supervisors of special education. *Journal of Exceptional Children, 12,* 209–210.

Martens, E. H. (1946b). State legislation for the education of exceptional children—Some basic principles. *Journal of Exceptional Children, 12,* 225–230.

Martens, E. H. (1951). Toward life adjustment through 'special education'. *Journal of Exceptional Children, 17,* 169–173.

Martz, C. (1993, spring). Educating European immigrant children before World War I. *Educational Horizons,* pp. 139–141.

Massachusetts Institution for the Idiotic and Feeble-Minded. (1885). *Annual Report.* Boston: Author.

Mattison, R. E., Hooper, S. R., & Glassberg, L. A. (2002). Three-year course of learning disorders in special education students classified as behavioral disorder. *Journal of the American Academy of Child and Adolescent Psychiatry, 41,* 1454–1461.

Maudsley, H. (1867). Illustrations of a variety of insanity. *Journal of Mental Science, 14,* 153.

Maudsley, H. (1868). *The physiology and pathology of mind* (2nd ed.). London: Macmillan.

Mazurek, K. (1981). *History, historiography, historical praxis.* Unpublished doctoral dissertation, University of Alberta.

McGann, J. B. (1863). *Home education for the deaf and dumb: First book of lessons.* Toronto: Author.

McGovern, C. M. (1986). *Masters of madness: Social origins of the American psychiatric profession.* Hanover, NH: University of New England.

McGrath, W. T. (1962). A new look at juvenile delinquency. *Canadian Forum, 42,* 55–57.

McGrath, W. T. (1965*). Crime and its treatment in Canada.* Toronto: Macmillan.

McKinley, A. M., & Warren S. F. (2000). The effectiveness of cochlear implants for children with prelingual deafness. *Journal of Early Intervention, 23,* 252–263.

McLaren, A. (1990). *Our own master race: Eugenics in Canada, 1885–1945.* Toronto: McClelland and Stewart.

McLaughlin, M., & Henderson, K. (2000). Defining U.S. special education into the twenty-first century. In M. Winzer & K. Mazurek (Eds.), *Special education in the 21st century: Issues of inclusion and reform* (pp. 41–61). Washington, DC: Gallaudet University Press.

McLeskey, J., Henry, D., & Hodges, D. (1999). Inclusion: What progress is being made across disability categories? *Teaching Exceptional Children, 31,* 60–64.

Meadow, K. P. (1980). *Deafness and child development.* Berkeley, CA: University of California Press.

Melcher, J. W. (1971). Some questions from a school administrator. In I. I. Meyen (Ed.), *Proceedings: The Missouri conference on the categorization-categories at issue in special education* (pp. 33–38). Missouri: University of Missouri, Columbia.

Melcher, J. W. (1976). Law, litigation, and handicapped children. *Exceptional Children, 43*, 126–130.

Mercer, J. R. (1973). *Labeling the mentally retarded: Clinical and social system perspectives on mental retardation.* Berkeley, CA: University of California Press.

Meredith, E. A. (1975). Separate report: Annual report of the Board of Inspectors of Asylums, Prisons etc., Province of Canada. In A. Prentice & S. Houston (Eds.), *Family, school and society in nineteenth-century Canada* (pp. 271–272). Toronto: Oxford University Press. (Original chapter published 1862)

Meyer, G. F. (1934). Excerpts from convention addresses. *Council Review/Journal of Exceptional Children, 1*, 45.

Meyers, C. E. (Ed.). (1978). *Quality of life in severely and profoundly mentally retarded people: Research foundations for improvement.* Washington, DC: American Association of Mental Deficiency.

Michigan loses a pioneer. (1942). *Journal of Exceptional Children, 8*, 123.

Midcentury White House Conference on Children and Youth. (1949). *Journal of Exceptional Children, 16*, 53–56.

Miller, M., & Moores, D. (2000). Bilingual/bicultural education for deaf students. In M. Winzer & K. Mazurek (Eds.), *Special education in the 21st century: Issues of inclusion and reform* (pp. 221–237). Washington, DC: Gallaudet University Press.

Miller, M. M. (1940). Spasticity. *Journal of Exceptional Children, 6*, 203–210, 222.

Miller, W. B. (1943). Education and the war. *Journal of Exceptional Children, 9*, 236–240, 252–253.

Mills v. Board of Education of the District of Columbia, 348F Supp. 866 (DDC, 1972).

The Minnesota Governor's Council on Developmental Disabilities. (2009). *Parallels in time II, 1950–2005: A place to call home.* Retrieved March 24, 2009, from http://www.mnddc.org/parallels2/one/022.htm

Mitchell, H. M. (1919). Child welfare, heredity and environment. *Social Welfare, 1*, 4.

Mitchell, S. H. (1971). *An examination of selected factors related to the economic status of the deaf population.* Unpublished doctoral dissertation, American University, Washington, DC.

Moats, L. C., & Lyon, G. R. (1993). Learning disabilities in the United States: Advocacy, science, and the future of the field. *Journal of Learning Disabilities, 26*, 282–294.

Moore, L. M. (1934). Caroline A. Yale—Pioneer and builder. *American Annals of the Deaf, 79*, 189–196.

Morgan, P. (1896). A case of congenital word blindness. *British Medical Journal, 11*, 378.

Morris, D. W., Ainsworth, S. S., & Pauls, M. D. (1944). Speech defectives. *Journal of Exceptional Children, 10*, 213–214.

Morrison, T. R. (1974). Reform as social tracking: The case of industrial education in Ontario. *Journal of Educational Thought, 8*, 87–110.

Moss, J. W. (1968). Research and dissemination. *Exceptional Children, 34*, 509–514.

Mostert, M. P., & Crockett, J. B. (1999–2000). Reclaiming the history of special education for more effective practice. *Exceptionality, 24*, 133–143.

Mostert, M. P. Kauffman, J. M., & Kavale, K. A. (2003). Truth and consequences. *Behavior Disorders, 28*, 333–347.

Mottez, B. (1993). The deaf-mute banquets and the birth of the deaf movement. In J. van Cleve (Ed.), *Deaf history unveiled: Interpretations from the new scholarship* (pp. 27–39). Washington, DC: Gallaudet University Press.

Mr. Stainer's London day schools. (1884). *American Annals of the Deaf, 29*, 252–254.

Mundie, G. S. (1919). Specialized care for the defective child. *Social Welfare, 2*, 5–6.

Munson, G. (1944). Finding the gifted child. *Journal of Exceptional Children, 11*, 3–6. 24.

National Coalition of Advocates for Students. (1985). *Barriers to excellence: Our children at risk*. Washington, DC: U.S. Department of Education.

The National Commission on Excellence in Education. (1983). *A nation at risk: The imperative for educational reform*. Washington, DC: U.S. Government Printing Office.

National Defense Education Act of 1958, Pub. L. No. 85-864, 20 U.S.C. § 401 *et seq.*

National Education Association. (1898, July). *Proceedings, thirty seventh annual meeting*. Washington, DC: Author.

National Research Council. (2001). *Educating children with autism*. Washington, DC: National Academy Press.

Nature of nurture? Actual improvement of the race impossible except through heredity—facts on which the eugenist bases his faith—the attitude of eugenics toward social problems. (1915). *Journal of Heredity, 6*, 227–240.

The neglected and dependent child. (1919). *Social Welfare, 2*, 78–80.

Neisworth, J. T., & Greer, J. G. (1975). Functional similarities of learning disability and mild retardation. *Exceptional Children, 42*, 17–21.

Nelson, C., & Huefner, D. S. (2003). Young children with autism: Judicial responses to the Lovaas and discrete trial training debates. *Journal of Early Intervention, 26*, 1–19.

Nelson, J. R., Benner, G. J., Lane, K. M., & Smith, B. W. (2004). An investigation of the academic achievement of K–12 students with emotional and behavioral disorders in public school settings. *Exceptional Children, 71*, 59–73.

New Jersey Commissioner of Education's Commission on the Education of the Handicapped (1965). *The education of handicapped children in New Jersey 1954–1964*. Trenton, NJ: New Jersey State Department of Education.

The New Jersey Training School. (1893). *Annual report of The New Jersey Training School*. Vineland, NJ: Author.

The New Jersey Training School. (1894). *Annual report of The New Jersey Training School*. Vineland, NJ: Author.

The New Jersey Training School. (1896). *Annual report of The New Jersey Training School*. Vineland, NJ: Author.

The New Jersey Training School. (1904). *Annual report of The New Jersey Training School*. Vineland, NJ: Author.

The New Jersey Training School. (1906). *Annual report of The New Jersey Training School*. Vineland, NJ: Author.

The New Jersey Training School. (1908). *Annual report of The New Jersey Training School.* Vineland, NJ: Author.

Newman, R. G. (1956). The acting-out boy. *Exceptional Children, 22,* 186–190, 204–206, 215–216.

New York Institution for the Blind. (1845). *Annual report.* New York: Author.

Nirje, B. (1976). The normalization principle. In R. B. Kugel & A. Shearer (Eds.), *Changing patterns in residential services for the mentally retarded* (pp. 231–240). Washington, DC: U.S. Government Printing Office.

Nirje, B. (1979). Changing patterns in residential services for the mentally retarded. In E. L. Meyen (Ed.), *Basic readings in the study of exceptional children and youth.* Denver, CO: Love Publishing.

No Child Left Behind Act of 2001, Pub. L. No. 107-110, 20 U.S.C. § 16301 *et seq.*

Not an asylum or place of detention, but a school for the deaf and dumb. (1902). In *Ontario School for the Deaf, annual report* (pp. 9–14). Toronto: Government Printer.

Notes from the twenty-second annual meeting. (1946–47). *Journal of Exceptional Children, 13,* 49–53, 57.

Numbers, F. C. (1927). Advantages and disadvantages in conducting a normal training class in connection with school work. *American Annals of the Deaf, 72,* 341–349.

Numbers, M. (1974). *My words fell on deaf ears.* Washington, DC: Alexander Graham Bell Association for the Deaf.

O'Brien, T., & Gurney, D. (2005). The problem is not the problem: Hard cases in modernist systems. In P. Clough, P. Garner, J. T. Pardeck, & F. Yeun (Eds.), *Handbook of emotional and behavioural difficulties* (pp. 141–153). London: Sage.

Oberti v. Board of Education of the Borough of Clemonton School District (1993). U.S. Court of Appeals, Third Circuit, 995F. 2d 1204.

Odom, S., Horn, E. M., Marquart, J. M., Hanson, M., Wolfberg, P., Beckman, P., et al. (1999). On the forms of inclusion: Organizational context and individualized service models. *Journal of Early Intervention, 22,* 185–199.

Olson, L. (2004, January 8). Enveloping expectations. *Education Week on the Web, 23*(17), 8–21.

O'Mahoney, P. (2005). Juvenile delinquency and emotional and behavioral difficulties in education. In P. Clough, P. Garner, J. T. Pardeck, & F. Yeun (Eds.), *Handbook of emotional and behavioural difficulties* (pp. 167–181). London: Sage.

Ontario Department of Education. (1903). *Annual report.* Toronto: Government Printer.

Ontario Department of Education. (1904). *Annual report.* Toronto: Government Printer.

Ontario Department of Education. (1906). *Annual report.* Toronto: Government Printer.

Ontario Department of Education. (1907). *Annual report.* Toronto: Government Printer.

Ontario Department of Education. (1925). *Annual report.* Toronto: Government Printer.

Ontario Department of Education. (1930). *Annual report*. Toronto: Government Printer.

Ontario, Inspector of Prisons, Asylums and Public Charities. (1876). *Annual reports of the Inspector of Asylums, Prisons and Public Charities for the Province of Ontario*. Toronto: Government Printer.

Ontario, Inspector of Prisons, Asylums and Public Charities. (1878). *Annual reports of the Inspector of Asylums, Prisons and Public Charities for the Province of Ontario*. Toronto: Government Printer.

Ontario Institution for the Education and Instruction of the Deaf and Dumb. (1884). *Annual report*. Toronto: Government Printer.

Ontario Institution for the Education and Instruction of the Deaf and Dumb. (1885). *Annual report*. Toronto: Government Printer.

Ontario Institution for the Education and Instruction of the Deaf and Dumb. (1891). How best to teach mutes. In Ontario Institution for the Education and Instruction of the Deaf and Dumb (Ed.), *Twenty first annual report* (pp. 12–17). Toronto: Government Printer.

Ontario Institution for the Education and Instruction of the Deaf and Dumb. (1891). *Annual report*. Toronto: Government Printer.

Ontario Institution for the Education and Instruction of the Deaf and Dumb. (1893). *Annual report*. Toronto: Government Printer.

Ontario Institution for the Education and Instruction of the Deaf and Dumb. (1895). *Annual report*. Toronto: Government Printer.

Ontario Institution for the Education and Instruction of the Deaf and Dumb. (1897). *Annual report*. Toronto: Government Printer.

Ontario Institution for the Education and Instruction of the Deaf and Dumb. (1900). *Annual report*. Toronto: Government Printer.

Ontario School Inspectors' Association. (1958). *Education of the gifted*. Toronto: Copp Clark.

Orlando, F. A., & Black, J. P. (1975). The juvenile court. In N. Hobbs (Ed.), *Issues in the classification of children: A sourcebook on categories, labels, and their consequences* (Vol. 2, pp. 349–376). San Francisco: Jossey-Bass.

Orton, S. T. (1925). Word-blindness in school children. *Archives of Neurology and Psychiatry, 14*, 581–616.

Orton, S. T. (1927). Studies in stuttering. *Archives of Neurology and Psychology, 18*, 671–672.

Orton, S. T. (1937). *Reading, writing and speech problems in children*. New York: Norton.

Osgood, R. (1997). Undermining the common school ideal: Intermediate schools and ungraded classes in Boston, 1838–1900. *History of Education Quarterly, 37*, 375–398.

Osgood, R. (1999). Becoming a special educator: Specialized professional training for teachers of children with disabilities in Boston, 1870–1930. *Teachers College Record, 161*, 82–105.

Osgood, R. L. (2000). *"Children who vary from the normal": Special education in Boston, 1838–1930*. Washington, DC: Gallaudet University Press.

Osher, D., Osher, T., & Smith, C. (1994). Toward a national perspective on emotional and behavioral disorders: A developmental agenda. *Beyond Behavior, 61,* 6–17.

Paden, E. P. (1970). *A history of the American Speech and Hearing Association, 1925–1958.* Washington, DC: American Speech and Language Association.

Palmer, B., & Sellars, M. (1993). The integration of hearing-impaired people in ordinary schools. *Education Today, 43,* 28–31.

Palmer D. S., Borthwick-Duffy, S. A., & Widaman, K. (1998). Parent perceptions of inclusive practices for their children with significant cognitive disabilities. *Exceptional Children, 64,* 271–282.

Palmer, D. S., Fuller, K., Arora, T., & Nelson, M. (2001). Taking sides: Parent views on inclusion for their children with severe disabilities. *Exceptional Children, 67,* 467–484.

Pare, A. (1982). *On monsters and marvels* (J. Pallister, Trans., from 1573 ed.). Chicago, IL: University of Chicago Press.

Passinen, T. M. (1974). Popular science and society: The phrenology movement in early Victorian Britain. *Journal of Social History, 8,* 1–20.

Passow, A. H. (1990). Letta Stetler Hollingworth: A real original. *Roeper Review, 12,* 134–136.

Paul, J. L., & Warnock, N. J. (1980). Special education: A changing field. *The Exceptional Child, 27,* 3–28.

Pearson, K. (1914). *The life, letters and labours of Francis Galton* (4 vols.). Cambridge: Cambridge University Press.

Peck, A. W., & Samuelson, E. E. (1936). Twenty-five years for the hard of hearing child. *Journal of Exceptional Children, 2,* 116–119, 124.

Pennsylvania Association of Retarded Citizens (PARC) v. Commonwealth of Pennsylvania 343 F Supp. 279 (E.D. Pa. 1972).

Pennsylvania certification of teachers of classes of the mentally retarded. (1941). *Journal of Exceptional Children, 7*(6), 248–249.

Pennsylvania Institution for the Feeble-Minded. (1868). *Annual report.* Media, PA: Author.

Penrose, L. S. (1966). *The biology of mental defect.* London: Sidgwick and Jackson. (Original work published 1949)

Percival, W. P. (1946–47). Special education in Quebec and Maritime provinces. *Journal of Exceptional Children, 13,* 237–241.

Perkins Institution for the Blind. (1834). *Annual reports of the trustees of the New England Institution for the Education of the Blind to the corporation.* Boston: J. T. Buckingham.

Perkins Institution for the Blind. (1837). *Annual reports of the trustees of the New England Institution for the Education of the Blind to the corporation.* Boston: J. T. Buckingham.

Perkins Institution for the Blind. (1851). *Annual reports of the trustees of the New England Institution for the Education of the Blind to the corporation.* Boston: J. T. Buckingham.

Perkins Institution for the Blind. (1856). *Annual reports of the trustees of the New England Institution for the Education of the Blind to the corporation.* Boston: J. T. Buckingham.

Perkins Institution for the Blind. (1858). *Annual reports of the trustees of the New England Institution for the Education of the Blind to the corporation.* Boston: J. T. Buckingham.

Perkins Institution for the Blind. (1861). *Annual reports of the trustees of the New England Institution for the Education of the Blind to the corporation.* Boston: J. T. Buckingham.

Perkins Institution for the Blind. (1881). *Annual reports of the trustees of the New England Institution for the Education of the Blind to the corporation.* Boston: J. T. Buckingham.

Perkins Institution for the Blind. (1895). *Annual reports of the trustees of the New England Institution for the Education of the Blind to the corporation.* Boston: J. T. Buckingham.

Peterson, F. (1896). The care of epileptics. In *Eighth report of the Vineland Institution for Feeble-Minded Boys and Girls* (pp. 43–45). Vineland, NJ: Vineland Institution.

Pfieffer, S. I. (2003). Challenges and opportunities for students who are gifted: What experts say. *Gifted Child Quarterly, 47,* 161–169.

Phelps, E. (1924). *Restriction of immigration.* New York: H. W. Wilson.

Piirto, J. (1994). *Talented children and adults: Their development and education.* New York: Merrill.

Pitkin, W. B. (1928). *Twilight of the American mind.* New York: Simon and Schuster.

Platt, A. (1969). *The child savers: The invention of delinquency.* Chicago, IL: University of Chicago Press.

Polloway, E. A. (1984). The integration of mildly handicapped students into the schools: A historical review. *Remedial and Special Education, 5,* 18–28.

Poole, F. (1955–56). The child with social and emotional problems. *Journal of Exceptional Children, 22,* 20–23.

Poponoe, P. (1915). Genealogy and eugenics. *Volta Review, 16,* 361–364.

Poponoe, P. (1928). Eugenic sterilization in California: The number of persons needing sterilization. *Journal of Heredity, 19,* 405–411.

Poponoe, P. (1934). The progress of eugenic sterilization. *Journal of Heredity, 25,* 19–25.

Porter, R. B. (1944–45). Exceptional children in rural schools. *Journal of Exceptional Children, 11,* 109–112, 126.

Porter, R. B. (1953). Clinical service extensions for rural area exceptional children. *Exceptional Children, 20,* 105–110.

Porter, R. B., & Milazzo, T. C. (1958). A comparison of mentally retarded adults who attended special class with those who attended regular class. *Exceptional Children, 24,* 410–412.

Postel, H. H. (1937). The special school versus the special class. *Journal of Exceptional Children, 4,* 12–13, 18–19.

Potter, H. (1922). The relation of personality to the mental defectives with a method for its evaluation. *Journal of Psycho-Asthenics, 27,* 27–38.

Potter, H. (1933). Schizophrenia in children. *American Journal of Psychiatry, 89,* 1253–1270.

Powell, F. (1882). Status of the work—Iowa. In *Proceedings of the Association of Medical Officers of American Institutions for Idiotic and Feeble-Minded Persons* (pp. 267–278). Philadelphia, PA: J. B. Lippincott.

Proctor, R. (1988). *Racial hygiene: Medicine under the Nazis.* Cambridge, MA: Harvard University Press.

Proposals for extending federal and state cooperative programs for children. (1945–46). *Journal of Exceptional Children, 12,* 147–151.

The psychological examination of recruits. (1917). *Science, 46,* 355–356.

Pugach, M., & Sapon-Shavin, M. (1987). New agendas for special education policy: What the national reports haven't said. *Exceptional Children, 53,* 295–299.

Pugach, M. C., & Seidl, B. L. (1996). Deconstructing the diversity-disability relationship. *Contemporary Education, 68,* 5–9.

Pugach, M. C. & Seidl, B. L. (1998). Responsible linkages between diversity and disability: A challenge for special education. *Teacher Education and Special Education, 21,* 319–333.

Pybas, A. (1909). Compulsory education for the deaf. *American Annals of the Deaf, 54,* 356–359.

Quay, H. C., & Peterson, D. R. (1960). Personality factors in the study of juvenile delinquency. *Exceptional Children, 26,* 472–476, 502.

Radford, J. P., & Park, D. C. (1995). The eugenic legacy. *Journal of Developmental Disabilities, 4,* 63–74.

Rae, L. (1847). Introductory. *American Annals of the Deaf and Dumb, 1,* 1–6.

Raftery, J. R. (1988). Missing the mark: Intelligence testing in Los Angeles public schools, 1922–32. *History of Education Quarterly, 28,* 73–93.

Reading First Initiative of 2002, Pub. L. No. 107-110, 20 U.S.C. § 6301 *et seq.*

Reagan, T. (1988). Multiculturalism and the deaf: An educational manifesto. *Journal of Research and Development in Education, 22,* 1–6.

Reeves, H. T. (1938). The later years of a mental defective. *Journal of Psycho-Asthenics, 43,* 194–200.

Reid, R., Gonzales, J. E., Nordness, P. D., Trout, A., & Epstein, M. H. (2004). A meta-analysis of the academic status of students with emotional/behavioral disturbance. *Journal of Special Education, 38,* 130–144.

Reid, R., Maag, J. W., & Vasa, S. F. (1993). Attention deficit hyperactivity disorder as a disability category. A critique. *Exceptional Children, 60,* 198–214.

Reinert, H. R. (1980). *Children in conflict* (2nd ed.). St. Louis, MO: Mosley.

Report of the New Jersey Commission on Epileptics. (1896). In *Annual report of the Vineland Institution for Feeble-Minded Boys and Girls* (pp. 30–38). New Jersey: New Jersey Training School for Feeble-Minded Boys and Girls.

Reymert, M. L. (1939–40). Prevention of juvenile delinquency. *Journal of Exceptional Children, 6,* 300–303, 306.

Reynolds, M. C., Wang, M., & Walberg, H. J. (1987). The necessary restructuring of special and regular education. *Exceptional Children, 53,* 391–398.

Reynolds, M. C., Zetlin, A. G., & Wang, M. (1993). 20/20 analysis: Take a closer look at the margins. *Exceptional Children, 59,* 294–300.

Rhodes, G. L. (1946). Wherein has the school failed? *Journal of Exceptional Children, 12,* 18–21.

Rinaldi, R. T. (1976). Urban schools and PL 94-142: One administrator's perspective on the law. In R. A. Johnson & A. P. Kowalski (Eds.), *Perspectives on implementation of the "Education for All Handicapped Children Act of 1975"* (pp. 135–152). Washington, DC: Council of the Great City schools. (ERIC Document Reproduction Service No. ED145599)

Robb, I. M. (1945–46). Segregation develops inadequacy. *Exceptional Children, 12,* 239–240.

Robinson, G. A., Palton, J. R., Polloway, E. A, & Sargent, L. R. (Eds.). (1989). *Best practices in mental retardation.* Reston, VA: Council for Exceptional Children.

Robinson, H. B., & Robinson, N. M. (1976). *The mentally retarded child: A physiological approach* (2nd ed.). New York: McGraw-Hill.

Robinson, S. (1936). *Can delinquency be measured?* New York: Columbia University Press.

Rogers, A. (1912). Book review of The Kallikak family. *Journal of Psycho-Asthenics, 17,* 83–84.

Rogers, J. A. (1972). Darwinism and Social Darwinism. *Journal of the History of Ideas, 33,* 265–280.

Rosen, C. (2004). *Preaching eugenics: Religious leaders and the American eugenics movement.* New York: Oxford University Press.

Rosen, M., Clark, G., & Kivitz, M. (1976). *The history of mental retardation.* Baltimore, MD: University Park Press.

Ross, I. (1951). *Journey into light: The story of the education of the blind.* New York: Appleton-Century Crofts.

Rothman, D. (1971). *The discovery of the asylum: Social order and disorder in the new republic.* Boston: Little Brown.

Rothstein, J. H. (1954). The California Youth Authority. *Exceptional Children, 21,* 42–46.

Rous, B. (2004). Perspectives of teachers about instructional supervision and behaviors that influence preschool instruction. *Journal of Early Intervention, 26,* 266–283.

Rudowski, V. A. (1974). The theory of signs in the eighteenth century. *Journal of the History of Ideas, 35,* 683–690.

Rusch, F. R., & Phelps, L. A. (1987). Secondary special education and transition from school to work: A national priority. *Exceptional Children, 53,* 487–492.

Rutherford, B. E. (1939–40). Where are we going? *Journal of Exceptional Children, 6,* 39–40.

Ryerson, E. A. (1848). Review of a report on a system of public elementary education for Upper Canada by E. A. Ryerson. *Journal of Education for Upper Canada, 1,* 175.

Rylance, B. J. (1997). Predictors of high school graduation or dropping out for youths with severe emotional disturbance. *Behavioral Disorders, 23,* 5–17.

Sagan, C. (1979). *Broca's brain*. New York: Ballantine Books.

The salary question. (1929). *American Annals of the Deaf, 74*, 260–272.

Saleeby, C. W. (1911). *Woman and womanhood: A search for principles*. New York: Mitchell Kennedy.

Salisbury, C. L. (1991). Mainstreaming during the early childhood years. *Exceptional Children, 58*, 146–155.

Samuels, C. A. (2006, February 22). Cardiac cases raise concerns over drugs for ADHD. *Education Week, 25*, pp. 5, 18.

Sanghavi, D. (2005, April 26). Time to calm down about Ritalin. *Boston Globe.* Retrieved February 26, 2009, from http://www.darshaksanghavi.com/columns/adhd.htm

Sarason, S. B., & Doris, J. (1979). *Educational handicap, public policy, and social history: A broadened perspective on mental retardation*. New York: Free Press.

Sargeant, B. B. (1935). The International Council for Exceptional Children. *Journal of Exceptional Children, 2*, 32–38.

Sasso, G. M. (2001). The retreat from enquiry and knowledge in special education. *Journal of Special Education, 34*, 178–193.

Sattler, J. (1974). *Assessment of children's intelligence*. Philadelphia, PA: Saunders.

Sattler, J. M. (1982). *Assessment of children's intelligence and special abilities* (2nd ed.). Boston: Allyn & Bacon.

Scheerenberger, R. C. (1981). Deinstitutionalization: Trends and difficulties. In R. H. Bruininks, C. E. Meyers, B. B. Sigford, & K. C. Lakin (Eds.), *Deinstitutionalization and community adjustment of mentally retarded people* (AAMD Monograph No. 4, pp. 3–13). Washington, DC: American Association of Mental Deficiency.

Scheier, S. (1931). *Problems in the training of certain special-class teachers*. New York: Columbia University.

Schein, J. D. (1989). *At home among strangers: Exploring the deaf community in the United States*. Washington, DC: Gallaudet University Press.

Schroeder, F. K. (1996). Perceptions of braille usage by legally blind adults. *Journal of Visual Impairment and Blindness, 90*, 210–218.

Schuller, E. & O'Reilly, F. (2003, May). *Building opportunities for students with disabilities* (Infobrief No. 23). Alexandria, VA: Association for Supervision and Curriculum Development.

Schwartz, H. (1952). Samuel Gridley Howe as phrenologist. *American Historical Review, 57*, 644–651.

Scruggs, T. E., & Mastroprieri, M. A. (2002). On babies and bathwater: Addressing the problems of the identification of learning disabilities. *LD Quarterly, 25*, 155–168.

Sedlak, M. W. (1983). Young women and the city: Adolescent deviance and the transformation of educational policy, 1870–1960. *History of Education Quarterly, 23* (Spring), 1–25.

Seguin, E. (1907). *Idiocy and its treatment by the physiological method*. New York: William Wood. (Original work published 1866)

Seigel, J. P. (1969). The Enlightenment and the evolution of the language of signs in France and England. *Journal of the History of Ideas, 30,* 96–115.

Seminary for female teachers. (1831). *American Annals of Education, 1,* 341–345.

Shapiro, S., Schlesinger, E. R., & Nesbit, R. E. (1968). *Infant, perinatal, maternal and childhood mortality in the United States.* Cambridge, MA: Harvard University Press.

Shattuck, M. (1946). Segregation versus non-segregation of exceptional children. *Journal of Exceptional Children, 12,* 235–240.

Shull, H. (1916). A family with abnormal hands. *Journal of Heredity, 7,* 224–228.

Sigmon, S. B. (1982–83). The history and future of educational segregation. *Journal for Special Educators, 19,* 1–11.

Simpson, R. L. (2001). Finding effective intervention and personnel preparation practices for students with autism spectrum disorders. *Exceptional Children, 70,* 135–144.

Singer, J. D. (1993). Are special educators' career paths special? Results from a 13-year longitudinal study. *Exceptional Children, 59,* 262–279.

Sisk, D. (1982). Educational planning for the gifted and talented. In J. M. Kauffman & D. P. Hallahan (Eds.), *Handbook of special education* (pp. 441–458). Englewood Cliffs, NJ: Prentice Hall.

The sixty-second summer meeting—June 16–20, 1952. *Volta Review, 54,* 491–500, 512–513.

Skeels, H., & Dye, H. (1939). The study of the effects of differential stimulation on mentally retarded children. *Proceedings of the American Association of Mental Deficiency, 44,* 114–136.

Sklar, K. (1973). *Catharine Beecher: A study in American domesticity.* New Haven, CT: Yale University Press.

Skrtic, T. M. (1991). The special education paradox: Equity as a way for excellence. *Harvard Educational Review, 61,* 148–206.

Slee, R. (1997). Inclusion or assimilation? Sociological explorations of the foundations of theories of special education. *Educational Foundations, 11,* 55–71.

Sleeter, C. E. (1986). Learning disabilities: The social construction of a special education category. *Exceptional Children, 53,* 46–54.

Sloan, W., & Birch, J. (1955). A rationale for degrees of retardation. *American Journal of Mental Deficiency, 60,* 258–264.

Smedley, A. (1998). *Race in North America: Origin and evolution of a worldview* (2nd ed.). New York: Perseus.

Smith, D. D. (2003). Welcome to the TESE special issue on the study of special education leadership personnel. *Teacher Education and Special Education, 26,* 163–164.

Smith, D. D., Pion, G., Tyler, N. C., Sindelar, P., & Rosenberg, N. (2001). *The study of special education leadership personnel with particular attention to the professorate.* Washington, DC: U.S. Department of Education, Office of Special Education Programs.

Smith, H. (1989). *Beyond the post-modern mind.* Wheaton, IL: Quest Books.

Smith, S. (1876). The silent community. *American Annals of the Deaf and Dumb, 21,* 137–145.

Smulker, D. (2005). Unauthorized minds: How "theory of mind" theory misrepresents autism. *Mental Retardation, 43,* 11–24.

Snider, V. E., Busch, T., & Arrowood, L. (2003). Teacher knowledge of stimulant medication and ADHD. *Remedial and Special Education, 24,* 45–56.

Snyder, W. G. (1947–48). Do teachers cause maladjustment:; A review, part 1. *Journal of Exceptional Children, 14,* 40–46, 63.

The socially inadequate. (1922). *American Annals of the Deaf, 67,* 348–349.

Social Survey Commission of Toronto. (1915). *Report of the Social Survey Commission of Toronto.* Toronto: Author.

Sokal, A., & Bricmont, J. (1998). *Fashionable nonsense: Postmodern intellectual abuse of science.* New York: Picador.

Sokal, M. M. (1984). Approaches to the history of psychological testing. *History of Education Quarterly, 24,* 419–430.

Soodak, L. C. (1998). Parents and inclusive schooling: Advocating for adolescents participating in the reform of special education. In S. J. Vitello & D. E. Mithaug (Eds.), *Inclusive schooling: National and international perspectives* (pp. 113–131). Mahwah, NJ: Lawrence Erlbaum.

Spencer, H. (1865). *Social statics.* New York: Appleton.

Spicker, H. H., & Bartel, N. R. (1968). The mentally retarded. In G. O. Johnson & H. Blank (Eds.), *Exceptional children research review* (pp. 39–109). Washington, DC: Council for Exceptional Children.

Spitzka, E. C. (1887). Insanity: Its classification, diagnosis and treatment. New York: E. B. Treat.

Spring, J. (1994). *The American school, 1642–1993* (3rd ed.). New York: Longman.

Springsteen, T. (1940). A Wyoming State Training School survey of emotional stability, intelligence, and academic achievement. *Journal of Exceptional Children, 77,* 54–64, 73.

Stainback, S., & Stainback, W. (1988). Educating students with severe disabilities. *Teaching Exceptional Children, 21,* 16–19.

Statistics of speech teaching in American schools for the deaf. (1900). *Association Review, 2,* 298–315.

Steiner, B. C. (1919). *Life of Henry Barnard, the first United States Commissioner of Education, 1867–1870.* Washington, DC: U.S. Government Printing Office.

Stephens, O. (1989). Braille—Implications for living. *Journal of Visual Impairment and Blindness, 83,* 288–289.

Stern, W. (1914). *The psychological methods of testing intelligence.* Baltimore, MD: Warwick and York.

Stevens, G. D. (1954). Developments in the field of mental deficiency. *Exceptional Children, 21,* 58–62, 70.

Stevens, G. D., & Birch, J. W. (1957). A proposal for clarification of the terminology used to describe brain-injured children. *Exceptional Children, 23,* 346–349.

Stewart, R. W. (1892). Report of the Standing Committee of the Board on the Deaf, State Board of Charities. *American Annals of the Deaf, 38,* 151.

Stogdell, R. M. (1938). Some behavior adjustment techniques in use with mentally retarded children. *Journal of Exceptional Children, 5,* 25–30, 45.

Stokoe, W. C. (1960). *Sign language structure: An outline of the visual communication system of the American deaf* (Studies in Linguistics, Occasional Papers No. 8). Buffalo, NY: Department of Anthropology and Linguistics, University of Buffalo.

Stone, C. (1848). On the religious state, and instruction of the deaf and dumb. *American Annals of the Deaf and Dumb, 1,* 133–149.

Stone, D. A. (1984). *The disabled state.* Philadelphia: Temple University Press.

Strauss, A. A. (1939). Typology in mental deficiency. *Proceedings of the American Association of Mental Deficiency, 39,* 44–85.

Strauss, A. A. (1941a). The incidence of central nervous system involvement in higher grade moron children. *American Journal of Mental Deficiency, 45,* 548.

Strauss, A. A. (1941b). Neurology and mental deficiency. *American Journal of Mental Deficiency, 46,* 192.

Strauss, A. A, & Lehtinen, L. (1947). *Psychopathology of the brain-injured child.* New York: Grune and Stratton.

Streng, A. (1964). Educating teachers of the deaf for the schools of tomorrow. *American Annals of the Deaf, 109,* 348–355.

Stribbling, F. T. (1842). Physician and superintendent's report. In *Annual report of the Court of Directors of the Western Lunatic Asylum to the legislature of Virginia.* Richmond, CA: Shephard and Conlin.

Struthers, J. (1981). A profession in crisis: Charlotte Whitton and Canadian social work in the 1930s. *Canadian Historical Review, 62,* 169–196.

Stullken, E. H. (1935–36). Special education in Chicago. *Journal of Exceptional Children, 2,* 73–75.

Sugai, G. (1998). Postmodernism and emotional and behavioral disorders: Distraction or advancement. *Behavioral Disorders, 23,* 171–177.

Summary analysis of state laws for gifted children. (1969). *Exceptional Children, 35,* 569–576.

Sutherland, I. M. (1938). How Los Angeles takes care of her exceptional children. *Journal of Exceptional Children, 4,* 159–166.

Sutherland, K. S., Wehby, J. H., & Copeland, S. R. (2000). Effects of varying rates of behavior-specific praise on the on-task behavior of students with EBD. *Journal of Emotional and Behavioral Disorders, 8,* 2–8.

Swanwick, R. A. (1998). Learning English as a second language: Opportunities and challenges for sign bilingual deaf children. *Deafness and Education, 22,* 3–9.

Szatz, T. (1961). *The myth of mental illness.* New York: Dell Press.

Talbot, M.E. (1964). *Edouard Seguin: A study of an educational approach to the treatment of mentally defective children.* New York: Teachers College, Bureau of Publications.

Tanenhaus, D. S. (2004). *Juvenile justice in the making.* New York: Oxford University Press.

Tashakkori, A., & Teddlie, C. (1998). *Mixed methodology: Combining qualitative and quantitative approaches.* London: Sage.

Taylor, H. (1900). The question of salary. *American Annals of the Deaf, 45,* 236–243.

Taylor Allen, M. B. (1986). "Let us live with our children": Kindergarten movements in Germany and the United States, 1840–1914. *History of Education Quarterly, 28*, 23–48.

Temkin, O. (1947). Gall and the phrenological movement. *Bulletin of the History of Medicine, 21*, 275–321.

Terman, L. M. (1975). *Genius and stupidity*. New York: Arno Press. (Original work published 1906)

Terman, L. M. (1916). *The measurement of intelligence*. Boston: Houghton Mifflin.

Terman, L. M. (1921). Intelligence and its measurement. *Journal of Educational Psychology, 12*, 127–133.

Terman, L. M. (1926a). *Genetic studies of genius: Mental and physical traits of a thousand gifted children* (2nd ed.). Stanford, CA: Stanford University Press.

Terman, L. M. (1926b). *Mental and physical traits of a thousand gifted children: Vol. 1. Genetic studies of genius*. Stanford, CA: Stanford University Press.

Terman L. M., & Childs, H. G. (1912). A tentative revision and extension of the Binet-Simon measuring scale of intelligence. *Journal of Educational Psychology, 3*, 61–74, 133–143, 198–208, 277–289.

Terman, L. M., & Oden, M. H. (1951). The Stanford studies of the gifted. In P. Witty (Ed.), *The gifted child* (pp. 20–46). Lexington, MA: D. C. Heath.

Thomas, G. (1997). Inclusive schools for an inclusive society. *British Journal of Special Education, 24*, 103–107.

Thomson, M. (1984). *Developmental dyslexia*. Melbourne, Australia: Edward Arnold.

Thurston, R. H. (1876). *Reports of the Commissions of the United States to the International Exhibition held in Vienna, 1873*. Washington, DC: U.S. Government Printing Office.

Tiessen, J. (1996, winter). Orthotics and prosthetics: Fit and fashion join a tradition of function. *Disability Today*, pp. 23–25.

Tillinghast, J. A. (1906). Reflections of an ex-educator of the deaf. *American Annals of the Deaf, 54*, 7–23.

Tinkle, W. J. (1933). Deafness as an eugenical problem. *Journal of Heredity, 24*, 13–18.

The Training and certification of teachers. (1929). *American Annals of the Deaf, 74*, 244–315.

The Training School. (1912). *Annual report of The Training School*. Vineland, NJ: Author.

The Training School. (1914). *Annual report of The Training School*. Vineland, NJ: Author.

The Training School. (1918). *Annual report of The Training School*. Vineland, NJ: Author.

Tredgold, A. F. (1908). *Mental deficiency*. London: Bailliere, Tindall and Cox.

Tredgold, A. F. (1929). *Mental deficiency (amentia)* (5th ed.). New York: William Wood.

Trent, J. W. (1994). *Inventing the feeble mind: A history of mental retardation in the United States*. Los Angeles, CA: University of California Press.

Tributes to Alexander Graham Bell at the Horace Mann School for the Deaf graduation exercises. (1923). *Volta Review, 25,* 49.

Tropea, J. L. (1987). Bureaucratic order and special children: Urban schools, 1890s–1940s. *History of Education Quarterly, 27,* 29–53.

Tuddenham, R. (1962). The nature and measurement of intelligence. In L. Postman (Ed.), *Psychology in the making* (pp. 469–525). New York: Alfred A. Knopf.

Tuke, D. H. (1968). *History of the insane.* Amsterdam: E. J. Basnet. (Facsimile of 1882 ed.)

Turner C. P. (1848). Expressions. *American Annals of the Deaf and Dumb, 1,* 78.

Turner, T. A. (1944). Crippled children. *Journal of Exceptional Children, 10* 215–216.

Turner, W. W. (1848). Causes of deafness. *American Annals of the Deaf and Dumb, 1,* 25–32.

Two out of five feeble-minded. (1917, September 15). *The Survey,* pp. 328–329.

Tyack, D. B., & Berkowitz, M. (1977). The man nobody liked: Toward a social history of the truant officer, 1840–1940. *American Quarterly, 29,* 31–54.

Tyor, P. L. (1977). "Denied the power to choose the good": Sexuality and mental defect in American medical practice, 1850–1920. *Journal of Social History, 10,* 472–489.

U.S. Department of Education. (1999). Assistance to states for the education of children with disabilities program and the early intervention program for infants and toddlers with disabilities: Final regulations.CFR Parts 300 and 303. *Federal Register, 64*(48), 12406–12672.

U.S. Department of Education. (2002). *Twenty-fourth annual report to Congress on the implementation of the Individuals with Disabilities Education Act.* Washington, DC: U.S. Government Printing Office.

U.S. Immigration Commission. (1911). *The children of immigrants in schools.* Washington, DC: U.S. Government Printing Office.

U.S. Office of Education. (1972). *Education of the gifted and talented: Report to the Congress.* Washington, DC: U.S. Government Printing Office.

U.S. Office of Education. (1993). *National excellence: A case for developing America's talent.* Retrieved March 21, 2009, from http://www.ed.gov/pubs/DevTalent/toc.html

Valentine, P. (1993). Thomas Hopkins Gallaudet: Benevolent paternalism and the origins of the American Asylum. In J. V. Van Cleve (Ed.), *Deaf history unveiled: Interpretations from the new scholarship* (pp. 53–73). Washington, DC: Gallaudet University Press.

Vedantam, S. (2006, September 5). Autism risk rises with age of father: Large study finds strong correlation. *Washington Post.* Retrieved March 28, 2009, from http://www.washingtonpost.com/wp-dyn/content/article/2006/09/04/AR2006090400513_pf.html

Vergason, G. A. (1972). Instructional practices in special education. In I. Meyen, G. A. Vergason, & R. J. Whelan (Eds.), *Strategies for teaching exceptional children.* Denver, CO: Love.

Vernon, M. L. (1942). Notes on the early days of the Training School. *Training School Bulletin, 39,* 22–25.

Victoria Industrial School. (1896). *Annual reports, 1896.* Toronto: Government Printer.

Wallin, J. E. W. (1911). A practical guide for the administration of the Binet-Simon Scale for Measuring Intelligence. *Psychological Clinic, 2,* 121–132.

Wallin, J. E. W. (1914). *The mental health of the school child: The psycho-educational clinic in relation to child welfare.* New Haven, CT: Yale University Press.

Wallin. J. E. W. (1924). *The education of handicapped children.* Boston: Houghton Mifflin.

Wallin. J. E. W. (1927). *Clinical and abnormal psychology.* New York: Houghton Mifflin.

Wallin, J. E. W. (1934). State provisions for mentally handicapped children in the United States. *Training School Bulletin, 30,* 56.

Wallin, J. E. W. (1936–1937b). Why not a special education efficiency rating committee? *Journal of Exceptional Children, 3,* 26.

Wallin, J. E. W. (1938–39). The nature and implications of truancy from the standpoint of the schools. *Journal of Exceptional Children, 5,* 1–6.

Wallin, J. E. W. (1945). A new approach toward the educational adjustment of the mentally retarded and specifically educationally handicapped in small schools. *Exceptional Children, 11,* 120–121.

Wallin. J. E. W. (1949). *Children with mental and physical handicaps.* New York: Prentice-Hall.

Wallin, J. E. W. (1955). *The odyssey of a psychologist.* Lyndalia, DE: Author.

Wallin, J. E. W. (1958). Some personal comments on the development of clinical psychology. *Exceptional Children, 24,* 413–420.

Wallin, R. (1962). New frontiers in the social perspective of the mentally retarded. *Training School Bulletin, 59,* 89–104.

Walton, J. K. (1979). Lunacy in the Industrial Revolution: A study of asylum admissions in Lancashire, 1848–50. *Journal of Social History, 13,* 1–22.

Wanted—Men in the school system. (1903). *Association Review, 5,* 81.

Ward, R. DeC. (1910). National eugenics in relation to immigration. *North American Review, 192,* 56–57.

Warner, M. L. (1940–41). Problems of the delinquent girl. *Journal of Exceptional Children, 7,* 102–107, 112–113.

Warner, M. L. (1942). Early history of the International Council for Exceptional Children. *Journal of Exceptional Children, 8,* 244–247.

Warner, M. L. (1944). Founders of the International Council for Exceptional Children. *Journal of Exceptional Children, 10,* 217–221.

Webb, J. T. (1994). *Nurturing social-emotional development of gifted children.* (ERIC Clearinghouse on Disability and Gifted Education No. H-E527)

Webster, N. (1839). *Dissertations on the English language, with notes, historical and critical.* Boston: Isaiah Thomas.

Wehmeyer, M. L. (2003). Eugenics and sterilization in the heartland. *Mental Retardation, 41,* 57–60.

Weintraub, F., & Abelson, A. (1975). New education policies for the handicapped: The quiet revolution. *Phi Delta Kappan, 55,* 526–529, 569.

Weld, L. (1848). History of the American asylum. *American Annals of the Deaf and Dumb, 1,* 7–14, 93–112.

Wepman, J. M., & Jones, L. V. (1961). *The Language Modalities Test for Aphasia.* Chicago, IL: University of Chicago Education Industry Service.

West, A. M. (1984). *The National Education Association: The power base for education.* New York: Free Press.

Whelan, R. J., & Kauffman, J. M. (1999). *Educating students with emotional and behavioral disorders: Historical perspectives and future directions.* Reston, VA: Council for Exceptional Children.

White House Conference on Children. (1910). Washington, DC: U.S. Government Printing Office.

White House Conference on Children in a Democracy. (1940). Washington, DC: U.S. Government Printing Office.

White House Conference Report. (1930). *Section 111, Education of the Handicapped and the gifted.* New York: The Century Company.

Whitton, C. (1919). Child labour. *Social Welfare, 1,* 142–144.

Widd, T. (1868). The deaf and dumb—of the past, present, and future. *New Dominion Monthly, 2,* 269–274, 354–359.

Wiebe, R. (1966). *The search for order.* New York: Hill-Wang.

Wiederholt, J. L. (1978). Adolescents with learning disabilities: The problem in perspective. In L. Mann, L. Goodman, & J. L. Wiederholt (Eds.), *Teaching the learning-disabled adolescent* (pp. 9–28). Boston: Houghton Mifflin.

Wiederholt, J. L., & Chamberlain, S. P. (1989). A critical analysis of resource programs. *Remedial and Special Education, 10,* 15–27.

Wilkinson, W. (1905). Day-schools, their advantages and disadvantages. *American Annals of the Deaf, 50,* 70–95.

Will, G. (1999, December 5). Don't just reach for Ritalin: New research finds old truth—sometimes, boys will be boys. *Calgary Sunday Sun,* p. C6.

Will, M. (1984). *OSERS programming for the transition of youth with disabilities: Bridges from school to working life.* Washington, DC: Office of Special Education and Rehabilitation Services, U.S. Department of Education.

Will, M. (1986). Educating students with learning problems: A shared responsibility. *Exceptional Children, 52,* 405–411.

Willard, de F. (1909, May). What shall we do with our cripples? Methods of the Widener Industrial Training School. *Medical Record,* pp. 780–782.

Williams, J. H. (1943–44). A decade of progress in special education: Behavior problems. *Journal of Exceptional Children, 10,* 195–197.

Wilson, A. (1972). *Diderot.* New York: Oxford University Press.

Wing, G. (1886). The associative feature in the education of the deaf. *American Annals of the Deaf and Dumb, 31,* 22–35.

Wing, G. (1902). Statistics of speech teaching in American schools for the deaf. *Association Review, 2,* 298–315.

Winzer, M. A. (1986). Early developments in special education: Some aspects of Enlightenment thought. *Remedial and Special Education, 7,* 42–49.

Winzer, M. A. (1993a). Education, urbanization, and the deaf community: A case study of Toronto, 1870–1900. In J. V. Van Cleve (Ed.), *Deaf history unveiled: Interpretations from the new scholarship* (pp. 127–145). Washington, DC: Gallaudet University Press.

Winzer, M. A. (1993b). *The history of special education: From isolation to integration.* Washington, DC: Gallaudet University Press.

Winzer, M. A. (1998). A tale often told: The early progression of special education. *Remedial and Special Education, 19,* 212–218.

Winzer, M. A. (2004). The history of special education: The past confronts new paradigms. In Z. Ruta (Ed.), *In the service of school and science* (pp. 65–71). Krakow: Polish Academy of Pedagogical Sciences.

Winzer, M. A. (2005a). *Children with exceptionalities in Canadian classrooms* (7th ed.). Toronto: Pearson.

Winzer, M. A. (2005b). The dilemma of support: Paraeducators and the inclusive movement. *Exceptionality Education Canada, 15,* 101–123.

Winzer, M. A. (2005c). International concepts and practices in the field of behaviour disorders. In P. Clough, P. Garner, J. T. Pardeck, & F. Yeun (Eds.), *Handbook of emotional and behavioural disorders* (pp. 21–30). London: Sage.

Winzer, M. A. (2007a). *Children with exceptionalities in Canadian classrooms* (8th ed.). Toronto: Pearson.

Winzer, M. A. (2007b). The ladies take charge. In B. J. Bruggerman & S. Burch (Ed.), *Women and deafness: Double visions* (pp. 110–129). Washington, DC: Gallaudet University Press.

Winzer, M. A., & Mazurek, K. (1998). *Special education in multicultural contexts.* Columbus, OH: Merrill.

Winzer, M. A., & Mazurek. K. (Eds.). (2001). *Special education in the 21st century: Issues of inclusion and reform.* Washington, DC: Gallaudet University Press.

Winzer, M., & Mazurek, K. (2005). Global agendas in special education: A critique. In J. Zajda & R. Zajda (Eds.), *International handbook on globalisation, education and policy research* (pp. 643–658). Netherlands: Springer.

Withrow, F. B. (1967). Public Law 87-276: Its effects on the supply of trained teachers of the deaf. *Volta Review, 69,* 656–663.

Witmer, L. (1907). Clinical psychology. *Psychological Clinics, 1,* 1–9.

Wolfe, M. (1925). The relation of feeble-mindedness to education, citizenship, and culture. *Journal of Psycho-Asthenics, 30,* 124–135.

Wolfensberger, W. (1975). *The origin and nature of our institutional models.* New York: Human Policy Press.

Wooden, H. Z. (Ed.) (1934–35a). Editorial comments on interesting statements made at the convention. *Journal of Exceptional Children, 1,* 20–21.

Wooden, H. Z. (Ed.). (1934–35b). The founding of the Clarke School. *Journal of Exceptional Children, 1,* 14–16.

Wooden, H. Z. (Ed.) (1936–37). Sight conservation progressing. *Journal of Exceptional Children, 6,* 60.

Wooden, H. Z. (Ed.) (1937–38). Divergent views. *Journal of Exceptional Children, 4,* 20–21.

Wooden, H. Z. (Ed.) (1940–41). Pennsylvania certification of teachers of classes of the mentally retarded. *Journal of Exceptional Children, 7,* 248–249.

Wooden, H. Z. (1946). Extremists have confused issue. *Journal of Exceptional Children, 12,* 238–239.

Woodring, P. (1975). The development of teacher education. In K. Ryan (Ed.), *Teacher education: The 74th yearbook of the National Society for the Study of Education* (pp. 1–24). Chicago: University of Chicago Press.

Woodsworth, J. S. (1921). *Strangers within our gate, or coming Canadians.* Toronto: Methodist Mission.

Wright, A. (1915). The manual and oral combination. *American Annals of the Deaf, 60,* 219.

Wyatt, J. M. (1919). Causes of juvenile delinquency. *Social Welfare, 2,* 10–11.

Wyatt v. Stickney 334 F. Supp. 131 (MD Ala. 1971).

Yale, C. (1931). *Years of building: Memoirs of a pioneer in a special field of education.* New York: Dial Press.

Yell, M. L., & Shriner, J. G. (1997). The IDEA amendments of 1997: Implications for special and general education teachers. *Focus on Exceptional Children, 30,* 1–19.

Yerkes, R. M. (1917). How may we discover the children who need special care? *Mental Hygiene, 1,* 252–259.

Yerkes, R. M. (Ed.). (1921). Psychological examining in the U.S. army. *Memoirs of the National Academy of Sciences, 15.*

Young, K. (1923). The history of mental testing. *Pedagogical Seminary, 31,* 1–48.

Ysseldyke, J. E., Algozzine, B., & Thurlow, M. L. (2000). *Critical issues in special education* (3rd ed.). Boston: Houghton Mifflin.

Zelder, E. Y. (1953). Public opinion and public education for the exceptional child— court decisions, 1873–1950. *Exceptional Children, 19,* 187–198.

Zenderland, L. (2004). The parable of The Kallikak Family: Explaining the meaning of heredity in 1912. In S. Nall & J. W. Trent (Eds.), *Mental retardation in America: A historical reader* (pp. 165–185). New York: New York University.

Zerler, M. L. (1938). The contributions of a speech program to the field of mental hygiene. *Journal of Exceptional Children, 4,* 85–88, 93.

Zetlin, A., & Murtaugh, M. (1990). Whatever happened to those with borderline IQs? *American Journal of Mental Retardation, 94,* 463–469.

Zettel, J. J. (1982). The education of gifted and talented children from a federal perspective, In J. Ballard, B. Ramirez, & F. Weintraub (Eds.) *Special education in America: Its legal and governmental foundations.* Reston, VA: Council for Exceptional Children.

Zigler, E., & Balla, D. (Eds.). (1982). *The developmental-difference controversy.* Hillsdale, NJ: Lawrence Erlbaum.

Zigler, E., & Hall, N. W. (1986). Mainstreaming and the philosophy of normalization. In C. J. Meisel (Ed.), *Mainstreaming handicapped children: Outcomes, controversies, and new directions* (pp. 1–9). Hillsdale, NJ: Lawrence Erlbaum.

Zilboorg, G., & Henry, G. W. (1941). *History of medical psychology.* New York: Norton.

Zirkel, P. (1990, December). Litigation forecast. *American School Board Journal, 177,* 16–18.

Zirkel, P. A. (1997). The 'explosion' in education litigation. *West's Education Law Reporter, 114,* 341–351.

Zirkel, P. A., & Osborne, A. G. (1987). Are damages available in special education suits? *West's Education Law Reporter, 37,* 497–508.

Zirkel, P. A., & Stevens, P. L. (1987). The law concerning public education of gifted students. *Journal for the Education of the Gifted, 10,* 305–323.

Appendix A

Chronology of Developments in Special Education

1760   Charles Michel de l'Epée opens the first permanent school for deaf students in Paris.

1784   Valentin Haüy opens a school for blind children in Paris.

1817   American Asylum for the Education and Instruction of Deaf and Dumb Persons opens; the Legislature of Connecticut appropriates the first funds from public money in America.

1817   Thomas Hopkins Gallaudet begins teacher training at the American Asylum.

1825   The New York House of Refuge opens.

1830   The Boston Disciplinary Day School is established.

1832   The New York Institution for the Blind is established.

1832   New England Asylum for the Blind is founded, which later becomes the Massachusetts Asylum for the Blind, then the Perkins Institution for the Blind in Watertown, Massachusetts.

1833   The Pennsylvania Institution for the Blind is organized.

1839   The Massachusetts Normal School is established.

1844   The Association of Medical Superintendents of American Institutions for the Insane is formed (now the American Psychiatric Association).

1845   Heinrich Hoffman describes childhood hyperactivity.

1848   An experimental school for teaching children with mental retardation is established with an appropriation of $2,500 from the Commonwealth of Massachusetts; an institution for the feeble minded opens in Barre, Massachusetts.

1848   Horace Mann establishes tax-supported common schools in Massachusetts.

1850   The term *feeble minded* is widely adopted throughout North America.

1850   The Convention of American Instructors of the Deaf and Dumb is formed.

1852   Massachusetts passes the first compulsory school law.

1852   The Pennsylvania Training School for Feeble-Minded Children opens in Georgetown. In 1859, the school moves to Media, Pennsylvania, and gradually assumes the name of the school's founder, physician Alfred L. Elwyn. In 1927, the name changes to The Elwyn Training School; in 1960, the Elwyn Institute.

1853   The first formal meeting of teachers of the blind takes place.

1855   The New York Asylum for Idiots at Syracuse opens; Columbus, Ohio, opens an institution for feeble-minded people.

1857   The National Education Association (NEA) is formed.

1858   The American Printing House for the Blind is formally established after quite a time of preparation and agitation.

1859   Charles Darwin publishes *On the Origin of the Species*.

1864   National Deaf Mute College is established to train teachers of deaf students.

1865   Francis Galton publishes *Hereditary Talent and Character*.

1866   Edouard Seguin publishes *Idiocy and Its Treatment by the Physiological Method*, which confirms a public attitude of hope and belief in the potential of people with disabilities.

1867   The Clarke Institution for Deaf-Mutes opens.

1867   A class for deaf children is started in the public school system of Boston.

1868   The Conference of Superintendents and Principals of American Schools for the Deaf and Dumb is founded at the urging of Edward Miner Gallaudet.

1869   The Horace Mann Day School for the Deaf in Boston opens.

1869   Francis Galton publishes *Hereditary Genius*.

1871   An ungraded class is formed in New Haven, Connecticut; Alexander Graham Bell arrives in Boston.

1871   The American Association of Instructors of the Blind is formally established.

1872   Alexander Graham Bell begins to teach Visible Speech and vocal physiology in Boston.

1874   The first class for truant boys is formed in New York City.

1875   William Wundt begins mental testing.

1876   The first day class for incorrigibles is founded in Cleveland.

1876   The Association of Medical Officers of American Institutions for Idiots and Feeble-Minded Persons is formed (which later, in 1933, becomes the American Association on Mental Deficiency, then the American Association on Mental Retardation in 1987). In 2006, it becomes the American Association on Intellectual and Developmental Disabilities.

1877   An "asylum branch" is added at the Pennsylvania Training School for Feeble-Minded Children.

1878   The National Conference of Charities and Corrections is established by members of state boards of charities dedicated to scientific charity, which includes institutions for deaf, blind, and mentally retarded students.

1879   Isaac Kerlin uses the term *moral imbecility*.

1880	The Second International Congress for the Amelioration of the Condition of Deaf-Mutes takes place in Milan.
1880	The National Association for the Deaf is founded.
1883	Detroit establishes an ungraded class for unruly students.
1883	Galton coins the word *eugenics*.
1884	Alexander Graham Bell presents his *Memoir Upon the Formation of a Deaf Variety of the Human Race*.
1884	Alexander Graham Bell coins the term *special education*.
1884	Formal training for teachers of the blind begins at Columbia University.
1886	The first class for the gifted is established in Elizabeth, New Jersey, followed by an acceleration class in Cambridge, Massachusetts, in 1891.
1887	The terms *deaf and dumb* and *deaf mute* are formally discarded.
1888	The New Jersey Home for the Education and Care of Feeble-Minded Children opens. In 1893, the name changes to the New Jersey Training School for Feeble-Minded Boys and Girls at Vineland. (Other variations are found in the literature.)
1890	The American Association to Promote the Teaching of Speech to the Deaf (AAPTSD) is founded.
1891	Galton addresses the Seventh International Congress of Hygiene and Demography and calls for new means of checking fertility.
1892	Chicago establishes a special class for delinquents.
1892	G. Stanley Hall founds the American Psychological Association, and the association holds its first annual meeting in Philadelphia. (Later, John Dewey would be elected president for one year at the association's eighth annual meeting.)
1893	The Children's Aid Society is formed in Toronto.
1895	Alfred Binet begins publishing on mental measurement.
1896	Clarke Institution for Deaf-Mutes changes its name to the Clarke School for the Deaf.
1896	Lightner Witmer establishes the Pennsylvania Psychological Clinic at the University of Pennsylvania, the first psychological clinic designed to help children with learning and behavior problems.
1896	Kraepelin describes dementia praecox (later referred to as schizophrenia).
1897	The Department of Deaf, Blind and Feeble Minded is formed as part of the National Education Association.
1898	The first class for children with mental retardation in Boston is established.
1898	College-based training for teachers of students with mental retardation begins.
1898	The first public school Department of Child Study opens in Chicago.
1899	The Snellen chart is introduced.
1899	The first public school orthopedic classes for crippled children begin in Chicago.
1899	First U.S. juvenile courts are established.
1900	Wisconsin and Michigan establish laws that allow for the formation of day classes for deaf children.

1900	The National Committee for Mental Hygiene is established.
1900	The first electronic hearing aid device invented by Ferdinand Alt.
1901	The first state inspector of classes for the deaf is appointed by the Wisconsin State Department of Public Instruction.
1904	The New Jersey Training School at Vineland begins to train teachers of the mentally retarded.
1904	G. Stanley Hall publishes *Adolescence*, a major event in the early child study movement.
1905	M. P. Groszmann, founder and director of the National Association for the Study and Education of Exceptional Children, first uses the word *exceptional*.
1905	Binet and Simon publish the first test of mental ability.
1906	The first trained visiting teachers begin working in Boston, Hartford, and New York; the first college program for the preparation of special educators is established at New York University.
1906	The Eugenics Section (later the Committee on Eugenics), part of the American Breeders Association, is formed in the United States; the New Jersey Training School for Feeble-Minded Boys and Girls at Vineland establishes a laboratory with Henry Goddard as director of research.
1906	Cleveland sets up its first public school classes for epileptic children; New York sets up its first classes for "cardiopathics."
1906	Eugene Blueler identifies autistic behaviors.
1907	Indiana passes the world's first compulsory sterilization law.
1908	Sante de Sanctis identifies schizophrenia in children.
1908	The New York Committee for the Prevention of Blindness is founded, which later becomes the National Society for the Prevention of Blindness.
1908	The Binet scale is revised for the first time.
1908	New York City begins a program for children with defective speech.
1908	The first child guidance bureau opens in a public school in Boston; an open-air class opens in Boston.
1909	The first compulsory school laws for children with exceptionalities are passed in the United States.
1909	William Healy establishes the Juvenile Psychopathic Institute in Chicago.
1910	Chicago, New York, and Buffalo establish their first public school open air classes.
1910	Henry Goddard translates the Binet scale for use in North America; the Dillingham Commission concludes that immigrants from southern and eastern Europe are biologically inferior to other immigrants.
1910	Classes for stammerers and other children with speech defects begin in Detroit and Chicago.
1910	Edward B. Nitchie founds the New York League for the Hard of Hearing.
1911	Jersey City begins its first speech therapy classes; New Jersey passes the first state law in special education; Arnold Gesell founds the Child Development clinic at Yale University.

1911   The second revision of the Binet scale is completed by Binet and Simon; William Stern coins the term *intelligence quotient*.

1912   First International Eugenics Congress is held at the University of London.

1912   The American Association of Social Workers is founded; the first public school guidance bureau is founded in Pittsburgh.

1912   The United Kingdom adopts the term *mental subnormality*.

1913   Roxbury (Massachusetts), Boston, and Cleveland establish the first sight-saving classes for partially sighted children.

1913   The earliest university-based program for teachers of the deaf is founded at the University of Wisconsin in Milwaukee.

1914   J. E. W. Wallin coins the term *special class*.

1916   Braille is officially adopted in schools in the United States.

1917   Braille is accepted in American schools for the blind.

1917   James Hinshelwood writes *Congenital Word-Blindness*.

1917   Goddard publishes Ellis Island data; the U.S. Army formulates and uses the Alpha and Beta tests.

1917   The American Association of Clinical Psychologists is organized by J. E. W. Wallin and others.

1917   The Canadian National Institute for the Blind is established.

1918   The Canadian National Committee for Mental Hygiene, an association of physicians, social workers, and wealthy patrons, is formed.

1919   The American Society for the Hard of Hearing is established.

1920   The term *gifted* appears in the literature.

1920   The first classes for hard of hearing children are formed in Lynn, Massachusetts, and Rochester, New York; the term *mentally retarded* is introduced.

1920   Americans begin to officially use the term *mental retardation*.

1922   Lewis Terman begins his longitudinal study on the gifted.

1921   Second International Eugenics Congress is held in New York; the United States passes the Emergency Quota Act of 1921 that temporarily restricts immigration.

1921   The American Foundation for the Blind is established.

1922   The Council for Exceptional Children is founded.

1922   Harry Laughlin publishes *Eugenical Sterilization*, the first book published in America on the topic of sterilization.

1924   The U.S. Congress passes the Johnson Act (Immigration Restriction Act).

1924   The American Orthopsychiatric Association is formed to encourage the dissemination of information on therapeutic and educational work with emotionally disturbed children.

1924   Audiometric testing begins in the United States; Great Britain initiates testing in 1928.

1926   Samuel Orton begins to publish on *strephosymbolia* ("twisted symbols").

1926   The American Association of Psychiatric Social Workers, aligned with psychiatry and medical practice, is formed.

1928   Seeing-eye dogs for the blind are introduced into the United States.

1929	National Committee on Nursery Education (later the National Association for the Education of Young Children) holds its first national conference in Washington, DC.
1931	The Conference of Superintendents and Principals of American Schools for the Deaf changes its name to Conference of Executives of American Schools for the Deaf.
1931	Third International Eugenics Congress is held in New York at the Museum of Natural History.
1933	The Cuyahoga County Ohio Council for the Retarded Child is established.
1935	Detroit public schools opens classes for epileptics.
1936	Blind people are included under the Social Security Act of 1935.
1939	The Seventh International Conference of Geneticists meets in Edinburgh and issues widely publicized condemnations of eugenics, racism, and Nazi doctrines.
1940	Eugenics Records Office at Cold Springs Harbor, New York, is closed.
1940	The White House Conference on Children in a Democracy is held.
1942	The John Tracy Clinic is founded to meet the needs of the parents of young deaf children.
1942	Council for Exceptional Children becomes a department of the National Education Association.
1943	The Industrial Rehabilitation Act of 1920 is amended to create the Office of Vocational Rehabilitation, intended to serve both mentally and physically disabled people.
1943	Leo Kanner describes the autistic syndrome.
1944	Bruno Bettelheim starts the orthogenic school in Chicago.
1946	The American Association for Gifted Children is established.
1950	The National Association for Retarded Children is formed.
1954	The National Association for Gifted Children is established.
1954	*Brown v. Board of Education* comes before the Supreme Court.
1955	Leonard Kornberg publishes *A Class for Disturbed Children*, the first book to describe classroom teaching of disturbed children.
1956	The American Association to Promote the Teaching of Speech to the Deaf becomes the Alexander Graham Bell Association for the Deaf.
1958	Public Law 85–926 provides grants for training special education personnel.
1962	The President's Panel on Mental Retardation is convened under the J. F. Kennedy administration.
1963	Samuel A. Kirk introduces the term *learning disabilities*.
1963	President Kennedy signs Public Law 88–164, which provides federal funds for teacher training in the area of emotionally disturbed children and which broadens earlier legislation (Pub. L. 85–926) to include most children with severe disabilities; Kennedy announces the formation of the Division of Handicapped Children and Youth (of which Samuel Kirk becomes director in 1964).
1965	The federal Economic Opportunity Act includes plans for Head Start as a demonstration program.

1965   The first annual conference on the education of emotionally disturbed children is held at Syracuse University.

1966   President Johnson appoints the President's Committee on Mental Retardation.

1966   The Bureau of Education for the Handicapped is created in the U.S. Office of Education with James Gallagher as director and Edwin Martin as assistant director.

1968   The *Declaration of General and Special Rights for the Mentally Retarded* international document is issued by the International League of Societies for The Mentally Handicapped.

1968   The *Diagnostic and Statistical Manual* of the American Psychiatric Association offers the first description of attention deficit hyperactivity disorder (ADHD).

1974   The Special Projects Act establishes an advocacy office titled the Office of The Gifted and Talented.

1975   Public Law 94–142 (Education for All Handicapped Children Act) is enacted.

1983   *A Nation at Risk*, a report by the National Commission on Excellence in Education is published.

1984   The term *inclusion* appears in the special education literature.

1986   The Regular Education Initiative is proposed by the U.S. Department of Education; Congress passes Public Law 99–457, the first amendment of Public Law 94–142, which stresses infant and preschool programs.

1990   Congress passes the Individuals With Disabilities Act (Pub. L. 101–336) and the Individuals With Disabilities Education Act (Pub. L. 101–476).

1991   The Individuals With Disabilities Education Act is amended.

1997   The Individuals With Disabilities Education Act is reauthorized.

2001   Congress passes the No Child Left Behind Act of 2001 (Pub. L. 107–110).

2003   The Human Genome Project is completed.

2004   The Individuals With Disabilities Improvement Act (Pub. L. 108–446) amends earlier versions of the Individuals With Disabilities Education Act.

Appendix B

Summary of U.S. Federal Legislation on Special Education, 1879–2004

1918   Pub. L. 65-178—The Smith-Sears Veterans Rehabilitation Act provided physical and vocational rehabilitation for veterans of World War I.

1920   Pub. L. 66-236—The Smith-Fess Act (also known as the Civilian Vocational Rehabilitation Act) authorized vocational rehabilitation services for civilians; initiated translation services for blind individuals.

1936   Pub. L. 74-732—Authorized blind people to operate vending stands in federal buildings.

1943   Pub. L. 78-113—The Barden-La Follette Act amended the Smith-Fess Vocational Rehabilitation Act of 1920. It allowed state commissions and other agencies to receive federal funding to provide services to people who were blind, and it provided services for those who were mentally retarded and mentally ill.

1945   Maternal and Child Welfare Act (which added to the Social Security Act) included services for crippled children.

1950   Pub. L. 81-597—National Science Foundations Act passed with the goal of improving the basic curriculum and encouraging gifted and talented students to pursue careers in mathematics and physical sciences.

1954   Pub. L. 83-531—The Cooperative Research Program allowed limited funding for cooperative educational research by the U.S. Office of Education and colleges, universities, and departments of education. Mental retardation was targeted.

1954   Pub. L. 83-565—Research and training promoted for the vocational rehabilitation of the disabled.

1958   Pub. L. 85-926—The National Defense Education Act provided for an appropriation of $1 million for federal grants to state governments and institutions of higher learning to encourage the education of college instructors who would in turn train teachers of the mentally retarded.

1961   Pub. L. 87-276—The Special Education Act signed by President Kennedy in September 1961 funded university-level programs designed to encourage and facilitate the training of more teachers of the deaf. It increased the number of teacher preparation programs and more than doubled the annual preparation of teachers in this field.

1962   Pub. L. 87-715—Provisions were made for the production and distribution of captioned films for the deaf.

1963   Pub. L. 88-164—The Mentally Retarded Facilities and Community Health Centers Act (Comprehensive Community Mental Health Centers Construction Act) signed by President Kennedy in October 1963 broadened Pub. L. 85-926 to include children with severe disabilities. It provided funding for teachers of handicapped children (mental retardation, deafness and hearing impairments, visual impairment, serious emotional disturbance, and physical and health impairments). It also provided funds for research into disability, permitted the establishment of the Division of Handicapped Children and Youth, and provided for demonstration programs for exceptional children. In addition, it provided federal money for the support and preparation of teachers of emotionally disturbed children.

1965   Pub. L. 89-10—The Elementary and Secondary Education Act was the first broad-scale education act enabled by Congress. It was an umbrella act affecting almost all aspects of education. The many facets included provisions relating to children with disabilities, low-income families, and teachers' salaries. It provided $1.3 billion in grants to states and localities in the first year alone to attack the problems of educationally disadvantaged and handicapped children.

1965   Pub. L. 89-36—Established the National Technical Institute for the Deaf.

1965   Pub. L. 89-313—Elementary and Secondary Education Act amendments (Title I) granted federal funds to state agencies for educating handicapped children and youth birth through age 20 in state-operated programs. It also provided support to assist handicapped children in state institutions.

1966   Pub. L. 89-522—Expanded talking-book services for the visually impaired to include those physically handicapped people who were unable to handle print material.

1966   Pub. L. 89-750—Under Elementary and Secondary Education Act amendments (Title IV), authorization was provided to establish the Bureau of Education for the Handicapped and a National Advisory Committee on the Handicapped as well as assistance to state and local agencies for the education of the handicapped.

1967   Pub. L. 90-35—The Education Professionals Development Act provided funds to be used to increase general educators' awareness of and sensitivity to the needs of students with disabilities.

1967   Pub. L. 90-170—The Mental Retardation Amendments, which amended the Mental Retardation Facilities and Community Mental Health Centers Construction Act of 1963 (Pub. L. 88-164), provided physical and recreational programs and professional training, including the training of leadership personnel, supervisors, and researchers.

1968   Pub. L. 90-247—Elementary and Secondary Education Act amendments created regional resource centers for the evaluation of the handicapped, services for deaf-blind children and youth, resource centers, and the expansion of media services for the handicapped; also established bilingual education.

1968   Pub. L. 90-576—Ten percent of vocational educational funds were earmarked for the handicapped population. It also provided for grants to other agencies in addition to colleges and universities as well as states.

1968   Pub. L. 90-538—Handicapped Children's Early Education Assistance Act (also known as the First Chance Program) covered children from birth to age 6 years effectively increasing the number of children receiving services; Also provided grants to agencies, colleges, universities, and states to establish experimental preschool programs for handicapped children and to fund assessment devices, curricula materials, and parent training materials.

1969   Pub. L. 91-61—authorized the National Center on Educational Media and Materials for the Handicapped.

1970   Pub. L. 91-230—Education Amendments of 1969 to the Elementary and Secondary Education Act of 1965 consolidated other federal special education programs. In addition, it consolidated all existing legislation related to students with disabilities into one section, Title VI, called the Education of the Handicapped Act. States were provided direct financial support to serve children with disabilities ages 3 through 5. Section 806, "Provisions related to gifted and talented children," provided two sources of support funds for the gifted. This law, which created a separate act and may be seen as the initial Education of the Handicapped Act, reinforced the federal commitment to the preparation of personnel to educate special children and recognized learning disabilities as a condition. The Children With Learning Disabilities Act amended Title VI (known as the Education of the Handicapped Act of 1967) of the Elementary and Secondary Education Act and specifically provided authority to the U.S. Office of Education to establish programs for learning disabled students.

1970   Pub. L. 91-205—Required facilities constructed with federal funds to be accessible to those who were physically handicapped.

1970   Pub. L. 91-517—Developmental Disabilities and Facilities Construction Amendment of 1970; coined the term *developmental disabilities* to describe the population of individuals who had historically been placed in state institutions.

1972   Pub. L. 92-424—Amended the Economic Opportunity Act to extend Head Start services to children with disabilities; ten percent of enrollment opportunities in Head Start were to be available to handicapped children.

1973   Pub. L. 93-112—Section 504 of the 1973 Rehabilitation Act was the first civil rights law to protect the rights of disabled people. The language was almost identical to that of the Civil Rights Act of 1964, which applied to racial discrimination, and of Title IX of the Education Amendment of 1972, which dealt with discrimination in education on the basis of gender. Section 504 stated that "no otherwise qualified handicapped individual in the United States shall, solely by reason of his (or her) handicap, be excluded from participation, be denied the benefits of, or be subjected to discrimination under any program or activity receiving federal financial assistance." In guaranteeing the rights of those with disabilities in employment and educational institutions receiving federal funds, Section 504 of the Rehabilitation Act had complex and far-reaching implications that covered both school-age individuals and adults. It served students who did not meet the eligibility requirements of the Education of the Handicapped Act.

1973   Pub. L. 93-233—Social Security amendments of 1973 included a focus on child abuse and neglect programs.

1974   Pub. L. 93-380—Amendment to the Elementary and Secondary Education Act; assured education in the least restrictive environment, identified the gifted and talented as part of the Special Projects Act, and stipulated that states should set the goal of serving handicapped children from birth to 21. It provided for personnel preparation with an influx of funds to provide inservice training that would assist practicing educators to serve students with disabilities in their classrooms. The legislation guaranteed provisions for due process procedures in placement, nondiscriminatory testing, and confidentiality of school records. Programs for the gifted and talented were authorized.

1975   Pub. L. 94-142—The Education for All Handicapped Children Act spoke specifically to free and appropriate education and included concerns for the education of children who were culturally and linguistically different in their native languages.

1976   Pub. L. 94-482—Education Amendments of 1976.

1977   Pub. L. 95-49—Amendment to the Elementary and Secondary Education Act included the approved federal definition of learning disabilities.

1977   Pub. L. 95-207—Career Education Incentive Act, though not applying specifically to people who were disabled, increased federal attention on career development and transition programming and led to later initiatives.

1978   Pub. L. 95-561—The education amendments to the Gifted and Talented Children's Education Act of 1978 provided funding to states for planning as well as grants for personnel training, model programs, and research through the Gifted and Talented Children's Education Act. Migrant programs funded through section 143 of Pub. L. 95-561. It also included a provision for identifying native American gifted and talented students.

1978   Pub. L. 95-602—The Developmental Disabilities Assistance Act, which served preschoolers and children up to age 22 years. Removed some categorical terms such as *cerebral palsy, epilepsy, autism,* and *dyslexia*.

1981   Pub. L. 97-35—Education Consolidation and Improvement Act.

1982   Pub. L. 97-300—The Job Training Partnership Act allowed 10% of the funds for disabled youth.

1983   Pub. L. 98-199—The Secondary Education and Transition Services for Handicapped Youth amendments, which amended the Education of the Handicapped Act, revised Pub. L. 94-142 to provide a variety of discretionary grants to expand services for the birth-to-3 age group, encourage programs to better prepare school-aged students for transition out of public education, and improve personnel preparation.

1984   Pub. L. 98-511—The Elementary and Secondary Education Act amendments introduced new programs such as developmental bilingual education; special alternative instructional programs; and preschool, gifted, and special education programs.

1984   Pub. L. 98-524—The Carl D. Perkins Vocational Education Act promoted high-quality vocational-technical education and included programs for people with disabilities as well as for those who were otherwise disadvantaged.

1984   Pub. L. 98-527—The Developmental Disabilities Act targeted supported employment and independent living as outcomes for those with severe disabilities.

1986   Pub. L. 99-372—The Handicapped Children's Protection Act clarified the original intent of Pub. L. 94-142 to other federal laws, especially Section 504, and amended Pub. L. 94-142 to allow courts to reimburse parents for costs in cases where they prevailed.

1986   Pub. L. 99-457—The Education of the Handicapped Act amendments in this legislation gave full services for 3 year olds and dramatically increased funding for preschool programs. It divided the population into two groups—infants and toddlers (birth to 3, Part H) and preschoolers (3 to 6, Part B). The section named Preschool Grants could be used by the states to plan, develop, or implement a comprehensive interagency system of services for infants and toddlers with developmental disabilities.

1986   Pub. L. 99-506—Rehabilitation Act Amendments.

1988   Pub. L. 100-297—The Jacob K. Javits Gifted and Talented Education Act clarified that these students need special education services in the schools but do not require special services for gifted and talented children. It authorized funding for a National Research Center and demonstration programs. It also focused on students from traditionally underserved populations, with a special focus on high ability learners in culturally and linguistically diverse and low socioeconomic groups. The Indian Education Act, a reauthorization of the Bilingual Act; expanded the Bilingual Education Act of 1968; used *Limited English Proficient* (LEP) rather than *limited English speaking ability*. Provided that LEP students could be instructed for up to 5 years in bilingual programs and provided funds for research.

1990   Pub. L. 101-336—The Individuals with Disabilities Act signed by President Bush in July 1990 to take effect in 1992 was based on the Vocational Rehabilitation Act of 1973. It primarily affected adults but reflected a continuing concern with the rights of all people with disabilities. The law governed disability policy in higher education and extended nondiscriminatory participation in public schools and private employment settings, public service, public accommodations, and telecommunication services. It also clarified the legality of the term *disability*.

1990   Pub. L. 101-393—Provided for vocational education for members of special populations.

1990   Pub. L. 101-476—The Individuals with Disabilities Education Act amendment abrogated state's immunity (under the 11th Amendment of the Constitution) from suits brought in federal courts for their violation of the act making it possible for parents and other advocates to sue the states more successfully for nonperformance. The law added autism and traumatic brain injury (TBI) as categories and included a transportation plan on Individual Education Plans. It retained all the basic provisions of the original legislation but expanded to include 13 types of disability. The title of the law was also changed to stress people-first terminology—for example, a *child with a disability* rather than *a disabled child*.

1991   Pub. L. 102-119—Amendment of Individuals With Disabilities Education Act included a title change to people-first terminology. It related particularly to early intervention services and provided for more early intervention services; stressed a family-centered approach; and identified the need to serve underrepresented populations such as minority, low income, inner city, and rural. It also added vision services, assistive technology, and transportation.

1992   Pub. L. 102-569—The Rehabilitation Act Amendments included programs to support people across the full range of types and extent of disability.

1994   Pub. L. 103-227—The Goals 2000: Educate America Act was a national framework for educational reform that included equity measures and initiatives for safe schools.

1994   Pub. L. 103-239—The School-to-Work Opportunities Act provided career awareness, career exploration, and counseling for all students.

1994   Pub. L. 103-382—The Improving America's Schools Act provided for greater targeting of students with high needs and provision to assist such students in reaching high standards.

1997   Pub. L. 105-17—Individuals With Disabilities Education Act Reauthorization. Although most of the general requirements of the 1997 Individuals With Disabilities Education Act had been in the law since 1975, the amendment refined the basics and addressed the issues of school discipline and the authority of school personnel to handle children who could be a danger to themselves and others. It put new discipline provisions in place, strengthened the role of parents, and added a new variable to the formula by changing the notion of a separate curriculum for individual children. The 1997 reauthorization required that the general education curriculum be a starting place for all students and that outcome measures on Individual Education Plans (goals and objectives) be tied directly to the general education curriculum goals and objectives. As students with special needs become more involved in the regular school curriculum, it was expected that most children with Individual Education Plans would take the standard proficiency tests beginning as early as fourth grade (see Yell & Shriner, 1997). The reauthorization also elevated the general classroom as the primary placement option where possible.

2000   Pub. L. 106-402—The Developmental Disabilities Assistance and Bill of Rights Act amended the developmental disabilities services legislation of 1970. It called for full community inclusion and self-determination for people with developmental disabilities.

2001   Pub. L. 107-110—No Child Left Behind Act, an amendment of the Elementary and Secondary Education Act. The legislation was designed to promote high standards in public education and to ensure that all youths receive high-quality services. In exchange for federal funding under the No Child Left Behind Act, states agreed to develop systems of accountability for schools and school districts.

2004   Pub. L. 108-446—The reauthorization of the Individuals With Disabilities Act as the Individuals With Disabilities Education Improvement Act passed into law on June 19, 2004. It explicitly aligned the provisions with the requirements of the No Child Left Behind Act.

Index